Mikhail Suslov

GEOPOLITICAL IMAGINATION
Ideology and Utopia in Post-Soviet Russia

With a foreword by Mark Bassin

Bibliografische Information der Deutschen Nationalbibliothek
Die Deutsche Nationalbibliothek verzeichnet diese Publikation in der Deutschen Nationalbibliografie; detaillierte bibliografische Daten sind im Internet über http://dnb.d-nb.de abrufbar.

Bibliographic information published by the Deutsche Nationalbibliothek
Die Deutsche Nationalbibliothek lists this publication in the Deutsche Nationalbibliografie; detailed bibliographic data are available in the Internet at http://dnb.d-nb.de.

Cover illustration: Paysage IX by Anton Semakin. Printed with kind permission.

ISBN-13: 978-3-8382-1361-3
© *ibidem*-Verlag, Stuttgart 2020
Alle Rechte vorbehalten

Das Werk einschließlich aller seiner Teile ist urheberrechtlich geschützt. Jede Verwertung außerhalb der engen Grenzen des Urheberrechtsgesetzes ist ohne Zustimmung des Verlages unzulässig und strafbar. Dies gilt insbesondere für Vervielfältigungen, Übersetzungen, Mikroverfilmungen und elektronische Speicherformen sowie die Einspeicherung und Verarbeitung in elektronischen Systemen.

All rights reserved. No part of this publication may be reproduced, stored in or introduced into a retrieval system, or transmitted, in any form, or by any means (electronic, mechanical, photocopying, recording or otherwise) without the prior written permission of the publisher. Any person who does any unauthorized act in relation to this publication may be liable to criminal prosecution and civil claims for damages.

Printed in the EU

Soviet and Post-Soviet Politics and Society (SPPS) Vol. 215
ISSN 1614-3515

General Editor: Andreas Umland,
Institute for Euro-Atlantic Cooperation, Kyiv, umland@stanfordalumni.org

Commissioning Editor: Max Jakob Horstmann,
London, mjh@ibidem.eu

EDITORIAL COMMITTEE*

DOMESTIC & COMPARATIVE POLITICS
Prof. **Ellen Bos**, *Andrássy University of Budapest*
Dr. **Gergana Dimova**, *University of Winchester*
Dr. **Andrey Kazantsev**, *MGIMO (U) MID RF, Moscow*
Dr. **Mykhailo Minakov**, Kennan Institute, Washington
Prof. **Heiko Pleines**, *University of Bremen*
Prof. **Richard Sakwa**, *University of Kent at Canterbury*
Dr. **Sarah Whitmore**, *Oxford Brookes University*
Dr. **Harald Wydra**, *University of Cambridge*

SOCIETY, CLASS & ETHNICITY
Col. **David Glantz**, *"Journal of Slavic Military Studies"*
Dr. **Marlène Laruelle**, *George Washington University*
Dr. **Stephen Shulman**, *Southern Illinois University*
Prof. **Stefan Troebst**, *University of Leipzig*

POLITICAL ECONOMY & PUBLIC POLICY
Dr. **Andreas Goldthau**, *Central European University*
Dr. **Robert Kravchuk**, *University of North Carolina*
Dr. **David Lane**, *University of Cambridge*
Dr. **Carol Leonard**, *Higher School of Economics, Moscow*
Dr. **Maria Popova**, *McGill University, Montreal*

FOREIGN POLICY & INTERNATIONAL AFFAIRS
Dr. **Peter Duncan**, *University College London*
Prof. **Andreas Heinemann-Grüder**, *University of Bonn*
Prof. **Gerhard Mangott**, *University of Innsbruck*
Dr. **Diana Schmidt-Pfister**, *University of Konstanz*
Dr. **Lisbeth Tarlow**, *Harvard University, Cambridge*
Dr. **Christian Wipperfürth**, *N-Ost Network, Berlin*
Dr. **William Zimmerman**, *University of Michigan*

HISTORY, CULTURE & THOUGHT
Dr. **Catherine Andreyev**, *University of Oxford*
Prof. **Mark Bassin**, *Södertörn University*
Prof. **Karsten Brüggemann**, *Tallinn University*
Dr. **Alexander Etkind**, *University of Cambridge*
Dr. **Gasan Gusejnov**, *Moscow State University*
Prof. **Georgii Kasianov**, NASU, Kyiv
Prof. **Leonid Luks**, *Catholic University of Eichstaett*
Dr. **Olga Malinova**, *Russian Academy of Sciences*
Dr. **Richard Mole**, *University College London*
Prof. **Andrei Rogatchevski**, *University of Tromsø*
Dr. **Mark Tauger**, *West Virginia University*

ADVISORY BOARD*

Prof. **Dominique Arel**, *University of Ottawa*
Prof. **Jörg Baberowski**, *Humboldt University of Berlin*
Prof. **Margarita Balmaceda**, *Seton Hall University*
Dr. **John Barber**, *University of Cambridge*
Prof. **Timm Beichelt**, *European University Viadrina*
Dr. **Katrin Boeckh**, *University of Munich*
Prof. em. **Archie Brown**, *University of Oxford*
Dr. **Vyacheslav Bryukhovetsky**, *Kyiv-Mohyla Academy*
Prof. **Timothy Colton**, *Harvard University, Cambridge*
Prof. **Paul D'Anieri**, *University of Florida*
Dr. **Heike Dörrenbächer**, *Friedrich Naumann Foundation*
Dr. **John Dunlop**, *Hoover Institution, Stanford, California*
Dr. **Sabine Fischer**, *SWP, Berlin*
Dr. **Geir Flikke**, *NUPI, Oslo*
Prof. **David Galbreath**, *University of Aberdeen*
Prof. **Alexander Galkin**, *Russian Academy of Sciences*
Prof. **Frank Golczewski**, *University of Hamburg*
Dr. **Nikolas Gvosdev**, *Naval War College, Newport, RI*
Prof. **Mark von Hagen**, *Arizona State University*
Dr. **Guido Hausmann**, *University of Munich*
Prof. **Dale Herspring**, *Kansas State University*
Dr. **Stefani Hoffman**, *Hebrew University of Jerusalem*
Prof. **Mikhail Ilyin**, *MGIMO (U) MID RF, Moscow*
Prof. **Vladimir Kantor**, *Higher School of Economics*
Dr. **Ivan Katchanovski**, *University of Ottawa*
Prof. em. **Andrzej Korboński**, *University of California*
Dr. **Iris Kempe**, *"Caucasus Analytical Digest"*
Prof. **Herbert Küpper**, *Institut für Ostrecht Regensburg*
Dr. **Rainer Lindner**, *CEEER, Berlin*
Dr. **Vladimir Malakhov**, *Russian Academy of Sciences*

Dr. **Luke March**, *University of Edinburgh*
Prof. **Michael McFaul**, *Stanford University, Palo Alto*
Prof. **Birgit Menzel**, *University of Mainz-Germersheim*
Prof. **Valery Mikhailenko**, *The Urals State University*
Prof. **Emil Pain**, *Higher School of Economics, Moscow*
Dr. **Oleg Podvintsev**, *Russian Academy of Sciences*
Prof. **Olga Popova**, *St. Petersburg State University*
Dr. **Alex Pravda**, *University of Oxford*
Dr. **Erik van Ree**, *University of Amsterdam*
Dr. **Joachim Rogall**, *Robert Bosch Foundation Stuttgart*
Prof. **Peter Rutland**, *Wesleyan University, Middletown*
Prof. **Marat Salikov**, *The Urals State Law Academy*
Dr. **Gwendolyn Sasse**, *University of Oxford*
Prof. **Jutta Scherrer**, *EHESS, Paris*
Prof. **Robert Service**, *University of Oxford*
Mr. **James Sherr**, *RIIA Chatham House London*
Dr. **Oxana Shevel**, *Tufts University, Medford*
Prof. **Eberhard Schneider**, *University of Siegen*
Prof. **Olexander Shnyrkov**, *Shevchenko University, Kyiv*
Prof. **Hans-Henning Schröder**, *SWP, Berlin*
Prof. **Yuri Shapoval**, *Ukrainian Academy of Sciences*
Prof. **Viktor Shnirelman**, *Russian Academy of Sciences*
Dr. **Lisa Sundstrom**, *University of British Columbia*
Dr. **Philip Walters**, *"Religion, State and Society"*, Oxford
Prof. **Zenon Wasyliw**, *Ithaca College, New York State*
Dr. **Lucan Way**, *University of Toronto*
Dr. **Markus Wehner**, *"Frankfurter Allgemeine Zeitung"*
Dr. **Andrew Wilson**, *University College London*
Prof. **Jan Zielonka**, *University of Oxford*
Prof. **Andrei Zorin**, *University of Oxford*

* While the Editorial Committee and Advisory Board support the General Editor in the choice and improvement of manuscripts for publication, responsibility for remaining errors and misinterpretations in the series' volumes lies with the books' authors.

Soviet and Post-Soviet Politics and Society (SPPS)
ISSN 1614-3515

Founded in 2004 and refereed since 2007, SPPS makes available affordable English-, German-, and Russian-language studies on the history of the countries of the former Soviet bloc from the late Tsarist period to today. It publishes between 5 and 20 volumes per year and focuses on issues in transitions to and from democracy such as economic crisis, identity formation, civil society development, and constitutional reform in CEE and the NIS. SPPS also aims to highlight so far understudied themes in East European studies such as right-wing radicalism, religious life, higher education, or human rights protection. The authors and titles of all previously published volumes are listed at the end of this book. For a full description of the series and reviews of its books, see www.ibidem-verlag.de/red/spps. **Editorial correspondence & manuscripts** should be sent to: Dr. Andreas Umland, Institute for Euro-Atlantic Cooperation, vul. Volodymyrska 42, off. 21, UA-01030 Kyiv, Ukraine **Business correspondence & review copy requests** should be sent to: *ibidem* Press, Leuschnerstr. 40, 30457 Hannover, Germany; tel.: +49 511 2622200; fax: +49 511 2622201; spps@ibidem.eu. **Authors, reviewers, referees, and editors** for (as well as all other persons sympathetic to) SPPS are invited to join its networks at www.facebook.com/group.php?gid=52638198614 www.linkedin.com/groups?about=&gid=103012 www.xing.com/net/spps-ibidem-verlag/	**Recent Volumes** *207* Per A. Rudling Tarnished Heroes The Organization of Ukrainian Nationalists in the Memory Politics of Post-Soviet Ukraine ISBN 978-3-8382-0999-9 *208* Kaja Gadowska, Peter Solomon (Eds.) Legal Change in Post-Communist States Progress, Reversions, Explanations ISBN 978-3-8382-1312-5 *209* Paweł Kowal, Georges Mink, Iwona Reichardt (Eds.) Three Revolutions: Mobilization and Change in Contemporary Ukraine I Theoretical Aspects and Analyses on Religion, Memory, and Identity ISBN 978-3-8382-1321-7 *210* Paweł Kowal, Georges Mink, Iwona Reichardt (Eds.) Three Revolutions: Mobilization and Change in Contemporary Ukraine II An Oral History of the Revolution on Granite, Orange Revolution, and Revolution of Dignity ISBN 978-3-8382-1323-1 *211* Li Bennich-Björkman; Sergiy Kurbatov (Eds.) When the Future Came The Collapse of the USSR and the Emergence of National Memory in Post-Soviet History Textbooks ISBN 978-3-8382-1335-4 *212* Olga R. Gulina Migration as a (Geo-)Political Challenge in the Post-Soviet Space Border Regimes, Policy Choices, Visa Agendas With a foreword by Nils Muižnieks ISBN 978-3-8382-1338-5 *213* Sanna Turoma, Kaarina Aitamurto, Slobodanka Vladiv-Glover (Eds.) Religion, Expression, and Patriotism in Russia Essays on Post-Soviet Society and the State ISBN 978-3-8382-1346-0 *214* Vasif Huseynov Geopolitical Rivalries in the "Common Neighborhood" Russia's Conflict with the West, Soft Power, and Neoclassical Realism With a foreword by Nicholas Ross Smith ISBN 978-3-8382-1277-7

Contents

Foreword by *Mark Bassin* 9
List of Figures 13
List of Tables 15
Acknowledgements 17

Introduction 19
    Studying Russian geopolitical imagination 19
    Renaissance of geopolitics 27
    Conspiracy, dialogue and political participation 33

Part I
Geopolitical Culture: Approaches to Understanding 39

Chapter 1
The Logic of Recognition, Confrontation and Exceptionalism in Russian Geopolitical Culture
    Russia's "perpetual geopolitics" 41
    Struggle for recognition and Russian geopolitical imagination 47
    "Large space" and isolationism 53
    The stigma of barbarism 62
    Geopolitical Messianisms 67
    Conclusions 76

Chapter 2
Creating Usable Spaces in Education: Textbooks on Geopolitics
    Introduction 79
    Geopolitics Redux: Studying, Teaching, Selling 81
    Geopolitics: Ideology or pragmatism? 87
    "Laws of geopolitics" 9
    Securitization in textbooks ....

Biopolitics and the rhetoric of "energy" 97
Spatialization of history and the anti-colonial rhetoric 103
Conclusions 108

Chapter 3
"Civilizationism" in Russian Geopolitical Culture

Introduction 111
The mainstream political debates, "sovereign democracy"
and the ideology of "Edinaia Rossiia" 119
ROC and civilizational discourses 131
The logic of fragility and security in civilizational discourses ... 138
Conclusions 142

Chapter 4
Geopolitical Imagination and Russian Imperial Science Fiction

Introduction 145
The Big Other of post-Soviet SF 151
Geopolitics of civilizations 156
The imperial sublime in Russian SF 160
Biology and energy 164
Engaging with Strugatsky brothers 167
Orthodox SF 174
Conclusions 178

Part II
Imaginary Places 181

˙apter 5
˙ Russia"

˙duction 183
y Russia" project 184
˙ Russia" as a civilization 190
ing Kirill's pastoral visits 198

Chapter 6
Continent Eurasia in Russian Geopolitical Imagination

Introduction 203
Defining Eurasian continentalism 206
"Naturalness" 209
Hyperbole of development 214
Hyperbole of autonomy 220
Hyperbole of authenticity 223
Conclusions 226

Chapter 7
Eurasian Symphony: Geopolitical Imagination and Alternative History

Introduction 227
Emplotment and enjoyment in alternative history 229
Irony in *Eurasian Symphony* 233
East and West in *Eurasian Symphony* 237
Conclusions 244

Chapter 8
"*Novorossiia*" in Russian Geopolitical Culture

Introduction 247
Methodological note: The brand "*Novorossiia*" and its
ideological meaning 250
Where is *Novorossiia*? Territorial indeterminacy 254
Ideology of *Novorossiia* 262
Novorossiia in online debates 268
Conclusions 274

Afterword: Amendments to the Constitution and
Geopolitical Visions, 2020 277

Index 287

Foreword

The term "geopolitics" — the subject of Mikhail Suslov's highly original collection of essays — has become remarkably popular since the end of the Cold War. It might therefore be useful to introduce his work by considering more generally where this popularity comes from. Perhaps the most basic source of the appeal of geopolitics is the fact that there is no fixed and universally-accepted definition of exactly what it is supposed to mean or represent. Very much to the contrary, across the century or so since the term made its entrance into public political discourses, it has consistently been used in ways that not only differ quite substantially but indeed not infrequently are simply mutually incompatible.[1] Paradoxically, this pronounced protean character is not a drawback but rather a key to geopolitics' broad appeal, for it enables the term to appear relevant and useful in a wide variety of different contexts and applications. Suslov's work does not escape these ambiguities; to the contrary it actively incorporates them — at least implicitly — at its very core. Thus, while the *subject* of his examinations involves one particular conceptualization of geopolitics, the *analytical method* he uses in order to examine this subject is "geopolitical" in an entirely different sense. The considerable skill that he deploys in navigating the undulations between these two alternatives is one of the features that make these essays so fascinating and insightful.

Suslov's subject is a geopolitics understood as the study of how the objective material conditions of the external world influence the character of political and national life. This perspective dates back to the origins of classical geopolitics as a positivistic and causal "science" that revealed how geographical features and conditions — physical size, location, topography, climate, maritime access, and so on — function as geopolitical "realities" to shape the political character and destinies of states and nations. The intense imperial and post-imperial competition of the Great Powers from the

---

1   Klaus Dodds and David Atkinson (eds.), *Geopolitical Traditions: A Century of Geopolitical Thought* (London: Routledge, 2000).

end of the 19th century through the first half of the 20th saw the flourishing of national schools of geopolitics in Britain, the USA, France, Germany, Italy, Japan, and (to a lesser extent) Imperial Russia.[2] The USSR, however, was a notable exception. In the form of Marxism-Leninism, the Soviet authorities opted for a very different set of causal explanations for the imperatives driving national politics, and they consistently resisted the principle of environmental determination inherent in geopolitics. After the collapse of the Soviet Union, however, *geopolitika* began to take hold in post-Soviet Russia, and it was precisely the reductionist insistence on the salience of environmental-geopolitical "realities" in explaining the twisted contours of Russia's national predicament that made it appealing. In another deep paradox, despite all the traditional Soviet castigation, the rigid causality and putative objectivity of geopolitics resonated on some subliminal level with the crude positivism of Soviet-Marxist materialism itself, and this made geopolitics seem an attractive candidate when the time came to replace the latter.

The proliferation of neo-classical geopolitics in Russia has been much facilitated by the activities and writings of Aleksandr Dugin, an extremist on the Russian far right who at an early point appreciated the potential appeal of a perspective emphasizing the primacy of geographical factors for understanding and managing Russia's national affairs. A thoroughly mediocre intellectual but a highly effective ideologue, Dugin carefully armed himself with a knowledge of Western geopolitical theory, readjusted it to fit the post-Soviet context of the 1990s, and emerged as an effective publicist — most notably as the author of a a highly popular and successful textbook *The Foundation of Geopolitics*.[3] By the beginning of Vladimir Putin's reign in the early 2000s, *geopolitika* had proven its appeal to a variety of constituencies in Russia: universities, the military, and perhaps most significantly of all to the ruling elite, which quickly came to appreciate the effectiveness of pointing to objective geopolitical realities and imperatives as the basis for its various

---

2   Geoffrey Parker, *Western Geopolitical Thought in the 20th Century* (London: Croom Helm, 1985).

3   Aleksandr Dugin, *Osnovy geopolitiki. Geopoliticheskoe budushchee Rossii. Myslit' prostranstvom*, 2nd ed. (Moscow: Arktogeia-tsentr, 2000).

political projects. As Suslov discusses, geopolitics has been and remains one of the great growth industries in Putin's Russia. Regardless of his origins on the extremist fringe and the enduring extremism of his politics, Aleksandr Dugin has today become Russia's chief geopolitician and an entirely mainstream figure.

If Suslov's *subject* is to be understood in terms of the mindsets of classical and neo-classical geopolitics, however, our author's own epistemological and analytical position comes from a much more recent geopolitical tradition. This is so-called "critical geopolitics," more specifically that part of critical geopolitics focused on the problem of geographical representation, or what Suslov calls in his title "geopolitical imagination".[4] Taking its initial inspiration from the precepts of post-modernism, this perspective begins by rejecting the assumption of an objective and external geographical world that shapes and conditions political life. To the contrary, critical geopolitics teaches that geography is always "constructed" in precisely the same way that history or identity are constructed. A geopolitical reality is therefore nothing of the sort, it is rather a phantom, a representation that makes a claim to objectivity and veracity in order to fortify narratives and interpretations that are in fact politically biased and interest-driven.

Critical geopolitics scrutinizes the arguments of classical or neo-classical geopolitics with a two-fold purpose: first, to reveal the subjective character of geopolitical narratives that claim to be dealing with genuine objective realities, and second to deconstruct them to reveal the underlying political intentions, projects, biases and prejudices that they support and reflect. The great inspiration for this endeavour was Edward Said's seminal deconstruction of Western narratives of "the Orient," which continues to inspire critical-geopolitical analyses of the contemporary policies of the traditional Western powers toward the rest of the world.[5]

As exemplified in the essays collected here, Mikhail Suslov's intervention into the field of critical geopolitics is distinguished by

---

4   Gearoid Ó'Tuathail and Simon Dalby (eds.), *Rethinking Geopolitics* (London: Routledge, 1998).
5   Edward Said, *Orientalism* (London: Routledge and Kegan Paul, 1978).

a significant nuance—one that might be illustrated by a comparison to Said's own analysis. Said emphasized that the authors of the Orientalist discourse on which he focuses—historians, ethnographers, poets, and artists—did not necessarily recognize the biased and constructed nature of the deeper perspectives they were representing, and so did not necessarily appreciate the hegemonic calculations of political power that underlay them. In other words, Orientalist discourse was not necessarily created with the express purpose of serving as an ideological vehicle for the political project of dominating the Orient. Suslov takes a very different approach. The common thread that runs through all of his analyses of post-Soviet society, whether focused on narratives devised by the political elite or on the work of academic "geopoliticians", is precisely that of intentionality. Whether the theme is "Eurasianism," "Holy Rus," "the Russian World," or something else, Suslov at all times is not only interrogating the narrative itself but beyond this is questioning who are its agents, what is the relevant political context, and what is the transactional goal that they are seeking to achieve? In the final analysis, what Suslov is offering is a different sort of critical geopolitics, one in which the geopolitical narratives and perceptions in question are understood not merely as expressions of social and political attitudes. Beyond this—and often more importantly—they represent practical ideological devices and strategies that are consciously developed and deployed as part of an effort to further a particular political objective or project.

As noted at the outset, geopolitics is a wide-ranging concept with a kaleidoscope of different meanings and associations. In this collection of essays, Mikhail Suslov offers us his own take on the subject: a brilliant exploration of how geographical images and visions work to shape our understanding, organization and signification of the political world.

Mark Bassin
Stockholm, August 2020

List of Figures

Figure 1.	The number of textbooks on geopolitics	32
Figure 2.	Flowchart of recognition	51
Figure 3.	Absolute numbers of mentions of the phrase "role of Russia" in the federal press, and "mission of Russia" in all media	71
Figure 4.	Total number of mentions of words "Danilevsky" and "Huntington" in the Russian central and regional press from 1990 to 2019	112
Figure 5.	Visualization of the network of the Youtube videos, containing the phrase "Russian civilization" in their descriptions	119
Figure 6.	Total number of usages of the terms "*rossiiskaia* civilization" (blue) as opposed to "*russkaia* civilization" (orange)	122
Figure 7.	Map of *gubernia Novorossiia*, 1800, and the territory of the pro-Russian rebellion in Donbas.	256
Figure 8.	Babai the Cossack	273

List of Tables

Table 1.   Components of Messianism in the official press 74
Table 2.   Contours of Eurasia 207

Acknowledgements

Publication of this book was made possible thanks to the financial help from the Department of Cross-Cultural and Regional Studies at the University of Copenhagen, and from the Baltic Sea Foundation, which supported part of this research in the framework of the research project "Continentalism, Geopolitics, and the Idea of 'Big-Space': Political Formations in Comparative Historical Perspective." Many of the ideas, developed in this volume, were previously discussed with and inspired by my colleagues on the project Mark Bassin, Andrés Rivarola Puntigliano, and Katharina Döring, and also with Iain Ferguson, Flemming Splidsboel Hansen, Fabian Linde, Mikhail Luk'ianov, Kåre Johan Mjør, Tine Roesen, Viktor Shnirelman, Greg Simons, Mette Skak, Vera Skvirskaja, Jørgen Staun, Igor Torbakov, Sanna Turoma, Nikolai Zakharov, and others. I would like to acknowledge a series of publishers and journals who kindly granted permissions to reproduce previously published chapters: *Ab Imperio*, *The Russian Review*, *Russian Politics and Law*, Frank&Timme, Rowman&Littlefield, and *Europe-Asia Studies*. I am additionally grateful to Mark Bassin for contributing the Foreword.

Introduction

Studying Russian geopolitical imagination

The analytical spotlight of this book is on the geopolitical imagination and its power to shape the geopolitical identity of a community. Geopolitical visions are building blocks of the geopolitical imagination. Gertjan Dijkink defines a geopolitical vision as "any idea concerning the relation between one's own and other places, involving feelings of (in)security or (dis)advantage (and/or) invoking ideas about a collective mission or foreign policy strategy."[1] But geopolitical imagination is a broader phenomenon than visions; it knits together "formal geopolitics" (i.e. expert theorization and ideologies), "practical geopolitics" (discourses of the political leadership), and "popular geopolitics" (grassroots' ideas, opinions and emotions).[2] In this sense, geopolitical imagination is important in three respects: as a language for political debates, as an access channel to understanding the political elite's style of thinking, and as crystallization of the grassroots' visions.

What defines geopolitical imagination in contrast to strategic culture,[3] geopolitical ideology, and popular geopolitics is its utopian aspect. Here utopia is understood not as irresponsible daydreaming but as a specific projective and normative orientation in the world. Two staples of utopian imagination are 1) rationalization (or "education") of desire and its streamlining into an imple-

---

[1] Gertjan Dijkink, *National Identity and Geopolitical Visions: Maps of Pride and Pain* (London: Routledge, 1996): 11.
[2] Gearóid Ó Tuathail, "Understanding Critical Geopolitics: Geopolitics and Risk Society," *Journal of Strategic Studies* 22, no. 2–3 (1999): 111.
[3] On Russian strategic culture see, for example: Jørgen Staun, *Russisk strategisk kultur under Putin* (Copenhagen: Forsvarsakademiet, 2018); Mette Skak, "Om russisk strategisk kultur før og nu," in L. Bisgaard et al. (eds.), *Utopi og Realiteter: Festskrift til Erik Kulavig* (Ødense: Syddansk Universitetsforlag, 2018): 121–132; Skak, "Russian Strategic Culture: The Role of Today's Chekisty," *Contemporary Politics* 22, no. 3 (2016): 324–341; Dmitry Adamsky, "Russian Campaign in Syria: Change and Continuity in Strategic Culture," *Journal of Strategic Studies* 43, no. 1 (2020): 104–125.

mentable program, and 2) articulation of discontent with the reality.[4] In contrast to the interpretation of a utopia as a static social ideal, Darko Suvin defines it as a method of contemplating the alternative.[5] Tom Moylan sides with Suvin and argues that contemporary utopia should first and foremost provide comprehensive criticism of the present world order.[6] At the same time, utopianism can be hijacked by the authoritarian regimes, portraying themselves as an alternative to the global hegemony of Western liberal democracies. In this case, the target of utopian criticism is externalized, whereas geopolitically strong "we" become the living utopian alternative. Utopianism in today's Russia is no longer concerned with global proposals for a more just, humane and prosperous world. It generally operates on the periphery of the central discussions now occupying Western intellectuals: ecology, artificial intelligence, exploration of cosmos and so on. Instead, it focuses almost exclusively on culture and identity: what is Russia? And what does it mean to be a Russian? These are the key questions for many Science Fiction (SF) writers today.[7] It is true that contemporary Russian utopianism is geopolitical to the same extent, as Russian geopolitics is utopian.

Utopian and geopolitical "styles of thinking"[8] manifest a certain "selective affinity," which goes beyond the mere etymology of the word "utopias" — coined by Thomas More from the Greek τόπος ("place") and with the addition of the consciously ambiguous

---

4   E.g.: Lucy Sargisson, *Fool's Gold? Utopianism in the Twenty-First Century* (Basingstoke: Palgrave Macmillan, 2012); Sargisson, "The Curious Relationship between Politics and Utopia," in Tom Moylan and R. Baccolini (eds.), *Utopia Method Vision: The Use Value of Social Dreaming* (Bern: Peter Lang, 2009): 27–30; Ruth Levitas, "Some Varieties of Utopian Method," *Irish Journal of Sociology* 21, no. 2 (2013): 41–50.
5   Darko Suvin, *Metamorphoses of Science Fiction: On the Poetics and Theory of a Literary Genre* (New Haven: Yale University Press, 1979).
6   Moylan, *Demand the Impossibe: Science Fiction and the Utopian Imagination* (New York: P. Lang, 1987).
7   See more on this in: Mikhail Suslov and Per-Arne Bodin (eds.), *The Post-Soviet Politics of Utopia: Language, Fiction and Fantasy in Modern Russia* (London: Bloomsbury Publishing, 2019).
8   Karl Mannheim, *Ideology and Utopia: An Introduction to the Sociology of Knowledge*: Transl. from the German by Louis Wirth and Edward Shils (New York: Routledge, 1972).

prefix—either εὖ ("good"), or οὐ ("not"). As a "good place, which does not exist," from its inception utopia became a powerful means of social and political experimenting and critically questioning the assumptions of the present way of life.[9] By the end of the 19th century, ways of utopia and geopolitics suddenly came together on the grounds of the common pursuit for a positivistic, science-like futuristic speculation.[10] Their symbiosis implied that geopolitics explains how the ideal international community should be organized, whereas utopia provides a method of extrapolating utopian theorization into the future.

Another important tenet is that utopias are self-reflective of their purpose to mix up "poetics and politics" and offer an argument in political debates.[11] Viacheslav Rybakov, an SF writer analyzed in this book, puts this in shrewd Hegelian terms: "culture recognizes (*osoznaet*) its dreams in utopias."[12] Elsewhere he compares SF to a prayer for attaining something essentially important or for protecting against something terrible.[13] This self-reflexivity enables utopias to mediate between "popular" and "formal" geopolitics:[14] designed as political arguments, utopias are intended not for consumption by the expert community but rather for a mass readership.

This brings us to the third point—utopias cannot be reduced to the description of the ideal alternative world, because in order to be seen as utopias, they have to resonate with the intellectual, cultural, emotional disposition of their readers and cater to their needs.[15] Seen from this angle, the key precondition for a utopia to

---

9   Ruth Levitas, *Utopia as Method: The Imaginary Reconstitution of Society* (New York: Springer, 2013); Tom Moylan and R. Baccolini, *Utopia Method Vision: The Use Value of Social Dreaming*.
10 Jason Dittmer and K. Dodds, "Popular Geopolitics Past and Future: Fandom, Identities and Audiences," *Geopolitics* 13, no. 3 (2008): 438.
11 Peter Fitting, "Positioning and Closure: On the 'Reading Effect' of Contemporary Utopian Fiction," *Utopian Studies* 1 (1987), 24; Fitting, "Narrating Utopian Space," *Science Fiction Studies* 30, no. 1 (2003), 100.
12 Viacheslav Rybakov, "Utopiia i upravlentsy," *Neva* 9 (2013). Available at: http://magazines.russ.ru/neva/2013/9/5r.html
13 Rybakov, *Rul' istorii* (St Petersburg: Soiuz pisatelei Sankt-Peterburga, 2012): 175.
14 Tuathail, "Understanding Critical Geopolitics."
15 Otherwise, as Emile Cioran noted, Fourier's falanster would be seen as "the most effective vomitive" (Emile Cioran, *History and Utopia* (New York: Simon&Schuster, 2015 [1969]).

happen as such (not as anti-utopia or dystopia) is successful engagement of the readership. This means that a utopian narrative is not just a literary representation among others — it is a practical relation between the author's description and the readers' intention. The author offering a model of an alternative and possible world creates a cognitive space in which ideological construction becomes possible, whereas the audience should find this space attractive and relevant to its experience.[16] The corollary is that a popular geopolitical utopia not only offers attractive images and ideas, but also overlaps meaningfully with people's non-representational experiences with space, time and power.

A utopia condenses what is "not-yet," but what is already considered as possible in principle; hence its heuristic role as an amplifier of the present tendencies in culture and society.[17] In this context, geopolitical imagination not only explains the past and legitimizes the present, but gives valuable hints for political forecasting. The approach of this book, however, does not operationalize geopolitical imagination as a predictor of the country's international behavior. Knowledge about geopolitical culture and its "nodes" — concepts — is not a crystal ball, but it is helpful for mapping out zones of high geopolitical risks and for excluding improbable options for the state's decisions. In other words, geopolitical imagination serves as "pre-propaganda," preparing and conditioning the audience into accepting a specific political move as a natural and reasonable thing.[18]

Geopolitical imagination rests upon a number of geopolitical concepts. Geopolitical concepts organize otherwise possibly disconnected visions, give them meaning and place in the system. Communicative connectivity, facilitated by the digital media, transforms the geopolitical concepts from the ideological toys of a select

---

16 Fitting, "The Concept of Utopia in the Work of Fredric Jameson," *Utopian Studies* 9, no. 2 (1998): 10; Fitting, "Narrating Utopian Space," 93; Suvin, "Locus, Horizon, and Orientation: The Concept of Possible Worlds as a Key to Utopian Studies," *Utopian Studies*, 1, no. 2 (1990): 76.
17 Ernst Bloch, *The Principle of Hope* (Cambridge, Mass.: MIT Press, 1995).
18 Jacques Ellul, *Propaganda: The Formation of Men's Attitude* (New York: Vintage Books, 1973).

few intellectuals into clogs of political ideas, think tanks, decision-making, art and literature, and online memes. The obvious example is Eurasianism's transformation in post-Soviet Russia from a highbrow esoteric political way of thinking into a conceptual hybrid, whose ideas trickled down to academia, education, the military, the media, and the arts, and began to inspire Russia's political leadership to such an extent that it came up with the working project of the Eurasian Economic Union.[19] Another example of the symbiosis between visionary projects and "Realpolitik" is how the "*Novorossiia*" project and the host of concomitant ideas (e.g. "Russian world," "Holy Russia," "Russian civilization") motivated the actual war in Donbas, confrontation with the West, and securitization of Russia's identity after 2014.

Unlike other political concepts, the geopolitical kind always deal with the community's identity, and—as soon as the identity is created—tend to reproduce their own ideological justification. Concepts, which describe (imaginary/imagined) communities, function as "names" of those groups, and thereby have self-legitimizing power. The imagined community of today's Russia and the imaginary communities of geopolitical utopias appear to be intimately related.[20] For example, the "Russian world" is both the name of an imaginary community, and the ideology, legitimizing its creation.[21] As a corollary, any territorial rearrangement has a substantial impact on Russia's identity-making. In this way, the annexation of Crimea in 2014 and the rhetorical question, "who does

---

19 Mark Bassin and G. Pozo (eds.), *The Politics of Eurasianism: Identity, Popular Culture and Russia's Foreign Policy* (Lanham: Rowman&Littlefield, 2017).
20 Cf. Phillip Wegner, *Imaginary Communities: Utopia, the Nation, and the Spatial Histories of Modernity* (Berkeley: University of California Press, 2002): 100. See also: Lyman T. Sargent, "Utopianism and National Identity," *Critical Review of International Social and Political Philosophy* 3, no. 2–3 (2000): 87–106; Sargent, "The Necessity of Utopian Thinking: A Cross-National Perspective," in J. Rüsen. M. Fehr and Rh. Rieger (eds.) *Thinking Utopia: Steps into Other Worlds* (New York: Berghahn Books, 2005): 1–14.
21 More on this see: Suslov, "'Russian World' Concept: Post-Soviet Geopolitical Ideology and the Logic of 'Spheres of Influence'," *Geopolitics* 23, no. 2 (2018): 330–353.

Crimea belong to?", became the primary marker of a person's identity and political persuasion.[22]

On the "formal" level of ideological conceptualization, the importance of the geopolitical imagination consists in the fact that it provides the main canvas for political debates, which elsewhere have been carried out in a different context. For example, geopolitics in Russia gave the language to discuss such controversies as identity politics and multiculturalism. Having renounced the class prism in its vision of global politics, the Russian leadership after 1991 adopted the perspective of recognition of the cultural differences in international relations. Russia, from this new viewpoint, has been seen as a "minority" of sorts, whose message to the "hegemonic" culture (here understood as the collective "West") reflected a variety of ideological responces. Among these responses, one can identify the claim in the 1990s to be fully accepted and assimilated by the dominant culture. Later on, this claim gave way to the different demand to be recognized as a valuable and valued "pole" in the "multipolar world." Simultaneously, this relatively liberal version of "multiculturalism" in international relations was supplemented by its conservative interpretation, according to which the community has the exclusive right to define what is good and what is bad for its members. Hence, we have theories of "spiritual sovereignty" and the "large space," substantiating precisely this. "State-civilization" discourses in the first half of the 2010s were intertwined with the demand for special treatment, a kind of "positive discrimination" in international affairs on the grounds of Russia's past accomplishments, such as saving the world from Nazism. In connection with this, opinions about Russia as having a Messianic quality were looming both on the political margins and in the mainstream. Finally, an inexhaustible geopolitical option for Russia lingers on the visions of isolationism, which is akin to the strategy

---

22 Suslov, "'Crimea Is Ours!' Russian Popular Geopolitics in the New Media Age," *Eurasian Geography and Economics* 55, no. 6 (2014): 588–609.

of some religious groups in the secular world (such as the Amish people), who just want to be left alone.[23]

So, Russia's geopolitical imagination tends to develop in step with global political debates. On the other hand, however, it also taps into the vast reservoir presented by the historical legacy of geopolitical conceptualization in Russia. Traditions of Orthodox and communist Messianisms, classic Eurasianism, "Holy Russia" and equivalent visions significantly shape the country's contemporary geopolitical imagination, but by no means provide a silver bullet for understanding the country's international behavior. Rather than this, the following book insists on a dialectical approach—according to which geopolitical ideas, past and present, should be understood as the ideological "software" of sorts. This "software" connects international politics with the "end users"—political leadership, thinkers and the general public. Geopolitical imagination gives a meaning to Russia's position in the global world, and it has powers to change this position, while it is also being changed by it.

Theoretically, this study is grounded in critical geopolitics and the constructivist approach to spatiality. This academic tradition rejects the realist reading of geopolitics as a positivist, pragmatic and objective "science" about the interconnection between politics and territoriality. Fighting with essentialism in representing "national interests," "nations," "international relations," critical geopolitics offers its own research program, which argues that practices of "geo-graphing" are social and discursive. From this perspective, space is a "a discursive subject, and whatever meaning or significance it may possess is not inherent or a priori, but rather is projected onto it—in a ceaselessly revolving kaleidoscope of signification—by political or geopolitical discourses."[24] Likewise, a national

---

23 Here the rendition of the debates around identity politics draws largely on Will Kymlicka, *Contemporary Political Philosophy: An Introduction* (Oxford: Oxford University Press, 2002).
24 Mark Bassin, "The Two Faces of Contemporary Geopolitics," *Progress in Human Geography* 28, no. 5 (2004): 620–626.

territory is seen as an ideational construct, produced by geopolitical representations and narratives.[25]

So, critical geopolitics is interested in discourses surrounding the creation of national territories and identities. Specifically, it zooms in on the construction of borders and boundaries, geographical images of the self and the other, geopolitical ideologies and expert knowledge about relations between politics and geography, as well as official discourses on this matter.[26] Virginie Mamadouh and Gertjan Dijkink call this analytical program the study of the "politics of geopolitical discourse."[27] Together with Michel Foucault, this scholarship claims that those social practices of knowledge production are permeated by power relations. Klaus Dodds succinctly sums up the essence of this research project as follows: "The politics of geographical knowledge and the power of geographical representation lie in the heart of these writings."[28] The normalizing power of geopolitical discourse is used by the political elite for the purposes of self-legitimization and positioning a country on the international arena.

This theoretical framework is operationalized by means of reconstruction of the discursive context of the geopolitical imagination. Quentin Skinner developed an approach to studying intellectual history, according to which an ideological statement is an "illocutionary act"; hence, to understand an ideological statement is to understand the "point" of the author's argument—that is, to understand the place and role of this statement in a historically

---

25 Tuomas Forsberg, "The Ground without Foundation: Territory as a Social Construct," *Geopolitics* 8, no. 2 (2003): 7–24; Colin Williams and A. Smith, "The National Construction of Social Space," *Progress in Human Geography* 7, no. 4 (1983): 502–518.
26 Gearóid Ó Tuathail and Simon Dalby, "Introduction: Rethinking Geopolitics: Towards a Critical Geopolitics," in G. Tuathail and S. Dalby, *Rethinking Geopolitics* (London: Routledge, 1998): 4–5.
27 Virginia Mamadouh and G. Dijkink, "Geopolitics, International Relations and Political Geography: The Politics of Geopolitical Discourse," *Geopolitics* 11, no. 3 (2006): 349–366.
28 Klaus Dodds, "Political Geography III: Critical Geopolitics after Ten Years," *Progress in Human Geography* 25, no. 3 (2001): 470.

specific political debate.[29] The present research is inspired by Skinner's analytical approach. It attempts to reconstruct the dynamics of the conceptual change by analyzing the post-Soviet geopolitical imagination as the never-ending and fluid polylogue about Russia's identity and its place in the world.

Renaissance of geopolitics

The term "renaissance of geopolitics"[30] — though inaccurate in many ways — grasps the fundamental post-1989 dynamics of understanding the political aspect of geographical knowledge within the analytical framework of "classic geopolitics." Shaped in the "high imperialist" late 19th to early 20th century, when it asserted itself as knowledge about great powers and their interrelations on the world arena, "classic geopolitics" is steeped in geographical determinism and nationalism.[31] Rudolf Kjellén, who coined the term "geopolitics," defined it as a "study of the state as a geographical organism."[32] In its classic understanding, geopolitics explains that the state's behavior depends on the qualities of the physical and political space it occupies. The geopolitical discourse of the time was dominated by four images: the world as an integral whole; the world as divided into unevenly developed parts; and the world as divided among states as homogenous units characterized by sovereignty and clear-cut borders.[33]

Following the post-war period — when geopolitics was castigated and academically ostracized as an intellectual pillar of National Socialism — a "revisionist" version emerged in the 1970s, and one that was informed by neo-Marxist and post-structuralist theories. First of all, it owes academic pertinence to Henri Lefebvre's

---

29 Quentin Skinner, *Visions of Politics. Regarding Method* (Cambridge: Cambridge University Press Cambridge, 2002): 103–105.
30 Bassin, "Two Faces of Contemporary Geopolitics."
31 Bassin, "Politics from Nature: Environment, Ideology, and the Determinist Tradition," in J. Agnew, K. Mitchell and G. ÓTuathail (eds.), *A Companion to Political Geography* (Oxford: Blackwell, 2003): 13–29.
32 Rudolf Kjellén, *Staten som livsform* (Stockholm: Hugo Gebers Förlag, 1916): 39.
33 John Agnew, *Geopolitics: Re-Visioning World Politics* (New York: Routledge, 1998): 49–66.

concept of the "production of space."[34] This interpretation represents space not as a "passive" zone in which action takes place, but rather as an "active" medium of social processes, possessing its own dynamic and agency. Trying to overcome geographical determinism, revisionists modified the object of research in order to focus on "social" aspects of spatiality, and to adjust their problematic to the "liquid" and "soft" ways of exerting power, to the "Jihad/McWorld" distinction instead of the East/West one, and to deterritorialized networks instead of territorially-bounded states.[35] In the late 1980s–90s the above-mentioned school of "critical geopolitics" emerged, which revamped not only the object but also methods of researching geopolitics. Much in line with Michel Foucault's and Henri Lefebvre's analysis, geographical knowledge itself became understood as politics,[36] so the key goal of contemporary theorists of "critical geopolitics" (e.g. John O'Loughlin, Gearóid Ó Tuathail, John Agnew, Gertjan Dijkink and some others) consists of uncovering power relations in what the hegemonic geographical culture takes for granted; in other words, this is the geopolitics of geopolitics.[37]

Geopolitical thought always had robust historical ties with ideology, especially to its conservative spectrum.[38] Its very appearance in the late 19th century was connected with the justification of imperialist expansionism and colonialism. Later on, geopolitics was tainted by connections with Nazi ideology, and denounced by both Soviet and Western scholars as pseudo-science in the service of

---

34 Henri Lefebvre, *The Production of Space* (Oxford: Blackwell, 1991[1974]).
35 Gearóid Ó Tuathail, "Postmodern Geopolitics? The Modern Geopolitical Imagination and Beyond," in Tuathail and Dalby, *Rethinking Geopolitics* (New York: Routledge, 1998): 28.
36 Cf.: "Simply to describe a foreign policy is to engage in geopolitics, for one is implicitly ... normalizing a particular world" (Ó Tuathail, *Critical Geopolitics: The Politics of Writing Global Space* (London: Routledge, 1996): 60). See also his exposé of critical geopolitics in: Ó Tuathail, "Understanding Critical Geopolitics: Geopolitics and Risk Society.")
37 For an overview of research in critical geopolitics within Russian studies, see: Nick Baron, "New Spatial Histories of Twentieth Century Russia and the Soviet Union: Surveying the Landscape," *Jahrbücher für Geschichte Osteuropas* 55, no. 3 (2007): 374–400.
38 E.g. Bassin et al., "Is There a Politics to Geopolitics?," *Progress in Human Geography* 28, no. 5 (2004): 620–626.

militarist regimes.³⁹ Post-war Marxist authors targeted this analysis against "bourgeois geopolitics" as an ideologically and class-biased false scholarship justifying American "imperialism."⁴⁰

The collapse of the Soviet Union opened the gate for the flux of geopolitical thinking and writing; a number of studies analyze these new developments in post-Soviet thought.⁴¹ In post-Soviet Russia, the term trickled down into everyday discourse and became fashionable shorthand for international relations. It also acquired an air of esoteric knowledge, and promised to provide the most penetrating insights into the essence of world politics. In a Preface to one of the textbooks on geopolitics, we can read that "knowledge of the bases of geopolitics helps people to see specific motives and decisions in the chaotic raft of international events."⁴² The flow of Western geopolitical concepts after 1991 resulted in a co-existence of "classic," "neo-classic" and "revisionist" geopolitics in Russia, whereas "critical geopolitics" did not become acclimatized in Russia, and references to it are sporadic.

The "renaissance of geopolitics" is not only a Russian phenomenon and could be explained by general disenchantment in ideological meta-narratives and increased international instability

---

39   Isaiah Bowman, "Geography vs Geopolitics," *Geographical Review* 32 (1942): 646–658. See on this: Tuathail, *Critical Geopolitics*, 151–160. See also: Petr Alampiev, "Voennaia geopolitika—orudie podzhigatelei mirovykh voin," in *Burzhuaznaia geografiia na sluzhbe amerikanskogo imperializma* (Moscow; Leningrad, 1951): 93–102; Iury Semenov, *Fashistskaia geopolitika na sluzhbe amerikanskogo imperializma* (Moscow, 1952): 60–81.
40   E.g.: Irina Ponomareva, *Geopolitika imperializma SShA* (Moscow, 1986): 4–16. For a short survey on the history of geopolitics in the Soviet Union see: Vladimir Kolossov and Rostislav Turovsky, "Russian Geopolitics at the Fin-de-siecle," *Geopolitics* 6, no. 1 (2001): 143.
41   E.g.: Olga Gritsai, Vladimir Kolossov, "Die Renaissance geopolitischen Denkens in Russland: Neue Ansätze und Forschungsfelder," *Geographische Zeitschrift* 81, no. 4 (1993): 256–264; Katia Kliouikova, "La géopolitique en Russie depuis 1991," *Outre-terre* 2, no. 19 (2007): 21–27; Andrei Tsygankov, "Mastering Space in Eurasia: Russian Geopolitical Thinking after the Soviet Break-up," *Communist and Post-Communist Studies* 35 (2003): 101–127.
42   Vladimir Staroverov, "Predislovie," in Nartov, *Geopolitika: Uchebnik dlia vuzov* (Moscow: IUNITI, 2000): 5. More on textbooks on geopolitics see Chapter 2 in this volume.

after the end of the Soviet rule in Eastern Europe.[43] A number of conservative and pro-governmental think tanks across the globe galvanized "classic geopolitics," — which is sometimes represented as non-ideological policy, based on "eternal truths" and invariant geographical "constants," and drawn from the writings of Rudolf Kjellén, Friedrich Ratzel, Halford Mackinder, Alfred Mahan and other "founding fathers".[44]

In Russia, however, the preeminence of geopolitics is especially salient. Here geopolitics supplanted official Marxism-Leninism in a daring promise to deliver an all-explaining, simple and operational "concise theory of everything."[45] Indeed, in today's Russia, disenchantment in both communist teleology and in the liberal hope of catching up with the West made the spatial imagery of the country more important than visions of the future.[46] Dissimilar from the future-oriented ideology of the Soviet Union, post-Soviet Russia is stuck in the "end of history." Decades of discourse about

---

43 Stefano Guzzini (ed.), *The Return of Geopolitics in Europe? Social Mechanisms and Foreign Policy Identity Crises* (Cambridge: Cambridge UP, 2011); Carl Marklund, "The Return of Geopolitics in the Era of Soft Power: Rereading Rudolf Kjellén on Geopolitical Imaginary and Competitive Identity," *Geopolitics* 20, no. 2 (2015): 248–266.

44 Bassin, "Between Realism and the 'New Right': Geopolitics in Germany in the 1990s," *Transactions of the Institute of British Geographers. New Series* 28, no. 3 (2003): 350–366; Pinar Bilgin, "'Only Strong States Can Survive in Turkey's Geography': The Uses of 'Geopolitical Truths' in Turkey," *Political Geography* 26, no. 7 (2007): 740–756; Gertjan Dijkink, *National Identity and Geopolitical Visions*; Petr Drulák, "Between Geopolitics and Anti-Geopolitics: Czech Political Thought," *Geopolitics* 11, no. 3 (2006): 420–438; Bertil Haggman, "Rudolf Kjellén and Modern Swedish Geopolitics," *Geopolitics* 3, no. 2 (1998): 99–112; Virginia Mamadouh, "Reclaiming Geopolitics: Geographers Strike Back," *Geopolitics* 4, no. 1 (1999): 118–138.

45 Cf: John Berryman, "Geopolitics and Russian Foreign Policy," *International Politics* 49, no. 4 (2012): 530–544; Eduard Solovyev, "Geopolitics in Russia — Science or Vocation?," *Communist and Post-Communist Studies* 37, no. 1 (2004): 85–96; Paul Goble, "In Moscow, Geopolitics Is the Scientific Communism of Today," *Estonian World Review*, 30 September 2005, available at: http://www.eesti.ca/in-moscow-geopolitics-is-the-scientific-communism-of-today/article11282

46 Cf.: "In distinction to Soviet identity, which was temporally defined … the post-Soviet debate about Russian identity has been couched in spatial metaphors of territory and geography" (Edith Clowes, *Russia on the Edge: Imagined Geographies and Post-Soviet Identity* (Ithaca: Cornell UP, 2011): xi). See also: Charles Clover, "Dreams of the Eurasian Heartland: The Reemergence of Geopolitics," *Foreign Affairs* 78, no. 2 (1999): 9–13.

stability and conservatism prepared the ground for constitutional change in 2020, which effectively legitimized Vladimir Putin's unchangeable stay in power.[47] Now, geopolitical ideas have more power to shape the community's identity than classic political concepts such as republicanism, equality, solidarity, freedom and so on. The antagonistic border separating "us" and "them" is now defined by the relation to Crimea, "the West," China, etc.

As of 2020, no less than 34 organizations sporting the word "geopolitics" are registered in Russia.[48] In fact, there are many more think tanks with a pronounced interest in geopolitics. As an example, we might mention the Center of Strategic Assessments and Prognoses, which seems to be allied with the Center of Military-Strategic Studies of the Military Academy of Russia,[49] and whose main interest is "geopolitics, domestic and international politics, ideology."[50] In Russia, as in many other countries (especially in Latin America), geopolitics is connected with the military. The first textbook on geopolitics, written in 1996 by Aleksandr Dugin, was first adopted for teaching in the military band of higher education. Likewise, the Academy of Geopolitical Problems, one of the key producers of geopolitical knowledge in Russia, founded in 1999, is dominated by former military officers such as its president Colonel-General Leonid Ivashov, and Lieutenant-General Vladimir Ostankov.[51]

When it comes to geopolitics in higher education—discussed in details in Chapter 2—the number of textbooks for universities grew steeply in the first half of the 2000s, reaching its peak of some

---

47 E.g.: "A Constitutional Ploy May Keep Vladimir Putin in Power until 2036," *The Economist*, March 10, 2020, available at: https://www.economist.com/europe/2020/03/10/a-constitutional-ploy-may-keep-vladimir-putin-in-power-until-2036.
48 Calculated with the help of the search engine on the webpage https://www.rusprofile.ru.
49 The founder of the Center, Sergei Griniaev, was the faculty member of the Military Academy; see his profile here: https://www.gubkin.ru/faculty/faculty-of-complex-safety-of-the-fuel-and-energy-complex/grinyaev-sergey-nikolaevich.php.
50 "O tsentre," no date, available at: http://csef.ru/ru/about.
51 "Istoriia akademii," no date, available at: https://akademiagp.ru/about/history/.

1100 published titles per year in 2006. After that, the number of textbooks gradually decreased, and in 2014 it was somewhat boosted but never reached the record of 2006, having stabilized around the mark of 600 titles per year (Figure 1).

Figure 1. The number of textbooks on geopolitics.

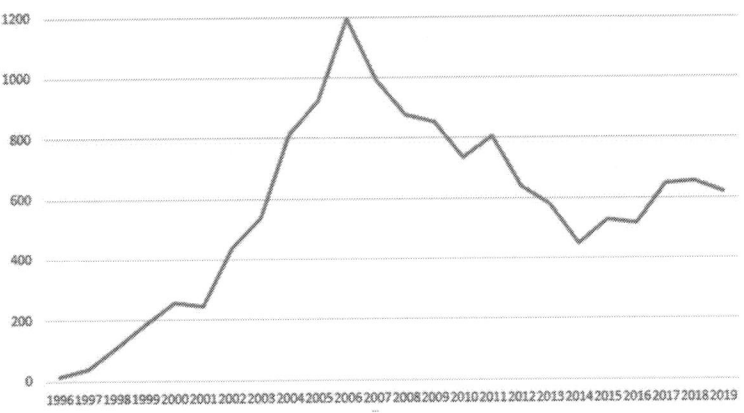

Calculated with the help of the search engine of the Russian State Library, www.rsl.ru.

Infatuation with geopolitics in Russia happened in pace with its capitalist transformation. By the end of the 19th century, perception of the world as an uncharted territory, waiting to be discovered and improved by bold explorers and entrepreneurial businessmen, was giving way to a new understanding that the frontier had stopped forever.[52] Now the world was seen as the single, finite, rationally understandable whole, in which increment of one's territorial possession could be only made at the expense of another. In this age, geopolitics appeared as both the modernist vision and the modernizing agent, translating the language of capitalism into notions by which people expressed their views on how the international system of states and their interrelationships were organized. Such words as competition, competitive advantages and disadvantages,

---

52   Fredrick Turner, "The Significance of the Frontier in American History [1893]," in Turner, *The Frontier in American History* (Auckland: The Floating Press, 2014).

monopolies, sovereignty (as the geopolitical parallel to property), geopolitical potential (as an equivalent to capital), national interest (cf. economic interest), began to dominate public discourses.

In post-Soviet Russia, the popularity of geopolitics came together with the rediscovered pleasures of capitalism and the clarion call "enrichissez-vous!," which supplanted ideological competition and the utopia of human perfection under communism. As a result, the crudest form of "Victorian-style" geopolitics became the orthodox way of thinking about the international world in Russia after communism. This kind of geopolitics only confirmed Russia in her intuitions — picked up during the first shocking experience of the market economy — that the world is a zero-sum game without rules, in which in order to survive you have to be stronger than your neighbor/adversary. Indeed, the strategic thinking of the Russian leadership seems to be consistently defined by Hobbesian, realist approaches to international relations, according to which the world system is in a state of anarchy, and the weaker part is beaten and crushed.[53]

Conspiracy, dialogue and political participation

Studying geopolitical culture, one cannot get rid of the impression that it is tightly connected with conspiratorial thinking. Conspiracy could be understood as form of social misrecognition.[54] In its elementary form, conspiracy means that "we" do not want or do not know how to communicate with the Other, and hence "we" securitize the Other's motivation, imagining it as an existential threat to "us" and the whole world. The concept of multiple civilizations with autonomous value systems, vying for dominance in today's Russian public sphere, is an ideal breeding ground for conspiratorial interpretations of the Other's actions.

---

53 Bobo Lo, "Two Worlds and the Return to World Disorder: Hobbesian Vision and Dysfunction of Russian Diplomacy," *Russian Studies* 2 (2016).
54 Mark Featherstone, "The Obscure Politics of Conspiracy Theory," in J. Parish and M. Parker (eds.), *The Age of Anxiety: Conspiracy Theory and the Human Sciences* (Oxford: Blackwell publishers, 2001): 31.

Recent scholarship departs from the view that conspiracy theories are synonymous with an irrational, "paranoid style" of understanding history and politics;[55] instead, it could be assumed that conspiracy theories are a sociological symptom of the "loss of agency,"[56] when "common" people perceive the lack of control over the overwhelming changes in the surrounding world. Peter Night argues that in the last decades, the vision of a conspiracy as a secret group of people, pursuing their rational goals has morphed into the ubiquitous atmosphere of anxiety, fuelled by the perception that there are some powerful and hostile forces plotting against "us." "In effect conspiracy theories have tended to restore a sense of agency, causality and responsibility to what would otherwise seem the inexplicable play of forces over which we have no control."[57] In Fredrik Jameson's words, conspiracy theory is the cognitive positioning of the "poor people," trying to attain control over the elusive world order.

In Russia, geopolitical conspiracy is the theory of "doubly poor people." First, they are stripped of the agency in the society of global capitalism, like other contemporary nations. Second, they feel dispossessed as a member of Russian society, represented as an international underdog, a semi-colony of the West. In this connection, moral panic around a Western conspiracy against Russia is augmented by the paranoia of physical integrity, which includes fear about addiction, viral penetration, sexual abduction, or the trade of organs. These conspiratorial discourses pay special attention to the biological and corporeal characteristics of the Russian people. For example, Aleksandr Prokhanov on many occasions spoke about the Western secret plan to fleece Russia of its "beautiful girls and talented mathematicians."[58] More recently, on the

---

55 E.g. Richard Hofstadter, *The Paranoid Style in American Politics and Other Essays* (New York: Knopf, 1966).
56 Mark Fenster, *Conspiracy Theories. Secrecy and Power in American Culture* (Minneapolis: University of Minnesota Press, 1999); Stefanie Ortmann and John Heathershaw, "Conspiracy Theories in the Post-Soviet Space," *The Russian Review* 71, no. 4 (2012): 551–564.
57 Peter Knight, "ILOVEYOU: Viruses, Paranoia, and the Environment of Risk," in arish and Parker (eds.), *The Age of Anxiety*, 21.
58 N.a., "Zagovor protiv Rossii," *AiF*, June 8, 2005.

wave of moral conservatism, state officials and activists spoke about practices of sexual abuse against children in the West. The infamous Irina Bergset, for example, maintained that "today, new kinds of information terrorism are moving on us from the West: incest, pedophilia and "Norwegian sex" (abuse of kids before they can speak, that is up to 3 years old)."[59]

Realist geopolitics could be viewed as a conspiracy theory of sorts, which promises "poor people" a shortcut to the hidden knowledge "of everything" and a sense of the control over politics. A geopolitical style of thinking frames the space as a constant factor in politics, so understanding of this factor and its impact on the behavior of states promises people the right key to the correct interpretation of the events in the past, present and future. For example, textbooks in geopolitics maintain that the fundamental law of geopolitics is the dualism of the land and the sea, which naturally develops into the eternal antagonism between continental and maritime powers. Having defined the Russia's territorial "constant" as an arch-continental power, those theorists reduce the complexity of Russian history to a never-ending battle of the country against the maritime power, whose contemporary embodiments are NATO and the US. Textbooks of geopolitics often directly refer to conspiracies as powerful driving forces in global politics, so the charm of "secret knowledge" lures readers into consuming some particular ideological product, most often of nationalistic provenience.[60] Thus, Vasilenko's textbook quotes the so-called "Dulles' Plan," the fake document which supposedly discloses aggressive aims of the postwar US against the Soviet Union.[61] Textbooks by Marinchenko, Vasilenko, Zubkov, and Nartov mention or imply the geopolitical "backstage" (*zakulisa*) and secret "agents of influence."[62] Dergachev includes a whole chapter entitled "Conspirology" in his textbook, defined as a "scholarly field studying conspiracies, secret societies

---

59 Sergei Vladimirov, "V Prezidentskom Sovete po pravam cheloveka kipiat strasti po 'delu Adagamova'," *Komsomol'skaia pravda*, January 10, 2013.
60 Laruelle, "Conspiracy and Alternate History in Russia: A Nationalist Equation for Success?" *The Russian Review* 71, no. 4 (2012): 565–580.
61 Irina Vasilenko, *Geopolitika sovremennogo mira* (Moscow, 2013): 64.
62 Anatolii Marinchenko, *Geopolitika: Uchebnoe posobie* (Moscow: Infra-M, 2009): 71.

and occult factors in history, which play a very important role in world geopolitics."[63]

However, ironically, geopolitics does not empower, but only further robs people from their agency, because in the geopolitical worldview reigning in today's Russia, people are mere cogs in the global mechanics of interaction among civilizations. In geopolitics, "geo" fully suppresses "politics," so that the central subject of the political processes is a geographically massive body you can belong, to but cannot control. For example, this big body could be a civilization, or a continent. On the level of morality, values of civic prowess, heroism, tragic opposition to the hostile collective are being reduced to the notions of faithfulness and treason. You can neither change nor control the "Eurasian Heartland," but you can betray it. Understandably, the geopolitical worldview is an ideal invention for the crackdown on the opposition. However, the reverse is true as well: by being faithful to one's "geo," a person acquires political might and (illusory) possibility to participate in the fate of humankind on the planetary scale.

***

This book is divided into two parts. The first part analyzes *how* the geopolitical imagination works, exposes mechanisms, principles and logics of production of geopolitical knowledge about a better Russia. It discusses sources and factors of the production of geopolitical culture in Russia. It starts with an overview of the central principles of geopolitical knowledge in and about Russia: mutual recognition, enlarging the scale, and the variety of Messianisms in geopolitics. Chapter 2, on the production of geopolitical knowledge in textbooks, outlines main features of the geopolitical "style of thinking" and points at the ascending importance of geopolitical education in Russia. Chapter 3 dwells on one of the central components of the Russian geopolitical culture, the concept of Russia as a "unique civilization." Then the spotlight shifts to the connections

---

63   Dergachev, *Geopolitika* (Moscow, 2007): 401–413.

between geopolitical concepts and the utopian imagination (Chapter 4).

Chapters 1 and 3 are written specially for this volume. Chapter 2 reproduces (with multiple revisions) the paper originally published as Mikhail Suslov, "'Urania Is Older than Sister Clio': Discursive Strategies in Contemporary Russian Textbooks on Geopolitics," *Ab Imperio*, no. 3 (2013): 351–387. Chapter 4 is an extended version of the article Mikhail Suslov, "Of Planets and Trenches: Imperial Science Fiction in Contemporary Russia," *The Russian Review* 75, no. 10 (2016): 562–578.

The second part discusses *what* is being imagined by focusing on four cases: "Holy Russia," "Eurasia" in cultural products, "Ordus" as a specific example of belletristic Eurasianism, and "*Novorossiia*." This part examines specific cases of "enlarging the scale" in the geopolitical imagination. Chapter 4 is devoted to the religion-inspired concept of "Holy Russia," which transcends the borders of the Russian Empire per se, embracing territories, belonging to Ukraine, Belarus, and possibly also Moldova and Kazakhstan. Chapter 5 considers Eurasianism from the viewpoint of continentalism. The chapter identifies three visions of the Eurasian continent and discusses their main ideological and rhetorical features, such as the metaphors of development, autonomy and authenticity. Specifically, it demonstrates pertinence of the continentalist thinking to the post-Soviet securitization of Russia's sovereignty, normative traditionalism and criticism of globalist liberal democracy. Due to its connection with the Russian imperial legacy, Eurasian continentalism tends towards conservative moral exceptionalism in the spirit of Carl Schmitt's ideas about *Großraum* and Mackinder's "Heartland" geopolitics. Chapter 6 analyzes the alternative history book series *Eurasian Symphony* by Viacheslav Rybakov and Igor Alimov as a literary exemplification of Eurasianism. The imaginary "place" constructed in these books is a union of ancient Russia and the Mongol Horde, predicted to develop—by the 21st century and in a parallel world—into powerful the continental empire *Ordus'*.

Chapter 5 is an extended version of the article Mikhail Suslov, "'Holy Rus': The Geopolitical Imagination in the Contemporary Russian Orthodox Church," *Russian Politics and Law* 52, no. 3 (2014):

67–86. Chapters 6 and 7 were published as Mikhail Suslov, "Bigger Is Better: Continent Eurasia in Russian Geopolitical Imagination," in Christine Engel and Birgit Menzel (eds.), *Russland und/als Eurasien: Kulturelle Konfigurationen* (Berlin: Frank&Timme, 2018): 19–44, and Mikhail Suslov, "*Eurasian Symphony:* Geopolitics and Utopia in Post-Soviet Science Fiction," in Mark Bassin and Gonzalo Pozo (eds.), *Politics of Eurasianism in Contemporary Russia* (Lanham: Rowman & Littlefield, 2016): 81–100. They are reproduced in this volume with many revisions. Chapter 8 was previously published as Mikhail Suslov, "The Production of 'Novorossiya': A Territorial Brand in Public Debates," *Europe-Asia Studies* 69, no. 2 (2017): 202–221.

Part I

Geopolitical Culture: Approaches to Understanding

1 The Logic of Recognition, Confrontation and Exceptionalism in Russian Geopolitical Culture

Russia's "perpetual geopolitics"[69]

Geopolitics returned to the Russian cultural soil, prepared by historical and geographical visions, which hark back to the medieval period. Speaking about the Russian traditions of geopolitics, we have to take into account a number of political emotions, such as the sense of vulnerability combined with admiration for territorial sublimity — or the sheer size of the country corresponding to a perception of the self as a less valuable and peripheral.

To start with, Russia's open borders and correspondent vulnerability to the invasions fostered certain aggressive-defensive attitudes to its neighbors. The steppe, the flat place of expansion and reconnection, represented the Russian "extraverted" side. During the whole of Russian history, the steppe belt across the Eurasian continent was the natural habitat for cattle-breeding nomadic tribes. Having mastered the technics of horse riding and wielding sables in the early Medieval Age, these tribes became a constant deadly threat to the neighboring forest-based Russian state. According to one of the calculations, during 150 years, in the 11th to the 13th centuries, Ancient Russia suffered 46 large raids by the Polovtsy (Cumans).[70] The devastating Mongol invasion of the 13th century put an end to the powerful Kiev principality and had a decisive impact on the popular imagination for centuries to come. The raids of the Turkic nomads on the centralizing Moscow principality continued well into the 16th century. For example, the massive foray

---

69 The term comes from the title of the article: Stephen Kotkin, "Russia's Perpetual Geopolitics: Putin Returns to the Historical Pattern," *Foreign Affairs* 95, no. 3 (2016): 2–9. In contrast to Kotkin's essay, this section does not purport to uncover objective factors of Russia's geopolitics; instead it focuses on how these factors were represented in the geopolitical imagination.

70 Petr Golubovsky, *Pechenegi, torki i polovtsy do nashestviia tatar* (Kiev: Un-t Sv. Vladimira, 1884): 37.

of Khan Davlet-Girei in 1571 into Russia brought him some 150,000 prisoners, and left many more dead. The vision of Russia as a victim of uncountable foreign invasions is deeply ingrained in the popular imagination. Historian Aleksei Miller, for example, dwells on the argument that the history of Russia's sufferings at the hands of external aggressors "shaped the Russian attitude to the defense of the Fatherland, its independence as a basic, key ... traditional value."[71] Curiously, the importance of the legendary tribes in the popular imagination found an unexpected confirmation in President Putin's recent speech on coronavirus (April 8, 2020), in which he talked on his country's resilience and ability to overcome all difficulties, such as the Polovtsy and the Pechenegs, who "tormented Russia."[72]

In response, the Russians developed an ingenious strategy to counter the nomadic mounted warriors by incorporating their pastures into the state territory. The Moscow principality slowly pushed its borders into the steppe by building fortresses and towns, followed by the peasants' colonization of the territories, secured by the state. After the fall of the Kazan and Astrakhan khanates in mid-16th century, large territories in the Volga basin and the Southern Urals became accessible for the Russian sedimentary colonists. By pursuing the expansionist policy, Russia discovered new threats, and in order to neutralize and control them, it used the usual strategy of absorbing the lands of its new enemies. This "expand to protect" method had a lasting effect on the country's political and geopolitical *imaginaire*. From the viewpoint of neorealism in international relations theory, "the flat geography of the Eurasian plain bred a genuinely Hobbesian international system in which a bias towards expansion was the only means of survival."[73]

By extension, the Historian Vasilii Kliuchevsky was the first to talk about Russia as a country built and maintained by colonizing

---

71 Aleksei Miller, "Reformatorskii konservatizm dlia sovremennoi Rossii," *Rossiia v global'noi politike*, May 2017: 35.
72 Vladimir Putin, "Soveshchanie s glavami regionov po bor'be s rasprostraneniem koronavirusa v Rossii," *kremlin.ru*, April 8, 2020, available at: http://kremlin.ru/events/president/news/63176.
73 William C. Wohlforth, "The Russian–Soviet Empire: A Test of Neorealism," *Review of International Studies* 27, no. 5 (2001): 217.

itself.[74] This colonization was carried out by the people on territories, and by the metropolitan state on the people. From the medieval times, when the only agricultural approach to forested areas was the "burn and slash" technique, the semi-nomadic lifestyle of the population and the association of expansion and economic prosperity were etched into the fabric of Russian life. In the 18th century, the Russian empire reached out to the southern and east-southern regions of virgin "black soil" lands, which became quickly colonized by the peasants from the Russian core lands. The last paroxysm of these colonization/expansion efforts came with Khrushchev's infamous virgin lands campaign in 1954–63.

Following Yu-Fu Tuan distinction between place and space, the forest remained the "place" for the sedimentary Russian people, the locus of security and confinement, where people could hide from the raids, or isolate themselves for the purpose of religious contemplation, whereas the steppe is the "space" of freedom and danger.[75] Unlike China, for example, which fenced itself from the Steppe, Russia embraced both, becoming a country of both "space and place," whose geopolitical imagination is dominated by mutually exclusive drives towards isolationism and expansionism, or, defined in more cultural and abstract terms: drives towards self-humiliation and self-aggrandizement, which will be discussed in the next chapter on Messianism.

The geopolitical metaphor of the retreat to the woods or to an island knits together visions of the feat of asceticism and protection from external enemies. The legend of the Invisible City of Kitezh encapsulates the Messianic aspect of this metaphor. In 1903–07 Nikolai Rimski-Korskakov composed an opera, based on the legend's plotline. In Rimski-Korsakov's rendition, the Mongol horde is advancing towards the glorious city of Kitezh. The traitor shows them the secret path to the city, but when the enemy approaches, thanks to the prayers of its inhabitants, Kitezh mysteriously disappears in the waves of the lake Svetloiar. Since then, on the shores of the lake,

---

74   Vasilii Kliuchevskii, *Kurs russkoi istorii* (Moscow: Iauza, 2018[1908]): 16–17.
75   Yu-Fu Tuan, *Space and Place: The Perspective of Experience* (Minneapolis: University of Minneapolis Press, 1977).

one has been able to hear the ringing bells or see churches in the water. The legend exposes the whole clog of visions about the intruding enemy, a besieged fortress, the enemy inside ("fifth column"), isolation, self-humiliation and Messianic sacrifice. These visions reverberate in many Russian cultural and ideological products, from the film *The Island* (2006) by Pavel Lungin to Vadim Tsymbursky's call for Russia to retreat to its continental "island."

The other extremity is the metaphor of Russia's territorial unboundedness and vastness, designed to evoke the feelings of sublimity, sometimes bordering on awe or rapture. Nikolai Berdiaev wrote about the "Russian soul, suppressed (*podavlena*) by the unbounded Russian fields," describing it as "sinking and dissolving in this unboundedness."[76] Andrei Belyi expressed the apprehension of the menacing Russian spaces in his poem of 1908 "Russia":

> ... The spreading army of spaces:
> There are spaces hiding in spaces.
> Russia, where shall I flee
> From famine, pestilence and drunkenness?[77]

Elsewhere Belyi wrote:

> Enough: do not wait, do not hope!
> Disperse, my poor people, my race!
> O torturous years without hope,
> Break up, disappear into space.[78]

Entitled "Despair," this poem reflects the writer's overwhelming disappointment in "Holy Russia"'s Messianism[79]. However, it also contains the metaphoric translation of the language of temporality

---

76 Nikolai Berdiaev, "O vlasti prostranstva nad russkoi dushoi," in Berdiaev, *Sud'ba Rossii: Opyty po psikhologii voiny i natsional'nosti* (Moscow: Filosofskoe obshchestvo SSSR, 1990 [1918]): 62–63.
77 Andrei Belyi, "'Rus'," in Belyi, *Stikhotvoreniia i poemy* (St Petersburg and Moscow: Akademicheskii proekt, 2006 [1908]), vol. 2: 116. In the original: "... prostorov prostertaia rat': // V prostranstvakh taiatsia prostranstva. // Rossiia, kuda mne bezhat' // Ot goloda, mora i p'ianstva?"
78 Andrei Bely, "Despair," in V. Markov and M. Sparks (eds.), *Modern Russian Poetry: An Anthology* (New York: Bobbs-Merrill, 1967): 191.
79 Vakana Kono, "Konets Sviatoi Rusi: Religioznaia problematika v 'Peple' Andreia Belogo," *Acta Slavica Iaponica* 19 (2002): 243–264.

into the language of spatiality, by which teleological optimism transfigures into "torturous years without hope" and "long centuries of serfdom and need."[80] The same troubled attitude to Russia's vastness found its expression in Alexander Blok's poem "On the Field of Kulikovo."

> Endless the battle! Blood and dust cover
> our dream of peace.
> The wild mare of the steppe sweeps on, on, over
> the feather-grass ...
>
> endlessly! Milestone and precipice flicker ...
> draw rein!
> The clouds in terror huddle closer, thicker,
> sunset's a bloodstain![81]

Following the research agenda of understanding maps as conveyers of political messages,[82] it could be assumed that the Mercator map projection has a lasting impact on the Russian geopolitical self-perception. Visually, on a Mercator map Russia's latitudinal extension is 2.5 times larger than that of China (in reality, it is only 1.4), 6.3 times larger than India (in reality it is 2.5), and 12.5 times larger than Spain (6.7 times in reality). It distorts the political map of the world and represents Russia as not just big, but enormously so, dominating all other countries, defying all geographical imagination and really standing out. Since imperial times, world maps have allocated the upper right quarter of the sheet to Russia, more or less in accordance with the golden ratio rule of composition. In this way, the observer's eye is drawn to somewhere in the South Urals. During Soviet times, the same geographical composition was improved by using the intensive red color, in which the country's territory was painted on maps, and which turned somewhat pale by the end

---

80 Bely, "Despair."
81 Alexander Blok, "On the Field of Kulikovo," translated by Jon Stallworthy and Peter France, *Critical Quarterly* 8, no. 1 (1966): 30.
82 Cf. the classic interpretation of maps as instruments of the political rhetoric by J.B. Harley (John Brian Harley, "Deconstructing the Map," *Cartographica: The International Journal for Geographic Information and Geovisualization* 26, no. 2 (1989): 1–20), and more recent studies on visualization of maps (e.g. Jeremy W. Crampton, "Maps as Social Constructions: Power, Communication and Visualization," *Progress in Human Geography* 25, no. 2 (2001): 235–252).

of the period. Surrounded by a motley horde of territorially smaller nations, the Soviet Union reigned on the world map from its prestigious upper right corner, visually conveying the message of exceptionality and global mission.[83] Even after the collapse of the Soviet Union, Russia's territory provides a symbolic pledge of Russia's future greatness and exceptionality. Aleksandr Ianov astutely observes that "gigantic size of Russia gave obvious points to Dugin and the revanchists. Geography worked for them."[84]

In Russia's medieval history, the country's latitudinal expansion across the Eurasian belt of steppes was an effective way to solve the security problem with the nomads, which contributed to the geopolitical imagination of impregnability and vastness. However, another security threat was more difficult to eliminate. Countries located more centrally in the world system had better access to technologies and economic capital.[85] In relation to them, Russia was permanently technologically backward and apprehensive of its intrinsic weakness. That is why geopolitical narratives about eternal antagonism with the West, territorial centrality, expansion and isolation, resonate with Russia's entrenched self-perception as a periphery of the global centers of culture, economy and technology. Dominic Lieven has noted, "the Russians were not simply more peripheral [than the Scandinavians] in geographical terms but were also — culturally — on the edges not of Latin Christendom but of Byzantium, which disappeared in the fifteenth century."[86] Also, Russian agriculture was historically exposed to high levels of production risks and relatively low profit level. The core of medieval Russia, situated in the forested and humid zone, dramatically lacked fertile soils for cultivation. Even when Russia gained access to fertile soils by acquiring vast swathes of the steppe in the 18th century,

---

[83] See, for example: A. Gorkina et al. (eds.), *Bol'shoi Sovetskii Atlas Mira*, 3 vols. (Moscow: NII VSAM, 1937), Vol. 1: 78–79–80.

[84] Aleksandr Ianov, *Russkaia ideia ot Nikolaia I do Putina* (Moscow: Novyi Khronograf, 2016), vol. 4, 13.

[85] Immanuel Wallerstein, *Mercantilism and the Consolidation of the European World-Economy, 1600–1750* (New York: Academic Press, 1980).

[86] Dominic Lieven, *Empire: The Russian Empire and Its Rivals* (London: John Murray, 2000): 203.

the recurring droughts in this semi-arid area made agriculture a risky business.

This perceived geopolitical weakness was cured by the repetitive cycles of state-induced, geopolitically-motivated modernization.[87] Geopolitical modernization became possible thanks to two of Russia's trademark methods: mimesis (imitation of a stronger opponent) and enlargement of scale. The first method aggravated already conflictual relations with the West and imparted to Russia the split and inauthentic identity of colonial underdog in the 19th century. The second gave rise to an already hypertrophic state apparatus, locked Russia into a vicious circle of state-driven reform and reaction, and inhibited the growth of the public sphere and the domestic market. This was the high price paid for control over Northern Eurasia. This geopolitical success (in spite of its massive negative economic and political consequences) had the decisive impact on the formation of Russian geopolitical culture, prompted the rise of Messianic visions, and inspired academic theorizations about Russia's "Grand Strategy" and invulnerability of the "Eurasian Heartland."[88]

Struggle for recognition and Russian geopolitical imagination

The mimetic theory reminds us of mimesis as the basic learning mechanism and major source of conflict among humans: "by obsessively imitating each other the rivals become increasingly similar ... Eventually they lose their chance of autonomy and become "mimetic doubles." This is the peak of the mimetic conflict, when the story of reciprocal imitation has escalated to the point that every difference has been erased and the rivals stand in from of each other as matching images."[89] In *Battling to the End* René Girard made an

---

87   For more on the idea of geopolitical modernization, see: Kotkin, "Russia's Perpetual Geopolitics."
88   John LeDonne, *The Grand Strategy of the Russian Empire, 1650–1831* (Oxford: Oxford University Press, 2004). Cf. Halford Mackinder, "The Geographical Pivot of History," *Geographical Journal* 170, no. 4 (1904): 298–321.
89   Roberto Farneti, *Mimetic Politics: Dyadic Patterns in Global Politics* (East Lansing: Michigan State University Press, 2015): 10.

attempt to translate the mimetic theory into geopolitical terms, speaking about France and Prussia's entangled history, and pointing to Fredrick II's infatuation with France, based on a bitter awareness that France looked down on Prussia. The mimetic rivalry between Germany and France ended in the Hall of Mirrors at Versailles on January 18, 1871. Likewise, Robert Farneti proposed to look at the Arabo-Israeli conflict through the mimetic prism. In this light, Russia's relation to the West represents a typical mimetic rivalry. "The admiration for Europe's economic and technological superiority turned into a mimetic competition for imitating Europe in order to overcome it."[90] The conflictual element in Russia's relation to the West was born not from the "actual" difference between Russia and the West, but from comparison, approximation, and mimesis; "it is not difference but sameness that is the problem."[91]

Mimesis exacerbates geopolitical conflicts, and raises existential questions about the community's identity: is it authentic, natural, organic? Is it dignifying to be Russian, if Russians are viewed as nothing more than wretched copycats of the Western model? Petr Chaadaev, the most controversial intellectual of Tsar Nicholas I's era, wrote in his famous *First Philosophical Letter* (1836):

> We are not a part of any of the great families of the human race; we are neither of the West nor of the East, and we have not the traditions of either. We stand, as it were, outside of time, the universal education of mankind has not touched us ... Everything passes, flows away, leaving no trace either outside or within us. In our homes, we are like guests; to our families, we are like strangers; and in our cities we seem like nomads ... Our memories reach back no further than yesterday; we are, as it were, strangers to ourselves.[92]

Russian intellectuals perceived Russia's relation to the West as undignifying, quasi-colonial, destructive of Russia's "inner self," cultural integrity and authenticity, and fed by a culture of *ressentiment*. Liah Greenfeld, in her controversial examination of Russian

---

90   Quoted from Farneti, *Mimetic Politics*: 126.
91   Cf. Jodok Troy, "Desire for Power or the Power of Desire? Mimetic Theory and the Heart of Twentieth-Century Realism," *Journal of International Political Theory* 11, no. 1 (2015): 29.
92   Petr Chaadaev, "Letters on the Philosophy of History: First Letter," in M. Raeff (ed.), *Russian Intellectual History: An Anthology* (New York: Harcourt, Brace and World, 1966): 162.

nationalism, argued that it was born from the spirit of *ressentiment*—"the rejecton of the West based on envy and the realization of the all-too-evident, and therefore unbearable, inferiority."[93] Classic Slavophilism provides ample evidence for this kind of attitude. For example, Aleksei Khomiakov, in his *Zapiska o vsemirnoi istorii*, argues that for time immemorial, the original population of Europe was Slavic, but that German intruders exterminated and enslaved and then wiped out its memory from history. From this viewpoint, the Germans have robbed Russians of their fatherland twice: first when they were expelled from their European native land, and second when Peter the Great violently transformed Russia into a kind of German province.[94]

Self-stigmatization and mimetic rivalry could be considered as part of the broader mechanisms of recognition. Axel Honneth claims that the struggle for recognition is almost an anthropological property of human identity. Keeping in mind the pitfall of comparing a state with a human, one can still argue that the theory of recognition is applicable for the international behavior of states.[95] This theory claims that states strive not so much for ascendancy, dominance or—for that matter—extermination of the rival, but rather for recognition from those whom they recognize as well. This vision of international politics is inspired by the emphatic rejection of realism and by the assumption that states' behavior crucially depends on performing their identities. From this viewpoint, the functioning of the world system comes down to a constant re-adjustment of self-image with reputation—that is, between the identity "mask" worn by the state, and the reception of this "show" by others.[96]

The idea of mutual recognition was engraved into the Westphalian system of international relations. As an outsider to this system, Russia has a long history of being treated as not fully

---

93   Liah Greenfeld, *Nationalism: Five Roads to Modernity* (Cambridge: Harvard University Press, 1994): 234.
94   Aleksei Khomiakov, *Polnoe sobranie sochinenii* (Moscow: Tip. Bakhmeteva, 1871), vol. 3, 96.
95   E.g. Christian Olsson, "Warfare and Recognition in IR: On the Potential Inputs of the Historical Sociology of the State," *Global Discourse* 4, no. 4 (2014): 539–542.
96   Thomas Lindemann and E. Ringmar (eds.), *The International Politics of Recognition* (Boulder: Paradigm Publishers, 2012): 7–8.

belonging nor fully recognized, which has left an indelible imprint on her geopolitical self-perception and international behavior.[97] In consequence, the Russian leadership was always concerned about status, prestige and honor.[98]

The theory of recognition displays its heuristic potential in a conflictual situation, such as one in which Russia and "the West" are stuck. Pointing to the fact that not the "small" states but "big" ones are likely to develop an inferiority complex, the theory of recognition explains why unsatisfied hubris of former empires is likely to cause international conflicts in the contemporary world.[99] With reference to the concept of "relative deprivation,"[100] one can identify the relative deprivation of recognition as the main source of tension in international relations. This concept points to two sets of factors that condition recognition-related conflicts: the decline of international reputation, and the heightening expectations that this recognition will be granted. The flowchart (Figure 2) visualizes the menu of possibilities beyond the simply and non-conflictual situation of mutual recognition. It identifies four possible outcomes from such a situation.

---

97 Iver Neumann, "Russia in International Society over the Longue Durée: Lessons from Early Rus' and Early Post-Soviet State Formation," in R. Taras (ed.), *Russia's Identity in International Relations: Images, Perceptions, Misperceptions* (London: Routledge, 2012): 24–41.

98 Andrei Tsygankov, "The Frustrating Partnership: Honor, Status and Emotions in Russia's Discourses of the West," *Communist and Post-Communist Studies* 47 (2014): 345–354.

99 Thomas Lindemann, "Interest, Passion, (Non)Recognition, and Wars: A Conceptual Essay", *Global Discourse* 4, no. 4 (2014); Lindemann, "Recognizing (Mis)Recognition from the Inside and the Outside: Some Criteria for 'Seizing' a Slippery Concept," *Global Discourse* 4, no. 4 (2014): 542; Lindemann and Ringmar (eds.), *The International Politics of Recognition*, 210–213; Richard Ned Lebow, *A Cultural Theory of International Relations* (Cambridge: Cambridge UP, 2008): 69.

100 This concept is taken from the field of the studies of protest movements. See, for example: Ted Gurr, *Why Men Rebel* (Princeton: Princeton UP, 1970).

Figure 2. Flowchart of recognition.

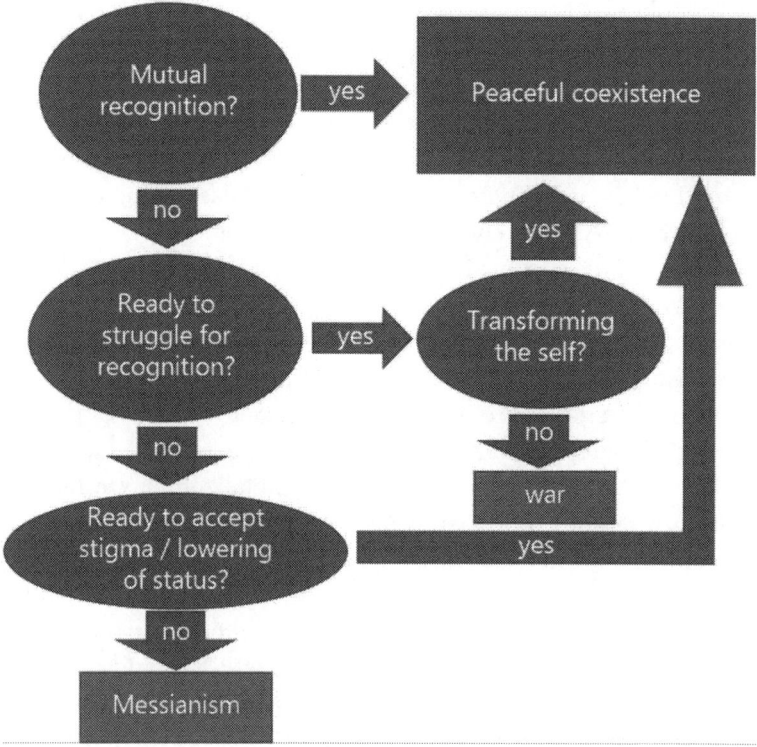

If the country is ready to fight for recognition, one option is to transform itself in order to revamp its reputation, typically by adjusting to the exalted self-image. This can take the form of the "actual" boosting of the country's economic, military or other kind of performance, or the "virtual" improvement of the country's soft power impact on the outside world. To put it slightly crudely, Russia's identity problems on the international arena would be solved if it had a GDP size comparable to that of the US and China, which is obviously not the case. As per the World Bank estimation of 2019, Russia's nominal GDP is only 7.9% from the US's economy, 11.9% from the Chinese, 34% from the Japanese and 44.7 from the German.[101] Likewise, according to the

---

101 World Bank, all countries and economies, 2019. Available at: https://data.worl dbank.org/indicator/NY.GDP.MKTP.CD?most_recent_value_desc=true.

"Soft Power 30," in 2019 Russia scored the unenviable 30th place out of 30 countries.[102]

Alternatively, the country can try to change the Other's attitude by physical force, which means war.[103] Despite a number of shockingly aggressive statements by Russia's leaders[104] and her second place among the world's most militarily powerful nations,[105] it is hard to believe that the Kremlin is seriously searching for a way to confront NATO in a full-scale military operation.

The third outcome is the realistic adjustment of the country's self-perception to her international reputation and factual performance. In spite of its sobering effect, in some most toxic contexts this means internalizing stigma, as explored by Ayse Zarakol. She explains imperial hubris among the latecomers to the Westphalian system of states—countries such as Russia, Turkey and Japan—by means of the psychological theory of stigmatization. On the one hand, she argues, these countries' inferior position vis-à-vis the Western core, "did not square well with self-understanding shaped by centuries of being the masters of their own domains."[106] On the other, Westernization was not imposed upon them externally, as a result of invasion and blatant colonialism, which would make the picture somewhat simpler: Western values would be taken as a foreign imposition. Instead, in the Russian case Western values were willfully emulated, and with them the country absorbed the humiliating self-perception as an outsider, as a backward, good-for-nothing loser in the historical game.

Finally, when the country refuses realistic realignment of its self-perception with its reputation, or when self-stigmatization

---

102 "The Soft Power 30," *USC Center on Public Diplomacy*, 2019, available at: https://softpower30.com.
103 Lindemann and Ringmar (eds.), *The International Politics of Recognition*, 8.
104 Cf. Putin's statement that in case of the nuclear Apocalypse, "we, as martyrs, will go to heaven and they [the Western aggressors] will just kick the bucket [*prosto sdokhnut*]" (Putin, "My popadem v rai, a oni—prosto sdokhnut," *Ria Novosti*, 18 October 2018, available at: https://ria.ru/20181018/1530999011.html.
105 E.g. "2020 Military Strength Ranking," *GlobalFirePower*, 2020, available at: https://www.globalfirepower.com/countries-listing.asp.
106 Ayse Zarakol, *After Defeat: How the East Learned to Live with the West* (Cambridge: Cambridge University Press, 2011): 10.

brings ideological fallouts, we can speak about Messianic self-aggrandizement and the "minimization of the Other," as Thomas Lindemann puts it.[107]

The rest of this chapter focuses on three of these outcomes: the struggle for recognition by means of re-imagining the "us"-community as being larger than its official territorial outline; playing with the stigma of being unworthy, low-status "barbarians"; and indulging in Messianic hubris.

"Large space" and isolationism

Enlarging the scale is the first outcome from the situation of relative deprivation of recognition. It means that the country attempts to transform itself by means of physical re-modeling or ideational re-considering in the way, which makes it larger than before. This strategy is especially doable for a country with an underdeveloped or blurred national identity and an undetermined shape of national territory. For a country like Russia, which has recently passed through the collapse of its land-based, contiguous empire, the question about its borderlines is a contested one. Vladimir Putin's bombastic statement that Russia's borders "do not end anywhere," or the popular joke: "Question: whom does Russia border with? Answer: With whom Russia wants, with them Russia borders" — both became thinkable in a post-imperial situation.[108] Such a situation is fraught with conflicts because a former empire stops recognizing its responsibility in relation to its former colonies, but does not stop perceiving itself as a "great power," whose lost dependencies become its "natural" sphere of influence and (predatory) interest.[109]

"Large space" projects provide a mental framework, within which the leadership and community traumatized by the lack of recognition gets a chance to position itself on a par with the

---

107 Lindemann, "Interest, Passion, (Non)Recognition, and Wars," 490–493.
108 Damien Sharkov, "Putin Claims Russia's Borders 'End Nowhere' at Geography Event," *Newsweek*, 24 November, 2016, available at: https://www.newsweek.com/putin-claims-russias-borders-are-endless-geography-event-524933.
109 Dmitri Trenin, "Of Power and Greatness," in P. Dutkiewicz and D. Trenin (eds.) *Russia: The Challenges of Transformation* (New York: New York University Press, 2011): 407–431.

"significant Other." This is pertinent for the entire "family" of the ideologies, related to the "larger space" (*Großraum*) visions. West-European continentalism developed in the 20th century as a response to the emergent non-European major players on the international arena: the US and Soviet Russia, whereas Latin-American regionalisms flourished in the anti-US atmosphere. Indeed, resizing "our" community to a larger, possibly continental scale would compensate for the fear of being on the periphery of the world and history. This function of *Großräume* was especially pertinent in the age of imperialism, especially in the late 19th–early 20th centuries, characterized by the fierce competition on the international arena, and by the meteoric rise of two most dynamic and aggressive nations — Germany and Japan — to global importance, in dangerous vicinity of the borders with Russia.

In the modern world, enlarging the scale should not necessarily take the form of the physical enlargement of the country's territory; it can also imply re-imagining the configuration of the self-community. In this way, the "we"-community emerges as a community, larger than the *de jure* state, and thereby craving more respect, power and ascendance in the family of other nations. Much of the Russian geopolitical imagination revolves around the visions of "us," whose identity spills over the actual border of the Russian Federation: the "Russian World," Eurasian continent, and Russian/East Slavic/Orthodox civilization. All these visions may or may not imply physical re-arranging of Russia's territory. Russia is not an outlier here. Since the first quarter of the 19th century, and especially by the end of that century, there was a persistent line of geopolitical argumentation in support of expanding existing borders in order to create geographically large states.[110] Indeed, the idea of *Großraum* ("large space") was conceptualized by two stalworts of German geopolitics of the 1930s: Carl Schmitt and Karl Haushofer.[111]

---

110 Friedrich Ratzel, "The Laws of Spatial Growth of States" (1898), in R. Kasperson and J. Minghi (eds.), *The Structure of Political Geography* (Chicago: Aldine Publishing Company, 1969): 17–28.

111 Carl Schmitt, *Völkerrechtliche Großraumordnung: mit Interventionsverbot für raumfremde Mächte: ein Beitrag zum Reichsbegriff im Völkerrecht* (Berlin: Duncker

In the "classic" Schmitt's understanding, *Großraum* is not just a "large space," but a space that is characterized by (1) a geographically specific location; (2) a state of exemption from the global normative order, and by extension—ultimate sovereignty; and (3) relative homogeneity in terms of culture and values.[112] One of the possible interpretations of Schmitt's ideas in today's world is the concept of multipolarity in international relations, vastly entertained by the Russian political elite.[113]

The most obvious and numerous "family" of *Großräume* is the continent. Continentalism implies the essentialization of continents—their reading as "naturally" given geographical phenomena which structure the surface of the earth, and which everyone is trained to see on a world map from childhood due it its seemingly "obvious" visual qualities.[114] A new continental infrastructure of pipelines and rapid railways, as well as the land-based migration and ascendance of the regional integration projects (EU, SCO, NAFTA, UNASUR and so on) gave rise to "new continentalism" in Eurasia.[115] As a specific type of scale-enlarging, continentalism is grounded on four ideological pillars: the idea of "naturalness" and homogeneity of a continental state; the idea that continental scale can better sustain the state's sovereignty; connection between the "large space" vision and the conservative-communitarian belief that cultural ties are more basic and strong than the formal rules of the game in international relations; and fourth, isolationism is an important component of the "large space" visions.[116]

& Humblot, 1941); Karl Haushofer, Geopolitik der Pan-Ideen (Berlin: Zentral-Verlag, 1931).
112 For example: William Hooker, *Carl Schmitt's International Thought: Order and Orientation* (Cambridge: Cambridge University Press, 2009).
113 Chantal Mouffe, "Schmitt's Vision of a Multipolar World Order," *South Atlantic Quarterly* 104, no. 2 (2005): 245–251; Robert Beyer, C. Schetter, J. Prinz, "Spatial Contestation?—The Theological Foundations of Carl Schmitt's Spatial Thought," *Geoforum* 43 (2012): 687–696.
114 Martin Lewis and Kären Wigen, *The Myth of Continents: A Critique of Metageography* (Berkeley: University of California Press, 1997).
115 Kent Calder, *The New Continentalism: Energy and Twenty-First-Century Eurasian Geopolitics* (New Haven, Conn.: Yale University Press, 2012).
116 For more on continentalism, see Chapter 6 of this volume.

First, the idea of the "naturalness" of the continental scale is connected with the perception of a continent as an organic habitat for a great nation. Geographer Carl Ritter, who was widely known and revered in Russia, was the first to introduce the concept of *Lebensraum*. Russian translations of his works consistently argued that the progress of civilization leads to a more harmonious interdependence between the culture and the territory on which it lives.[117] The German school of new, social geography, which emerged around 1870s, was an attempt to comprehend the creation of the German Empire. Sergei Solov'ev's theory of geographical determinism connected the progress of the Russian people and the development of its territory. For him a "historical people" is one capable of territorial expansion. He was among the first Russian intellectuals who, contrary to the canon of imperial geography of the 18th century, emphatically stressed the unity, compactness and naturalness of the Russian geographical space, which he saw as the primary cause of the greatness of the Russian state.[118]

The second constitutive element of continentalism is the idea of ultimate sovereignty, supported by the large, continental territory. It sounds counter-intuitive, but the most obvious reason for a *Großraum*-thinking is the perception of an existential threat on the one hand, and apprehension of "our" weakness. In this sense, a "large space" is the weapon of the weak. States try to compensate deficiencies of their economic performance, international reputation and geopolitical power by means of territorial enlargement. Moreover, the idea of a continental right-sizing of a country is fueled by the perception that in the age of globalization, nation-states cannot sustain their sovereignty. The ideological thread running through various visions of Eurasianism consists in the striving to exclude this territory from the internationally accepted model of

---

117 Natalia Sukhova, *Karl Ritter i geograficheskaia nauka v Rossii* (Leningrad: Nauka, 1990); Karl Ritter, "Ob istoricheskom elemente v nauke zemlevedeniia," *Geograficheskii sbornik*, no. 2 (1853). Ritter also exerted much influence on the classics of geopolitical thought: Rudolf Kjellén and Karl Haushofer (Cornelia Lüdecke, "Carl Ritters (1779–1859): Einfluß auf die Geographie bis hin zur Geopolitik Karl Haushofers (1869–1946)," *Sudhoffs Archiv* 88, no. 2 (2004): 129–152).
118 Mark Bassin, "Turner, Solov'ev, and the 'Frontier Hypothesis': The Nationalist Signification of Open Spaces," *The Journal of Modern History* 65, no. 3 (1993): 22.

the politics, and thereby to outlaw all possibilities of external interference into Russian affairs. The vision of Eurasia as a community of common values was entertained already by the classic Eurasianists, who spoke about "brotherhood" and natural affinity among the Eurasian nations or even insisted on the existence of the single, multi-ethnic Eurasian nation.[119] Drawing on the ideas of Carl Schmitt, Vladislav Surkov theorized sovereignty as the central political value of absolute importance. According to Surkov, "sovereign democracy" provides equal rights in the global (geo)political competition, in which the "West" all too often capitalizes on its normative power: "to be a sovereign nation is profitable."[120]

Third, the vision of *Großräume* taps into the ideology of conservative communitarianism, which privileges cultural contexts over the rules of the game. An example of the alliance between *Großräume*-thinking and anti-liberal communitarianism can be found in the book *The Politics of Virtue* (2016) by John Milbank and Adrian Pabst. In their view, nation-states fail to counter the pervasive but corrosive influences of global liberalism, and therefore leaders of the former empires have embarked on projects of restoring premodern state structures and imperial traditions in Turkey, Iran, China, and Russia. What can arise from this, the authors argue, is the "associationist approach" to international relations. This approach engages with the creation of a society of nations and peoples who are bound together by social ties and cultural bonds that are more primary than state-guaranteed rights and market contracts. Up to a point, this is true of the countries that compose the British Commonwealth, members of the Francophonie, or the association of Ibero-American states, or certain parts of the post-Soviet space.[121]

The intellectual evolution of the "Russian world" concept perfectly illustrates the point about ideological alignment between the

---

119 Nikolai Trubetskoi, *Izbrannoe* (Moscow: ROSSPEN, 2010): 457–459.
120 Vladislav Surkov, *Suverenitet – eto politicheskii sinonim konkurentosposobnosti* (Moscow: Lenand, 2006): 10.
121 John Milbank and Adrian Pabst, *The Politics of Virtue: Post-Liberalism and the Human Future* (Lanham, MD: Lexington Books, 2016): 334.

vision of a "large space" and conservatism.[122] The political need to make sense of the 25-million-strong Russian-speaking communities outside Russian borders stimulated ideologists to produce a usable concept of the diaspora. In the mid-1990s the first attempts were made to conceptualize Russia's "compatriots" as a deterritorialized, cultural, borderless community. This vision, resembling Milbank and Pabst's theorization above, included both the Russian emigrants in Western Europe, North America, and other parts of the world, and the "post-Soviet" Russians—the last of whom had not physically moved, although state borders had moved across them in 1991, which effectively separated them from Russia proper.

The bottom line of this vision of the "Russian world" is the idea that diaspora Russians are natural agents of globalization, so it is a great boon for Russia to have them. With their hybrid identities, linguistic competence, business activities, and access to Western capital and technologies, they would pave a highway for Russia toward a new globalized world. In the 2000s, the ideological climate in Russia changed. Reconceptualized by the theory of "sovereign democracy," the "Russian world" was now understood as an instrument of state, facilitating Russia's "soft power" abroad. Hopes for alternative "Russianness" waned with the ascension of a realist political worldview, in which Russia uses its compatriots abroad as a competitive edge in its struggle with other global players. Finally, the Ukrainian conflict of 2013–14 and the domestic "conservative turn" prepared the ground for the second conceptual shift in the meaning of the "Russian world." It is now seen as a civilizational entity with a precise (but debatable, of course) geographical location. This location might well spill over the state borders of the Russian Federation—as happened with the annexation of Crimea—but the new concept ushers in the era of conservative retreat from the global presence of the "Russian world" into the location of "our civilizational platform"—a Russian *Großraum* of sorts, embracing

---

[122] For more on the "Russian world" concept, see: Mikhail Suslov, "'Russian World' Concept: Post-Soviet Geopolitical Ideology and the Logic of 'Spheres of Influence'," *Geopolitics* 23, no. 2 (2018): 330–353.

Russia per se, Berlaus, Eastern and Southern parts of Ukraine and North Kazakhstan.

Fourth, this "large space" vision implies an introspective gaze, concentration on the self, and a certain degree of isolationism. Aleksandr Solzhenitsyn offered this ideal in his geopolitical theorization, as did Vadim Tsymbursky, who thought of Russia as an island. Theorizing on the painful dilemma between fascist and colonial paths for Russia, Tsymbursky argued in favor of the isolationist way out of this dilemma.[123] He intuited that Russia's geopolitical predicaments stemmed from the the tendency to become entangled with life in the West, whether the intention was to save it, to demolish it, or to offer it a model of "true Europe."[124] Instead, after the failure of yet another attempt to engage the West during the time of communism, Russia should try another path, retreat to its civilizational core and partially encapsulate itself within its "island," strictly observing its borders and differences.

Tsymbursky's proposals sound in tune with Solzhenitsyn's call for the cultivation and preservation of Russia proper, instead of dangerously stretching its sinews in a futile attempt to project its powers abroad. Vadim Tsymbursky's theory of Russia as an "island" is a projection of the striving toward authenticity into the language of geopolitics. His analysis is grounded on an insightful foray into the history of Russian-European relations. Tsymbursky identifies five stages of these relations, which tend to repeat again and again. The circle starts with Russia's striving to participate actively in European politics, which quickly leads to the Western invasion of Russia in the second stage, and Russia's reciprocal conquest of Europe in the third stage. Finally, Europe consolidates and repels Russia (stage four), which, then, indulges in what Tsymbursky calls "Eurasian interludes,"[125] when Russia tries its luck in Asia. The "Eurasian interlude" is an apt description of Russia's

---

123 Vadim Tsymbursky, "Poka—ne vkhodit' v mirovoe tsivilizovannoe ...," *Tetradi po konservatizmu*, no. 1 (2015): 39–40.
124 Tsymbursky, "Tsikly pokhishcheniia Evropy," in *Inoe: Khrestomatiia novogo rossiiskogo samosoznaniia* (Moscow: Argus, 1995), vol. 2.
125 Tsymbursky, *Morfologiia rossiiskoi geopolitiki i dinamika mezhdunarodnykh sistem XVIII–XX vekov* (Moscow: Knizhnyi mir, 2016): 68.

recent turn to China, seen by the Russian leadership not as a goal in itself but rather as leverage in its game with the West.[126] Inevitably, he argues, sooner or later, Russia again jumps at a chance to participate in European affairs and the vicious cycle repeats.

Tsymbursky believes that there is a way out of this cycle, which is for Russia to resist the temptation to be part of Europe and to retreat to its naturally isolated position on the continent. Here Tsymbursky dwells on the argument *ad naturum* in a way that is very similar to Savitsky's line of thinking: Russia is naturally situated on a gigantic island of sorts. This island is separated from the rest of the world by icy waters in the north and east and impenetrable mountains and deserts in the south. In the west, he continues, Russia is separated from the European continent by a broad "strait" of small nations, which do not belong fully either to "the Russian core," or to the Romano-Germanic West. He calls this "strait" the "Great Limitrophe."[127] It is the obsessive struggle for spheres of influence in the "Great Limitrophe" that powerfully draws Russia into European politics. This means that first and foremost, Russia should withdraw from the Great Limitrophe into its insular retreat. Tsymbursky shapes his vision of Russia as a state-continent in terms of isolationism and autarchy, but he also emphasizes the importance of regaining its "true self," to stop dissolving "ourselves" into amorphous spaces of Eurasia. He likewise draws on Aleksandr Panarin's civilizational jargon, arguing that the "[tectonic] platform of Russia" has its own civilizational identity, and as such it is a part of the bigger Eurasian continent.[128] As we can see from this, the "island of Russia," in spite of its polemics with Eurasianism,

---

126 "If Moscow perceives its interests are being ignored by Washington, a partnership with China, itself a powerful outsider, enhances Moscow's ability to challenge the legitimacy of an international order based on liberal democracies." Jeffrey Mankoff, *Russian Foreign Policy: The Return of Great Power Politics* (Lanham, MD: Lexington Books, 2012): 183; see also Bobo Lo, *Russia and the New World Disorder* (London: Brookings Institution Press, 2015).

127 Tsymbursky, *Morfologiia*, 411–420; Tsymbursky, "Zemlia za Velikim Limitrofom: Ot 'Rossii – Evrazii' k 'Rossii v Evrazii'," *Biznes i politika*, 1995, no. 9.

128 Vadim Tsymbursky, *Ostrov Rossiia: Geopoliticheskie i khronopoliticheskie raboty* (Moscow: ROSSPEN, 2007); Tsymbursky, *Morfologiia rossiiskoi geopolitiki i dinamika mezhdunarodnykh sistem XVIII–XX vekov* (Moscow: Knizhnyimir 2016): 401–403.

epitomizes the central traits of continentalist visions, and is actually a restatement of the early Eurasianists' theory of the "third continent"[129] that rests on the *Großraum* logic of civilizational exemption from the universal world order.

Although Tsymbursky's worldview was not conservative but leftist, his ideas were eagerly assimilated in conservative circles, which have understood Tsymbursky's concept as powerful opposition to liberal universalism and support for cultural authenticity.[130] More broadly speaking, for Tsymbursky all civilizations are lonely, isolated, and sovereign. Juggling the ideas of Carl Schmitt and Tsymbursky, Boris Mezhuev argues that if Russia wants to be a civilization, it should have the sovereign right to choose its friends and enemies, without complying with any external power.[131] Similarly, Mikhail Remizov maintains that large, continental-scale economies tend toward quasi-autarky, which means that smaller economies should embark on regionalist projects of creating "world-economies" (with the reference to Fernand Braudel) in order to better uphold their sovereignty. He suggests that "geo-economic competition obviously shifts from the international level into the level of macro-regions."[132] Vladislav Surkov's most recent theorizing follows the same line of *Großräume*-thinking. The former chief ideologist of the Kremlin intimates that after centuries of engaging with either East of West, now it is about time for Russia to remain in isolation and solitude, which well befits such a culturally hybrid and territorially continental state.[133]

---

129 See more on this in Chapter 6 of this volume.
130 Andrei Tsygankov, "'Ostrovnaia' geopolitika Vadima Tsymburskogo," *Tetradi po konservatizmu*, no. 1 (2015): 14.
131 Boris Mezhuev, "Suverennoe bessoznatel'noe," *Tetradi po konservatizmu*, no. 3 (2016): 33.
132 Mikhail Remizov (ed.), *Konservatizm kak factor "miagkoi sily" Rossii* (Institut natsional'noi strategii, n.d.), 28. Available at: http://www.instrategy.ru/pdf/245.pdf.
133 Vladislav Surkov, "Odinochestvo polukrovki (14+)," *Rossiia v global'noi politike*, April 9, 2018, http://globalaffairs.ru/global-processes/Odinochestvo-polukrovki-14-19477.

The stigma of barbarism[134]

The second outcome from the situation of non-recognition is the lowering of self-status. The following section discusses this strategy and its pitfalls by the example of the stigma of barbarism. Coping with the internalized image of a "barbarian" provides an excellent example of the struggle for recognition on the global periphery. Center and periphery constitute the most primary and basic structure of human spaciality. The center provides security, peace and self-assuredness, whereas the periphery is fraught with conflicts, aggression, but also with possibilities for self-realization and adventure. Our homes follow the same model: the hearth and the threshold. The hearth is the center of family life, giving us warmth and comfort. The threshold is the place of liminality, where we encounter with strangers, dangerous and intriguing. This is where we can meet barbarians. Barbarians are not just any strangers—fabulous exotic far-away lands are, of course, strange, but not barbarian, they promise unheard of riches and powerful knowledge. By contrast, barbarian is half-familiar and half-strange.[135] The Germanic tribes inhabiting borderlands and provinces of Orbis Romanus were eponymic barbarians for the dwellers of the metropolis. The Romans used them not only to defend the frontier of their vast empire, but also to construct their own identity, the self-image as being "in the center," being civilized, knowledgeable, cultivated.

From this perspective, Russia's entire history is the history of struggle with the stigma of barbarism.[136] Byzantine authors left

---

134 This section is inspired by the article Mikhail Suslov and Tine Roesen, "Barbarens selvforsvar: Historien om Ruslands identitetskamp," in B. Nielsen and M. H. Roesgaard (eds.) Vis mig din barbar. Tværkultur Nr. 9. Årbog for ToRS (Copenhagen: ToRS, 2019): 90–103. The author acknowledges Tine Roesen for productive discussions and valuable ideas on this topic.
135 Anne Norton, *Reflections on Political Identity* (Baltimore, MD: The Johns Hopkins University Press, 1988): 54–55.
136 Iver Neumann, *Uses of the Other: "The East" in European Identity Formation* (Minneapolis: University of Minnesota Press, 1999); Mark B. Salter, *Barbarians and Civilization in International Relations* (London: Pluto Press, 2002); Larry Wolff, *Inventing Eastern Europe: The Map of Civilization on the Mind of the Enlightenment* (Stanford: Stanford University Press, 1994); Maxim Khomiakov, "Russia between East, West and North: Comments on the History of Moral Mapping," in

numerous accounts on the life and mores of the Slavic peoples — the "northern barbarians," filled with repulsive descriptions of their language, lack of restraint, outlandish and morally crooked traditions, and so on. Later on, West Europeans travelling to Moskovia, dwelled on the slavish nature, sexual laxity, and lack of education among the Russians.[137] Looming on the threshold of European civilization, Russia was ideally suited to the role of "constitutive barbarians," akin to the role of the monstrous siblings in archaic cultures: familiar but alien. Internalization of this stigma of barbarism locked Russia into a toxic love-hate relation with the West, prompted self-Orientalization,[138] and preconditioned a raft of possible, sometimes creative, sometimes (self-) destructive responses. Two among them will be briefly discussed below and taken for a more detailed examination in Chapter 7 of this volume.

The Messianic response to the stigma of barbarism can take the form of ironic internalization, leading to self-exoneration. Political reading of this ironic position suggests that it reveals an over-identification with the source of power. The brave soldier Svejk from Jaroslav Hasek's novel, is an excellent example of how the tactic of excessively meticulous observation of the state regulations covertly undermines and ridicules the authorities. Irony is an effective weapon to resist the hegemonic Western gaze on Russia. Poet Aleksandr Blok famously asserts in "the Scythians" (1918, in Kurt Dowson's translation):

> Yes, we are Scythians — leafs of the Asian tree,
> Our slanted eyes are bright aglow with greed.

Blok enumerates historical grievances, which Russia suffered from the West, and calls for reconciliation and mutual respect

---

P. Wagner (ed.), *The Moral Mapping of South and North* (Edinburgh: Edinburgh University Press, 2017): 72–106.

137 E.g.: Sigismund Herberstein, *Notes upon Russia* (London: Hakluyt Society, 1852); Jerome Horsey, "Travels," in L. Berry and R. Crummey (eds.), *Rude and Barbarous Kingdom: Russia in the Accounts of Sixteenth-Century English Travel Voyagers* (Madison: University of Wisconsin Press, 1968): 202–369.

138 On self-Orientalizing attitudes see, for example: Valeria Sobol, "Internal Orientalism in Radishchev's 'Journey from St Petersburg to Moscow'," *Zeitschrift für Slavische Philologie* 68, no. 2 (2011): 241–269.

Come to our hearth, join our festive meal.
Called by the strings of our Barbarian lyres.

Or, if this call is unheeded, he threatens the West:

Advance, advance to Ural's crest,
We offer you a battleground so neat
Where your machines of steel in serried ranks abreast
With the Mongolian savage horde will meet.[139]

The "yes, we are Scythians" narrative juxtaposes the vigorous, passionate youthful energy of the coming barbarian race with the decrepit civilization of old Europe. The well-established Russian literary tradition of anti-Western and anti-bourgeois criticism and the Christian belief that "the last shall be first, and the first last," and Blok's infatuation with revolution of 1917 coalesce here into a powerful metaphor of the "Mongolian savage horde" as God's weapon of rectifying historical injustices, rejuvenation of the world and achieving unlimited freedom.[140]

Another response is the reversal of the stigma and the claim the "West" is "barbarian." There is a subtle difference between reinterpretation of a barbarian as a positive hero, and reattribution of barbarianism to the source of hegemony: "you call us barbarians, but this is you who are real barbarians, not we!" The "you are the barbarian" narrative powerfully entered the public debates with the beginning of the WWI. In the war-time press were accounts of the Germans as barbarians galore. German "wildness," "inhumanity," destruction of the world cultural heritage, blasphemous sacrileges were widely discussed and castigated. A pamphlet entitled "The Germans-Barbarians" (1915) claimed that the Germans were

---

139 Alexandr Blok, "The Scythians," *International Socialism* 6 (1961), 24. See more on this poem in: Judith Kornblatt, "Eschatology and Hope in Silver Age Thought," in G.M. Hamburg and R.A. Poole (eds.), *A History of Russian Philosophy: Faith, Reason and the Defense of Human Dignity* (Cambridge: Cambridge University Press, 2010): 297–299.

140 See examination of Scythianism in pre-revolutionary Russia in: Ekaterina Bobrinskaya and A. Tait, "Scythianism in Early Twentieth-century Russian Culture and the Scythian Theme in Russian Futurism," *Art in Translation* 8, no. 2 (2016): 137–168; A.P. Romanova, S.N. Iakushenkov and O. S. Iakushenkova, "Metaforicheskoe ispol'zovanie obraza varvara v obshchestvennom diskurse," *Gumanitarnye issledovaniia* 40, no. 4 (2011): 28–35.

an alien, non-autochthonous tribe in Europe—the infamous barbarians, as described by ancient historians, who had dared to desecrate the great achievements of Roman culture and now were committing the same crime against a common European civilization.[141] Philosopher Nikolai Berdiaev argued that in spite of the great achievements of German culture, it remained barbarian in its essence. Berdiaev called Luther and Kant "great barbarians," who had destroyed the organic connectedness of the people by means of extreme individualism and rationalism—their modern equivalent of the physical destruction wrought by historical barbarians on civilized Roman cities.[142]

Authors of both high-brow philosophy and literature for entertainment jumped at the opportunity to settle scores with "the German"—Russia's long-time teacher and master. During centuries, "the German" was the metonymy of Europe for Russia (cf. the Russian word for the German is "nemets," i.e. a dumb person, someone who does not speak—any foreigner). By putting forward the idea that "in actuality" the Germans are barbarians, and hence are not truly Christian, not truly European, and not truly civilized, this narrative powerfully reverses the hegemonic relations, claiming that this is Russia, which is truly European, truly Christian, and truly civilized.[143]

During the Great Patriotic War the same idea was expressed with utmost clarity. Musa Jalil's poem "Barbarity" (1943) is a piercing description of a mass shooting of civilians, including women and kids, by the SS officers:

---

141 See, for example: *Nemtsy-varvary. Tvorimye imi uzhasy v nashi dni nad nashimi ottsami, brat'iami i sestrami* (Moscow, 1914); P. Kovalevskii, S. Syromiatnikov and A. Mikhailov, *Nashi vragi. Ocherki* (Petrograd, 1915): 4–9. On the "German the barbarian" narrative in political debates see: Suslov, "'Obezlichil nas i vlastvoval nad nami …': Poniatiie 'nemets' v rossiiskikh pozdneimperskikh politicheskikh debatakh," *The Herald of the Perm State University (History)* 27, no. 4 (2014): 180–193.
142 Nikolai Berdiaev, *Smysl tvorchestva* (Moscow: AST, 2018 [1916]): 483–485.
143 On the Orthodox discourses about "the barbarian West" see: Vasilios Makrides, "'The Barbarian West': A Form of Orthodox Christian Anti-Western Critique," in A. Krawchuk and T. Bremer (eds.), *Eastern Orthodox Encounters of Identity and Otherness: Values, Self-Reflection, Dialogue* (New York: Palgrave Macmillan, 2014): 141–158.

> My land, tell me, what is happening?
> [...] Have you ever seen
> Such a shame and such barbarism?
> [... Should be] Pitilessly destroyed
> These barbarians and savages
> Who greedily gulp blood of our children,
> And blood of our mothers ...[144]

The "conservative turn" in Russia (since the beginning of the third presidency of Vladimir Putin in 2012) made "you the barbarian" narrative prevailing. Russia's leadership emphatically asserts Russia as one of the global "civilizations" and "poles" in the multipolar world, and not a wretched periphery of the West. The chosen tactic is the tactic of denigrating "the West," representing it as unworthy of its position at the center of the map. Russia's state-sponsored propaganda and public opinion both are at pains to portray Western Europe as the locus of moral corruption—the decay of all traditions and family values. Out of this attitude, the word "Gayrope" was coined, conflating "Europe" and "gays" in one concept.[145]

Out of this also comes a focus on a certain kind of story about the West in the Russian media. In February 2014, for example, the giraffe Marius was killed in order to exclude inbreeding, and fed to the lions in the zoo of Copenhagen. Coverage of this episode acquired biblical proportions in the Russian press and social media. For example, the search on the Russian central and regional press for the words "giraffe Marius" returned nearly 2000 hits.[146] People were raging at the decision of the zoo's administration, unanimously calling it "barbarism." Even the Russian central press and highest officials, such as the Minister of the Natural Resources Sergei Donskoi referred to this episode as a "'civilized' barbarianism."[147]

---

144 Musa Jalil, "Varvarstvo," in Jalil, *Moabitskaia tetrad'* (Moscow: Khudozh.lit., 1969).
145 Tat'iana Riabova and O. Riabov, "'Geiropa': Gendernoe izmerenie obraza Evropy v praktikakh politicheskoi mobilizatsii," *Zhenshina v rossiiskom obshchestve* 68, no. 3 (2013).
146 *Integrum Profi*, July 1, 2020.
147 Svetlana Basharova, "Minprirody ne pozvolit raschleniat' nashikh zverei v zarubezhnykh zooparkakh," *Izvestiia*, October 20, 2015; Evgeny Shestakov, "Oni ubivaiut vsekh, kogo zovut Marius?" *Rossiiskaia gazeta*, February 14, 2014.

Geopolitical Messianisms

Messianism is the fourth outcome from the situation of relative deprivation of recognition (see **Figure 2**). To put it bluntly, Messianism can arise from a situation of an acutely perceived discrepancy between the nation's self-perception and its reputation worldwide. Whereas the struggle for recognition is grounded on the idea of "honor" and fears of "losing face," Messianism, by contrast, emerges as a radical negation of the need for recognition, grounded on the assumption that "we" are cardinally different from and better than all others, and therefore immune to what others think about "us." Political Messianism in this sense is a method for the ideological reimagining of the self as a community of hidden, non-transparent, or even transcendental importance. Lindemann points to the fact that "self-glorification often is the result of a process of stigmatization by which excluded actors transform their negative difference into something particularly positive, transforming a 'pariah people' into an 'elected people'."[148]

The working definition of Messianism in (geo)politics includes the following elements. First, the belief in the community's uniqueness, which acquires the proportion of exceptionalism. Second, the idea that this status of exceptionalism has salvific effects for others, possibly also for the whole world. Third, the futuristic orientation, which, in the ultimate case, borders with eschatological vision of the end of the world. Fourth, Messianic imagination necessitates the vision of a nemesis, from which the nation is predestined to save the world.[149]

Messianism is a complex and fluid phenomenon, and the above-mentioned components may have different meanings and interrelations. For example, the historical form of the "Moscow —

---

148 Lindemann, *International Politics of Recognition*, 210. Cf. with the concept of "cognitive cocoon" of Messianism, which allows a state to position itself as a great power, even if it is not recognized as such by others (in relation to Russia, this concept was explored by Alicja Curanovic, "Russia's Mission in the World," *Problems of Post-Communism* 66, no. 4 (2018): 254.)
149 Alicja Curanovic identifies a somewhat similar set of distinctive features of Messianism: special destiny, moral superiority and non-pragmatic motivation of the political actions (Curanovic, "Russia's Mission in the World," 254.)

Third Rome" doctrine proved to be flexible enough to accommodate different, sometimes mutually incommensurable, Messianic visions.[150] These visions included concepts such as the Russian people as the bearer of the only true faith in the world, the legitimization of expansionism and seizing Istanbul from the Ottoman Empire, self-perception as a guarantor of peace and stability in the world, and many more. As an attempt to work out a taxonomy of Messianisms, this research identifies the following ideological iterations of Messianism:

First, the "weak" and the "strong" Messianisms. The "weak" version of Messianism deals with the vision of the national uniqueness, such as the concept of a "state-civilization." "Weak Messianism" helps to avoid comparisons or even excludes a community from the international order. Russia as a "unique civilization" is a typical representative of the ideological conceptualization, characteristic for "weak Messianism."[151] Sociological surveys identify that 50 to 60% of the Russians believe in the country's *Sonderweg*.[152] There could be a long roster of Russia's unique features, catering to different ideological and political needs. These features may include the special role of the state, the unique "spirituality" of the people, the exceptional role of Christianity in the life of the nation, the extraordinary territorial expanse of the country and its unique strategic position in Eurasia, and so on.[153] The "strong" version of Messianism argues that the community is not just one of many different "civilizations," but it is like nobody else: the only country keeping the true faith, for example.

Second, positive and negative exceptionality Positive exceptionality is grounded on the assumption that "we" are the best. The

---

150 See, among other studies of the doctrine: Jardar Østbø, *The New Third Rome: Readings of a Russian Nationalist Myth* (Stuttgart: ibidem-Verlag, 2015); Dmitry Sidorov, "Post-Imperial Third Romes: Resurrections of a Russian Orthodox Geopolitical Metaphors," *Geopolitics* 11, no. 2 (2006): 317–347.
151 See Chapter 3 in this volume.
152 "Osobyi rossiiskii put'," *Levada-Tsentr*, April 7, 2014, available at: https://www.levada.ru/2014/04/07/osobyj-rossijskij-put/.
153 For example: Boris Dubin, "Mifologiia 'osobogo puti' v obshchestvennom mnenii sovremennoi Rossii," in E. Pain (ed.), *Ideologiia "osobogo puti" v Rossii i Germanii: Istoki, soderzhanie, posledstviia* (Moscow: Tri kvadrata, 2010): 211–229.

negative one emerges, when the community sees itself as the worst, the most wretched and unhappy nation in the world. Negative exceptionality, grounded on the Biblical assumption that "the last shall be first" (Mathew 20:16) and "blessed are the poor" (Luke 6:20) — can be no less powerful than the positive Messianism.[154] The idea that "we" are the most suffering and humiliated nation, and precisely *because of that* "we" are chosen by God, was a long-time favourite in the 19th-century Russian political thought. In any case, the "strong version" of Messianism revolves around the idea of being chosen by God and playing some providential mission in the history of humankind.

Third, "saving others" can happen in the historical and transcendental planes of interpretation. On the one hand, Messianism can instill the vision of the country, vested with a mission to spread the right ideals or institutions across the globe. One can think of the American exceptionalism or the Soviet internationalistic communism. On the other hand, Messianism can take the shape of serving God, or fulfilling God's will in the world, not serving other people. For example, a country can entertain a Messianic vision of itself as the ultimate destroyer of the world, which is part of the God's design.

Fourth, proactive Messianism and status quo Messianism. In relation to plans for the future, Messianism can motivate people to actively do something, for example, transform the self and the world around them. However, there is an opposite belief in a powerful conservative and self-legitimizing potential — the assumption that a community is fulfilling its Messianic task by simply being, keeping true to itself and its original "agreement" with God. Anthony Smith came up with the distinction between covenant and missionary Messianisms, which grasps the distinction between doing something and just being. The latter promises salvation to the chosen people, if it is faithful to the "covenant" with God, whereas

---

154 Cf. Andrei Zorin, "'Osobyi put' Rossii' — ideia transformatsionnogo proryva v russkoi kul'ture," in T. Atnashev, M. Velizhev and A. Zorin (eds.), *"Osobyi put'": ot ideologii k metodu* (Moscow: NLO, 2018): 43–49; Dirk Uffelmann, *Der erniedrigte Christus: Metaphern und Metonymien in der russischen Kultur und Literatur* (Köln: Böhlau Verlag, 2010).

others are predestined to perish. The task of saving the self, in this vision, acquires universal importance as part of God's plans about this world. The former, missionary Messianism, advances the imperative to save others by spreading the word of truth and instilling righteous mores among them (peacefully or otherwise).[155]

Fifth, the image of the enemy can be couched in abstract religious and ethical terms (e.g. Antichrist), or—and more often than not—it is embodied as a specific geopolitical entity, such as—the "Great Satan" (i.e. the US) for some Islamic movements. At the same time, Messianism implies that "Others" should be saved. This ambiguity prods Messianic ideologists to create "doubles": "true Europe" and "false Europe,"[156] for example, in order to separate those who should be destroyed from those who should be saved.

From a bird's eye view, Messianic ideas have gradually populated the post-Soviet intellectual landscape. **Figure 3** shows that mentions of a "Russian mission" and "Russian role" multiplied during Putin's presidencies, especially around 2005–2008 and 2014–2018, when debates about official ideology coincided with the country's decisive moves on the international stage. Of course, these discussions are not equivalent to Messianism, but they created the communicative environment in which the circulation of Messianic ideas became possible.

---

155 Anthony Smith, *Chosen Peoples* (Oxford: Oxford University Press, 2003): 49.
156 The distinction between "true" and "false Europe" is elaborated in: Iver Neumann, *Russia and the Idea of Europe: A Study of Identity and International Relations*. 2nd ed. (New York: Routledge, 2017).

Figure 3. Absolute numbers of mentions of the phrase "role of Russia" in the federal press, and "mission of Russia" in all media.

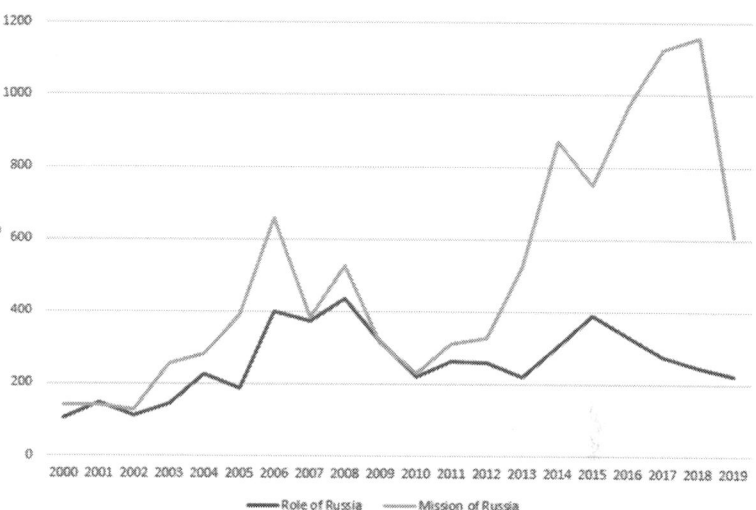

Data source: Integrum Profi. Calculated and plotted by the author.

Rejection of Soviet communism in the early 1990s motivated intellectuals and the public to reject any ideology and any Messianic or utopian vision out of hand. The prevalent view on the matter was that "the best ideology is one hundred sorts of tea in a food store, and preferably with sugar."[157] This anti-ideological stance found its expression in the Constitution (1993), article 13, paragraph 1 and 2, which states: "ideological diversity shall be recognized in the Russian Federation. No ideology shall be proclaimed as state ideology or as obligatory." This standpoint resonated with Putin's public speeches during his first and second presidencies (2000–2008), and especially with his ironic remark about "Russian ancient folk entertainment—searching for the national idea," which he made in his State of the Nation address of 2007.[158] In the same year, deputy prime minister and the would-be President of Russia Dmitry

---

157 Konstantin Kedrov, "Chelovek razumnyi i chelovek bezumnyi," *Novye izvestiia*, March 3, 1998.
158 Vladimir Putin, "Poslanie Federal'nomu Sobraniiu," April 26, 2007, available at: http://www.kremlin.ru/events/president/transcripts/24203.

Medvedev admonished to stop talking about Russia's Messianic role, which could only distract people from the important domestic issues.[159]

In opposition to the official resistance to Messianism, the margins of the political arena had developed into hotbeds of Messianic ideas already by the mid-1990s. The patriotic opposition from both left and right was developing a strong opinion that ideological strategic vision and a belief in Russia's global mission are instrumental for the country's existence and prosperity. In this milieu, the vision of Russia as a *Katechon* gained currency, which comes down to the idea that Russia is preordained to play an exceptional role in the apocalyptic history of the last days of the world. Russia either somehow saves the world from the influence of Satan, thereby preventing the coming of the Antichrist, or it provides the "infrastructure of salvation" in its territory, when the Antichrist is already in full control elsewhere in the world. In the post-Soviet context, visions of Russia as a *Katechon* acquired much ascendance in the group of thinkers, who could be identified with the camp of "political Orthodoxy."[160] This group came up with a flurry of Messianic concepts, whose common trait was geopolitization of the religious imagination about Russia, and the call for expansionism: the larger Russia is, the more peoples' souls it can save from going to hell. For example, historian and science fiction writer Dmitry Volodikhin claims that Christianity lies in ruins across the whole of Europe, and it is therefore incumbent upon Russia as *Katechon* to re-Christianize "colossal territories" and turn them into "territories of salvation."[161] Mikhail Nazarov developed another, perhaps the most articulated vision of Messianic expansionism. He is one of the "tsar-worshipers" with a noticeable slant towards anti-Seminism. Instead, this means the hard problem of responsibility for the destinies of humanity: "… the Russian idea transformed from the idea of salvation for our own people only into the idea of salvation of as many

---

159 Dmitry Vladimirov, "U komissarov," *Rossiiskaia gazeta*, July 27, 2007.
160 Anastasia Mitrofanova, *The Politicization of Russian Orthodoxy: Actors and Ideas* (Stuttgart: ibidem-Verlag, 2005).
161 Dmitry Volodikhin, "Dve Moskvy," *Nash sovremennik*, no. 9, September 30, 2012.

people of the world as possible. Here lies the historiosophic meaning of successful expansion of Russia ... This is the nature of Russia's geopolitical miracle — its enormous expanses."[162]

The concept of *Katechon* powers is not only expansionist Messianism, but also Messianism of covenant, according to which Russia fulfills its mission as a Retainer even if it "just is." At this point, visions of *Katechon* and the besieged fortress may coincide. *Katechon* as a "besieged fortress" gained prominence in the mid-2000s, when the fundaments of post-Soviet conservatism were crystallized on the grounds of *Young Conservatives* and the "Russian Doctrine" movements. For example, in the beginning of the 2010s, Egor Kholmogorov drifted from the expansionist towards a different interpretation of Messianism. For him, Russia's historical mission comes down to that of the killer of global hegemons, who purported to replace Russia from its position as the "Third Rome": Napoleon and Hitler. "We are the destroyers of the Towers of Babel," says he elsewhere.[163] Elaborating on this point, Kholmogorov ponders on Russia's today's role as a "spoiler" of all plans of the Western powers to establish the global order. So, by simply being and sticking with its traditional ways, Russia prevents the Last Days to come.[164] In his blog post, reproduced on the pages of *Vzgliad*, Kholmogorov reflected on the change of his opinion: "now I understand that there isn't any mission. What is left is to "spoil" [*ostalos' meshat'*]. [Russia is] just a spoiler."[165]

Consolidation of Putin's authoritarianism, the Orange revolution in Ukraine, and the polemics about the ideological identity of the United Russia party created the intellectual clout for the cautious reception of some Messianic ideas in 2005–2008. In this period,

---

162 Nazarov, *Vozhdiu Tret'ego Rima: K poznaniia russkoi idei v predapokalipsicheskoe vremia* (Moscow: Russkaia ideia, 2004). See also: Nazarov, "Zapad, kommunizm i russkii vopros," *rusidea.org*, 1995, available at: https://rusidea.org/12005.
163 Egor Kholmogorov, "Osobaia missiia Russkogo naroda," December 22, 2017, available at: https://bditelnost.info/2017/12/22/egor-holmogorov-osobaya-missiya-russkogo-naroda/.
164 Kholmogorov, *Russkii proekt. Restavratsiia budushchego* (Moscow: Eksmo-Algoritm, 2005): 175.
165 Kholmogorov, "Geroi dolzhen umeret'," *Vzgliad*, December 4, 2013, available at: http://admin.vz.ru/columns/2013/12/4/662621.html.

the leaders of the United Russia and pro-Kremlin thinkers tested the Messianic ground by dropping three ideas. The first pertains to Russia's global role as a peacekeeper in the context of her more assertive foreign policy of this period. The second feeds on growing anti-Westernism, connected with searches for a global moral-conservative alternative to the liberal West. The third also capitalizes on anti-Westernism, but here is associated with criticism of Western multi-culturalism and with the promotion of the imperial (mostly the Soviet-like) model for internal national harmony (see **Table 1**).

Table 1. Components of Messianism in the official press.

Levels of interpretation	Intellectual and political sources	Ideological content
Doctrinal level	Conservative official ideology, contribution of the ROC	Defender of the traditional morality against Western left liberalism and secularism
International level	Russia's international assertiveness, Putin's "Munich speech"	Stabilizer of the global order, promoter of the multipolar world model and opposition to the US hegemony
Domestic level	Crackdown on radical nationalism, appropriation of the Soviet past	Alternative model for multi-culturalism: harmony of intra-state national and confessional relations

The leadership of the United Russia proved to be receptive to these ideas. In 2006–2008, Iury Shuvalov, one of the leaders of this party and the head of the Center for Social Conservative Politics, presented his two visions of Russia's mission. First, he nailed down Russia's uniqueness as a multinational country, whose model of peaceful coexistence should serve as the global alternative to "Western" left-liberal multiculturalism.[166] Shuvalov expressed this idea by speaking about the unique Russian historical experience of tolerance and co-existence of many nations and religious within the single imperial political body. In his view, "this is the vision of the

---

166 Cf.: Aleksandr Dugin, "My — imperiia osvoboditel'," *Krasnaia Zvezda*, March 20, 1999.

future world, which we have to promote."¹⁶⁷ Later on, he said: "Russia's mission is the mission of benevolence [*missiia dobra*], especially in the context of our multi-national country," which implies harmonious intra-state relations.¹⁶⁸ Secondly, he presented his vision of Russia's mission as a provider of "peaceful development and the progress of humanity," and a supporter the balance of powers on the international stage.¹⁶⁹

In 2009 debates about the party's program intensified, and one of its leaders Andrei Isaev came up with a new Messianic proposal to consider Russia's role in the world as "somehow connected with the concept of justice." He specified that his understanding of justice had nothing to do with social justice, fraught with revolutionary potential, but rather as justice in international relations, namely as the struggle against a unipolar world.¹⁷⁰ Konstantin Kosachev fleshed out the idea of justice in international relations by arguing that Russia would not participate in the unfair accumulation of riches by those who are already rich, but instead would become the "lobbyist of ... developing economics" in the world.¹⁷¹

Preparations for the new electoral circle and the wave of mass protests in 2011/12 created a new political climate. In November 2011, Medvedev seemingly renounced his previous anti-Messianic statements by ruminations about Russia's historical mission.¹⁷² Laying out his understanding of Russia as a "state-civilization," Vladimir Putin pointed at Russia's ability to maintain "harmony of identities [*garmoniia samobytnosti*] of the peoples of Russia."¹⁷³ Sergei Naryshkin, then the speaker of the State Duma, believes that Russia's mission consists in "maintaining justice in the world," and

---

167 N.a., "Suverennaia demokratiia: pervye itogi diskussii," *Edinaia Rossiia: ofitsial'nyi sait*, September 21, 2006.
168 Anna Zakatnova, "Missiia dobra," *Rossiiskaia gazeta*, February 26, 2008.
169 Maria Sokolova, "Ne upustit' shansa stat' liderom," *Parlamentskaia gazeta*, February 7, 2008.
170 Andrei Isaev, "Russkaia missiia—spravedlivost'," *Izvestiia*, February 16, 2009.
171 Konstantin Kosachev, "'Bol'shaia vos'merka' i arkhitektura mira," *Izvestiia*, July 7, 2008.
172 Ivan Afinogenov, "S nami pravda," *Vzgliad*, November 27, 2011, available at: https://vz.ru/politics/2011/11/27/541919.html.
173 Vladimir Putin, "Rossiia—strana-tsivilizatsii," *Komsomol'skaia pravda*, October 4, 2019.

specifically, in defending the weak against the strong.[174] Elsewhere he voiced another popular idea about the Messianic claims of the West, and especially—U.S.[175] In this context, Russia's mission comes down precisely to refutation of these claims and establishing genuine equality among the subjects of international relations.[176] Elsewhere he repeated that Russia's mission was "defense of justice in the whole world,"[177] whereas Shuvalov pronounced the plan of consolidating all traditionalist forces of the world under Russian guidance.[178]

So, on the qualitative level, two most important developments could be described as: first, a gradual rapprochement between the mainstream Messianism and the right-left patriotic one; and second, Messianic discourses in the mainstream debates. These discourses were crystallized from a disconnected set of ideas into a more or less consensual vision of Russia's global mission as a combination of three elements: the guarantor of the global peace and stability, the keeper of true (i.e. traditional, authentic, conservative) values, and the model for a healthy intra-state national and confessional relations.

Conclusions

This chapter outlined the main parameters of the Russian geopolitical culture, which are fleshed out in the rest of the book. This analysis reveals the central concern with the issue of international recognition, which builds upon the geopolitical insecurities and

---

174 Sergei Naryshkin, "Naryshkin nazval missiei Rossii zashchitu spravedlivosti v mire," *lenta.ru*, April 2, 2016, available at: https://lenta.ru/news/2016/04/02/naryshkin/.
175 N.a., "ES v pokhod sobralsia," *Izvestiia*, September 20, 2016; Aleksandr Khramchikhin, "Mira Ukraine ne vidat'," *Nezavisimaia gazeta*, December 16, 2016.
176 Sergei Naryshkin, "Tret'ia mirovaia voina dlia chelovechestva stanet poslednei," *Izvestiia*, July 30, 2015. Cf. Maria Zakharova's speech on "Tolstoi. Voskresen'ie", *Pervyi kanal*, December 23, 2018, available at: https://www.1tv.ru/shows/tolstoy-voskresene/vypuski/vypusk-programmy-tolstoy-vosk resene-v-21-00-ot-23-12-2018.
177 Naryshkin, "Naryshkin nazval missiei Rossii zashchitu spravedlivosti," *Lenta.ru*, April 2, 2016.
178 Elena Chinkova, "Frantsuzy prosiat Rossiiu vozglavit' bor'bu s gei-lobbi," *Komsomol'skaia pravda*, June 19, 2013.

political-religious ideas of the Russian exceptionalism. Today, the perceived lack of recognition pushes geopolitical imagination towards the panoply of Messianic ideas, civilizational rhetoric, enlarging the territorial scale and reversing the "civilization-barbarism" duality in a way, which portrays the Western nemesis as the genuine barbarian.

The following vignette illustrates this intertwined complex of Messianic ideas. On May 5, 2016 the Mariinsky orchestra performed a concert amidst the ruins of recently re-captured Palmyra, Syria. The orchestra was conducted by Valery Gergiev and played — among others — Prokofiev's piece. At that time, it was seen as the icing on the cake of Russia's military operation in Syria, which involved some 50,000 troops and several dozens of aircrafts. The concert in Palmyra sent a double message, which was powerful and easy to decipher.

Firstly, by bringing the best of its artistic achievements to Palmyra — the cradle of Western culture and a place which had been pillaged and destroyed by ISIS — Russia defies evil and death.[179] The documentary "Palmyra," produced by propagandist Evgeny Poddubnyi,[180] highlighted the role of Russian field engineers, who painstakingly cleared the entire city of mines, risking their lives. The storyline about sappers reinforces the main thread of the "Palmyra narrative": Russia brings peace, high culture and restored normalcy, whereas the Western support of the Syrian opposition only wreaked havoc and invited barbarians into this land. Secondly, meddling in the Syria conflict rehearses the age-old narrative about Russia's role as a bridge and a reconciler of East and West. With this narrative in mind, war correspondents and political figures portray NATO's military operation in Syria as a tragic misunderstanding and violent suppression of the East by the West.

---

179 For more on the "Syria spectacle" see: Andrey Makarychev and Alexandra Yatsyk, "The Sword and the Violin: Aesthetics of Russia's Security Policy," *The Journal of Slavic Military Studies* 30, no. 4 (2017): 543–560.
180 "Pal'mira. Dokumental'nyi fil'm Evgeniia Poddubnogo," May 21, 2016, available at: https://www.youtube.com/watch?v=U6FbV7nDXjA.

2 Creating Usable Spaces in Education: Textbooks on Geopolitics

Introduction

Geopolitics in Russia seems to be climbing the pedestal of toppled Marxism. Its gurus and pontifices claim it to be an all-explaining and all-embracing discipline, or rather an analytical strategy for the whole corpus of social sciences, and a "worldview" supplying people with ready-made interpretations of the past and prognostications for the future.[181] Besides, geopolitics benefits from its reputation as a "prohibited science" under the Soviet regime, and from its scent of arcane knowledge about the fundamentals of world order. Together with its aesthetic appeal to the imperial "sublime," all these made it an intellectual vogue of sorts, and the object of a fixed look from the top of the political elite.[182]

Discursive strategies of shaping a "usable space" in textbooks on geopolitics constitute the analytic focus of this research, which operates on the methodological borderland reclaimed by "textbook studies" and critical geopolitics. These two fields neatly correspond to the form and content of textbooks on geopolitics; their dialectical interrelationship brings methodological specificity to the study of such an object. On the one hand, university textbooks have a peculiar status as semiofficial documents, usually approved by the authorities, and effectively shaping the mass consciousness on important social and political issues. On the other hand, textbooks on geopolitics are read in a classroom (and usually written) by intellectual "proletarians," thereby mirroring their idiosyncratic protest (directed not against their own government but against the West). So, if "embedded in textbooks are narratives and stories that nation

---

[181] Eduard Solov'ev, *Rossiia v meniaiushchemsia mire: Geopoliticheskie aspekty formirovaniia rossiiskoi natsional'noi identichnosti* (Moscow: IMEMO RAN, 2010): 39–41.
[182] Harsha Ram, *The Imperial Sublime. A Russian Poetics of Empire* (Madison: University of Wisconsin Press, 2003).

states choose to tell about themselves,"[183] the crucial question arises: who are those, who speak on behalf of a "nation state," and how is their subjectivity being formed through the social background and institutional affiliations of the authors of textbooks?

The focus of textbooks raises another question about the ideological function of pedagogical media in general. Textbook studies scholarship promotes a research strategy of uncovering assumed epistemologies and power relations in education, building upon the assumption that textbooks are capable of forming the ideological worldviews of the audience.[184] To be sure, the "ideological" impact of a textbook is never unequivocal and unidimensional, and a large part of ideological meaning is constructed in contextualized interaction between textbooks and audiences,[185] but in case of geopolitics, the thesis of "ideological impact" could be accepted without a great stretch. The reason is that texbooks on geopolitics not only function in the role-defined setting of higher education in which a teacher is raised to a position of an "authority" and a textbook—authoritative source of information, but also in the media environment, in which they have no competition. Unless the audience has wide access to non-Russian language sources (which it generally has not), textbooks on geopolitics remain the most comprehensive and easily accessible source of information on geopolitical knowledge for the whole of the Russian readership, not only for the students.

The ideological content of textbooks on geopolitics is explored by methods of critical geopolitics, which helps to emphasize that textbooks do not merely describe international relations and its

---

183 Keith Crawford, "The Role and Purpose of Textbooks," *International Journal of Historical Learning, Teaching and Research* 3, no. 2 (2003): 5.
184 E.g. Egil B. Johnsen, *Textbooks in the Kaleidoscope: A Critical Survey of Literature and Research on Educational Texts* (Oslo: Scandinavian UP, 1993). See also the UNESCO guidebook, prepared by the Georg Eckert Institute: *UNESCO Guidebook on Textbook Research and Textbook Revision*, 2nd ed. (Braunschweig: GEI, 2009): 7–8.
185 On this: Veronika Kalmus, "What Do Pupils and Textbooks Do with Each Other? Methodological Problems of Research on Socialization through Educational Media," *Journal of Curriculum Studies* 36, no. 4 (2004): 469–485; Simone Lässig, "Textbooks and Beyond: Educational Media in Context(s)," *Journal of Educational Media, Memory and Society* 1, no. 1 (2009): 1–23.

theories, but themselves constitute a political discourse: textbooks on geopolitics are geopolitics too, so the way in which textbooks organize their epistemology and ethic is also (geo)political. In this chapter, as many as 40 textbooks have been analyzed — including their different editions.[186]

Geopolitics Redux: Studying, Teaching, Selling

The surge of post-Soviet writings on geopolitics gives a hint of an almost psychoanalytical irony: the very existence of this "discipline" became possible only after the destruction of its "object of desire" — the Soviet Union. In the early 1990s, however, geopolitics made relatively modest advances into the Russian society, academia and education. Geographers and economists were among the first to stake out this new terrain of research. Sergei Lavrov (1928–2000), the president of the Russian Geographic Society in the 1990s, wrote an authoritative series of articles on the necessity to rehabilitate and revitalize geopolitics as an academic field,[187] and organized the first conference on geopolitics in Russia in October 1994.[188] At the same time Elgiz Pozdniakov from the Institute of

---

186 Nikolai Ashenkampf and S. Pogorel'skaia, *Geopolitika* (Moscow, 2010 [2005]); Tat'iana Beidina, *Osnovy geopolitiki* (Chita, 1999); Ivan Blokhin, *Politologiia. Sovremennaia geopolitika* (Moscow, 2003); Vladimir Dergachev, *Geopolitika* (Moscow, 2007 [2004]); Aleksandr Dugin, *Geopolitika Rossii* (Moscow, 2012); Kamalutdin Gadzhiev, *Geopolitika* (Moscow, 2013 [2012, 2011, 2000, 1998]); Vitalii Karpov, *Geopolitika* (St Petersburg, 1999); Elena Kharitonova et al., *Geopolitika* (Samara, 2010); Vladimir Kolosov and N. Mironenko, *Geopolitika i politicheskaia geografiia* (Moscow, 2005 [2001]); Natalia Komleva, *Osnovy geopolitiki* (Yekaterinburg, 2008); Galina Lebedeva, *Geopolitika* (St Petersburg, 2012); Nikolai Luk'ianovich, *Geopolitika* (Moscow, 2011 [2004, 2003]); Viacheslav Mikhailov (ed.), *Geopolitika* (Moscow, 2010 [2007]); Rashid Mukhaev, *Geopolitika* (Moscow, 2012 [2010, 2007]); Nikolai Nartov, *Geopolitika* (Moscow, 2012 [2010, 2007, 2002, 1999]); Naum Sirota, *Geopolitika* (St Petersburg, 2009[2006]); Andrei Tuzikov, *Osnovy geopolitiki* (Moscow, 2013 [2004]); Irina Vasilenko, *Geopolitika sovremennogo mira* (Moscow, 2013 [2003, 2006]); Viktor Zheltov, *Geopolitika: Istoriia i teoriia* (Kemerovo, 2007); Aleksandr Zubkov, *Geopolitika i problemy natsional'noi bezopasnosti Rossii* (St Petersburg, 2004).
187 Sergei Lavrov, "Geopolitika: vozrozhdenie zapretnogo napravleniia," *Izv. RGO* 4 (1993); Lavrov, "Eto strashnoe slovo 'geopolitika'," in Lavrov, *V kakom mire my zhivem: Razmyshleniia geopolitika* (St Petersburg, 2001).
188 Lavrov (ed.), *Geopoliticheskie i geoekonomicheskie problemy Rossii. Materialy nauchnoi konferentsii* (St Petersburg, 1995).

World Economy and International Relations of the Russian Academy of Science (Moscow), Konstantin Pleshakov from the Institute of the USA and Canada, and Vladimir Razuvaev, the head of the Institute of Europe at the same Academy published first monographs on geopolitics.[189] But the greatest public resonance has been evoked by Aleksandr Dugin's bestseller *Foundations of Geopolitics* (1996),[190] whose ideas and style reverberated in tens of textbooks to be written later.

In Russia, geopolitics is being taught at each single university in a continually increasing number of specializations.[191] Like "kul'turologiia," which in the 1990s professionally accommodated teachers from the Marxist disciplines,[192] some sources of Russian geopolitics could be traced back to the Soviet time; for example, one of the biggest centers for teaching and studying geopolitics is the Department of National Security at the Russian Academy for State Service which before 1991 was the Academy of Social Sciences of the Communist Party of the Soviet Union. However, in many cases geopolitics became a niche, providing jobs for young scholars, who received their first academic degrees (*Kandidat nauk*) in the 1990s

---

189 Elgiz Pozdniakov (ed.), *Geopolitika: Teoriia i praktika* (Moscow, 1993); Vladimir Razuvaev, *Geopolitika postsovetskogo prostranstva* (Moscow, 1993); Konstantin Pleshakov, *Geo-ideologicheskaia paradigma* (Vzaimodeistvie geopolitiki i ideologii na primere otnoshenii mezhdu SSSR, SShA i KNR v kontinental'noi Vostochnoi Azii, 1949–1991 gg.) (Moscow, 1994).

190 See the analysis of his textbook in: Alan Ingram, "Alexander Dugin. Geopolitics and Neo-Fascism in Post-Soviet Russia," *Political Geography* 20, no. 8 (2001): 1029–1051; John Dunlop, "Aleksandr Dugin's 'Neo-Eurasian' Textbook and Dmitry Trenin's Ambivalent Response," *Harvard Ukrainian Studies* 25, no. 1–2 (2001): 91–127.

191 Sirke Mäkinen, "Geopolitical Teaching and Worldview. Making the Future Generation in Russia," *Geopolitics* 19, no. 1 (2014): 86–108. As of 2012, in the Perm State University, for example, geopolitics was taught for students majoring in the State and Municipal Administration in the 5th semester (3rd year of education) and it is allocated 144 hours, including 29 hours of lectures and 28–seminars. In the end of the course formal examination is held.

192 Marlène Laruelle, "The Discipline of Culturology: A New 'Ready-Made Thought' for Russia," *Diogenes* 51, no. 4 (2004), 23; Jutta Scherrer, "The Cultural/Civilizational Turn in Post-Soviet Identity-Building," in Per-Arne Bodin et al. (eds.), *Power and Legitimacy: Challenges from Russia* (London: Routledge, 2013): 153–154; Scherrer, *Kulturologie: Russland auf der Suche nach einer zivilizatorischen Identität* (Göttingen: Wallstein Verlag, 2003), especially pp. 36–44.

and 2000s. A random sample of six teachers' background shows that their first degrees were obtained after 1991.[193]

Geopolitics as a "scholarship" and university course has made a spectacular entry into Russian academia and the book market in the last two decades. The most popular textbook has been written by Nikolai Nartov in 5 editions with the total running to 135,000 copies; more than 30,000 copies of Vladimir Dergachev's textbook were printed in two editions; Irina Vasilenko's textbook has 4 editions with a total run 10,000 copies, and so on. At least up to now, the market for textbooks has undergone very little regulation by authorities. University professors are free to choose, depending on their tastes and the availability of textbooks in university libraries, which have no single policy for acquiring them. Thus, for example, the mass textbook in geopolitics at the Perm State University is Gadzhiev's edition of 1998, which has been acquired more than 1000 times; in Vladivostok University for Economy and Services, the basic textbook is Dergachev's (2004) — ca. 50 copies; in the Moscow City Pedagogical University it is the textbook by Rashid Mukhaev (2007) — ca. 50 copies, and so on. With the exception of Kolosov, Mironenko, and Gadzhiev, authors of these textbooks have no academic reputation; given the considerable capacity of the market, writing textbooks is a self-sustainable and rewarding activity.

The development of geopolitical language was instigated by a boom in Kremlin and rightist think tanks at the turn of the 2000s — which almost invariably employed this novel terminology. Gleb Pavlovskii's Foundation for Effective Politics (1995) became a breeding ground for a bunch of pro-Putin's organizations with an

---

[193] In Saratov State University "geopolitics" is taught by Vera Semenova, PhD in political science (2004), Denis Krelenko, PhD in history (1999), and Olga Tsoberg, PhD in sociology (1995). A Special course, "Geopolitics and world culture," is taught at the North Caucasus Federal University (Stavropol) by I. Babin, PhD in history (2001). Geopolitics is taught at the Military University of the Ministry of the Defense by Iaroslav Volkov, PhD in history (1997). Peoples' Friendship University of Russia offers a course in geopolitics taught by Mikhail Grachev, PhD in philosophy (1994). Years of obtaining the first academic degree *(Kandidat nauk)* are in parenthesis. Source: webpages of the respective universities and the catalogue of defended dissertations at the Russian State Library.

interest in geopolitics such as the State-Patriotic Club, the Russian World Foundation, and so on. On the extreme right, the geopolitical theme is being developed by *Pravaya.ru*, the Information agency *Russian People's Line* (www.ruskline.ru), the *Agency of Political News* (www.apn.ru), and so on.[194] In these conditions, a number of textbooks on geopolitics was prepared, including, among others, Anatolii Marinchenko's manual. He is connected with the Academy of National Security, which was established in 1997 with the assistance of the State Security services; today it is affiliated with a number of obscure organizations such as the Ufological Association of the Union of Russian Higher Officers, the Club of Veterans of the Criminal Investigation and so forth.

The camp of right-wing geopolitical theorists includes the Academy of Geopolitical Problems (1999), headed by Colonel General Leonid Ivashov, which actively participated in shaping the Concept of National Security and the War Doctrine of Russia. This NGO was established in 1999 and became known for its nationalist, fundamentalist and pan-Slavic views. It boasts of having more than 200 scholars with doctoral degrees in five branches. Its St Petersburg branch was founded by Igor Kefeli,[195] who is a head of the department of cultural and global studies at the Baltic State Technical University, and an editor of the journal *Geopolitika i bezopasnost'* (in 2010 this journal was entered in the list of journals, approved by the Highest Attestation Commission).[196] The academy's Yekaterinburg branch is headed by Professor Natalia Komleva, an author of another textbook. Nikolai Nartov, who wrote the most popular series of textbooks on geopolitics, is another "academician" of the Academy of Geopolitical Problems.

---

194 See in detail: Laruelle, *Inside and Around the Kremlin's Black Box: The New Nationalist Think Tanks in Russia* (Stockholm: Institute for Security and Development Policy, 2009), available at: https://www.isdp.eu/content/uploads/images/stories/isdp-main-pdf/2009_laruelle_inside-and-around-the-kremlins-black-box.pdf.
195 Igor Kefeli, *Sotsiokul'turnaia dinamika rossiiskoi geopolitiki. Uchebnoe posobie* (St Petersburg, 2001).
196 Other "geopolitical" journals include *Vestnik MGU. Ser. Globalistika i geopolitika*; *Vek globalizatsii*; *Voennaia mysl'* (rubric "Geopolitika i bezopasnost'"), etc.

The second type of producers of geopolitical discourse pertains to the "departmental" (*vedomstvennyi*) institutes of higher education, sometimes associated with military and security services such as the Military University of the Ministry of the Defense, the Border Guard Institute of the Federal Security Service, and sometimes with public administration (the North-Caucasus Academy of State Service in Rostov-on-Don[197]). One of the most popular textbooks has been edited by V. A. Mikhailov in 2007 and 2010, with the total run of 20,000 copies, and appeared under the aegis of the Russian Academy of State Service of the President of Russia, where in 2012 a Faculty of National Security—another hub of geopolitical studies, was established. A. I. Zubkov's textbook (2011) was published by the Academy of State Service of the Ministry of the Interior in St Petersburg. N. V. Luk'ianovich's textbook (2011) was published by the University of Finance of the Russian Government. The textbook by N. Ashenkampf and S. Pogorel'skai represents the Academy of State Fire-Protection Service at the Emergency Control Ministry.

Finally, there are "purely" academic institutions at the Russian Academy of Science (RAS) and specialized departments at the state universities. The Institute of World Economy and International Relations of the RAS hosts Kamalutdin Gadzhiev, another author of a textbook. Vladimir Kolosov works at the Institute of Geography at the RAS, where he heads the Center of Geopolitical Studies. Irina Vasilenko and Nikolai Mironenko teach at the Moscow State University. There are also many textbooks, published by provincial universities in the "genre" of "methodical manual."[198]

So, in the 2000s and 2010s, geopolitics has been institutionalized through university teaching, academic research in state-sponsored institutions of higher education, and think-tanks from the conservative and radical right-wing political spectrum. This

---

197 Now the South-Russian Branch of the Russian Academy of National Economy and State Service at the President of Russian Federation.
198 N. M. Golunov, *Geopoliticheskaia dinamika* (Novosibirsk, 1999); E. A. Kharitonova et al., *Geopolitika* (Samara, 2010); T. E. Beidina, *Osnovy geopolitiki* (Chita, 1999), etc. Because titles of the textbooks are similar, thereafter all references are given with the name of the author, year and page numbers.

"discipline" meets all formal criteria of academism, including institutionalization, teaching at the university, a semblance of a professional community (e.g. availability of doctoral degrees for those writing in geopolitics), adherence to the academic style of writing and quoting. Authors try to get approvals by state authorities on their textbooks; most of the textbooks in geopolitics are recommended by the Ministry of Education (e.g. Nartov, Gadzhiev), others—by the Education and Methodic Council of the Universities' Union in different academic fields (e.g. Marinchenko, Vasilenko, Luk'ianovich), or by the Academic Council of a particular university (e.g. Komleva), or by the non-governmental "Education and Methodic Center 'Professional Textbook'"(Dergachev). However, similarly to *kul'turologiia*, geopolitics "became institutionalized before it was conceptualized"; its academic status remains ambiguous due to unclear criteria of professionalism, dubious heuristic merits, conspicuous connections with ideology, and relative isolation of Russian geopolitics from the international academia.[199] As the corollary of all the aforementioned deficiencies and ironies, geopolitics generally features low academic standards.

The lowering of academic standards has not passed unnoticed by theorists of geopolitics in Russia;[200] some of whom proposed to distinguish between "vulgar geopolitics" of Duginite style, and "respectable geopolitics."[201] The latter, purged from "mythology," propaganda, and dilettantism, should produce pragmatically workable interpretative schemes, similar to how the theory of Mackinder provided "adequate geopolitical substantiation from the viewpoint of the British hegemonic [power] of the end of the 19th century."[202] To be sure, from the viewpoint of critical geopolitics,

---

199 Sergei Serebrianyi, "Est' li takaia nauka—'kul'turologiia'?" in N. Kocheliaeva (ed.), *Filologiia – iskusstvoznanie – kul'turologiia: Novye vodorazdely i perspektivy vzaimodeistviia* (St Petersburg, 2009): 147.

200 Eduard Solov'ev, *Rossiia v meniaiushchemsia mire: Geopoliticheskie aspekty formirovaniia rossiiskoi natsional'noi identichnosti* (Moscow, 2010): 35–54.

201 A. Bogaturov, "Poniatie mirovoi politiki v teoreticheskom diskurse," *Mezhdunarodnye protsessy* 2, no. 1 (2004): footnote 24.

202 A. Elatskov, "Geopolitika: Nauka i mifologiia," *Oikumena. Regionovedcheskie issledovaniia* 16, no. 1 (2011): 72 (the author is mistaken, Mackinder's "pivotal" work appeared not "in the end of 19th century" but in 1905).

the last statement is an object of critical analysis itself rather than analysis per se. For critical geopolitics, "classic geopolitics" is inescapably ideologically biased, because any geopolitical knowledge produces or reinforces power and is therefore geopolitical in itself. But it is not its ideological character as it is which prejudices geopolitics as an academic enterprise, but its pretention to be non-ideological—that is the lack of critical awareness of its own analytic instruments, which makes geopolitics essentially a spurious science. Having embraced a much broader interpretation of "false science," this chapter argues that unlike international relations theory or political geography, geopolitics fails to develop a critical and self-reflective approach to its field, to distinguish between its object of research and itself, and to pass the tests of verification and falsification.

Geopolitics: Ideology or pragmatism?

Close reading of textbooks on geopolitics uncovers two seemingly irreconcilable viewpoints, that geopolitics is "ideological science," and that it is "pragmatic science." On the one hand, Dugin's phrase "geopolitics is the worldview of [those in] power; [this is] science about power and for the power," reverberated in a number of textbooks.[203] In this context, "ideological" stands for the Marxist principle of "*partiinost*" (party-mindedness, or broader: partisanship) in science. Its Leninist interpretation points to two things: the impossibility of non-ideological standpoint for an analyst, and—according to his notion of "the criterion of practice in the theory of knowledge"—the necessity of an operationally effective theory. Both moments are embraced by Dugin in his reasoning on geographically-determined theorization in geopolitics. So, if the United States can only develop the doctrine of "Atlanticism" (i.e. justification for the dominance of maritime power in history), Russia is "predestined" to develop Eurasianism which substantiates Russia's position as the holder of the "geographical pivot of history" and

---

[203] Dugin, 1997, 13; Vasilenko, 2013. 43 (in earlier editions: 2003, 22–23; 2006, 31); Nartov, 1999. 38; Komleva, 2008, 4.

consequently as the hegemon of the world.[204] Reminiscent of the divide between "Soviet science" and "bourgeois science," the idea of relativity in geopolitics, according to those authors, does not prejudice geopolitics as a science.

On the other hand, for many an author geopolitics became almost a synonym of the liberation from the ideological fetters and "down to earth" "healthy pragmatism," based on national interest and calculations of advantages and disadvantages of (geo)political decisions. "Pragmatism" in this context should sustain anti-liberal and anti-Western criticism, according to which Russia has its own national interests, not always coinciding with ideological principles, violently imposed on Russia "first by Peter the Great, than by the Bolsheviks and in our times by the latter-day liberals."[205] At this juncture it becomes especially clear that "ideology" and "pragmatism" in geopolitical discourses is one and the same designator of an authentically Russian theory, which pays heed to national interests and fights all externally imposed concepts, inorganic and hostile to true "Russianness."

By extension, anti-Westernism is ubiquitous on the pages of textbooks. Thus, Gadzhiev's textbook of 2012 features chapters on the recent Russian-Georgian war of 2008, including a chapter entitled "The Role of the West in Unleashing the Georgian-Russian War."[206] This war is interpreted as "salvation of national honor" and the signal that "the period of endless retreats and concessions has ended."[207] Putin's period is commonly contrasted with the period of geopolitical weakness in the 1990s. Mikhailov writes that "starting from 2000 [Russia] is carrying out its steady policy of healthy pragmatism and defense of its national interests."[208] Like many other authors, she supports her statements by references to such right-wing intellectuals and web-resources as General Leonid Ivashov, Sergei Kara-Murza, Aleksandr Panarin, Natalia Naroch-

---

204 E.g. Dugin, 1997, 92. See also: Zubkov, 2004, 23; Dergachev, 2004, 117–118.
205 Zheltov, 2007, 221.
206 Gadzhiev, 1997, 380. Cf.: Gadzhiev, 2012, 36, 374, and especially on Russian-Georgian war, 436–443.
207 Gadzhiev, 2012, 442–443.
208 Mikhailov, 2010, 169, 366. Cf.: Mukhaev, 2010, 523.

nitskaia, Gennady Ziuganov, and neglects to even mention an opposite point of view.[209] Another textbook, written by general major of the Internal Service A. Zubkov, features radical right-wing and fundamentalist attitudes, resembling the position of such Orthodox fundamentalist organizations as *Narodnyi Sobor* (People's Assembly). He attacks the idea of "new world order," defined as the "global dictatorship of the West in the name of perpetuation of American political, economic and military hegemony"; he opposes to the concept of multiculturalism, cosmopolitanism, family planning and sexual education of children.[210]

Trying to represent a geopolitical version of the "authentic" Russian ideology, authors are constructing Russia's own geopolitical historiography. New editions of the textbooks in geopolitics boast of having improved chapters, in which they unscrupulously appropriate prominent thinkers of the past as precursors of "Russian geopolitical thought."[211] Nartov's textbook, for example, mentions Mikhail Lomonosov, Vladimir Dal, Dmitry Mendeleev and others in this context; including Vasilenko — Gogol, Tiutchev, Nikolai Berdiaev.[212] The central figure in Russian geopolitical thought is, however, Nikolai Danilevsky, "the great Russian scholar," represented as the founding father of the "civilization approach" and by extension as geopolitics in general, whose ideas continue to be keenly relevant for the 21st century.[213]

After Dugin, authors write about Eurasianism as the Russian school of geopolitics par excellence.[214] Eurasianist ideas lie in the

---

209 Cf.: Kharitonova, 2010, 86–89; Beidina, 1999, 19; Tuzikov, 2004, 128–129; Zubkov, 2011, 24, 38.
210 Zubkov, 2011, 25–32; Dergachev, 2004, 4.
211 Cf. in Nartov's textbook of 2002 23 pages were devoted to the Western schools in geopolitics and 23 to the "Russian school"; in his textbook of 2010 the proportion is different — 27 and 42 correspondingly. See also: Irina Alekseeva, *Geopoliticheskaia mysl' v Rossii: Genezis i osnovnye etapy razvitiia, konets XVIII–nachalo XX vv.* Dissertation (St Petersburg, 1999).
212 Nartov, 2010, 119; Vasilenko, 2013, 172.
213 Luk'ianovich, 2011, 10. Nartov, 2010, 8, 124.
214 On the interrelationship between geopolitics and Eurasianism see: Natalia Morozova, "Geopolitics, Eurasianism and Russian Foreign Policy under Putin," *Geopolitics* 14, no. 4 (2009): 667–686. Studies on Eurasianism are abundant; to name just a few which made for an influence on this paper: Graham Smith, "The Masks of Proteus: Russia, Geopolitical Shift and the New Eurasianism,"

conceptual center of the majority of textbooks in geopolitics. Among the most earnest "Duginite" textbooks is a work by Nikolai Nartov, which features a whole sub-chapter entitled "Eurasian Counter-globalism [Is] Russia's Future," in which students can read that there is a "great distance" between Russia and Europe, and in order to maintain Russia's authenticity and to control the Eurasian landmass, Russia has to unite with Kazakhstan, Tadzhikistan, Iran and Afganistan. In conclusion, Nartov quotes from Lev Gumilev's last interview: "If Russia is to be saved, it would happen only as a Eurasian country and only through Eurasianism.[215]

The popularity of this theory could be explained by its notion of a "geographical pivot of history" which lies in Eurasian landmasses (also called "the Heartland") and which is paradoxically derived from Mackinder's analysis (1904), designed politically to support the other side of the "Whale–Elephant" controversy — the British Empire against the Russian Empire.[216] Eurasianism gives a hint of optimism to the geopolitical meta-narrative of Russian history; although climaxed in the "greatest geopolitical catastrophe," this was just a lost battle not the war — the struggle between the Whale and the Elephant will continue for times to come, so as long as Russia possesses the "geographical pivot of histor," its Eurasian landmasses, she is invincible and still has all necessary "material preconditions" to claim the status of super-power or even the Messianic world leader if not now, but invariably — given the geographical determinism of those theorists! — one day in the future. But even today, Russia's territorial position raises her to the role of the world's "balance of powers."

Eurasianism, in other words, provides such an intellectual context, in which Russia continues to occupy the central place on the mental maps of the Russians. General Major Zubkov, in his textbook, paraphrases Mackinder: "who controls the heartland, he

---

Transactions of the Institute of British Geographers 24, no. 4 (1999): 481–500; Laruelle, *Russian Eurasianism: An Ideology of Empire* (Washington, DC: Woodrow Wilson Center, 2008).

215 Nartov, 2010, 172–174.
216 See on this: Bassin and Aksenov, "Mackinder and the Heartland Theory in Post-Soviet Geopolitical Discourse," *Geopolitics* 11, no. 1 (2006): 99–118.

controls the world politics, and first of all he has means to maintain geopolitical ... balance in the world."[217] Likewise, the rhetoric of the confrontation with the West elevates Russia to the position of an equal rival and the last bastion on the way of Americanization of the world; as Iakunin, Bagdasarian and Sulakshin write, Russia stands "in the epicenter of the world conflicts."[218] Even the narrative of mourning of the defunct Soviet Union, when its obliteration is pictured as the "key event of the 20th century,"[219] locates Russia in the center.

"Laws of geopolitics"

Eurasianism is associated with two intellectual tendencies in textbooks: legitimization of the Russian political regime as long as it is able to confront the West, and radicalization of the concept of geopolitical struggle. The latter means that if classic geopolitics tends to explain the world in terms of balance of powers, or maintaining the status quo with its view on the war as an extreme episode of the "Great Game," its revisionist version offers a sort of Trotskyite picture of the "permanent war" which flares all the time in the spheres of culture or economy, and occasionally envelops the military too. Unlike the Hobbesian *bellum omnium contra omnes*, geopolitics pictures global warfare as the orderly system of confrontations with Russia in the center. Similarly to Marxist analysis of the "permanent revolution," in geopolitical discourses Russia has to sequentially overcome rivals on her way to world dominance.

Professor Sergei Smul'skii, the head of the department of National Security at RASS defines geopolitics as "the system of theoretical knowledge about spatial expansionism of the states. We speak not only about territorial expansionism, but also about expansionism in other spaces."[220] Kamaludin Gadzhiev quotes Cecil

---

217 Zubkov, 2004, 75. Cf: Tuzikov, 2013, 5; Kolosov and Mironenko, 2001, 215.
218 Vladimir Iakunin et al., *Zapadnia: Novye tekhnologii bor'by s rossiiskoi gosudarstvennost'iu* (Moscow, 2010): 397; Marinchenko, 2013, 3; Luk'ianovich, 2011, 299.
219 Mikhailov, 2010, 135.
220 Sergei Smul'skii, "Geopolitika kak sistema teoreticheskikh znanii i metodologiia analiza mezhdunarodnykh otnoshenii," in Mikhailov (ed.), *Aktual'nye*, 14.

Rhodes, "expansion is everything," arguing that any country "of historical importance" inevitably embarks on expansionism.[221] "Trotskyite geopolitics" argues that expansionism is the "fundamental law of geopolitics,"[222] or the main property of the relations between states and spaces, regardless of the type of the political regime; disguised by lofty rhetoric of human rights and freedoms, liberal democracies act in geopolitics exactly as totalitarian regimes do.[223] In 2004, Leonid Ivashov started the conference on Russian geopolitical doctrine in St Petersburg as follows: "The world permanently lives in global fight. This fight reflects the fundamental opposition between powers of the Continent and powers of the Sea, [which] structures the world geopolitics and geopolitical processes."[224]

Eurasianist geopolitics specifies the "law of expansionism" as the never-ending struggle between the continental and maritime powers. The "first law of geopolitics," modeled after Halford Mackinder's (in)famous analysis, has deeper implications in culture: "the land is something which is always steady, stable, solid. This steadiness forms firmness in morals and laws, firmness of traditions."[225] Russia and "Eurasia" in general clearly belong to the rubric of continental powers. Maritime powers, associated with the West, are, by contrast, characterized by "the spirit of individualism,

---

221 Gadzhiev, 2013, 51.
222 Ashenkampf, 2010, 26; K. Sorokin, *Geopolitika sovremennosti i geostrategiia Rossii* (Moscow, 1996): 31–32.
223 Komleva, 2007, 42–44; Komleva, *Geopoliticheskaia ekspansiia. Sushchnost', aktory, formy osushchestvleniia*. Dissertation (Yekaterinburg, 2003): 9, 14. Alla Bakina's dissertation, supervised by Komleva, addresses exactly the theme of the "liberal-democratic paradigm of human rights and freedoms as an instrument of geopolitical expansionism" (Bakina, *Liberal'no-demokraticheskaia paradigma prav i svobod cheloveka kak instrument geopoliticheskoi ekspansii*. Dissertation (Yekaterinburg, 2008).) Cf.: Mikhailov, 2010, 14; Ashenkampf, 2010, 293; Luk'ianovich, 2011, 301.
224 Leonid Ivashov, "Geopoliticheskoe protivoborstvo: Mesto i rol' Rossii," in Kefeli et al. (eds.), *Geopoliticheskaia doktrina Rossii: Realii i problemy vybora* (St Petersburg, 2004), 4.
225 Halford Mackinder, "The Geographical Pivot of History" [1904] in K. R. Cox (ed.), *Political Geography: Critical Concepts in the Social Sciences* (London: Routledge, 2005), vol. 1, 124–139. Many authors claim that Mackinder's analysis retained academic significance up to the moment (e.g.: Blokhin, 2003, 7).

greed, entrepreneurship ... In such a civilization moral and juridical norms, principles and laws are relative."[226] By extension, maritime powers strive for expansion, colonization, military adventures.[227] The "law" of fundamental geopolitical controversy provides readers with the sense of dynamism and conflict, seamlessly connecting geopolitics with the Marxist discourses on class struggle.[228]

The thesis of expansionism also means that the West has been waging war with Russia for ages, regardless of whether Russia was called the Russian Empire, the Soviet Union or the Russian Federation. Russia's geopolitical problems are usually explained as results of hostile encroachments of the Western powers so that the textbooks create the alarmist atmosphere and represent the West as an impending threat to Russia's existence.[229] As Luk'ianovich's textbook transparently states, "in the course of centuries the West was attacking Russia and bringing her on the edge of catastrophe."[230]

With the unfolding of the processes of globalization, expansionism against Russia will become more violent.[231] But at the moment, as Nartov and Marinchenko write, this war is "soft," it is mostly "information war," which consists in "most immoral methods ... including misrepresentation of the role of the Soviet Union in the Second World War ...," spreading of negative stereotypes about Russia, hostile interpretation of any event which takes place in or around Russia, exporting of the most lowbrow mass culture in order to distort and corrupt the Russian culture, and finally to

---

226 Marinchenko, 2009, 15–16. Cf.: Mikhailov, 2010, 12. Nartov, 2010, 26–29; Lebedeva, 2012, 14.
227 Blokhin, 2003, 11.
228 Dugin outspokenly compares geopolitics with Marxism, saying: "Yes, this means war ... geopolitics as an academic discipline is as conflictological as Marxism." See: Dugin, "Voina i smert' Aleksandra Dugina" (http://www.arctogaia.com/public/txt-yanov.htm). Cf.: Sorokin, *Geopolitika sovremennosti*, 5–9.
229 Karpov, 1999, 38.
230 Luk'ianovich, 2004, 301. Such statements are typical for the secondary education as well; one of the articles in *Uchitel'skaia gazeta* (*Schoolteachers' Newspaper*) quotes Minister of Defense Sergei Ivanov: "we cannot exclude the possibility that ... [some] states or groups of states will be encroaching on Russia's territorial integrity ..." (A. Kolganov, "Geopolitika: Tendentsii Novogo Veka," *Uchitel'skaia gazeta*, 6 July 2004).
231 Mikhailov, 2010, 360; Nartov, 2010, 199.

destroy Russia's national identity and to take control over people's consciousness by means of inculcating foreign principles, values and ideas.[232] Some textbooks are more explicit on what exactly those "foreign principles" mean; thus, the textbook by Zubkov from the Academy of Management at the Ministry of the Interior, explains that they include multiculturalism, "limitless cosmopolitism," lack of patriotism, sexual education among the school pupils, juvenile justice and family planning.[233] Consequently, the key target of the Western "information war" against Russia is school and university education, academic research, arts and literature, mass media, religion, representation of history.[234] Revisionist geopolitics claims that encroachments on "spiritual security" can lead to violations of national security as such.[235]

Securitization in textbooks

Classic geopolitical theorization remains at the centre of textbooks' narratives, but recent editions pay increasingly greater attention to revisionist versions of geopolitics, which pay heed to the "production of space" thesis and expand the field beyond physical geography. Thus, Viacheslav Mikhailov, professor at the Russian Academy of State Service (RASS), formulated the task of contemporary Russian geopolitical research as "a move away from classic

---

[232] Nartov, 2010, 575, 607–612. Cf.: Marinchenko, 2013, 437–438, 472; Mikhailov, 2007, 14.
[233] Zubkov, 2011, 25, 31–32. In another version, these are "permissiveness, vulgarity (*poshlost'*), violence, sadism, pornography and other features of the Western lifestyle" (Marinchenko, 2009, 125.)
[234] Komleva, 2007, 97–105; Vasilenko, 2006, 62; V. Buianov, E. Kovaleva, "Mezhdunarodnaia bezopasnost' Rossii v usloviiakh globalizatsii," in V. Mikhalov (ed.), *Globalizatsiia i Rossiia* (Moscow, 2007): 119; V. Zav'ialov, "Informatsionnye ugrozy natsional'noi bezopasnosti Rossii," in V. Gutorov et al. (eds.), *Sovremennye geopoliticheskie protsessy: Novye vyzovy i poiski reshenii* (St Petersburg, 2011): 52.
[235] E.g. Bela Biragova, *Mobilizatsionnyi potentsial sredstv massovoi informatsii kak aktora etnokul'turnogo vzaimodeistviia na geopoliticheskom prostranstve*. Dissertation (Moscow, 2012): 3; Aleksandr Tonkonogov, *Dukhovnaia bezopasnost' rossiiskogo obshchestva v usloviiakh sovremennogo geopoliticheskogo sopernichestva*. Dissertation (Moscow, 2011): 4–7. Tonkonogov teaches geopolitics at the Military University of the Ministry of Defense.

concepts, [which are] outdated to a great extent, towards principally new problematic, related to new[ly conceptualized] spaces: military, economic, ecologic, cosmic, information."[236] Following this call, textbooks broadened their take on the prefix "geo", informing it with the interpretation of space as a social product.[237] Having stepped into the mainstream of international human geography, Russian geopolitics, however, floats if not in the opposite then in a very idiosyncratic direction. The idea of the social "production of space" has been mobilized in order to create such an interpretative frame, in which Russia and the West relations are understood as essentially or potentially colonial and hegemonic. So, Russian revisionism tends towards the problematic of "information and spiritual security," which highlights the importance of preserving Russia's "civilizational identity" in order to maintain the sovereignty.

Textbooks on geopolitics foster the rhetoric of civilization, often overlapping with Eurasianism.[238] For example, Mikhailov regrets that after 1991 Russia "has lost its civilizational identity."[239] Gadzhiev developed a specific concept of "civilization," which according to his analysis is based on an "axial ideal," around which "a whole complex of systemic values and norms" revolves.[240] In the context of geopolitics, the civilizational approach "upgrades" Russia's status to that of a separate civilization, capable of negotiating with the "Western civilization" on equal terms. The assumed idea behind this analysis is that Russian/Eurasian "civilization"

---

236 Mikhailov (ed.), *Aktual'nye problemy rossiiskoi geopolitiki* (Moscow, 2004): 5. Cf.: Mikhailov, 2007, 7.
237 Zheltov, 2007, 7; Vasilenko, 2013; Komleva, 2007, 6, 41; Gadzhiev, 2013, 41; Ashenkampf, 2010, 10.
238 Cf.: Scherrer, *Kulturologie*, 127–151; Scherrer, "The Cultural/Civilizational Turn," 159–161. See more on the rhetoric of "civilizations" in Chapter 3 of this volume.
239 Mikhailov, *Globalizatsiia i Rossiia*, 2007, 123. More on civilizational rhetoric in Chapter 3 of this volume.
240 Gadzhiev, 2013, 149. Cf. also: Vasilenko, 2013, 54; Mukhaev, 2007, 210. In the 1990s, following the retreat of the Marxist "theory of formations," "civilizational" approach secured its central place in methodology of teaching history in the secondary schools. More on the civilizational rhetoric in geopolitics in Chapter 3 of this volume.

represents a homogenized single whole, characterized by cultural authenticity and political agency.[241]

However, as a theory of Russian authenticity, geopolitics has an internal irony (which Eurasianism per se may or may not have): Dugin's statement on geopolitics as a worldview of rulers, affiliates it with ideological conservatism through its "anthropology of imperfection" and disregard of the grassroots' agency in general. In the long run, this means that geopolitics is "authentic" as long as the ruler expresses anti-Western and anti-liberal viewpoints, not caring a bit about public opinion and society's self-governing initiatives. Denying the agency of the grassroots, theorists in geopolitics are generally hostile towards mass protest movements, which are usually attributed as being instigated from abroad by some hostile forces. The irony doubles when negativism towards the grassroots' rights and ability to self-organize is expressed by intellectual "proletarians" themselves — that is by underpaid university teachers whose social status has drastically diminished in recent decades.

Thus, for example, Vasilenko's textbook centers around the "colored revolutions" and provides an interpretation of them as a geopolitical scenario of external aggression, whose objective is taking power by the "fifth column" with the help of foreign grants (information on the grant-giving organization is usually enclosed).[242] Earlier editions of Vasilenko's textbook covered the events in somewhat less intransigent style: versions of 2006 and 2007 defined the "velvet revolution" as a strategy to utilize spontaneous processes of self-government for somebody else's purposes; eventually they lead to "geopolitical destabilization" and the submissiveness of these countries to the external hegemonic power (i.e. the United

---

[241] According to Vladimir Medinskii, the former grey eminence in ideological sphere, the cultural policy of Ministry of Culture would be to forge a single culture on the Russian territory, "with common goals and values" (Vladimir Medinskii, "Kul'tura imeet znachenie," *Kul'tura*, October 5, 2012). Elsewhere, trying to repudiate the idea that Russia was an oppressive colonial empire, he argues that Russia used to incorporate only those peoples which had had close ties with Russia, or kindred culture, or "common historical destiny" (Medinskii, *O russkom rabstve, griazi i tiur'me narodov* (Moscow, 2010)). See also: Medinskii, *Teoretiko-metodologicheskie*, 83.

[242] Vasilenko, 2013, 47, 101.

States and the West in general).[243] An Analogous interpretation of the "colored revolutions" as a US "strategy of the anaconda" to suffocate Russia can be found in a textbook by Komleva,[244] which neatly corresponds to the "official," pro-Kremlin version of the protest movement on the post-Soviet space.[245] The pronounced anti-intelligentsia moods in the textbooks on geopolitics are being developed along the two lines of argumentation: distrust towards agency of the masses, and the anthropology of imperfection. Vasilenko is very explicit in her aversion towards Westernized intelligentsia; she claims that Russian "geopolitical tragedies" of 1917 and 1991 resulted not from the clash with a mighty enemy but from "erroneous choices [made by] Russian intelligentsia."[246]

Biopolitics and the rhetoric of "energy"

Putin's catchword about the collapse of the Soviet Union as the "greatest geopolitical catastrophe" reverberated in dozens of textbooks on geopolitics thereafter, and determined the "emotional regime" of the geopolitical narrative as a story of the protagonist (the Russian state) who dramatically rose to power through ages of military struggle, but ultimately fell a prey of the insidious adversary.[247] This is a tragic story. The unanimous equation of Russia with the Soviet Union prompted the interpretation of its breakup not as a birth of new Russia's sovereignty, but in terms of the loss of Russian territories (e.g. "loss of Ukraine," "loss of land outlets to Western Europe,"[248] or even "cutting off" (*urezanie*) of Russia),[249] shrinking of her spheres of influence, and breaking off of parts of her "legacy." Textbooks focus on Russia being thrown back to the borders of pre-Petrine Rus',[250] with an impending danger of further

---

243 Vasilenko, 2007, 76 (Vasilenko, 2006, 34–35).
244 Komleva, 2008, 109. On the "fifth column" see also: Blokhin, 2003, 21
245 E.g. Iakunin, *Zapadnia*, 20–22.
246 Vasilenko, 2013, 62, 88. Cf.: Zheltov, 2007, 221; Marinchenko. Geopolitika, 125.
247 Marinchenko, 2009, 4; Luk'ianovich, 2011, 299.
248 Beidina, 1999, 75.
249 Zubkov, 2004, 86.
250 Tuzikov, 2004, 65; Mukhaev, 2007, 5; Mukhaev, 2010, 582; Luk'ianovich, 2011, 299; Buianov, "Geopolitichskoe polozhenie sovremennoi Rossii: v 'kruge

contraction.[251] Many textbooks offer a sort of inventory of losses, listing territories, sea outlets, military bases, dependent states and spheres of influence, which have gone—"probably for good."[252] Poet Nikolai Zinov'ev penned often quoted verses, in which Russia's geopolitical losses evoke an image of the mutilated dead body of a dear one:

> At the map of the former [Soviet] Union
> With clapping thunder in my heart
> I stand. I neither cry, nor pray
> But I have no strength to leave.
> I caress mountains and rivers.
> I touch seas by fingers
> As if I were closing the eyelids
> Of my unhappy Motherland.

Mourning of geopolitical losses has cathartic meaning; it usually triggers redemptive mechanism, which provides explanation, prognosis and a practical guide to getting out of the impasse. So geopolitical studies in Russia set their goal in explaining the "contraction of Russia"; they develop a universal theory of history, accounting for and reducing history to circles of "expansion" and "contraction."[253] Explanatory strategies could be different but they all reduce historical contingency to a single theory and they capitalize on the idea that some kind of the "iron law of nature" controls socio-political developments, so the point is to find it out and turn it to Russia's advantage. The rhetoric of "loss" and "contraction" translates the geopolitical concepts into the "body language" of "vital force" or "energy."[254]

"Energy discourses" in Russian geopolitics underlie the civilization approach in Gadzhiev's textbook; the author argues that vital force powers self-organization of civilizations, but this energy is

---

pervom' i posleduiushchikh," in Mikhailov (ed.), *Globalizatsiia i Rossiia*, 2007, 121–122.
251 Lavrov, "Prostranstvo Rossii: Mify i real'nost'," *Ostrov Krym*. 61 (999); Beidina, 1999, 76; Marinchenko, 2009, 118.
252 Marinchenko, 2009, 111–112; Nartov, 2010, 182–183; Beidina, 1999, 75.
253 Sirota, 2006, 5; Sirota, 2009, 134; Gadzhiev, 2013, 36; Mukhaev, 2010, 582.
254 On the discourses of "ethno-vitalism" see: Oushakine, "Vitality Rediscovered," 171–193. Cf: Mäkinen, "Geopolitical Teaching," 8–9.

not unlimited and it is controlled by the second law of thermodynamics; the attenuation of "social energy" explains decline and obliteration of civilizations.[255] Gadzhiev connects "social energy" with the cultural sphere and information in general, and maintains that in historical terms, waning of "social energy" implies corrosion of the "axial ideal" and the corresponding values system of a civilization. By extension, radical re-definition of the "axial ideal" can reinvigorate the civilization; the decline of the West, in this context, "does not mean the end of the Western rationalistic civilization," but its transformation or perhaps hybridization with the east.[256] Gadzhiev does not extrapolate his speculations on Russia, but others do so, asserting that Russian identity (read: energy) is "fading away," so Russia has to activate the "energy and information (*energoinformatsionnyi*) resource of its culture and language."[257]

A more straightforward, "ethno-vitalist" interpretation is offered by followers of Lev Gumilev's theory of "passionarity," according to which "ethnogenesis," i.e. evolution of ethnoses, is determined by the level of energy, residing in "passionary" people. The whole history is thereby reduced to the story of counteraction of different ethnic communities, which all pass through the same stages of passionarity, from the initial explosion of energies, through the apex of territorial expansion to the phases of recession, to the final low-energy period of homeostasis when a nation lives peacefully and in harmony with the environment.[258]

As Igor Kefeli, the head of the department of geopolitics and globalists at the Baltic State Technical University puts it, "Gumilev is 'our everything' in contemporary Eurasianism," because he "performed a great synthesis" of ethnography and geopolitics.[259]

---

255 Gadzhiev, 2013, 148–149.
256 Gadzhiev, 2013, 153–154.
257 Mikhailov, 2007, 365; Marinchenko, 2013, 468.
258 On Gumilev's impact on geopolitics see: Bassin, "The Emergence of Ethno-Geopolitics in Post-Soviet Russia," *Eurasian Geography and Economics* 50, no. 2 (2009): 135–136.
259 Igor Kefeli, "Istoki evraziiskoi geopolitiki v otechestvennoi nauke," in S. Goncharov (ed.), *Nasledie L. N. Gumileva i sud'by narodov Evrazii: istoriia, sovremennost', perspektivy* (St Petersburg, 2012): 132. On Eurasianism in Gumilev's

Gumilev's follower Sergei Lavrov was one of the fathers-founders of post-Soviet Russian geopolitics, and today some authors explicitly acknowledge the Gumilevian influence on their theorization, or contend that they were acquainted with or disciples of Gumilev.[260] Karpov's textbook argues that Gumilev's theory is the most important contribution to the understanding of Russia's place in the world, which raises geopolitics to a new level of synthesis of "natural and political systems." Karpov interprets the collapse of the Soviet Union accordingly, as the inevitable process of "ethnogenesis" of the Russian people, which entered the "inertial" phase of its development, characterized by the political dissolution of the Russian *"super-ethnos"* with the marked possibility of its physical extinction. However, according to Karpov's textbook, if Russians survive this phase, they will have five hundred years of the "golden autumn" of prosperity and cultural productiveness in Russia's history.[261] Likewise, Mukhaev's textbook assert that Gumilev's theory "meets objective regulations of the development of the world."[262]

Even if the presence of Gumilev's theories is not explicit in many other textbooks, the Gumilevian language is ubiquitous. The textbook of Kolosov et al., prepared at the Russian Academy of Science, refers to the subjects of geopolitics as "passionary individuals," borrowing Gumilev's notion in quotation marks.[263] Mikhailov et al.'s textbook says about "the dynamic of extinction of national identity of the Russian people," which has no logical meaning unless we interpret it in Gumilevian sense as fading away of "passionarity," i.e. of national "energies."[264] Irina Vasilenko makes sense of the term *mestorazvitie* (locus of development), introduced by Eurasianist Savitskii and promoted by Gumilev; this is "the central category of Russian geopolitics," because it reflects the multifaceted interdependence of Russia's historical evolution with it

---

thoughts see: Martin Beisswenger, "Was Gumilev a 'Eurasianist'? A New Look at His Postwar Contacts with Savitskii," *Ab Imperio*, no. 1 (2013): 85–108.
260 Andrei Orekhov, "Evraziiskii geopolitik (Zapiski o Sergee Lavrove)," *Zavtra*, no. 31 (2001); Dergachev, 2004, 47.
261 Karpov, 1999, 39.
262 Mukhaev, 2007, 241.
263 Kolosov, 2005, 18.
264 Mikhailov, 2010, 365.

geography.²⁶⁵ Many textbooks and "methodical manuals" contain lists of special terms, which usually include notions like "passionarity," "ethnogenesis," "passionarists" (people with high level of "passionarity"), "positive/negative compementarity" of ethnic communities and so on.²⁶⁶ The latter term refers to the emotional comfort or lack thereof, which nations "feel" in regard to the neighboring nations. Thus, Eurasianists argue that Russian people has "positive complementarity" with the Turkic peoples. This concept underpins one of the most ominous deductions from Gumilevian discourses, namely anti-Semitism; according to Gumilev, Russians have "negative complementarity" with the Jews, so the existence of two nations with negative complementarity in one "ecological niche" produces lifeless "chimeras."²⁶⁷

Dergachev develops his own theory, based on Gumilevian "energies." In his revision of classic geopolitics, Deragachev purports to overcome geographic and economic determinism by means of "uncovering hidden potential of human energies."²⁶⁸ In his attempts to apply a paradigm from natural sciences as an all-explaining strategy in social sciences, Dergachev ironically lapses into mysticism.²⁶⁹ Drawing on geology, meteorology, oceanology and a number of other natural disciplines, he asserts that border zones (between tectonic plates, weather fronts, etc.) have the highest energy levels; having to extrapolate this onto the social sphere, he argues that borders, liminality (or communicativeness in his arcane terminology) in general is the source of social "energies." Thus, ethnography and geopolitics are controlled by the fundamental laws

---

265 Vasilenko, "Vlast' prostranstva i ideia messianizma," *Vlast'*, no. 2 (2001).
266 Kharitonova, 2010, 84; Marchenko, 2012, 417–420.
267 Marinchenko, 2013, 123, 420.
268 Dergachev, 2004, 97.
269 Here is an extract from his idiosyncratic prose, which is supposed to be consumed by the students: "In geopolitics, an attempt to find the spiritual pole of the Earth and to [find a way to] Gods has become widespread ... On the heights of power one cannot cheat the human nature and reach physical immortality. Perhaps, geopolitics exaggerates the role of political, economic, and military force in the formation of world order, which [in fact] is being formed by Nature on the borders of rational and sensual perception of the world. Here traditional geopolitics ends and new horizons of the Great Ocean of Big Multidimensional spaces open" (Dergachev, 2004, 412–413).

common for all "Earthly entities": civilizations exist like cyclones or oceans, they are limited by weather fronts and seismic fault lines; like the borders of oceans whose number is approximately the same as the number of civilizations, borders of civilizations are characterized by "unconfounded interaction" or "negative complementarity," at the same time borderlands accumulate energies, be this the energy of confessional conflicts or the energy of cultural creativity. So, Dergachev's twist of logic puts borderlands into the center of analysis as key geopolitical players; he asserts that there are two main high-energy zones: the Eurasian "contact zone" called Euramar, and the "contact zone" of the Atlantic world (Moremar), corresponding roughly to Russia and the "Western civilization."[270]

As a core land of "Euramar" Russia was one such unique, high-energy liminal zone, where several civilizations hybridized, but ultimately much of her energy dissipated in vain when her leaders in the 18th to 20th centuries tried to project her influence abroad (e.g. in Alaska in the imperial period, or Cuba during the post-war period). Today, Russia has to re-kindle her burnt away passionarity by means of the Russian diaspora—the newly emerged energy-rich communicative zone. All this obscure theorization is important not only because one can read it in one of the most popular textbooks on geopolitics in Russia, but also due to its "reverse geopolitical synecdoche," as Boris Mezhuev calls it—that is, when a part of the geopolitical entity (borderland) stands for the whole.[271] Dergachev's concept is itself a "synecdoche" of post-Soviet revisionist geopolitics, which aims to reconsider centripetal imperialist geopolitics, but in so doing restores revanchist Eurasianism. Having admitted that Russia is essentially the periphery, Dergachev reshuffles the logic of geopolitics in such a way that this periphery becomes a true center—the "communicative zone" of "Euramar."[272]

The "energy" discourse in geopolitics reframes the popular imagination. Like "kul'turologiia," another brainchild of the post-

---

[270] Dergahev, 2004, 107–126.
[271] Boris Mezhuev, "Geopolitika marginal'nosti", available at: http://www.archipelag.ru/authors/mezhuev/?library=1178.
[272] Attempts to rethink Russia as a liminal zone have been brilliantly discussed in: Clowes, *Russia on the Edge*.

Soviet academia, geopolitics supports an idea of uniqueness of the "Russian civilization" but it reinterprets it differently. First, it lies behind an important move towards "enthno-geopolitics" among Russian intellectuals.[273] Second, married with the "ethno-vitalist" discourses on demography,[274] "civilizational genotype," and "national genofond,"[275] geopolitical theorization changes the perception of Russian space as something "eternally womanish," amorphousness, and limitlessness,[276] and advances an alternative imagery of a well-organized, consolidated and coherent space and political entity, possessing willpower and agency, and sturdily embedded into the force fields of the global world. Unlike contemplative isolationism of "kul'turologiia" with its "historiosophy" of the "Russian destiny," geopolitics offers a simple and easily understandable guide for practical steps which the state has to make in order to regain the status of a "great power," and it seems that this is namely what the Russian population wants of its state today.[277]

Spatialization of history and the anti-colonial rhetoric

Interwoven with Marxist discursive debris, geopolitics tries to play the same function for the society as Marxism previously did; it provides people with the "big picture" of the world around us, gives some sense and meaning to historical processes and explains the past.[278] The important difference, however, is that Marxism was by and large a specific philosophy of history with the time arrow heading towards the future. Geopolitics, by contrast, translates history

---

273 Bassin, "The Emergence of Ethno-Geopolitics," 132.
274 Zubkov, 2004, 31–32, 38–40.
275 Zubkov, 2004, 40.
276 The metaphors of Russia's horizontal unboundedness are researched in: Elena Hellberg-Hirn, "Ambivalent Space: Expressions of Russian Identity," in J. Smith (ed.), *Beyond the Limits: The Contept of Space in Russian History and Culture* (Helsinki, 1999): 49–70.
277 Cf.: according to VTsIOM's press-release of 26 June 2013, 43% of respondents want Russia to become a prosperous great power by 2020, while democracy, social justice, lack of corruption lag far behind with only 5 to 4% of answers (http://wciom.ru/index.php?id=459&uid=114258).
278 This, to be sure, does not mean that geopolitics occupies similarly central place in social life and politics.

into geography, time into space; it may have explanatory devices for the future events, but its thrust is not towards the future but much rather towards the past, when the powerful Soviet Union and earlier Russian Empire existed. The end of history and history-based ideological meta-narrations, proclaimed by scholars and public intellectuals in the 1990s,[279] and the ascendance of "presentism" as the dominant historical sensibility have been superimposed on the particularly Russian situation of troubled and divisive historical memory.[280] Geographic discourses, in this sense, are more stable and its facts are easier verifiable than historical ones.

This means, among other things, that the history of Russia can be retold as the story of territorial gains and losses, thereby avoiding pitfalls of unshared memories and normative assessments. The whole geo-historical narrative is reduced to the problem of effectiveness in managing, or "mastering" (*osvoenie*) territories, because "inability to master territory leads to its loss."[281] Gadzhiev reverentially quotes conservative thinker Ivan Il'in, who said that "the greatness of the state depends on its ability to take upon itself the burden of great international tasks ..."; so, the "greatness" is here reduced to the ability of the state to project its power onto vast territories.[282] From the vantage point of the collapse of the Soviet Union, the whole of the Russian history is retrospectively explained and interpreted as failure to "master" the space. Likewise, textbooks in geopolitics supply students with a sense of teleology, give the picture of Russia's future and provide prognostic function.[283]

---

279 See, e.g.: Francis Fukuyama, *The End of History and the Last Man* (New York, 1992); P. Nora, *Realms of Memory* (New York, 1996–1998): 2–12.
280 Nikolai Koposov, *Pamiat' strogogo rezhima: Istoriia i politika v Rossii* (Moscow, 2011): 128; Igor Torbakov, "'Nepredskazuemoe' ili 'neopredelennoe' proshloe? Mezhdunarodnye otnosheniia i rossiiskaia istoricheskaia politika," in O. Malinova (ed.), *Simvolicheskaia politika. Sb. nauchn. trudov. Vyp. 1: "Konstruirovanie predstavlenii o proshlom kak vlastnyi resurs"* (Moscow, 2012): 91–125.
281 Cf.: Ashenkampf, 2005, 64; Beidina, 1999, 75; Tuzikov, 2013, 72.
282 Gadzhiev, 1997, 380. Russian presidents often quote from Il'in as well, e.g.: "Zasedanie po voprosu podgotovki k prazdnovaniiu 1150-letiia zarozhdeniia rossiiskoi gosudarstvennosti," July 22, 2022, available at http://www.kremlin.ru/news/12075.
283 Cf.: Mikhailov, 2007, 8; Beidina, 1999, 76; Vasilenko, 2006, 138.

Professor Natalia Komleva, the head of the Yekaterinburg section of the Academy of Geopolitical Problems has developed an idiosyncratic concept of totalitarianism as a result of "dramatic contraction ... of a great power"; according to this logic, Nazi and Stalinist totalitarianisms are explained as "natural" consequences of territorial squeezing of Germany and Russia by external geopolitical forces. And by extension, the greater territorial, cultural, ideological, and economic spaces have been appropriated by the Soviet Union after the World War Two, the milder its political regime became. Thus, Komleva reinterprets historical events in purely geopolitical terms and reduces the plethora of historical factors to a self-discovered "iron law" of geopolitics.[284] Vasilenko also reduces history to geopolitics. She argues that two fundamental elements govern the Russian history: Slavic anarchism and love of freedom, and the Russian geopolitical "instinct"; and that the waning of this instinct in the early 20th century led to "two bloody world wars and two revolutions," before finally the Russian geopolitical space was restored. "Several decades afterwards," however, "the geopolitical will of the nation weakened again," which resulted in the breakup of the Soviet Union.[285] Likewise, Leonid Ivashov uncovers the "geopolitical imperative" in Russia's history, which consisted in her mission to achieve her "natural borders"; it happened in the late 19th century, and the subsequent "Soviet history [is] the history of regaining and reinforcing the ... Russian state in the borders of the Russian Empire."[286]

John Agnew, one of the leading theorists of critical geopolitics, argues that modernity tends to interpret spatial differences as a by-product of temporal differences, the West as the "advanced," "developed" place, and non-Western societies as "backward."[287] John Agnew identifies three features of such a colonial gaze: essentialization ("identify[ing] one trait as characterizing a particular spatial unit"), exoticization ("focus[ing] on differences as the single

---

284 Komleva, *Geopoliticheskaia ekspansiia*, 21–22.
285 Vasilenko, "Vlast' prostranstva i ideia messianizma," *Vlast'*, no. 2 (2001).
286 Ivashov et al., *Global'nye vyzovy XXI veka – geopoliticheskii otvet Rossii* (Moscow, 2012): 200–201.
287 Agnew, *Geopolitics: Re-Visioning World Politics*, 32–48.

criterion for comparison"), and totalization (i.e. "turn[ing] relative differences into absolute ones").[288] However, with the growth of post-colonial awareness and anti-Eurocentric criticism, geopolitics has reversed this paradigm: indeed, underdevelopment is being read as the spatial difference, as "just the other place." Both revisionist and Eurasian schools of Russian geopolitics concur in exactly this interpretation, powered by the morbid sensitivity to the (imaginary) threat of Russia's becoming a colony of the West. Repudiation of all teleologies—"communist future," "nation-building," "catch up with the West," etc.—in the regime of "presentism" signifies the reconsideration of the place of the West in Russian imagination. For centuries, the West was cast in temporal terms as either the goal for the future development, or the capitalist backwater, stuck on the phase, which (Soviet) Russia got over long time ago. Today's interpretation of the West says that it is just a different place; and its differences preconditioned mostly by its geographical location and the peculiarities of "Western civilization"; not by the "stage" it is going through in world history. Russia, by extension, is not an underdeveloped "Third" world, but yet another place, the true "Second (i.e. alternative) World." On the one hand, these discursive strategies abolish the necessity to account for Russia's inability to compete with the West economically and develop similar standards of political participation and human rights' protection. On the other hand, considered as a kind of anti-colonial criticism, the "time into space" narrative transforms the "colonial gaze" but does not abolish it altogether, so it still "essentializes the difference" by identifying one trait, e.g. the Russian "continentality" as characteristic for the whole place ("essentialization"), juxtaposing it to European maritime character ("exotization"), and representing this confrontation as the keynote of Russian—or even world—history. So, the cumulative ideological effect of this kind of geopolitical theorizing is predominantly conservative; unlike the (hi)stories of

---

288 Agnew, "Time into Space: The Myth of 'Backward' Italy in Modern Europe," *Time & Society* 5, no. 1 (1996): 28. Eventually, these charactristics can be reduced to the formula: essentialization of the difference, in which "essentialization" stands for the "false consciousness," representing accessory characteristic of an object as an essential one.

nation-building, which raise the questions of political representation and legitimacy, the geopolitical narrative substitutes these questions with the question of the "effectiveness" of mastering the space, expansion and contraction.[289]

The rhetorical strategy of revisionist geopolitics adopts elements of anti-colonial criticism as long as colonialism is associated with the Western hegemony. Unlike the "classic" anti-colonialism of Franz Fanon or Aimé Césaire, this Russian geopolitical anti-colonialism scares readers into a particular ideological agenda by arguing that Russia is under a perennial threat of becoming a colony of the West.[290] This strategy usually posits the question as a dilemma: either Russia will become an underdeveloped and colonial territory, or reemerge as a great power.[291] The dilemma is whether to be the colonizer or the colonized, with no intermediate option available; the possibility of being an advanced democratic country but not a great power is not discussed. Revisionist geopolitics broadened the problematic of Russia's dependency on the West,[292] so that it pertains now not only to economic dependency or to (the fear of) political dependency, but also to multifaceted "Gramscian" hegemonic relations. The societal importance of this interpretation consists in inscribing the idea of dependency into the concepts of autonomy and authenticity,[293] which closely corresponds to the Slavophile reading.

---

289 On parallels between categories of history and geography: Andrei Treivish, *Geograficheskaia polimasshtabnost' razvitiia Rossii*. Dissertation (Moscow, 2006): 12.
290 Nartov, 1999, 21; Nartov, 2010, 168; Mukhaev, 2010, 524; Zubkov, 2004, 76. Cf. Similar rhetoric in: "Doktrina informatsionnoi bezopasnosti Rossii," 2000, available at: http://www.rg.ru/oficial/doc/min_and_vedom/mim_bezop/doctr.shtm.
291 Luk'ianovich, 2011, 292; Ashenkampf, 2010, 183; Zubkov, 2011, 25; Marinchenko, 2009, 4, 125; Nartov, 1999, 146.
292 Vadim Kaliuzhnyi, *Sistemologiia poznaniia mirovogo poriadka i geopoliticheskogo protivoborstva* (Syzran', 2011): 255; Luk'ianovich, 2011, 287; Mukhaev, 2010, 524.
293 See in full: *Scherrer, Kulturologie*, 16–17.

Conclusions

The Russian leadership consistently tries to instrumentalize history education,[294] and to toy with the concept of "patriotism." "Patriotism" is inclusive enough to embrace ideological developments of the past 15 years, such as sovereignty, "civilization-state," and "traditional values." It also implies a specific model of history, massively tailored by Putinism as an ideological tool, legitimizing Russia's leading position in contemporary international world order. On April 4, 2017, the roundtable at the State Duma discussed the law proposal on patriotic education. One of the participants expressed the main ideas of this documents as loyalty to the president and veneration of the traditions.[295] The official version of history and its undisputed character are now enshrined in the amended Constitution as of July 1, 2020.

What passed relatively unnoticed for the observers of Russia's current affairs is the state's long-term and consistent effort to work out the official version of Russian geography, primarily by means of the textbooks on geopolitics. Dissimilar from the battles on history, the geographical "grand narrative" is less contestable because it is rooted in the (seemingly) unyielding nature of territoriality. There could be hesitations on the matter of the Soviet Union's role in the World War Two, but the fact that the Russian Federation today occupies 17 million square kilometers in Northern Eurasia, and borders with the EU and China, among other countries—these are undeniable geographical "facts." By connecting these "facts" in a systematic storyline, the "discipline" of geopolitics produces a

---

294 On the state policy of history teaching, see, inter alia: Joseph Zajda, "The New History School Textbooks in the Russian Federation: 1992–2004," *Compare: A Journal of Comparative and International Education* 37, no. 3 (2007): 291–306; Lina Klymenko, "Narrating the Second World War: History Textbooks and Nation Building in Belarus, Russia, and Ukraine," *Journal of Educational Media, and Society* 8, no. 2 (2016): 38–57; Zajda and J. Whitehouse, "The Russian Revolution in School History Textbooks," *World Studies in Education* 18, no. 2 (2018): 61–88; Li Bennich-Björkman and Sergiy Kurbatov (eds.), *"When The Future Came." The Collapse of the Soviet Union and the Emergence of National Memory in Post-Soviet History Textbooks* (Stuttgart: ibidem-Verlag, 2019).
295 Marina Lemutkina, "Nad patriotizmom naseleniia reshili vvesti zakonodatel'nyi kontrol'," *Moskovskii Komsomolets*, April 5, 2017.

"usable space" out of the land of the Russian Federation and supply its leadership with a powerful legitimizing geopolitical narrative. Promoting geopolitics of identity (for example, in the form of civilizational rhetoric, examined in the next chapter), textbooks on geopolitics effectively eliminated questions of legitimacy of the regime and people's democratic participation. Instead, they instilled ideas about the importance of political stability, perpetuation of status quo, and being "faithful" to your "civilization" in the post-Cold War battles for global ascendance.

At the same time, geographical contours of this "usable space" evoke a sense of loss, thereby calling for reshaping the territory of Russia. The point is that the contemporary Russian borderline has no historical precedent, so the popular geopolitical imagination and affection alike have no strong attachment to Russia in its present shape. Popular journalist Oleg Kashin observed:

> Russia has never existed in the way it is pictured on contemporary maps. [It has] Tyva [Republic] and Chechnya but no Ukraine and North Kazakhstan—this is like picturing the United States with Texas, Hawaii, and Alaska but without Alabama and West Virginia. The Russian border in its present state is ideally suited for debates and fantasies of the "what if?" style.[296]

Written in this "what if?" modus, textbooks on geopolitics became an important factor of justifying Russia's aggressive international policies in the past two decades.

---

296 Oleg Kashin, "Rossiia—urodlivoe detishche Belovezhskogo dogovora," October 28, 2013, available at: https://republic.ru/posts/1/1010793.

3 "Civilizationism" in Russian Geopolitical Culture

Introduction

In the 1990s the civilizational approach in understanding global history replaced the formation approach. In parallel, discourses about Russia as a unique civilization first engulfed academic studies and thereafter thoroughly saturated the political rhetoric.[297] "Civilizations" brought the windfall profits to the right wing and pro-government political thinkers, because now they can think about Russia as a political entity, which is both nationally oriented and imperially inclusive. In other words, the civilizational frame allowed them to 1) underline the importance of Russian culture, ethnos and language, 2) align present-day Russia with historically diverse forms of "Russian" statehood (primarily, the Soviet Union), and 3) to exclude the Muslim population of Central Asia by portraying non-Russian peoples of the Soviet Union as "co-travelers," who may or may not be part of the "Russian civilization," depending on their own will and behavior. The "Russian civilization," thus, becomes yet another ideological cover for the attempt to define Russia as an entity, which is larger than the Russian Federation, and which includes Belarus, parts of Ukraine and Kazakhstan, and some other territories, populated by "Russians" through language, culture and self-identification. In this sense, the "Russian civilization" is essentially the same as visions of the "Russian world" and "Holy Russia." However, political usages of the civilizational rhetoric are broader than this.

The concept of "civilization" can be used with multiple adjectives, such as the "Orthodox civilization," the "Eurasian civilization," the "Nordic civilization" and others. They all include the

---

[297] On the connection between civilizational discourses in PhD dissertations and in Russian politics see: Mikhail Suslov and Irina Kotkina, "Civilizational Discourses in Doctoral Dissertations in Post-Soviet Russia," in Sanna Turoma and Kåre Johan Mjør (eds.), *Russia as Civilization: Ideological Discourses in Politics, Media and Academia* (London: Routledge, 2020): 164–185.

Russian Federation as their central component, and they all rest upon the organic vision of a community. As organisms, civilizations are autonomous, self-sufficient, sovereign, but at the same time, they are also fragile and perishable, and they require strong defense mechanisms to survive. Civilizational logic feeds into the idea of radical incommensurability of civilizations and provides argumentation for anti-globalist and anti-Western criticism. In post-Soviet Russia two intellectual streams concurred on the same "civilizational" ground: the left-wing multiculturalism with its attention to identity politics and cultural differences, and the right wing anti-globalism. In this context, the 19th-century pan-Slavist thinker Nikolai Danilevsky was successfully exhumed and galvanized by the injection of Samuel Huntington's interpretation of the clash of civilizations. The resulting product was warmly received in both left and right camps: among the post-Soviet "red-brown" opposition to the liberal and reformist course of President Boris Yeltsin. **Figure 4** illustrates the surging interest in Danilevsky and Huntington in the Russian central and regional press with two steep ascensions in the beginning of the 2000s and between 2013 and 2016.

Figure 4. Total number of mentions of words "Danilevsky" (dark) and "Huntington" (grey) in the Russian central and regional press from 1990 to 2019.

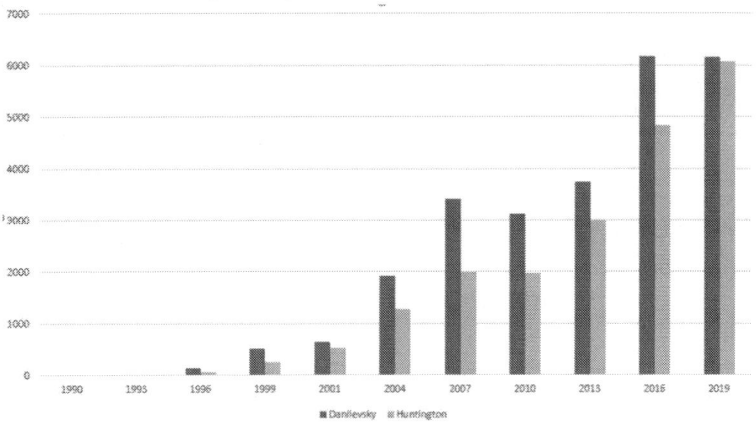

Source of data: Integrum Profi. Calculated and plotted by the author.

The concept of "Russian civilization" in its both variants: *russkii* and *rossiiskii*, forced its way into the public debates in the middle 1990s. Such nationalists as Oleg Platonov and Evgeny Troitskii[298] developed the identitarian reading of civilizations,[299] which buttresses anti-Western identity politics. The term was picked up by the representatives of the "red-brown" movement, such as National-Bolsheviks and the patriotic newspaper *Zavtra,* and the "Orthodox" communists. In the "Manifesto for Russia's Regeneration" (1995), penned by Sergei Pykhtin, Andrei Savel'ev, and edited by Dmitry Rogozin, civilization was seen as the highest development of a "great nation" — a project for future Russia, which is called not a civilization per se, but part of the larger Orthodox civilization.[300] In the same vein, mathematician and public intellectual Nikita Moiseev pontificated that the "unique Russian civilization" was an "alternative" to the West.[301] In an article from 1997 Aleksandr Prokhanov mused on the Soviet Union being "pregnant with *russkaia* civilization," seen as a special path of development on the grounds of "newest science, [industry of] hydrogenous energy, space travels, and also on the unity of nature, God and humans." In Prokhanov's vision, the Soviet Union "was killed" in order to destroy this would-be yet-unborn civilization: "this is how a mother is being killed in order to prevent her from giving birth. A knife pierces the womb and transfixes the fetus."[302] This metaphor condenses much of the civilizational discourses about Russia in the next two decades: the Russian civilization is portrayed as fragile, wounded,

---

298 Kåre Johan Mjør, "A Morphology of Russia? The Russian Civilisational Turn and Its Cyclical Idea of History," In *Philosophical and Cultural Interpretations of Russian Modernisation* (London: Routledge, 2016): 101; E.g. Platonov, *Russkaia tsivilizatiia: Uchebnoe posobie dlia formirovaniia russkogo natsional'nogo soznaniia* (Moscow: Roman-gazeta, 1995).
299 The term "identitarian" is connected with the "Identitarian movement," but here we use it broader, as a concept, embracing all kinds of right-wing concerns with preservation of community's identity against left-liberal agenda of multiculturalism and tolerance.
300 https://bb.velikoross.org/forums/topic/manifest-vozrozhdeniya-rossii-1995
301 Nikita Moiseev, "Russkii vopros," *Moskva,* no. 7 (1997): 147–148.
302 Aleksandr Prokhanov, "Chetvertaia russkaia revoliutsiia—vperedi," *Zavtra,* November 4, 1997. Cf. with the similar speculations in: Prokhanov, "Kop'e natsii," *Zavtra,* March 24, 1998, available at: http://zavtra.ru/blogs/1998-03-2422answer.

dying or even already killed by powerful enemies. A similar rhetoric was heard on the congress of the People's Patriotic Union of Russia—an electoral bloc rooting for Gennady Ziuganov at the presidential elections in 1996. The union's address "To the patriots of Russia," mourned that the "unique (*nevidannaia*) *russkaia* civilization has been pillaged overnight' by the criminals and oligarchs.[303]

In 1997, the committee on geopolitics at the Russian State Duma hosted a conference entitled "Russian-Slavic civilization Historical Roots and Contemporary Geopolitical Problems," which followed the tracks of Danilevsky, but focused mostly on the idea of Slavic unity rather than Russian civilizational uniqueness.[304] In the same year, the publishing house *Entsiklopediia russkoi tsivilizatsii* was launched in Moscow by Oleg Platonov. In 2003 the publishing house became an "institute," whose advisory board includes some of the most intransigent anti-liberals, such as Iury Begunov, a conspirologist who propagates actively *The Book of Veles*, a well-known literary forgery,[305] and the Protocols of the Elders of Zion; Jürgen Graf, a well-known Holocaust denier; Vladimir Osipov, an underground right-wing dissident; Anatolii Stepanov, the editor of the fundamentalist online news agency Russkaia Narodnaia Liniia; and Igor Shafarevich, a famous conservative publicist.[306] However, in the 1990s the term "Russian civilization" became contested among the nationalist opposition. For example, Aleksandr Panarin, the main proponent of the idea of the "Orthodox civilization" in the 1990s, was cautious about applying this term to Russia. He saw a possibility for a civilizational reading of Russian culture, but for him the "Russian civilization" was not the reality, but rather a

---

303 "K patriotam Rossii," *Pravda-5*, August 9, 1996.
304 Evgeny Troitskii (ed.), *Russko-Slavianskaia tsivilizatsiia: Istoricheskie istoki, sovremennye geopoliticheskie problem, perspektivy slavianskoi vzaimnosti* (Moscow: AKIRN, 1998): 478.
305 The *Book of Veles* is a literary counterfeit claiming to be a text of ancient Slavic religion and history supposedly written on wooden planks. The content proves historical supremacy of Slavs, the antiquity of their race and vastness of the territories.
306 See more on the Institute for Russian Civilization in: Kåre Johan Mjør, "An Eternal Russia: Oleg Platonov, the Institute for Russian Civilization and the Nationalization of Russian Thought," in Mjør and Turoma (eds.), *Ideological Discourses in Politics, Media and Academia, 186–205.*

project for future development, pledged by the possibility to align the Orthodox culture and Eurasian geopolitics with the present Russian state.[307]

Dmitry Rogozin merged together nationalistic rhetoric and the concept of the "*rossiiskaia* civilization" in his legislative proposal "On the national-cultural development of the Russian (*russkii*) nation" (1999).[308] Rogozin came up with the same rhetoric once again in 2003, when he commented on the amendments to the law of citizenship; he argued that the revamped version of the law would allow people to obtain Russian citizenship "according to the fact of their belonging to the *rossiiskaia* civilization."[309] In this context, visions of Russia's cultural uniqueness became amalgamated with another newcomer in the academic and pseudo-academic world, the "discipline" of geopolitics, which surged shortly after 1996, when Dugin published his first manual *Basics of Geopolitics*. Quite early, in the beginning of the 2000s, the civilizational rhetoric emerged on the pages of professional military writers.[310] They drew on Dugin's geopolitics but also quoted from the *Book of Veles* and claimed that the Russian civilization harks back into the pre-historical Slavic paganism.[311] One of the examples is the doctoral thesis of Aleksandr Kan'shin, who defended it at the Military University in 2000.[312] Thus, during President Yeltsin's second term in power, 1996–1999, all necessary elements were there: geographic determinism, Russian integral nationalism, and the logic of antagonism between Russia and the West. The concept of the "Russian civilization" successfully glued together explanatory principles of culture, nation, and territory.

---

307 Aleksandr Panarin, *Rossiia v tsiklakh mirovoi istorii* (Moscow: MGU, 1999): 14–15, 221–222.
308 Dmitry Rogozin, "Grazhdanskoe obshchestvo ili rai dlia biurokratov," *Parlamentskaia gazeta*, February 27, 1999.
309 "Rossiia budet prirastat' svoimi grazhdanami," *Parlamentskaia gazeta*, October 16, 2003.
310 Valery Petrov, "Bezopasnost' rossiiskoi tsivilizatsii," *Krasnaia zvezda*, no. 5 (2000).
311 Boris Kaverin, "'Megapir' ob"edinil filosofov," *Krasnaia zvezda*, no. 63 (2003).
312 Aleksandr Kan'shin, *Dukhovnye osnovy sotsial'nogo upravleniia*. Dissertation (Moscow: Military University, 2000). See also: *Russkaia tsivilizatsiia: Istoriia i sovremennost'* (Moscow: Megapir, 2003).

In the 2000s, the term "Russian civilization" continued to be used by various political thinkers across the right-left divide. The Church-oriented ideologists emphasized the original, "Huntingtonian" sense of the term "civilization" as primarily a confessional unity, whereas the socialist flank of the right-wingers unobtrusively mentioned "civilization" and the "Soviet Union" in one breath and stressed the importance of the Soviet period of Russian history.[313] In general, however, both camps entertained a surprisingly similar set of ideas, with some minor variations. Aleksandr Prokhanov professed about the victory of the "*russkaia* civilization" in the Great Patriotic War,[314] and about the feat of Stalin who resuscitated the "half-dead *russkaia* civilization" by means of harsh state centralism.[315] On the other hand, we have the religiously-motivated party "People's Assembly," which puts the concept of the "*russkaia* civilization" as the cornerstone of its program, characterized by anti-Westernism, Messianism and geopolitical irredentism. They identified the main "threats to the Russian civilization": the attack on the Russian traditional values and national identity, weakness of the state, "information-related aggression" from the West.[316]

For both poles of the political spectrum, "Russian civilization" became shorthand for the "Russian nation," but in a more "politically correct," inclusive and — at the same time — irredentist way, which provides for the possible incorporation of non-Russian parts of the former Soviet Union, which "openly gravitate towards Russian civilization."[317] The concept of "civilization" is an ideational ground on which supporters and adversaries of the Soviet past can

---

313 Cf. the program of the people's movement "Russkii Lad" ("Russian style"), established by the Communist Party in 2012 ("Proekt programmy," 2012, available at: http://kprf13.com/gazeta-nasha-pravda/105-sajty/)
314 Aleksandr Voznesenskii, "22 iunia, rovno v chetyre chasa," *Nezavisimaia gazeta – NG Ex Libris*, June 22, 2006.
315 Valery Vyzhutovich, "Ot anarkhii k zhestkoi vlasti," *Rossiiskaia gazeta*, February 28, 2007.
316 "Osnovy natsional'noi strategii Rossii," August 2, 2010, available at: https://www.km.ru/news/v_rossii_sozdano_narodnoe_sobran.
317 "Predvybornaia platforma politicheskoi partii 'Narodnyi Soiuz'," *Patriot*, September 27, 2007; Sergei Baburin, "Russkaia ideologiia v usloviiakh sovremennoi rossiiskoi politiki," *Patriot*, September 20, 2007. See also the open letter to Vladimir Putin from the party "Rus'."

concur.[318] Oftentimes, "Russian civilization" with an adjective is used to stress a particular aspect of its inclusiveness. One can read, for example, about "Nordic Russian civilization," embracing Yakuts;[319] or "Russian Orthodox civilization," which would encompass Ukraine and Belarus in the discourses of the ROC (see below). In any case, the circular idea that a Russian is someone who belongs to the "Russian civilization" gained much currency.

Both the socialist and religious agendas seamlessly fused in the program of the so-called "Young conservatives," who coalesced around the web portal APN.ru — *Agentstvo Politicheskikh Novostei* and its editor-in-chief in 2005-2007 Boris Mezhuev. The movement was intellectually heterogeneous; what united them was the identitarian orientation with its nationalistic implications. Mezhuev specified that for the "Young conservatives" identity had not a cultural but rather a "civilizational meaning," i.e. it had a geopolitical projection and a clearly isolationist overtone: "Russia has always existed as a separate, isolated civilization, and in the future, this isolationism should be preserved."[320] This position was propped up by a variety of ideological scaffoldings — nationalism, political Orthodoxy, Great Power imperialism, resistance to the liberal reforms, and anti-globalism.

By the mid-2000s, the concept in its multiple forms decisively entered the discourses of various public figures and high-level bureaucrats. Film director Karen Shakhnazarov spoke about the Soviet period as the apex of the "Russian [*russkaia*] civilization."[321] Minister of Communication Igor Shchegolev, speculating on the inventor of radio Aleksandr Popov, called it an important milestone

---

318 Cf.: *Sovetskaia Rossiia* interprets the socialist period of Russia history as acme of the Russian civilization: N. F. Bondarenko, "Narod-otets," *Sovetskaia Rossiia*, March 22, 2016, available at: http://www.sovross.ru/articles/1369/23878.
319 Prokhanov, "Rus' sobornaia," *Izvestiia*, November 3, 2015.
320 Boris Mezhuev, "Konservatizm eto ostorozhnoe i opaslivoe otnoshenie k progressu," *Kommersant-vlast'*, August 21, 2006: 24.
321 Karen Shakhnazarov, "Vmeste s imperiei ischezla i logika," *Argumenty i fakty*, February 20, 2008. Cf. similar statements by another film director: Aleksandr Sokurov, "Ne nado smotret' trebukhu," *Komsomol'skaia pravda*, September 12, 2011.

of the "Russian [*russkaia*] civilization."[322] Today, the language of civilizations spills over from the sphere of the political debate to permeate everyday talks, as well as popular and pseudo-science. **Figure 5** demonstrates the network of Youtube videos, which mention the term "Russian civilization." Only a relatively marginal part of this network contains information and political channels, whereas the center and the most densely "populated" part of the picture is represented by Youtube channels, devoted to conspirology and pseudo-history, such as a channel hosted by Valery Chudinov, who traces the roots of Russian civilization to distant planets, or Sergei Sall, who claims to expose esoteric "discoveries" about ancient Rus'. For them and their followers, the invention of the ancient roots of the "Russian civilization" serves as an instrument to reclaim Russia.

---

322 Igor Shchegolev, "Genial'nye professionaly — glavnyi resurs Rossii," *Argumenty i fakty*, March 11, 2008.

Figure 5. Visualization of the network of the Youtube videos, containing the phrase "Russian civilization" in their descriptions.

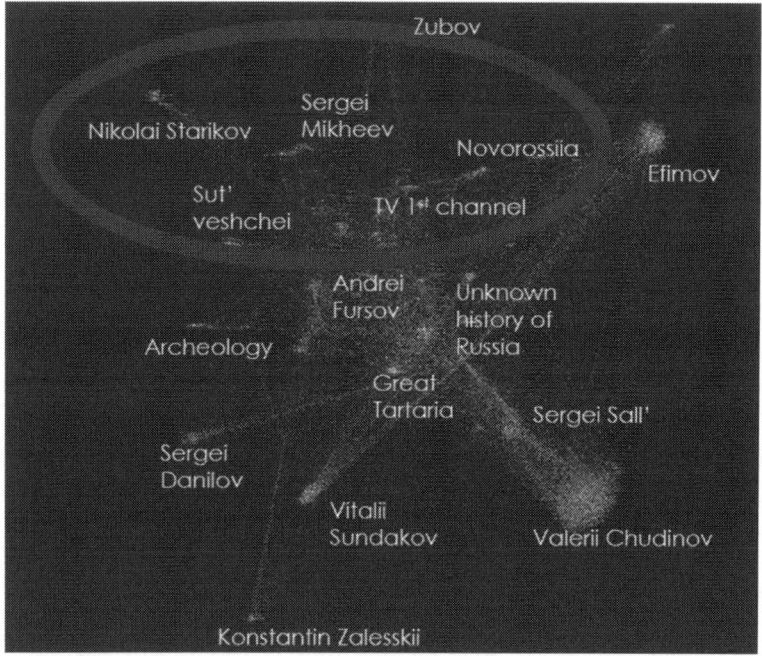

The "political" part of the network is identified by the blue oval. The network includes 50 seed videos, 2000 nodes, 28,000 edges.
Source of the data: Youtube Data Tools (https://tools.digitalmethods.net/netvizz/youtube/), visualized by the program Gephi in May 2019. Data collection and visualization by the author.

The rest of this chapter will focus on the usages of the "Russian civilization" concept in the mainstream political debates, in the language of the Russian Orthodox Church, and specifically in its identitarian-conservative interpretation, offered by Boris Mezhuev.

The mainstream political debates, "sovereign democracy" and the ideology of "Edinaia Rossiia"

This rhetoric of Russia's civilizational uniqueness gradually made its way to the official documents during Vladimir Putin's second term as the President of Russia, and especially by the end of the

2000s. This happened in the context of the pursuit of an official ideology of the ruling party United Russia, and the growing popularity of Vladislav Surkov's concept of "sovereign democracy." There were two spheres of applicability of the concept: international relations and domestic politics. For the debates on the international relations, the key function of the civilizational rhetoric was to fight against the US's hegemony and to stand for a vision of the world as a collection of large, independent and relatively isolated civilizations. For the debates on Russian internal affairs, the language of "civilizations" mediated searchers for a third way between ethnic Russian nationalism and post-Soviet imperial inclusiveness.[323]

Leaders of the United Russia party began to toy with the concept in 2004–2007. The party's leader Boris Gryzlov, spoke for the first time of the "Russian (*rossiiskaia*) civilization" in his article dedicated to the Victory day celebration in 2005,[324] and then again at the end of the year. The rhetorical context of the term was shaped by the debates about "sovereign democracy," and thus, the accent was made on "self-sufficiency" (*samostoiatel'nost'*) of the "Russian civilization."[325] Other party leaders, Andrei Isaev and Iury Shuvalov, made similar statements, carefully wording the term in an inclusive civic-national way ("*rossiiskaia* civilization"), and stressing that its hallmark was its ethnically heterogeneous nature. The term "multinational *rossiiskaia* civilization" gained much currency in the party discourses as a substitute for the previously popular term "multinational Russian nation."[326] Influential Moscow mayor Iury Luzhkov changed his language during the year 2006. In his strongly-worded anti-Western article "We and the West" in *Rossiikaia gazeta*, he dwelled on the ideas of Nikolai Danilevsky and Ivan Il'in, and related them to the contemporary debates about Russia as a "sovereign

---

323 Aleksandr Verkhovskii and E. Pain, "Tsivilizatsionnyi natsionalizm: Rossiiskaia versiia 'osobogo puti'," in Pain (ed.), *Ideologiia "osobogo puti" v Rossii i Germanii: Istoki, soderzhanie, posledstviia* (Moscow: Tri kvadrata, 2013): 171–210.
324 Boris Gryzlov, "Preobrazhenie pobedoi," *Trud*, May 6, 2005, available at: http://gryzlov.ru/index.php?page=publications&id=121.
325 Gryzlov, "Kazhdaia strana idet k demokratii svoim, osobym putem," *Parlamentskaia gazeta*, December 21, 2005.
326 "Edinaia Rossiia zadala russkie voprosy," *Komsomol'skaia pravda*, February 5, 2007; "Ne upustit' shans stat' liderom," *Parlamentskaia gazeta*, February 7, 2007.

democracy" and an autonomous geopolitical player, whose special role in the world was secured by its position as a "bridge between different world civilization."[327] A few months later in the same year, Luzhkov renounced this vision of Russia as a "bridge" and described it as the multinational "Russian civilization."[328] The idea of "multinationality" as the hallmark of the "Russian civilization" gained much currency among the academic discourses as well.[329]

The following **Figure 6** compares the total number of mentions of either "*rossiiskaia* civilization" or "*russkaia* civilization" in the federal press. It demonstrates that after a period between 2005 and 2010—when both terms had roughly the same popularity—the ethno-national version of civilization discourse has prevailed over the inclusive and civic one. It also shows that until 2014 the frequency of these terms steadily grew from ca. 100 hits annually (both versions) in 2005 to 300 in 2014.

---

327 Iury Luzhkov, "My i Zapad," *Rossiiskaia gazeta*, June 15, 2006.
328 Luzhkov, "Usloviia razvitiia rossiiskoi tsivilizatsii," *Strategiia Rossii*, no. 12 (2006), available at: http://www.fondedin.ru/sr/new/fullnews_arch_to.php?archive=1166779714&id=1166779476&start_from=&subaction=showfull&ucat=14.
329 Oksana Gaman-Galutvina, "Tvorcheskoe nasledie N.A. Berdiaeva i dialektika russkoi politicheskoi istorii," *Tetradi po konservatizmu* 1, no. 2 (2014): 43.

Figure 6. Total number of usages of the terms *"rossiiskaia* civilization" (grey) as opposed to *"russkaia* civilization" (dark).

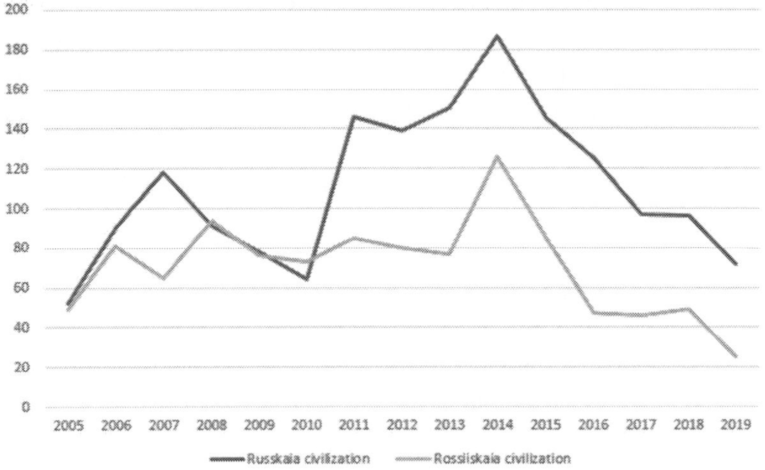

Source: Integrum World database, prepared by the author.

In 2005, the advent of the concept of "sovereign democracy" signaled the decisive turn of the regime from declared pragmatism in its first years to ideology.[330] The Presidential Address of 2005 did not mention the concept "sovereign democracy," but it emphasized Russia's state priority as "striving to increase the national independence of Russia, to strengthen its sovereignty."[331] Vitalii Tret'iakov reflected on the Address, distilling its central ideas as follows: Russia is and will remain a European democracy; democracy was not artificially implanted in Russia after the collapse of the Soviet Union, but rather Russia has come to it naturally in the course of its thousand-year history and as a result of the free choice of its people. This means that Russia needs no foreign teachers of democracy; it should be strong and independent, and it has all historical and moral rights to define its own way to, and its own understanding of democracy. Tret'iakov's article is entitled

---

[330] Cheng Chen, *The Return of Ideology: The Search for Regime Identities in Postcommunist Russia and China* (Ann Arbor: University of Michigan Press, 2016): 72.
[331] "Poslanie Prezidenta Rossiiskoi Federatsii", April 25, 2005, available at: http://www.kremlin.ru/acts/bank/36354.

"Sovereign democracy," and he was the first who introduced the term into the public debates.[332] Elsewhere, Tret'iakov accentuated the idea of the continuity of Russian history and acceptance of the Soviet past as valuable if not the most precious period.[333] Later in this year, the leader of Nashi, the youth branch of the United Russia party, used this term to strike the balance between the leftists who underestimated democracy, and the liberals who, in his interpretation, underestimated country's independence; hence his formula was "sovereign democracy ... in which liberties of a person and liberties of the state are necessary and equal."[334]

In 2006 the United Russia party was carried away by this fashionable concept. It was picked up and propagated by some experts,[335] as well as by the main ideologist of the Presidential Administration Vladislav Surkov, who in February 2006 gave a talk for the United Russia activists. By summer 2006, the "sovereign democracy" concept had ideologically consolidated the political elite and was widely seen as the most obvious starting point for the development of the official ideology of a United Russia or—broader still, and as Vladimir Medinsky, the former Minister of Culture, saw it— of a Russian state ideology.[336] Surkov repeats Tret'iakov's point about organic and natural growth of democracy in Russia,[337] but unlike Tret'iakov, he emphasized the word "sovereign" in "sovereign democracy." To be more specific, in pace with the changing international agenda, "sovereign democracy" acquired a new geopolitical meaning: to be "independent from the West." Andranik

---

332 Vitalii Tret'iakov, "Suverennaia demokratiia," *Rossiiskaia gazeta*, April 28, 2005, available at: http://www.kremlin.ru/acts/bank/36354; Vitalii Tret'iakov, *Nauka byt' Rossiei: Nashi natsional'nye interesy i puti ikh realizatsii* (Moscow: Russkii mir, 2007): 424–425.
333 Tret'iakov, "Nuzhen li nam Putin posle 2008 goda?," *Politicheskii klass*, May 15, 2005.
334 Vasilii Iakemenko, "My za suverennuiu demokratiiu," *Komsomol'skaia pravda*, October 26, 2005, available at: https://www.kompravda.eu/daily/23602/46035/.
335 Cf. Aleksandr Tsipko, "Prezidentskaia filosofiia," *Literaturnaia gazeta*, February 8, 2006.
336 "Strasti po ideiam," *Izvestiia*, March 10, 2006.
337 Vladislav Surkov, "Natsionalizatsiia budushchego," in *Suverennaia demokratiia: Ot idei k doktrine* (Moscow: Evropa, 2006): 30; Surkov, "Politika—eto prezhde vsego tekst", in Surkov, *Teksty 97–07* (Moscow: Evropa, 2008): 60.

Migranian saw it as a tool, which non-Western rising powers could use to fight back against the US's interference in their domestic affairs.[338] Dmitry Orlov emphasized another important aspect of the concept, which would resonate later in the 2010s: the idea to positively reassess and recycle the Soviet past.[339] However, the keynote of the concept remained liberal, democratic and oriented towards reforms and all-embracing modernization. In his programmatic paper "Natsionalizatsiia budushchego" (2006), Surkov geared the "sovereign democracy" concept to the classic liberal doctrine. For him, a dignified and free person requires that her political community would also be independent from external pressures.[340]

In the same year 2006, pro-Kremlin political analyst Aleksei Chadaev came up with the book about Putin's ideology, which revolved around the concept of "sovereign democracy." Chadaev aptly pinpointed that its core idea was geopolitical: autonomy from the West and the issue of Russia's sphere of influence in Eurasia and Eastern Europe. He specifically dwelled on three levels of state sovereignty: absolute sovereignty, nuclear sovereignty and sovereignty by proxy. Without nuclear sovereignty a state has at best sovereignty by proxy as a satellite of the state with absolute sovereignty.[341] Chadaev maintains that the actual stumbling stone in Russia's relations with the West is precisely Russia's striving for absolute sovereignty with the possibility to dominate the post-Soviet space, while the West can agree on only nuclear sovereignty for Russia.[342] The book was designed as a normative statement (hence the subtitle "Manifesto"), rather than an analysis of the actual ideological trends, and it is significant that both Surkov and Volodin, the doyens of state ideology,

---

338 Vladislav Surkov, "Natsionalizatsiia budushchego," 32; Andranik Migranian, "Istoricheskie korni suverennoi demokratii," in *Suverennaia demokratiia: Ot idei k doktrine*, 12. Andranik Migranian is a pro-Kremlin political analyst. In 2008–2015 he chaired the New York branch of the Institute for Democracy and Cooperation.

339 Dmitry Orlov, "Politicheskaia doktrina suverennoi demokratii," *in Suverennaia demokratiia: Ot idei k doktrine*, 8. Orlov is the chair of the United Russia's "in-house" think-tank the Agency for Political and Economic Communication.

340 Surkov, "Natsionalizatsiia budushchego," in *Suverennaia demokratiia: Ot idei k doktrine*, 27.

341 Aleksei Chadaev, *Putin. Ego ideologiia* (Moscow: Evropa, 2006): 49–51.

342 Aleksei Chadaev, *Putin. Ego ideologiia*, 141–144.

endorsed the book as an expression of the Russian state ideology of "sovereign state, democracy and quality of life."[343]

After some attempts to ground the United Russia ideology in the "sovereign democracy" concept, by summer 2006 the party leadership decided to work out its own, original political platform, which would be better suited to the party's socially-oriented constituency.[344] Gryzlov, Isaev and Morozov decided in favor of "social conservatism"; as far as we can gather from the press, the party even considered to avoid the term "conservatism" altogether in order not to push its mass electorate away into the embraces of the socially-oriented political movements, such as Sergei Mironov's *Just Russia* party.[345] After a period of wavering, a few months ahead of the State Duma elections, the United Russia finally embraced a very eclectic version of conservatism. In his programmatic article in July 2007, Boris Gryzlov made a cautious advance towards the social agenda, but the center of gravity of his paper lay in the identitarian idea of a strong state and national identity. It is remarkable, that in his article names of Ivan Il'in, Dmitry Likhachev, Nikita Moiseev and Lev Gumilev popped up as useful references, backing up the idea that Russia had to fight back against globalization and to preserve its culture and traditions.[346]

In this period, a number of patriotic experts and publicists entertained the idea of reformatting the concept of "sovereign democracy" into the concept of "sovereign civilization." In this interpretation, nation-states were fading away, and statehood would instead be concentrated in the larger entities—civilizations. Russia, thus, should strive to become such a sovereign civilization.[347] In 2007 the party has published a collection of policy papers *Russia's Vector: Contemplations on the Ways of Russia's Development*. Among

---

343 Iury Politov, "'Nuzhny teksty, kotorye ob"ediniaiut liudei'," *Izvestiia*, February 13, 2006, available at: https://iz.ru/news/311122.
344 Vitalii Luzov, "Partizatsiia vlasti prodolzhaetsia," *Nezavisimaia gazeta*, July 19, 2006.
345 Natalia Kostenko, "Edinorossy vstupaiut v polosu uskoreniia," *Nezavisimaia gazeta*, August 29, 2006; Kostenko, "Edinorossy smenili protivnika," *Nezavisimaia gazeta*, September 26, 2006.
346 Gryzlov, "Dve partii v odnoi," *Nezavisimaia gazeta*, July 20, 2007.
347 Vitalii Tret'iakov, *Nauka byt' Rossiei: Nashi natsional'nye interesy i puti ikh realizatsii* (Moscow: Russkii mir, 2007): 426.

other things, the book featured an important an important chapter by Maksim Shevchenko, which elaborated on the vision of Russia as a multicultural civilization, which is self-sufficient and unique.[348] Another party leader Andrei Isaev spoke about "Edinaia Rossiia" as a "party of the *russkii* people and the *russkaia* civilization."[349] Gryzlov also voiced the invective against the "unipolar world." He spoke in support of the "multipolar world" instead, in which Russia would assume the role of "one of the centers of civilizational development,"[350] — the hallmark of the Russian official rhetoric, especially after Putin's renowned "Munich speech" of 2007. In this year, Gryzlov "firmly and consistently" stated that Russia is a "unique and great civilization."[351] This formula reemerged in the party's discourses on multiple occasions.[352]

The identitarian trend was epitomized in the party's election program, adopted on October 1 2007. The program identified as its primary goal the "further development of Russia as a unique civilization" through "defense of [our] common cultural space, Russian language and historical traditions," but at the same time, does not mention "conservatism" whatsoever.[353] A tendency towards identitarian and isolationistic reinterpretation of conservatism shows a distinctive move of the official ideology towards positions previously occupied by the patriotic left opposition, such as "Rodina."[354] In September 2011, the Center for Social-Conservative Policy launched a new discussion platform for experts, the "Social-Conservative Union," which was moderated by the usual suspects Shuvalov and Isaev, together with the representative of the "political Orthodoxy," Sergei Volobuev. Its political agenda was vocally anti-

---

348 Gryzlov et al., *Vektor Rossii*, 63–105.
349 Efim Andriushin, "'Edinaia Rossiia' zadala russkie voprosy," *Komsomol'skaia pravda*, February 5, 2007.
350 Gryzlov, "Doklad predsedatelia [...] partii 'Edinaia Rossiia'."
351 Gryzlov, "Vystuplenie [...] na otkrytii pamiatnika prepodobnomy Savve Storozhevskomu," 2005, available at: http://gryzlov.ru/index.php?page=publications&id=121.
352 "'Plan Putina' izmenit stranu," *Izvestiia*, May 23, 2007.
353 "Plan Putina—dostoinoe budushchee velikoi strany," *Rossiiskaia gazeta*, November 9, 2007, available at: https://rg.ru/2007/11/09/er.html.
354 Cf. Vladimir Rudakov, "Ideologiia Vos'mogo goda,' *Profil'*, no. 12 (2006), available at: http://nomad.su/?a=3-200604050112.

liberal and grounded mostly on the rhetoric of Russia as a unique civilization, confrontation with the West, Eurasianism and "Orthodox values."[355] The collection of policy papers, edited by Shuvalov, and prepared by the St Petersburg branch of the CSCP, dwells on the revamped definition of conservatism as a "wholehearted reception of the system of values of the Russian civilization."[356]

In the international relations, the concept of Russia as a "civilization" reinforced isolationist and anti-Westernist tendencies. The vision of "multiple civilizations" in the international arena is not new.[357] It is built upon the negation of Western liberalism and upon the foundation of the "Inter-Traditional" — the claim that all traditional religions have essentially the same moral mainstays. Surely, the Russian leadership and pro-Kremlin intellectuals would be happy to discover a universalist project similar to the project of global communism or liberal democracy.[358] Bare anti-Westernism lacks positive content, whereas the idea of the "Inter-Traditional" lacks depth. As the result, the civilizational rhetoric in international relations is paradoxical. It is a universalist appeal for particularity, a call to fight against universal liberal hegemony and to promote a system of sovereign, local civilizations.

As we can observe in the official documents, the language of civilization had evolved from the idea of multipolarity in international relations to the concept of securitization of Russia's unique civilization from the hegemonic West in most recent documents, such as the Foreign Policy Concept of 2013 and the Bases of Russia's Cultural Policy of 2014.[359] For the Russian leadership, the concept

---

355 Viktor Khamraev, "'Edinaia Rossiia' nauchit grazhdan konservatizmu," *Kommersant*, September 19, 2011.
356 Shuvalov, "Novyi etap razvitiia rossiiskoi demokratii," in Sergei Volobuev (ed.), *Sovremennyi rossiiskii konservatizm: Sbornik statei* (Moscow, 2011): 5.
357 Natalia Morozova, "Particularism and Universalism in Russian Post-Soviet Foreign Policy: Russia's Discourse on Humanitarian Cooperation in the CIS," *Higher School of Economics Research Paper No. WP BRP 24* (2015); Lauri Mälksoo, *Russia and European Human-Rights Law: The Rise of the Civilizational Argument* (Leiden: Brill, 2014).
358 Kristina Stoeckl, *The Russian Orthodox Church and Human Rights* (New York: Routledge, 2014).
359 Kaarina Aitamurto, S. Turoma and S. Vladiv-Glover (eds.), *Religion, Expression, and Patriotism in Russia* (Stuttgart: ibidem-Verlag, 2019); Turoma and Aita-

of "civilizations" became a handy ideological tool to fight against the Western hegemony, and an invitation to think about international relations as a playground of civilizations, possessing equal value and enjoying equal rights.[360] Pro-Kremlin spin-doctor and analyst Sergei Markov argued that the idea of Russia as a unique civilization emerged from the anti-colonial protest against colonization of Russia by the West.[361]

The civilizational discourse as articulated in Russian official documents is an adaptation of Samuel Huntington's notorious post-Cold War vision. According to Huntington, a civilization is a "highest cultural grouping of people and the broadest level of cultural identity." Civilizations have different and often incommensurable value-systems, and thus, they approach the most fundamental questions of human life differently — such as peoples' relations to groups, to the state, to the transcendental, to partners, and so on. These differences are "far more fundamental than differences among political ideologies and political regimes."[362] The Concept of the Foreign Policy of the Russian Federation of 2013 offers an almost verbatim restatement of Huntington's argument: "for the first time in modern history, global competition acquires a civilizational dimension, and it is manifested in competition of various value reference points [*tsennostnye orientiry*] and models of development ... Cultural and civilizational multiplicity of the contemporary world is becoming more obvious."[363] The Concept warns that in this context any attempt to impose a hegemonic normative order will exacerbate already conflictual international relations. The most recent Concept, adopted in 2016, rewords the same principles but also

---

murto, "Renegotiating Patriotic and Religious Identities in the Post-Soviet and Post-Secular Russia," *Transcultural Studies* 12, no. 1 (2016): 1–14.

360 See Putin's speech at the World Russian People's Assembly in 2018 ("Golos Rossii v mire budushchego," *Izvestiia*, November 2, 2018).

361 *Tetradi po konservatizmu* 1, no. 2 (2014): 41.

362 Samuel Huntington, *The Clash of Civilizations? The Debate* (New York: Council of Foreign Relations, 1996): 4.

363 "Kontseptsiia vneshnei politiki Rossiiskoi Federatsii," February 12, 2013, available at: https://www.garant.ru/products/ipo/prime/doc/70218094/. See also Sergei Lavrov's statements, analyzed by Fabian Linde (Linde, "The Civilizational Turn in Russian Political Discourse: From Pan-Europeanism to Civilizational Distinctiveness," *The Russian Review* 75, no. 4 (2016): 612).

articulates the Spenglerian *Untergang des Abendlandes*, arguing that against the backdrop of ascendance of non-European great powers, the West's role in global politics and economy is now shrinking.[364] Both Concepts add a tinge of Messianic universalism to this big picture of radical relativism and cultural incommensurability. Hinting on Eurasianism, they insist that Russia has always played the role of the balancer in this world of disparate and conflictual interests.

Another important development of the civilizational rhetoric is the advent of the concept of Russia as a "state-civilization." This term sporadically popped up in political discussions in the 2000s in the writings of such conservative thinkers as Mikhail Remizov, Stanislav Belkovskii, Vitalii Tret'iakov, Mikhail Iur'ev, Mikhail Leont'ev and Andrei Okara.[365] By the upcoming presidential elections in 2012, it became clear that the civilizational rhetoric had entered the intellectual, academic and political mainstream, seconded by the "conservative turn" in the official ideology and growing alienation from the West in the aftermath of the Russo-Georgian war of 2008.[366] One of Vladimir Putin's articles, deployed in the electoral campaign of 2011/2012, was entitled "Russia: The National Question." In this paper, Putin maintained that Russia was a unique, "multi-ethnic 'state-civilization', glued together by the Russian (*russkii*) cultural core."[367] In his state of the nation address in

---

364 "Kontseptsiia vneshnei politiki Rossiiskoi Federatsii," November 30, 2016, available at: http://www.mid.ru/foreign_policy/news/-/asset_publisher/cK NonkJE02Bw/content/id/2542248.
365 E.g. Mikhail Remizov, "Proekt 'gosudarstvo-tsivilizatsiia'," *Intelros*, September 2, 2005, available at: http://www.intelros.org/drevo/remizov1.htm; Aleksandr Gamov, "Kurs: V Evropu nel'zia v Aziiu," *Komsomol'skaia pravda*, July 18, 2005, available at: https://www.kompravda.eu/daily/23546/42240/; Vitalii Tret'iakov, "Neizbezhnost' Soiuza," *Profil'*, September 15, 2008; Tret'iakov, "Kto meshaet pokonchit' s 'kholodnoi voinoi'," *Izvestiia*, April 2, 2009; Iur'ev, Leont'ev, "Poekhali!," *Profil'*, February 16, 2009; Iur'ev, "Rossiia zavoiuet Evropu v 2020 godu," *Komsomol'skaia pravda*, February 19, 2009. Andrei Okara mentioned it in: Andrei Okara, "Gde iskat' osnovaniia dlia novoi chelovecheskoi solidarnosti," *Nezavisimaia gazeta*, March 30, 2010.
366 In 2009, United Russia adopted conservatism as its ideology. See, for example: "Rossiia: Sokhranim i priumnozhim," *Edinaia Rossiia: Ofitsial'nyi sait partii*, November 21, 2009, available at: http://archive.li/WWJGg.
367 Vladimir Putin, "Rossiia: Natsional'nyi vopros," *Nezavisimaia gazeta*, January 23, 2012, available at: http://www.ng.ru/politics/2012-01-23/1_national.html. See on this: Fabian Linde, "The Civilizational Turn in Russian Political

December 2012, Putin accentuated issues about morality and "spiritual values," and mentioned the concept of Russia as a "state-civilization" again.[368] In September 2013 Putin refined the concept in this speech at the Valdai discussion club, when he referred to pre-revolutionary conservative philosopher Konstantin Leont'ev and his ideal of the "blossoming complexity." Building on this Putin interpreted Russia as a "state-civilization, cemented by the Russian people, Russian language, Russian culture, Russian Orthodox Church and other traditional religions of Russia."[369] "State-civilization" in this rendition continues to highlight universalist inclusivity of Russia, while adding to this meaning four important overtones: 1) Russianness in its ethnical dimension (*russkii*, not *rossiiskii*), 2) the idea of unity, 3) the importance of the statehood, and 4) the hint on the traditional religious morality.

This phrase was eagerly adopted by the Russian political leadership.[370] The same formula entered the pages of many pro-government newspapers and journals, such as *Krasnaia Zvezda*, published by the Ministry of the Defense.[371] Picking up on Putin's term, Orthodox activists signed the open letter to him in 2013, urging him to include a mention of Orthodoxy as a spiritual foundation of Russia in the Preamble to the Constitution. The letter, signed by

---

Discourse: From Pan-Europeanism to Civilizational Distinctiveness," *The Russian Review* 75, no. 4 (2016): 604–625; Kåre Johan Mjør, "A Morphology of Russia? The Russian Civilisational Turn and Its Cyclical Idea of History," in K. Lehtisaari and A. Mustajoki (eds.), *Philosophical and Cultural Interpretations of Russian Modernisation* (New York: Taylor & Francis, 2016): 56–70; Mjør and Turoma (eds.) *Russia as Civilization: Ideological Discourses in Politics, Media and Academia*; Andrei Tsygankov, "Crafting the State-Civilization Vladimir Putin's Turn to Distinct Values," *Problems of Post-Communism* 63, no. 3 (2016): 146–158.

368 Daniil Dondurei, "O defitsite dukhovnykh skrep," *Rossiiskaia gazeta*, December 14, 2012. See also Putin's talk at the Valdai forum on September 18, 2013.

369 "Zasedanie mezhdunarodnogo diskussionnogo kluba 'Valdai'," September 19, 2013, available at: http://www.kremlin.ru/events/president/news/19243.

370 E.g. Ramazan Abdulatipov, "Kul'turnyi kod mnogonatsional'noi Rossii," *Izvestiia*, December 17, 2014, available at: https://iz.ru/news/580931; Valentina Matvienko, "Rossiia: sil'naia i otkrytaia," *Parlamentskaia gazeta,* May 22, 2014, available at: https://www.pnp.ru/archive/2014/05/22/rossiya-silnaya-i-otkrytaya.html; Vladimir Medinskii, "Eto ne ugolovnyi kodeks kul'tury," *Kommersant,* April 15, 2014.

371 Vladimir Mokhov, "Nas dolzhno byt' bol'she," *Krasnaia Zvezda*, December 13, 2012.

Konstantin Malofeev, Leonid Reshetnikov, Aleksandr Bokhanov and Mikhail Isaev, identified Russia as a "unique state-civilization," whose "civilizational code" is determined by the Orthodox Church.[372] Likewise, nationalists found the new parlance convenient to mitigate the ethno-centrism of their ideology while at the same time saying what they wanted to say. Egor Kholmogorov, for example, chose to utter in one breath his description of the Russian identity: "Russia as a nation and Russia as a state-civilization."[373]

ROC and civilizational discourses

In 2001, in the context of the 9/11 attack, Metropolitan Kirill (Gundiaev) dwelled on the concept of the "clash of civilizations." Kirill argued that Russia had been called to reconcile the "civilization of the West" and the "world of Islam." In his assessment, Russia's status as a civilization was a "work-in-progress," something which the present-day Russia should become the ground for.[374] His address to the World Russian Assembly was cautiously worded; Russia was evaluated as "one of the pillars of the East-Christian world, and a center of the original civilization";[375] elsewhere in the documents of the Assembly, Patriarch Aleksii II spoke about the "Orthodox civilization."[376] At the same Assembly Aleksandr Dugin spoke about the "Euro-Asian Orthodox civilization."[377] Civilizational discourses at this stage revolved around two ideas: Russia as a part of a larger, religiously-defined Orthodox civilization, and Russia as a Eurasian civilization in statu nascendi. In the next few years, the World Russian Assembly continued this line of thinking, while political

---

372 Konstantin Malofeev et al., "Obrashchenie," n.d., available at: https://repu blic.ru/images/doc/obrashenie.pdf.
373 Egor Kholmogorov, "Rozhdenie novoi zvezdy," *Izvestiia*, May 12, 2015.
374 "Russia's experience should become the ground for shaping the original civilization" (Metropolitan Kirill, "Vystuplenie ...," December 13–14, 2001, available at: https://vrns.ru/documents/59/1232).
375 "Sobornoe slovo VI Vsemirnogo Russkogo Narodnogo Sobora," December 13–14, 2001, available at: https://vrns.ru/documents/59/1229.
376 Patriarch Aleksii II, "Slovo ...," December 13–14, 2001, available at: https:// vrns.ru/documents/59/1230.
377 "Plenarnye zasedaniia v Khrame Khrista Spasitelia," December 13–14, 2001, available at: https://vrns.ru/documents/59/1233.

leaders, invited to give talks to the Assembly, assimilated its rhetoric. For example, in addresses to the Assembly by Boris Gryzlov (then the speaker of the State Duma) and Minister of the Foreign Affairs Igor' Ivanov, Russia was inscribed into the "history of the East-Christian civilization."[378]

Around the same time in the beginnings of the 2000s, the ROC became part of the discussions in the framework of the Forum "Dialogue of Civilizations," run and financed by the railway "king" Vladimir Iakunin. Metropolitan Vladimir (Ikim), for example, was invited for the first meeting of the "Dialogue" in 2003 and in connection with it, he spoke vocally about the importance of the "Russian [*russkii*] civilization."[379]

The Assembly of 2006 visibly changed its rhetoric. In its general address, as well as in Metropolitan Kirill's talk, the words about the "original *russkaia* civilization" appeared,[380] leaving no doubt about who stood behind this conceptual shift. Contrary to his previous talks at this forum, this time Kirill spoke positively about the "original *russkaia* civilization" as a fait accompli, not a blueprint for the future, which has its own package of basic ideas and principles, different from other civilizations.[381] In his civilizational discourses, Kirill appeals to historical roots and traditions. Elsewhere, he spoke about the "civilization of Ancient Rus'" — the cultural and territorial trunk out of which modern Orthodox nations sprouted.[382] At the same time, for Kirill, Russian civilization is a "powerful project," designed by St Prince Vladimir, and launched into the future.

---

378 Gryzlov, "Privetstvie ...," February 3-5, 2004, available at: https://vrns.ru/documents/61/1224; Igor' Ivanov, "Vystuplenie ...," February 3-5, 2004, available at: https://vrns.ru/documents/61/1223.
379 Petr Pavlov, "Russkii vektor dialoga tsivilizatsii," *Argumenty i fakty*, September 3, 2003.
380 "Sobornoe slovo X VRNS," April 4-6, 2006, available at: https://vrns.ru/documents/63/1162. See also: Mikhail Moshkin, "Zhivaia liubov' i zhivaia sovest'," *Nezavisimaia gazeta*, April 28, 2006; Metropolitan Kirill (Gundiaev), "Vystuplenie ...," April 4-6, 2006, available at: https://vrns.ru/documents/63/1190.
381 Metropolitan Kirill, "Vystuplenie ...," April 4-6, 2006, available at: https://vrns.ru/documents/63/1190.
382 *Sviataia Rus' – Vmeste ili vroz'? Patriarkh Kirill na Ukraine* (Moscow: Danilovskii muzhskoi monastyr', 2009): 214.

Even today, he argues, this "project" keeps the momentum and provides Russia with a global mission.[383] The Declaration of the Rights and Dignity of Humans was adopted at this Assembly "in the name of the original *russkaia* civilization,"[384] and as an expression of its own interpretation of this matter, dissimilar from the classic documents of the Western liberal tradition.

Since his enthronement in 2009, Patriarch Kirill eloquently gave his opinion on the unity of the "civilizational space" with the center in Moscow. Elsewhere he called this space the "Russian world"[385] and, in this case, the civilizational rhetoric served the purpose of providing the common cultural denominator for Russia and Ukraine (and secondarily, to all other parts of the "Russian world," such as Belarus, Kazakhstan, and Moldova).[386] For him, the "question of Russian civilizational identity is [...] first and foremost the question of unity of our civilizational space (*edinstvo nashego tsivilizatsionnogo prostranstva*)."[387] This formula allowed him to resort to the language of fragility: if the civilizational space splits, it will be an "enormous civilizational catastrophe."[388]

Following Putin's idea about Russia as a "state-civilization," Patriarch Kirill gave a keynote speech at the World Russian People's Assembley in 2013. In this speech, Patriarch emphatically argued that Russia was a member of the "family" of original civilizations. Referring to Ivan Il'in and Nikolai Danilevsky, he dwelled on the question if Russia is a "great civilization," given its relative insignificance in the world economy, Kirill responded by saying that greatness should

---

383 *Sviataia Rus' – Vmeste ili vroz'?* 242.
384 "Deklaratsiia o pravakh i dostoinstve cheloveka," April 4–6, 2006, available at: https://vrns.ru/documents/63/1179.
385 Patriarch Kirill (Gundiaev), "The Russian World Is a Special Civilization," *Russkiymir.ru*, September 9, 2014, available at: HTTP://RUSSKIYMIR.RU/EN/NEWS/149812/
386 Patriarch Kirill (Gundiaev), "Vystuplenie ... na torzhestvennom otkrytii III Assamblei Russkogo Mira," November 3, 2009, available at: http://www.patriarchia.ru/db/print/928446.html.
387 Patriarch Kirill (Gundiaev), "Slovo [...] na otkrytii XXII Vsemirnogo Russkogo Narodnogo Sobora," *Zhurnal Moskovskoi Patriarkhii*, no. 11 (2018): 38; Patriarch Kirill (Gundiaev), "Slovo ...," *Zhurnal Moskovskoi Patriarchii*, no. 11 (2018), 38; *Sviataia Rus' – Vmeste ili vroz'?* 183, 204.
388 Kirill, "Interview ... ukrainskim telezhurnalistam," July 19, 2010, available at: http://www.patriarchia.ru/db/print/1223635.html

be measured by the civilization's ability to offer a global alternative. In this sense, "the Russian [*russkaia*] civilization" is a great one, because it, first, emphasizes non-material, spiritual values, and second, shows an example of peaceful, non-hegemonic coexistence of various nationalities, cultures and confessions. In this connection, Patriarch raised the issue of "spiritual sovereignty" — the concept, which grasps the need to protect the "Russian civilization" from the hostile foreign information and propaganda.[389] The concept of "spiritual sovereignty" added new colors to the rhetoric of civilizations, pushing it decisively towards geopolitical isolationism.

The term "spiritual sovereignty" was discussed in the milieu of Young Conservatives around 2005. For example, Oleg Matveichev paralleled it to the concept of the country's uniqueness and global mission. The ultimate guarantee of the country's existence, he argued, was the high value of this country in the eyes of other nations.[390] In 2007–2008, the term was used by the Ukrainian President Viktor Iushchenko, who saw it as legitimation of Ukraine's religious independence from Moscow.[391] In 2009 "spiritual sovereignty" was adopted by the radical right-wing party "For Our Motherland," whose Manifesto with words about "spiritual sovereignty and spritirual freedom of the Nation" was banned as extremist by the decision of the Ministry of Justice.[392] The Orthodox-nationalistic movement "People's Assembly" (*Narodnyi Sobor*) put the concept in the center of its political program. The Assembly's document "Declaration on the Defense of Spiritual Sovereignty" (May 2009) insisted that Russia had already lost its "spiritual sovereignty" because of its Westernization and exclusion of the state ideology from Constitution of 1993. Still, one can tease out from the "Declaration," that the struggle was not hopeless. Namely, Russia as part of its fight for "spiritual sovereignty," Russia had to reject Western "juvenile justice," moral laxity, sexual education,

---

389 Patriarch Kirill, "Rossii est', chto predlozhit' miru," *Zhurnal Moskovskoi Patriarkhii*, no. 12 (2013): 28–31.
390 Oleg Matveichev, "Novaia missiia Rossii," *APN.ru*, December 13, 2005.
391 E.g.: Aleksandr Sidorov, "Pravo, slavnyi iubilei," *Tribuna*, August 1, 2008.
392 N.a., "Federal'nyi spisok ekstremistskikh materialov," *Rossiiskaia gazeta*, December 14, 2009.

"vulgarity" in arts, re-consideration of Russia's history, and normalization of sexual "pervesions."[393] In other words, activists of the "People's Assembly" aligned "spiritual sovereignty" with the ideological agenda of moral conservatism.

In 2012 the term entered the religious and political mainstream during the 16th World Russian Assembly in 2012, chaired by Patriarch Kirill.[394] It was understood as an important addition to the concept of state sovereignty. In Kirill's words, "spritutual sovereignty" implies the country's impregnability in terms of stability of its basic values and identity, its indepdendence from foreign cultural impact.[395] In the next year, Patriarch Kirill opened the 17th Assembly with another speech on the necessity of "spiritual sovereignty" in the context of understanding Russia as a unique civilization.[396] He specified, that "spiritual sovereignty" meant securitization of Russia's "traditional values," which were supposedly threatened by alien values and lifestyles.[397] The confrontational aspect of this term was highlighted by the monarchist think-tank Russian Institute for Strategic Research (RISI), which in 2013 appealed to the Russian President with a demand to revamp the Constitution by mentioning "spiritual sovereignty" in its Preamble. "Orthodox oligarch" Konstantin Malofeev voiced this position by saying that Russia needed a shield against Western "Godless ideology," alien to the traditional understanding of a family, child-rearing and morals.[398]

For Church leaders, "spiritual sovereignty" implies that Russia should shun Western values simply because they are Western, "not ours." Concepts of "spiritual sovereignty" and "spiritual

---

393 "Deklaratsiia o zashchite dukhovnogo suvereniteta Rossii," *Ruskline.ru*, May 20, 2009, available at: https://ruskline.ru/analitika/2009/05/20/materialy_konferencii_dvizheniya_narodnyj_sobor/
394 "Sobornoe slovo XVI Vsemirnogo Russkogo Narodnogo Sobora," October 1–2, 2012, available at: https://vrns.ru/documents/69/896.
395 Kirill, "Vremia tiazhelykh ispytanii," *Zhurnal Moskovskoi Patriarkhii*, no. 11 (2013): 8.
396 "Slovo Sviateishego Patriarkha Kirilla na XVII Vsemirnom Russkom Narodnom Sobore," *Vsemirnyi Russkii Narodnyi Sobor*, October 31, 2013, http://www.vrns.ru/news/2237/?sphrase_id=5018; Kirill (Vladimir Gundiaev), *Propovedi. 2009–2010* (Sergiev Posad, 2010): 182. See also Chapter 5 of this volume.
397 E.g., Kirill (Gundiaev), *Preodolenie smuty* (Moscow: 2013): 41.
398 Konstantin Malofeev, "Davaite vernem sebe pravo nazyvat'sia narodom-bogonostsem," *Komsomol'skaia pravda*, December 24, 2013.

security" resonated in academia as well.[399] Professor of the Russian Presidential Academy (RANEPA) Aleksei Sitnikov analyzed "spiritual sovereignty" in the context of Carl Schmitt's concept of "Church sovereignty" in Catholicism, which meant the sovereign right of Vatican to define moral aspects of the political terms, such as justice. With references to Russophobia in the West, Sitnikov argued that "spiritual sovereignty" would provide rights of the Russian Orthodoxy to deny "common liberal norms."[400]

The vision of the Russian civilization received a powerful boost after the Ukrainian crisis. For the ROC, the "Russian civilization" is convenient language with which to express their ambivalence about the "Russian world" as an identitarian entity: it is defined by ethnicity, culture and language, but at the same time is inclusive and internationalistic. Patriarch Kirill pronounced many times on his understanding of the "Russian [*russkii*] civilization," which is "not only Russian and not only Orthodox and Christian, in spite of the decisive contribution of the Russian people [*russkii narod*] and the Russian Orthodox Church into its creation."[401]

Another programmatic speech by Patriarch Kirill of 2015 restated his previous thoughts about the "Russian civilization" as a world of solidarity and international cooperation, and introduced a new concept of the "civilizational choice."[402] This concept helps him to problematize the Ukrainian crisis as a struggle against the ROC's attempts to build an Orthodox civilization. On his TV show *Slovo pastyria* of September 6, 2014, Kirill emphasized the importance of preserving Russian civilization in today's global world, and referred to the military conflict in Ukraine as a "struggle for East European space"—while one side was struggling for its civilizational identity,

---

[399] E.g. in 2012 the faculty of national security was established at RASS. See also RASS's publications: S. Smul'skii (ed.), *Natsional'naia bezopasnost' Rossii: Problemy i puti obespecheniia* (Moscow, 2012).
[400] Aleksei Sitnikov, "Karl Shmitt i model' politicheskogo upravleniia," *Obozrevatel'*, March 15, 2015.
[401] Patriarch Kirill, "Fundament nashei tserkvi—v Kieve," *Argumenty i fakty*, November 18, 2015.
[402] Patriarch Kirill, "Prinimaia khristianstvo, Rus' sdelala shag navstrechu istine," *Zhurnal Moskovskoi Patriarkhii*, no. 12 (2015): 20–23; Kirill, "Kniaz' Vladimir: Tsivilizatsionnyi vybor," *Zhurnal Moskovskoi Patriarkhii*, no. 1 (2016): 39–45.

the other, unfaithful to its civilizational roots, was fighting on the side of an alien civilization."[403] Elsewhere Patriarch Kirill labeled the pro-Ukrainian side of the conflict as "traitors" of their own historical roots and civilizational principles.[404] Viacheslav Nikonov articulated this idea with utmost clarity: we cannot choose our civilizational identity, we can only uncover and become aware of it, because that civilizational choice was made long before us, by St Prince Vladimir in 988.[405]

Boris Mezhuev's sophisticated interpretation of the "Russian civilization" demonstrates the conceptual change from the secular ideology of "sovereign democracy" from the mid-2000s, to the religiously-colored and geopolitically-informed understanding, characteristic for the post-2014 Russian ideology. From the viewpoint of "sovereign democracy" "we" are sovereign because "we" are adult, and can well decide for ourselves what constitutes a good life for us.[406] It might be that "we" decide on a life that is different from others. This is the liberal way of thinking. From the viewpoint of Mezhuev's theory of "civilization" "we" are sovereign *because* we are different from others, unique. Here the causal relationship is reversed: "our" primordial difference makes us sovereign, not the other way around. "We" have not chosen this uniqueness, it just has always been this way, and "we" can only belong, we can only step into this "stream of history," as he puts it. Mezhuev argues that "civilization" means a particular relation of a nation to its place in the world and history, namely, the adamant conviction that this nation has a special path and therefore cannot be put on the same footing with others.[407]

---

403 "Patriarkh Kirill rasskazal rossiianam, chto takoe Russkii mir," *Vlasti.Net*, September 9, 2014); "Slovo pastyria," TV show, September 6, 2014, available at: https://www.youtube.com/watch?v=Qile_bwVp9U.
404 "Patriarkh: Tragediia Ukrainy sviazana s poterei obshchego ponimaniia istorii," *Vsesmi.Ru*, November 11, 2014.
405 "Russkii mir: Kod tsivilizatsii," *Strategiia Rossii*, no. 12 (2015): 5–26.
406 Vladislav Surkov, *Suverenitet – eto politicheskii sinonim konkurentosposobnosti* (Moscow, 2006).
407 Boris Mezhuev, "Po tu storonu dvoinogo standarta," *Izvestiia*, August 18, 2014.

The logic of fragility and security in civilizational discourses

The rhetoric of civilizations is a specific ideological language, used to express various positions about Russia, its identity and place on the planet. At the same time, "civilizations" convey broader epistemological characteristics of the political language in today's Russia. This section uncovers these characteristics by analyzing academic dissertations, defended in Russia.[408] Namely, "civilization" is used to relate the feeling of insecurity and fragility of the current political regime. This vision stems from the interpretation of civilizations as organic bodies. Such a "body" was born at some point in time, it will die sometime in the future, and now it is coming through an ordeal of potentially deadly crises or is under an internal or external threat.[409] Sometimes, theorists of the civilizational approach elaborate on the ongoing or forthcoming crisis of the global human civilization.[410] Oksana Galkina's dissertation, for example, dwells on the idea of a "deep civilizational crisis" and the "crisis of civilizational identity" in which contemporary Russia has become entrapped. The fragility and vulnerability of the Russian civilization is conditioned by the encroachments of the powerful Western nemesis, but also by internal weakness.[411]

Following Huntington's assessment of Russia as a civilizationally "torn country," on a par with Turkey and Mexico, many Russian dissertations elaborate on Russia's "civilizational status" as unclear, contested, undetermined, or not fully-fledged and liminal. Unlike other civilizations, Russian civilization's full autonomy and self-sufficiency is not something already given, but is—rather—a

---

408 This section is partial reprint of the chapter Suslov and Kotkina, "Civilizational Discourses in Doctoral Dissertations in Post-Soviet Russia," in Turoma and Mjør (eds.), *Russia as Civilization: Ideological Discourses in Politics, Media and Academia*.
409 Mikhail Svistunov, *Rossiiskaia tsivilizatsiia i pravoslavie: Dialektika ikh vzaimootnoshenii i perspektivy razvitiia*. Dissertation (Moscow: Moscow University for the Humanities, 2005): 285.
410 Aleksandra Il'ina, *Territoriia kak resurs preodoleniia tsivilizatsionnykh krizisov*. Dissertation (Vladivostok: Federal University of the Far East, 2017): 12.
411 Oksana Galkina, *Rossiiskaia tsivilizatsiia v kontekste sovremennogo globalizatsionnogo protsessa*. Dissertation (Armavir: Armavir Orthodox-Social Institute, 2011).

project for the future.[412] Galkina identifies the task of her dissertation as an investigation of the "reasons for the civilizational crisis."[413] She argues that the Russian civilization "has not been shaped" yet (*nedooformlennaia*), that Russia's "civilizational status is chronically undetermined" and "amorphous."[414] Specifically, it was the "geopolitical catastrophe [i.e. the fall of the Soviet Union] which dimmed Russia's self-awareness as a civilization, so that the sense of civilizational self-sufficiency has been lost," and Russia has entered a condition of "civilizational anxiety."[415]

The idea of the fragility and immaturity of Russian civilization provides for the multiple opportunities for securitization, while at the same time it imparts a teleological vision to the history of Russia. It explains, why the concept of civilizational uniqueness is seamlessly connected with the concept of "state-civilization": a weak, underdeveloped "body" of civilization requires a powerful protective shell of the state. For example, Svetlana Nikitova's dissertation qualifies Russia as "a dependent civilization" (*nesamostoiatel'naia tsivilizatsiia*), and dwells on the necessity to have a strong state in order to counter the West, which "feels the need to sneeze Russia's properties, resources and territories."[416] Albert Ianakov would probably disagree with the qualification of Russia as a "dependent civilization," but he still makes two similar points, the first being the uncritically accepted assumption that Russian civilization is "in crisis," while the second is the argument about its "intermediate" (*promezhutochnyi*) character.[417] Having stated this, Ianakov likewise calls for the state protection.[418]

---

412 Svetlana Nikitova, Kharakter rossiiskoi tsivilizatsii: Sotsial'no-filosofskii analiz. Dissertation (Moscow: Moscow State Technical University, 1999): 21, 24; Iury Iaretskii, Rossiiskoe obshchestvo i razvitie tsivilizatsii: Sotsial'nye sostavliaiushchie istoricheskogo protsessa. Dissertation (Moscow: Russian State Social University, 2002): 372.
413 Galkina, *Rossiiskaia tsivilizatsiia*, 10.
414 Galkina, *Rossiiskaia tsivilizatsiia*, 11, 29–30.
415 Galkina, *Rossiiskaia tsivilizatsiia*, 49, 31.
416 Nikitova, *Kharakter rossiiskoi tsivilizatsii*, 24, 50.
417 Albert Ianakov, *Dukhovnyi potentsial rossiiskoi tsivilizatsii kak faktor voennoi*. Dissertation (Moscow: Air Force Academy, 2004): 204, 372.
418 Ianakov, *Dukhovnyi potentsial*, 372.

Mikhail Svistunov points at the democratic reforms of the 1990s, which as he argues, made "civilizational processes more difficult" (*tsivilizationnye protsessy* [...] *byli otiagoshcheny*), while the "scientific and intellectual potential of the Russian civilization was considerably undermined."[419] He identifies the West as a political subject, which consciously spoiled the Russian civilization in the 1990s by means of pouring into Russia the most immoral and corrupt products of the Western civilization. Following this logic, Svistunov comes to the conclusion that only a strong state can "ward Russia off all intrigues and attacks (*proiski i naskoki*) of its external and internal enemies."[420] Mourning various threats, which beset the Russian civilization, Maria Milovzorova entices its readers to "recover and shudder" (*ochnut'sia i sodrognut'sia*) deep inside their souls.[421] Nadezhda Butenko also connects the fact that the Russian civilization has been "disbalanced" (*rasbalansirovanie*) because of the West's interference, and because of Russia's own pro-Western course in the 1990s.[422] Likewise, Vladimir Lepekhin interprets the period of the 1990s as "de-civilizationization" (*rastsivilizovyvanie*) of the post-Soviet space.[423]

Andrei Shuklin adds one more layer to this idea, claiming that due to the heterogeneity of the Russian civilization, only the strong centralized state power is capable of keeping together its disparate parts, which will otherwise gravitate toward other civilizations: Islamic, Buddhist, West-European, etc. To justify his argument, he stipulates further on that strong power should be combined with dialogue, which—as we know—is an oxymoron.[424] Here, the idea of the Russian civilization as "power-centric" comes from the same

---

419 Svistunov, *Rossiiskaia tsivilizatsiia*, 3, 15.
420 Svistunov, *Rossiiskaia tsivilizatsiia*, 267.
421 Mariia Milovzorova, *Aksiologicheskie osnovania russkoi tsivilizatsii kak dialekticheskogo otritsania globalizma*. Dissertation (St Petersburg: Baltic State Technical University ("Voenmekh"), 2016): 33.
422 Nadezhda Butenko, *Russkii etnos i rossiiskaia tsivilizatsiia: Sotsial'no-filosofskoe issledovanie samosoznaniia*. Dissertation (Surgut: Surgut State University, 2003): 92.
423 Vladimir Lepekhin, *Antropologicheskii podkhod v issledovanii problemy sushchnostnykh priznakov rossiiskoi tsivilizatsii*. Dissertation (Moscow: Moscow State University, 2015): 13, 26.
424 Andrei Shuklin, *Perspektivy rossiiskoi tsivilizatsii i globalizatsiia*. Dissertation (Tiumen': Tiumen' State University, 2014): 120.

assumption that this civilization is incomplete, torn asunder by more accomplished civilizational centers. When discussing what can help the Russian civilization to "preserve itself" (*sokhranit'sia*) in the future,[425] Shuklin's choice of words instigates a moral panic that Russia is facing a real threat of *not* being able to preserve itself. The same word is used by Butenko. For her, the state priority should become the politics of "preservation" of Russia's civilizational space. Otherwise Russia as a civilization "may stop to exist."[426]

Securitization of the Russian civilization gave a stimulus for the whole subfield of studies and opinion journalism, dubbed "civilization security" (*tsivilizatsionnaia bezopasnost'*). Eleven of our dissertations deal directly with civilizational security. One of them is the *Doktor nauk* dissertation in political science (2005), written by Konstantin Feofanov, professor at the Diplomatic Academy of the Ministry of the Foreign Affairs. In this work, saturated with esoteric language and general words about Russia's role in the world, Feofanov introduces the concept of "security of the civilizational development." This concept condenses the whole gamut of civilizational imaginary: The vision of civilizations as organism, whose natural development could be effectively stemmed not only by the direct "mechanical" intervention, but also in the more subtle ways. For example, a civilization could be exposed to the hostile information impact, or, as he puts it, the lack of "necessary domestic and international conditions."[427] Logically, in order to securitize the "civilizational development," a "civilizational policy" should be developed.[428] In a more recent *Doktor nauk* dissertation in philosophy by Farid Mustafaev (2014), the idea of civilizational (in)security is expressed by the concept of "civilizational risks."[429]

It should be noted that the language of crisis and insecurity is characteristic for all Russian political debates, especially touching

---

425 Shuklin, *Perspektivy rossiiskoi tsivilizatsii*, 6, 129.
426 Butenko, *Russkii etnos*, 95.
427 Konstantin Feofanov, *Bezopasnost' tsivilizatsionnogo razvitiia Rossii v usloviiakh globalizatsii*. Dissertation (Moscow: Academy of FSB, 2005): 37, 89, 112.
428 Feofanov, *Bezopasnost' tsivilizatsionnogo razvitiia*, 60, 279.
429 Farid Mustafaev, *Mezhnatsional'noe obshchenie v kontekste obespecheniia tsivilizatsionnoi bezopasnosti Rossii*. Dissertation (Rostov on Don: South Federal University, 2014): 4.

upon such topics as "spiritual security" and "civilization code." For example, in 2013, Nikita Mikhalkov spoke about the revolution 1917 as the "breakdown (*slom*) of the Russian (*russkii*) civilizational code."[430] Vladislav Kononov, the executive director of the pro-Kremlin "Russian Military-Historical Society" in 2015–2018, insisted that the film *The Death of Stalin* should not be shown in Russia on the grounds that it is a "disgusting parody on the whole Russian (*rossiiskaia*) civilization."[431] One can infer from Kononov's intransigence that the "Russian civilization" is so fragile that a foreign film can seriously damage it.

Conclusions

This chapter examined one of the central components of contemporary Russian geopolitical culture — the concept of "civilizations." Its conceptual development reflects on the multiplicity of the political actors, ideological contexts and debates, in which it was used. Today, its meaning depends on a specific situation. It can mean the inseparability of the Soviet period from the rest of the Russian history. It can imply criticism of the Western hegemony and the US leadership in international relations. It can become a weapon against the liberal "fifth column" and the argument in favor of the "strong hand" in politics and annexationism in the "near abroad." The common denominator of all these ideological iterations is the claim that Russia is larger than the Russian Federation, and that there are peoples and lands *outside* of the RF, which belong to the "Russian civilization," and at the same time, there are no peoples and lands *inside* the current RF, which do not belong to this "civilization." In this way, a "civilization" is the substitute concept for a "nation" in the post-imperial reality, which provides for a nation-like cohesiveness among parts of the "civilization," while at the same time, it cements together non-Russian (ethnically) parts of the

---

430 "V ramkakh foruma 'Moia istoriia. Romanovy' proshla konferentsiia," November 10, 2013, available at: http://monarhist.info/news/2271.
431 Nikolai Kornatskii, "V Rossii ne uvidiat 'Smert' Stalina'," *Izvestiia*, January 23, 2018, available at: https://iz.ru/699318/nikolai-kornatckii/v-rossii-ne-uvidiat-smert-stalina.

present political body of Russia. However, the importance of the "Russian civilization" concept exceeds its purely political instrumentalization; it also displays an attempt to contemplate a universal doctrine, which would be a counterpart to Western liberalism both in international relations and in its general meaning as an ideology. In this sense, we can speak about the nascent ideology of "civilizationism," which taps into two main intellectual sources: religious communitarianism and left-wing anti-globalism. In post-Soviet Russia, these two intellectual streams met. In this context, the 19th-century pan-Slavist thinker Nikolai Danilevsky was successfully exhumed and galvanized by the injection of Samuel Huntington's interpretation of the clash of civilizations.

4 Geopolitical Imagination and Russian Imperial Science Fiction

Introduction

This chapter inquires into the ways in which contemporary Russian science fiction (SF hereafter) interacts with the processes of identity-making, and participates in shaping of the post-Soviet subjectivity. The initial premise of the research consists in the idea that the post-Soviet SF narrative is connected with the post-Soviet geopolitical subjectivity, similarly to how the classic novel is connected with Victorian imperialism,[432] or early SF — with colonialism.[433] In Russia today, SF repeatedly trespasses on the border with political engineering, so that it is becoming more than just a literary genre, but rather a specific type of projective thinking. Many authors of SF are close to ideological think tanks and participate in state-sponsored or dissident initiatives to manipulate the mass consciousness.[434] Konstantin Rykov is one example of the symbiosis between SF literature and political engineering; being a member of the ruling party, United Russia, and a State Duma deputy, he stood behind many pro-Kremlin media projects, and is known for promoting the literary franchise *Ethnogenesis*, which is responsible for more than 50 books written by some three dozens of SF authors, and an online video game.[435]

---

432 Edward Said, *Culture and Imperialism* (London: Vintage, 1994).
433 John Rieder, *Colonialism and the Emergence of Science Fiction* (Middletown CT: Wesleyan University Press, 2008); Patricia Kerslake, *Science Fiction and Empire* (Liverpool: Liverpool University Press, 2007).
434 E.g. Sergei Norka, the author of popular political SF Russia the Damned (Moscow, 2000) is the former officer of the Soviet military intelligence, and the head of his own agency "Norka", specializing on political analysis (http://www.norkag.ru/ru/about/index.php). Mikhail Iur'ev, the State Duma deputy and an influential businessman, is also known for his much-talked-of SF book *The Third Empire: Russia as It Should Be* (Moscow, 2007). Sergei Dorenko is a prominent political journalist and analyst who published a SF novel, discussing Russia's nearest future, *2008* (Moscow, 2005).
435 Mark Bassin and Irina Kotkina, "The Etnogenez Project: Ideology and Science Fiction in Putin's Russia," *Utopian Studies* 27, no. 1 (2016): 53–76.

Another example is a series of edited volumes put together by Sergei Chekmaev (oftentimes with Dmitry Volodikhin) and published under the overarching series title "Close Range Social Science Fiction."[436] For example, in the Preface to one of the books, called *Liberal Apocalypse,* the purpose of the book is defined as exploration of the "liberal tendencies," stretched to their absurd and terrifying extremity, which, according to the volume, implies "horrors of globalization, losing of the national identity, spiritless world of material [values], substitution of traditional values by artificially created [ones]."[437] Conservative writers have eagerly dubbed this dystopian sub-genre "liber-punk."[438] Some of these volumes were published with financial support from pro-government foundation "Interaction of Civilizations," whose mission is to "promote moral foundations for non-conflictual interaction among civilizations."[439] The foundation maintains liaisons with the arch-conservative *Russian People's Council,* and the Synodal PR Department of the Moscow Patriarchate.

Most of contributors of these books come from the conservative SF club "Bastion." It emerged in 1999 by the initiative of Dmitry Volodikhin, and its first convention, Bastkon, was held in 2001. "Bastion" does not only produce fiction books but also serves as an organizational shelter for nonfiction manifestoes and policy papers promoting such values as imperial order, traditionalism, Orthodox

---

436 The term "close range science fiction" *(fantastika blizhnego pritsela)* comes from a trend in Soviet SF of the 1940s–early 1950s, which focuses on relatively near future, technological accomplishments, and as few fantastic assumptions as possible. It was associated with the Stalinist mandate to limit the genre of science fiction to socially useful fantasies illustrating technological progress and social goals that might be achieved in the "close range" or "near horizons." It is noteworthy that the rebooting of the term serves the same purpose: to limit the iconoclastic potential of the genre and to highlight its usefulness for the pragmatic goals of the state. I thank Yvonne Howell for drawing my attention to this remarkable parallel.
437 Sergei Chekmaev and Roman Silant'ev, "Preface," available at: https://royallib.com/read/chekmaev_sergey/liberalniy_apokalipsis.html#0.
438 The term was invented around 2005 and propagated by the community liberpunk.livejournal.com until 2017. Among other participants, there were Dmitry Volodikhin and Konstantin Krylov. See: Sergei Chuprinin, *Russkaia literatura segodnia: Zhizn' po poniatiiam* (Moscow: Vremia, 2007).
439 "Nashi tseli i zadachi," available at: http://cif-russia.ru/ru/.

fundamentalism, anti-globalization, imperial revanchism and monarchism. Dmitry Volodikhin claims that he knows of "many attempts to correct public opinion with the help of a [SF] novel" and some of his interviews sound like invitations to get contracts from the government.[440] In 2014, he was appointed as an advisor of the head of the think-tank Russian Institute for Strategic Research (RISI), and took some of his fellow SF writers on board of this institution. RISI was created in the 1990s but became prominent after 2012, when the new chief ideologist of Kremlin Viacheslav Volodin was at pains to provide a greater ideological legitimacy to Putin's third term in power in spite of the wave of protests in the winter 2011/2012.

The Institute for Socio-Economic and Political Research (ISEPI) is another think-tank, catering to the needs of the Presidential Administration. It hosts the web-newspaper *Vzgliad* and the analytical webpage "Political conservatism," previously edited by Konstantin Rykov and Kirill Benediktov, both renowned authors of SF. ISEPI was established in 2012 as an heir to inactive Gleb Pavlovsky's Foundation for Effective Politics.[441] The new institute staffed with the former and present employees of the Presidential Administration, was designed as a pro-government think-tank vested with the macro-task of supporting the federal electoral circle in 2016-18. Its publishing outlets are especially vocal in ridiculing migrant policies of the EU and supporting Western rightists and migrantophobes.[442]

In terms of numbers, the genre of SF enjoys unprecedented popularity in today's Russia, which is still on raise, resulting in 400 to 900 titles of SF novels annually.[443] Research on the readers'

---

440 Volodikhin, 2007, 140; Volodikhin, "Imperskie gumanoidy," *Politicheskii zhurnal*, no. 20 (2006).
441 More on pro-Kremlin think-tanks: Laruelle, "Inside and Around the Kremlin's Black Box: The New Nationalist Think-Tanks in Russia."
442 See, for example, his recent interview to another conservative SF writer Igor Shengal'ts (November 14, 2017). Available at: http://russkoepole.de/ru/ru briki/tochka-zreniya/4167-k-benediktov-ssha-zagnali-sebya-i-rossiyu-v-situ-atsiyu-kogda-ustupki-vosprinimayutsya-kak-kapitulyatsiya.html.
443 E.g. V. Berezin, "Fantastika," *Knizhnoe obozrenie*, no. 52 (2008); Maria Cherniak, "Fantastika kak aktual'noe chtenia," *Bibliotechnoe delo*, no. 16 (2013): 4. It is hard

preferences shows that a typical portrait of a SF reader is a young or middle-aged man of relatively low social status (44% of countryside teenagers, 34% of all teenagers, and 19% of all population prefer SF over all other genres).[444] Analysts observe a lowering of intellectual standards among both authors and readers of SF, compared to in Soviet times; once a literature aimed at critically thinking intelligentsia, it is becoming pulp fiction aimed at the grassroots. During Soviet time, authors and readers of SF were recruited mostly from the groups of qualified engineers, scientists, university teachers[445] — that is, from the groups affected most seriously by the socio-economic transformations of the late 1980s to the 1990s and suffered from the dramatic lowering of their social statuses. The advent of the market economy in the book publishing industry ushered in an epoch of uncertainty and low wages for the majority of SF writers.[446] Besides, during the 1990s the market was totally dominated by non-Russian, mostly American SF, which had advantages both in quality and novelty for the former Soviet reader. Russian SF

---

to give precise figures, but some indicative numbers pertain to popular series of SF, such as "SF action novel" by the publishing house "Alfa-kniga" (1992–2014) which counts now 913 books; "The Magic of Fantasy" (2004–2014) by the same publisher — 534; "The Alternative" (2003–2014) by AST publishing house — 291, and so on. A simple calculation of the SF novels published in the Russian language (including translations from non-Russian authors), which appeared in series gives 4100 titles (http://fantlab.ru/autorseries).

444 A. Stepanova, V. Ialysheva, *Chtenie v bibliotekakh Rossii. Issue 7* (St Petersburg, 2007): 46, 53, 64. See also: Birgit Menzel, "Russian Science Fiction and fantasy Literature," in Stephen Lovell and B. Menzel (eds.), *Reading for Entertainment in Contemporary Russia: Post-Soviet Popular Literature in Historical Perspective* (München: Sagner, 2005): 118–119.

445 See: Patrick McGuire, *Red Stars. Political Aspects of Soviet Science Fiction* (Ann Arbor: UMI Research Press, 1977): 87.

446 There are ca. 10–15 top authors whose royalties may reach the level of some 60,000 USD per book. The rest of thousands of authors can rely on hardly more than 2,000 USD per book. Analysts diagnose repetitive overproduction of SF on the market. This accounts for both lowering of literary perfection of SF, and marginalization of its writers, many of whom have no stable source of income and live literally from hand to mouth. See: Elena Luk'ianova, "Mir spasut mutanty," *Argumenty i fakty – Ufa*, May 15, 2013; correspondence with Iulia Andreeva (April 12, 2014) — from the personal archive of the author. Cf.: "SF authors have sunk into the very bottom of the food chain in publishing business." (Pavel Vinogradov and Tat'iana Alekseeva, "Zhizn' posle Strugatskikh," *Nevskoe vremia*, February 6, 2014.)

has been slowly emerging from under the rubble of translated literature since around the year 2000.[447] Digital literacy among Russian fans, and the availability of virtually all SF books in pirated editions have consolidated the popularity of some authors and enlarged their readership,[448] but have definitely not increased print-runs of paper books and royalties.

This study focuses on 15 of the most popular and/or reviewed genre-specific SF books, published since 1999; mainstream literature, even if it has elements of SF, is excluded from this analysis.[449]

The chapter argues that SF exposes the structure of contemporary Russian identity. Recent studies have researched Russia's internal colonization, targeted at creation of cultural distances between westernized elites and Russia's own "simple people."[450] On top of that, Russian intellectuals developed a kind of "imaginary self-coloniality," when they painfully observed Russia's (real or imaginary) backwardness and submission to the West. The West in

---

[447] Some authors adopted pseudonyms which sounded in Anglo-Saxon way in order to increase marketability of their books; thus, "Madeleine Simons" was Elena Haetskaia, "Henry Lion Oldie" — Dmitry Gromov and Oleg Ladyzhenskii. See on this: Vitalii Kaplan, "Zaglianem za stenku: Topografiia sovremennoi russkoi fantastiki," *Novyi mir*, no. 9 (2001).

[448] One of the pirate hubs "flibusta.net" ranges books by popularity; interestingly, that out of top 10 Russian books, nine belong to SF genre plus the tenth is Bulgakov's The Master and Margarita. (http://flibusta.net/stat/b).

[449] Books under the scrutiny include: Oleg Divov, *Vybrakovka [Reject Control]* (Moscow, 2009 [1999]) — 9 editions; Pavel Krusanov, *Ukus angela [Angel's Bite]* (St Petersburg, 2013 [2000]) — 5 editions; Sergei Norka, *Rus' okaiannaia [Russia the Damned]* (Moscow, 2000); Dmitry Volodikhin, *Konkistador [The Conquistador]* (Moscow, 2004); Andrei Stoliarov, *Zhavoronok [The Lark]* (Moscow, 2004); Kholm van Zaichik, *Delo zhadnogo varvara [The Case of a Greedy Barbarian]* (St Petersburg, 2000) — 5 editions; Roman Zlotnikov, *Vivat, imperator! [Long Live the Emperor!]* (Moscow, 2001) — 4 editions; Kirill Benediktov, *Voina za 'Asgard' [The Battle for 'Asgard']* (Moscow, 2003); Aleksandr Zorich, *Zavtra voina [Tomorrow There Will Be War]* (Moscow, 2004) — 7 editions; Zakhar Oskotskii, *Posledniaia bashnia Troi [The Last Tower of Troy]* (Moscow, 2004); Sergei Dorenko, 2008 (Moscow, 2005); Mikhail Iur'ev, *Tret'ia imperiia. Rossiia, kotoraia dolzhna byt' [The Third Empire. Russia As It Should Be]* (Moscow, 2007); Ilia Briz, *Krasnye polkovniki. Derzhava prevyshe vsego [Red Colonels. Empire Is Above Everything!]* (Moscow, 2011); Oleg Izmerov, *Deti imperii [Empire's Children]* (Moscow, 2012); Zakhar Oskotskii, *Utrennii, rozovyi vek [Rosy Age of Morn]* (St Petersburg, 2012).

[450] E.g. Aleksandr Etkind, *Internal Colonization. Russia's Imperial Experience* (Cambridge UK: Polity, 2011); A. Etkind, D. Uffelmann, and Il'ia Kukulin, *Tam, vnutri. Praktiki vnutrennei kolonizatstii v kul'turnoi istorii Rossii* (Moscow, 2012).

this sense functioned as the Lacanian "mirror," which—on a certain stage of Russia's intellectual development—helped to construct an integral self-image, but proliferated so deep into Russia's identity that it structured debates on identity-making for centuries to come,[451] serving as the model to stage its own colonial attitude towards grassroots, and as a repressive Father, prohibiting Russia from living in her own way.

The Russian tradition of utopianism and political SF goes back to the late 18th century, but until the end of the imperial period this genre lacked readership and its rare exemplars remained mostly internationally unknown until today.[452] Students of utopianism insist on interaction between the "imagined community" as a form of social cohesion, and "imaginary community" of a literary utopia.[453] In Phillip Wegner's view, modern utopias enable readers to effectively imagine subjectivity and its spatial parameters.[454] This interaction accounts for the relative weakness of the political SF in pre-revolutionary Russia, where the formation of national political subjectivity was impeded by the preeminence of imperial and monarchist allegiances.

In today's globalized world, securitization of identity is playing the role of ideology, so the task of successful imagining of "national identity" has been raised to the position of national ideology; this, however, entails an unseen of discursive perplexity, related to Russia's "Oedipal" complex towards the West. SF sensitively reflects this perplexity. Just as fin-de-siècle Russian utopianism

---

451 Cf.: "The West [has] become the most important ingredient of modern Russian identity." (Vera Tolz, "Russia and the West," in William Leatherbarrow and Derek Offord (eds.), *A History of Russian Thought* (Cambridge UK: Cambridge University Press, 2010): 197–216.

452 In the last three decades before the revolution of 1917, ca. 30 original utopian novels and short stories were published in Russia, in the US and Britain there were by order more. See: Suslov, "Spisok russkikh utopii XIX–nachala XX veka," in V. Shestakov (ed.), *Russkaia utopia v kontekste mirovoi kul'tury* (St Petersburg, 2013): 301–304; Lyman T. Sargent, *British and American Utopian Literatures, 1516–1985* (New York: G. K. Hall, 1988): 17–34.

453 Sargent, "Utopianism and National Identity," *Critical Review of International Social and Political Philosophy* 3, no. 2–3 (2000): 87–107; Maxim Shadurski, "Debating National Identity in Utopian Fiction (Morris, Benson, Read)," *Trames* 15 (65/60), no. 3 (2011): 300–316.

454 Phillip Wegner, *Imaginary Communities*, xvi–xvii.

discussed the perspectives and dangers associated with modernity and westernization,[455] so today's SF offers perspectives on post-modernity cum West-centric globalization, more often than not dealing with perceived threats therein. If in the early 20th century, the socialist dream of a peripheral empire plucked up the nerve of modernity and triggered processes of imagination and construction of the "Second World" alternative, so contemporary Russian SF entertains the idea of an alternative globalization, and who knows how far it could lead political engineers and top intellectuals.

The Big Other of post-Soviet SF

In the mid 19th century, Slavophiles articulated the importance of being true to Russia's original inner-self as a precondition for historical self-esteem. Cultural authenticity was vital in this context, asserted against an "imaginary self-coloniality," so vividly expressed by Petr Chaadaev's "Philosophic Letters" (1836). Slavophilism, which smoldered on the right-wing underground in the 1960s, flared up during Prestroika and helped intellectuals to define their post-Soviet condition as "unauthentic," based on a series of massive losses: the loss of the empire with which Russians identified themselves, of communist teleology and of the status of an alternative, "Second" World. The loss of Russia's authenticity – all too much unbearable in the present "culture of authenticity" – is at the center of post-Soviet SF.[456]

The loss of authenticity is likely to injure self-esteem and dignity, and to cause emotional reactions such as rage and wrath.[457] As

---

[455] Anindita Banerjee, *We Modern People. Science Fiction and the Making of Russian Modernity* (Middletown CT: Wesleyan University Press, 2012).

[456] Viktor Mart'ianov, Leonid Fishman, *Rossiia v poiskakh utopii: Ot moral'nogo kollapsa k moral'noi revoliutsii* (Moscow, 2010): 127. On the "culture of authenticity": Charles Taylor, *The Ethics of Authenticity* (Cambridge Mass.: Harvard University Press, 1992).

[457] On the emotions, associated with "honor" or lack thereof: Ute Frevert, *Emotions in History – Lost and Found* (Budapest: CEU Press, 2011): 80–85; Dominique Moïsi, *The Geopolitics of Emotion: How Cultures of Fear, Humiliation, and Hope Are Reshaping the World* (New York: Doubleday, 2007); Sergei Oushakine, *The Patriotism of Despair: Nation, War, and Loss in Russia* (Ithaca: Cornell University Press, 2009).

one of the leading SF authors Dmitry Volodikhin puts it, contemporary "imperial SF was born from pain, anxiety and *ressentiment* of millions of people."[458] Iury Nikitin's SF book about Russia's resistance to NATO's advancement to the east is called exactly *The Rage* (1997). In his novels, Russians adopt Islam, which helps them to regain dignity and develop the ethic of proud and independent warriors, and ultimately to fight back the West.[459] The utmost humiliation from fantasized NATO's military aggression is exemplified in Dmitry Iankovskii's book with another telling title—*The Rhapsody of Wrath* (2000).

The personal life experience of many authors of SF heightens the sense of displacement and unauthenticity of their post-Soviet lives. Marginalization of the Russian fandom is accountable for the adaptive model of behavior and the perceived loss of agency.[460] This means that a typical SF writer is an intellectual proletarian, whose literary production reflects his or her déclassé social position and generally depressive emotional backdrop. Il'ia Briz, whose books were published in "Russian imperial SF" series, reflects on the collapse of the Soviet Union as follows: "This is as if you put on sunglasses in a bright sunny day, and forget to take them off in the evening—and forever. All colors faded out. [So that now] you feel a bitter aftertaste of an irreversible loss."[461] To adduce an example: Zakhar Oskotskii, born in 1947, graduated from celebrated Technological Institute in Leningrad (now St Petersburg) and became a leading engineer of a closed institute where he worked for twenty years and patented many inventions in military equipment. With the collapse of the Soviet Union and disappearance of defense contracts, he had to break off his career in the institute and re-trained to become a fireman in a boiler house for two more decades to come.[462] Little wonder that his anti-utopian books stage Russia's

---

458 Dmitry Volodikhin, *Intellectual'naia fantastika* (Moscow, 2007): 195.
459 On this: Leonid Fishman, "Smena orientirov," *Politicheskii zhurnal*, no. 20/115 (2006).
460 On the adaptive behavior in post-Soviet Russia: Boris Dubin, *Rossiia nulevykh: Politicheskaia kul'tura, istoricheskaia pamiat', povsednednaia zhizn'* (Moscow, 2011): 291–292.
461 Il'ia Briz, *Krasnye polkovniki. Derzhava prevyshe vsego!* (Moscow, 2011): 30.
462 Interview with Zakhar Oskotskii (March 26, 2014).

collapse and despicable misery as its rulers continue to neglect the sciences and education.[463]

Gleb Eliseev, one of the commentators and reviewers of SF, has identified Russia's problem as that of being "under the foreign yoke" — similar to the "Mongol Yoke" of the 13th to 15th centuries.[464] Agreeing with Eliseev's analysis, Eduard Gevorkian, another SF author, points at the perils of decolonization: "Experience of the former colonies in Africa and South America (sic!) shows that after [colonizers] went away, chaos and a wretched parody on the metropolis had remained."[465] In this vein SF has been eagerly developing themes of Russia becoming a "raw material appendage" to the West.[466] In Zakhar Oskotskii's *Rosy Age of Morn* Russia's technological degradation and increasing dependence on the West lies in the thematic center of the novel, which pictures the formation of the anti-terrorist alliance, incorporating all economically advanced Western countries. Excluded from this alliance, Russia became a world's outsider. The decision of the West to stop supplying Russia with high-tech products wreaked havoc on Russia's economy.[467]

SF sensibility towards Russia's "second worldly" status is exemplified in another Oskotskii's novel *The Last Tower of Troy*. The story is set in 2085, after the third world war between the "First World" and "the Third World." This war was, however, a bloodless one, because the canny Westerners spread a viral pandemic, which affected the genitals and the procreative ability of those who had not been vaccinated, but only Westerners and their satellites were treated with this vaccine. So 90% of the Third World population died out in the next several decades and the remaining elderly people were kept in the UN's camps, which supplied all their needs and high living standards, with the only exception that their inhabitants could have no children. Russia was accepted in the "family of the civilized nations" and got the vaccine, although it was looked

---

463 Oskotskii, *Utrennii, rozovyi vek. Rossiia – 2024* (St Petersburg, 2012); Oskotskii, *Posledniaia bashnia Troi* (Moscow, 2004).
464 "My u sebia doma," Spetsnaz Rossii, no. 1/100 (January 15, 2005).
465 "My u sebia doma."
466 E.g. Briz, *Krasnye polkovniki*, 18.
467 Oskotskii, *Utrennii*, 285–302.

down upon to some degree, as a sort of younger sister of the triumphant Anglo-Saxons and an insignificant and inactive partner of the West.[468] A strikingly similar narrative structure could be uncovered in Kirill Benediktov's novel *The Battle for "Asgard."* His storyline is developing in the year 2053; by that time the fascist and fundamentalist movement "White Revival" prevails in the West, having conquered the whole world. Two billion racially and genetically impure and imperfect humans have been detained behind the colossal wall, somewhere in southern Siberia. The purpose of this object called Tollan, is to construct a huge collider on its walls, in order to move Tollan and all its inhabitants one hundredth part of a second in the past. This would transfer Tollan to a parallel world, locked by the impenetrable time barrier from the prosperous world of the White Revival. The theme of time travel in this context fleshes out the trope of stages of progress — one of the most typical science fiction devices, according to which spatial Otherness is defined by temporal synchrony: the underdeveloped tribe represents the past of the industrial nation. In *The Battle for "Asgard"* the Third-World inhabitants of Tollan should be physically sent to the past, thereby staging the ultimate resolution of the colonial difference. In this story, territorially reduced and politically declining Russia lingers on the periphery of the globalized world — spared from the "final solution" but not invited to the feast of winners.[469]

On a more abstract plane of interpretation, the loss of the Soviet Union and the loss of one's own social status become tightly interconnected and comes to the same thing: the perception of Russia's national authenticity as being stolen by the Big Other, by the West. This interpretation evokes a paradigm of Russia's (imaginary) colonial status vis-à-vis the West, according to which the loss of authenticity is concomitant with disempowerment and the loss of agency. In the late 19th to early 20th century, Russian SF shared the Kantian fear of the Westerners that one day a higher civilization would conquer them and treat them similarly to how they used to

---

468 Oskotskii, *Posledniaia bashnia*, 5–97.
469 Kirill Benediktov, *Voina za "Asgard"* (Moscow, 2003).

treat their colonies.[470] Today the underlying anxiety of Russian SF is more than simply the reversal of the colonial situation. It manifests a fear that when the Second World passed away, Russia shared its destiny, neither automatically becoming the "First," nor willing to downgrade itself to the position of the "Third World." So the colonial anxiety in SF is not only about "foreign yoke," but rather a perception that—having stolen Russia's agency—the West has deprived her of her very historical existence.[471] This sensibility still remains within the boundary of the colonial situation, but in its most dramatic "Fanonian" extreme, in which the relationship between the colonizer and the colonized are antagonized to the point, in which the whole story boils down to "who will bury whom." In this sense anti-utopian SF which pictures Russia's military defeats or economic collapse,[472] is consumed with much pleasure not only because it gives vent to people's rage, but also because it still reserves Russia a place in world history, and treats it as being worthy of destruction—in any case, better than a nonentity. By contrast, in the late 19th to early 20th century Russian SF often indulges into "imaginary war" stories in emotionally pessimistic register; they pictured Russia's military defeat and political collapse, but the literary device of "victory out of defeat" served to re-establish Russia's status as the world pivot: hated by others and capable of recoiling and striking back.[473]

---

470 E.g. John Rieder, *Colonialism*, 5–10.
471 Cf.: "The former imperial human [is] certain about her own superiority, [but in the post-Soviet case] she suddenly becomes stranded, excluded from historical process ... So globalization persists in post-Soviet imagination in its most terrific and unique form ... [as] the violent reduction of our country and its population to the situation of non-existence ..." (Madina Tlostanova, *Postsovetskaia literatura i estetika transkul'turatsii: Zhit' nikogda, pisat' niotkuda* (Moscow, 2004): 98).
472 On the preeminence of anti-utopianism in post-Soviet SF: A. Vorob'eva, *Russkaia antiutopiia XX–nachala XXI veka v kontekste mirovoi antiutopii*. Dissertation (Samara, 2009).
473 E.g. stories by Konstantin Sluchevskii ("Poverzhennyi Pushkin," 1898) and Dmitry Ilovaiskii ("Bolee tridtsati let spustia," 1897).

Geopolitics of civilizations

Winding up in megalomania and persecution mania in international relations, a geopolitical style of thinking exposes the structure of the collective identity and sutures together a post-Soviet social sensibility and the utopian desire of SF. Thus, commenting on Kirill Benediktov's SF, Dmitry Volodikhin pointed at the fact that "his books could be fully understood only by those readers who know basics of geopolitics and civilization approach. Not knowing, say, [theories of Samuel] Huntington, [Karl] Haushofer or at worst [Aleksandr] Dugin, you can comprehend only half of what Benediktov intended to say."[474]

In the big picture of the world provided by geopolitics, there is no place for individual agency: "eternal laws" of geopolitical struggle among "great powers" supply us with the comprehensive theory of everything, capable of explaining the past and predicting the future.[475] The centerpiece of this theorization is the concept of the perpetual warfare between maritime and continental powers, or more specifically, between Eurasian cum Russian "civilization" and "Atlanticist" cum Western "civilization." In Eduard Gevorkian's *The Dark Mountain* the plot is structured by the conflict between expansionist maritime civilizations and morally sturdy civilizations of the "heartland."[476] Mark Lipovetsky argues that the notion of eternal war dominates the post-Soviet imagination and functions as a master-narrative, holding together a disintegrating picture of the Russian history.[477] Dmitry Volodikhin's own SF, for example, his space opera *Konkistador* (*The Conquistador*, 2004) is rife with a whole set of geopolitical stereotypes, extrapolated on the outer space and subsumed under the title of the "discipline" of "cosmopolitics." The plotline focuses on the military conflict among the "great powers" of the Russian Empire, the Geneva

---

474 Volodikhin, *Intellektual'naia fantastika*, 49.
475 More on the "laws of geopolitics" see in Chapter 2 of this volume.
476 Volodikhin, "Mesto vstrechi ... Fantastika i literatura osnovnogo potoka: Konvergentsiia?" *Znamia*, no. 12 (2005); Eduard Gevorkian, *Temnaia gora* (Moscow, 1999).
477 Mark Lipovetsky, *Paralogii: Transformatsii (post)modernistskogo diskursa v kul'ture 1920–2000-kh godov* (Moscow: NLO, 2008): 738.

confederation (i.e. Western Europe), China, Terra-2 (Russian-speaking independent planet) and some others over the virgin Earth-like planet Terra-10. The only reason for the conflict is the demographic situation in the human Oikumene, namely the pressing need to resettle the surplus population on a newly discovered stellar system. To do justice, Volodikhin questions if resettlement as a final goal justifies military losses, but he does so in a way of moralistic speculation, which has nothing to do with *Realpolitik*. Alternating battle scenes with discourses on "cosmopolitics" (who allies with whom and fights with whom, and why), he creates a background, against which all international subjects are embedded into the immutable network of lines of geopolitical force, and interact with one another either friendly or antagonistically, depending on their "national interests." Volodikhin relocates "laws of geopolitics" into space, where their specifically geographic parameters (e.g. continental or maritime character) loses its preeminence, so *Konkistador* explains antagonism in "cosmopolitics" by unalterable civilizational differences. For example, the civilization of the "Russian world" (the Russian empire and Terra-2) is characterized by religiosity and the high profile of traditional values, while the civilization of "New-Scotland" (probably representing a US projection into space) is renowned for its entrepreneurial spirit, and technological advancement.

SF books by brothers Arkadii and Boris Strugatsky were the single most important source of inspiration for the majority of contemporary writers of this genre, who by and large share their preoccupation with the ethics of "progressing" (from *progressory* – people from the future communist Earth who interfere with historical processes on more backward planets).[478] If the Strugatskies effectively questioned the right of a "higher civilization" to define "progress," today's authors deny this right altogether,[479] because what they observe looming behind the topic of *progressing* is blatant West-centric universalism – the quintessence of today's Russian

---

478 E.g. Yvonne Howell, *Apocalyptic Realism: The Science Fiction of Arkady and Boris Strugatsky* (New York: P. Lang, 1994): 9–10.
479 E.g.: Ol'ga Belova, "Viacheslav Rybakov: Na budushchii god v Moskve," *Novoe Literaturnoe Obozrenie*, no. 65 (2004).

preoccupation with the loss of authenticity. So, post-Soviet SF is unanimously driven by the "civilization approach," which rejects universalism and the paradigm of the arrow-like progress.[480] From this viewpoint, the West is just the other place among a dozen of other equal civilizations on Earth, and not Russia's teleological goal, so this is not possible to apply the same moral yardstick to them.

Commentators argue that repudiation of the "Euro-American project of globalization" occupies the center of today's SF concerns.[481] Inspired by the ideology of Eurasianism and Samuel Huntington's theorization, such SF writers as Kirill Benediktov (*The Battle for "Asgard"*), Dmitry Volodikhin (*The Conquistador*), and Aleksandr Zorich (*Tomorrow There Will Be War*) reduce their plotlines to clashes of civilizations. As a result, lacking a common moral denominator, their protagonists are involved in a zero-sum game by which, and in contradistinction to all traditions of Russian literature, the mightiest wins. In *The Conquistador*, for example, one may sympathize with the societal values of "our" civilization, but its ultimate victory has no moral substantiation and results solely from the free play of choice and cunning application of force.[482]

The civilization approach in SF manifests passivity.[483] We can observe a shift of political subjectivity from states or nations, which implies some kind of participation, to the level of "civilizations," whose cohesion is preconditioned by essentialized and securitized identity,[484] and has nothing to do with the "common cause," *res publica*. A complete alienation from politics in longview of the

---

480 Cf. in Oleg Izmerov's *Empire's Children*, a protagonist finds himself in the Soviet Union of 1958, but in contradistinction to the stereotypical storyline, employing such a device, he is as much in a position to teach people from the past, as to learn from them. The authors thereby denies superiority of Russia of 2000s before the Soviet Union of the 1950s.
481 Dmitry Volodikhin, "Khram i kosmodrom," *Politicheskii zhurnal*, no 3 (2008).
482 Volodikhin, *Konkistador*.
483 More on the civilizational rhetoric see in Chapter 3 of this volume.
484 For application of Barry Buzan's concept of "securitization of identity" to post-Soviet Russia see: Viacheslav Morozov, "Resisting Enthropy, Discarding Human Rights: Romantic Realism and Securitization of Identity in Russia," *Cooperation and Conflict: Journal of the Nordic International Studies Association* 37, no. 4 (2002): 409–429.

"civilization approach" can be observed in various among SF books, but particularly in Volodikhin's *The Conquistador*, which presents political decision making on Terra-2 as enacted by an obscure council of elders of clans with an irremovable chair at the top with not a single reference to democratic procedure.[485] The similar lack of political agency in the fantastic visions of civilizations is observable in the book series Eurasian Symphony by Kholm van Zaichik's (Viacheslav Rybakov and Igor' Alimov).[486]

As an empire, embedded into the network of geopolitical relations, imaginary Russia acquires the capability to revenge itself upon the West for stealing its agency. The problem with this narrative strategy lies in Russia's quasi-post-colonial split of identity, which is not sufficiently different from the West to effectively separate one from another.[487] Ultimately, this means that "burying" the West is explicitly suicidal, as Pavel Krusanov's *Angel's Bite* shows. In the novel an alternative history of the 20th century is presented; in which the Russian Empire expanded its borders in Europe and Asia but at some point its armies got stuck in Western Germany, South Italy and Egypt. The whole world took up arms against Russia and its military defeat became imminent. The Emperor Ivan Nekitaev applied to his court magician for help and was advised to let the "Hounds of Hecate" into the world. They are the embodiment of other-worldly primordial evil and rage, who can devour millions of souls in a second and leave bodies agonizing for five more months, and the magician promised to set them on Russia's enemies but could not warrant that they will do no harm to Russians. During the spiritualist session, the imperial council was shown the Hounds of Hecate and they were so despicably horrible that some people squeezed their eyes out and crumbled their teeth in the mouth, but the emperor remained inflexible and ordered the magician to let the hounds in the world.[488]

---

485 Cf. Aleksandr Zorich, *Zavtra voina*, and dozens of others.
486 See Chapter 7 of this volume.
487 Tlostanova, *Postsovetskaia literatura*, 44.
488 Pavel Krusanov, *Ukus*, 279–285.

The imperial sublime in Russian SF

In the age of "high imperialism" pre-revolutionary Russian political SF was—although commersially insignificant—on a par with Western SF thematically. Having absorbed geopolitical ideologies of pan-Slavism and proto-Eurasianism, it discussed promises of expansionism, indulged in the "imperialist pleasures" of listing acquired territories and spheres of influence, and excited its readers by portraits of "imaginary war."[489] Out of fashion during the Soviet period, the imperial theme gained traction soon after the dissolution of the Soviet Union and, since the year 2000, has been tremendously popular. Without a great stretch, imperial SF could be called the predominant subgenre of post-Soviet SF—rife with patriotism, anti-Westernism, and nostalgia for the Soviet Union.[490] The popularity of this kind of literature prompted "Eksmo" publishing house to launch a series "Russian imperial SF" in 2011, within which 32 books have been published ever since.

The surge of the imperial theme has not passed unnoticed by critics and SF authors themselves, who point to the connection between imperial theme in this genre and the post-Soviet sensibility of millions of Russians. As one commentator suggests, mainstream literature failed to cater to the tastes of "simple people" who want to indulge in feelings of pride about their native land, to reinforce self-identification with protagonists, who are like themselves: ordinary teenagers, soldiers, policemen, security officers,[491] but who— unlike themselves—possess the agency to control their life and

---

489 Suslov, *Russian Geopolitical Utopias in Comparative Perspective, 1880–1914*. PhD thesis (Florence: European University Institute, 2009).
490 "All writers are more or less preoccupied with the topic of the vanished empire" (Menzel, "Russian Science Fiction," 149). Cf.: Kovalev, "Rossiiskaia fantastika kak politologiia"; Viktor Shnirelman, "Vozvrashchenie ariistva: nauchnaia fantastika i rasizm," *Neprikosnovennyi zapas*, no. 6 (2008); Dmitry Mikhailovich, "Bol'shaia restavratsiia?" *Politicheskii zhurnal*, no. 2/179 (2008).
491 As SF writer Vasilii Zviagintsev penned, "In the last 20 years there has been no book [of mainstream literature] which would give a positive image of a Russian soldier. But humans remain the same, and he cannot read only negative [things]; he wants to see his history and state glorious. This mission has been assumed by SF which speaks of patriotism and other things which simple reader needs" (V. Ialysheva, L. Glukhova, "Fantastika kak aktual'noe chtenie," *Informatsionnyi biulleten' RBA*, no. 67 (2013): 99–102).

world around them, and to actively transform these. True, as Olga Slavnikova, another SF writer, observes, "imperial SF replaces the feat of holiness [i.e. confrontation of an individual with overwhelming forces of environment], by the feat of conformity [with environment],"[492] but through conformity with the imperial "body politic," a protagonist accesses the source of strength and the feeling of significance of his or her life. This is especially important for a post-Soviet audience, whose quasi-post-colonial disempowerment is augmented by social disintegration, diagnosed both by sociologists and some SF writers.[493] An utmost manifestation of the failure of post-Soviet subjectivation is the common trope of the liberal intelligentsia, which separates two "Russias": the Russia of the Russian people, and the Russia of the Russian government, whose interests may be contradictory.[494] In this context, the idea of an empire becomes an attractive device to restore self-identification with the "common cause" and to reenact the organicist metaphor of "body politic."[495]

Thus, in SF an empire functions as both an unfathomably wide horizon of personal activity, and a structural framework, providing an individual with a natural and appropriate niche. The paradoxical combination of empowerment and conformity is what the audience is looking for in imperial SF, striving to symbolically restore pre-revolutionary and Soviet experience. As Aleksandr Roife argues, imperial SF is not a dream of a "strong hand," but rather "longing for normal life."[496] In a similar vein, Volodikhin explains the skyrocketing of imperial SF in Russia as a sign that a previously silent majority are learning to speak; he argues that democracy and

---

492 Olga Slavnikova, "Ia liubliu tebia, imperiia," *Znamia*, no. 12 (2000).
493 Cf., for example, Eduard Gevorkian's statement: "As a SF writer who has been writing on societal themes the whole life, I see how far social differentiation had gone in Russia. The Soviet people was once a single whole, and now there are absolutely isolated castes" (Gevorkian, "Ideiia imperii uzhe vbroshena v massy," *Novye izvestiia*, no. 132 (July 27, 2004)).
494 Discourses on "two Russias", the ruling and the ruled, evoke the concept of "internal colonization".
495 Cf. an idea to revitalize medieval estates in Mikhail Iur'ev's *Third Empire*.
496 Aleksandr Roife, "Iz tupika, ili Imperiia nanosit otvetnyi udar," *Esli*, no. 3 (2000).

liberalism are "anomalous" for humankind, so imperial SF is the comeback of normality.[497] In the context of "imaginary coloniality" of Russia, the return of empire in SF is equal to the return to historical existence.

In low- and middlebrow SF the loss of agency finds its literary expression in the vilification of the West. In psychoanalytic terms, the West for Russian SF is the Other who has stolen Russia's "imperial pleasures," so the narrative boils down to equating empire with enjoyment and reclaiming Russia's imperial status back from the West. Andrei Stoliarov in the novel *Zhavoronok* (*The* Lark, 1999) wrote: "bitter is the taste of national humiliation and disturbing is the drone of military machines of NATO, moving eastwards ..." What cures the emotional loss in Stoliarov's narrative is acquisitions of parts of Crimea — a half-hearted victory due to Russia's dependence on the West. The striking parallel (but not too uncommon in the history of world literature) with Russia's recent policy towards Ukraine suggests that Crimean discourses are especially important for Russia's imperial sensibility.[498] Stoliarov's story has, however, a more important aspect — the way in which "reclaiming" of imperial pleasures is enacted. In *Zhavoronok* the main protagonist is a young lady named Zhanna (an explicit reference to Jeanne d'Arc) who conceives of herself as being "called" to restore Russia's glory and who possesses almost supra-human faculty to persuade people by speech. On her own initiative she foments people's anti-government protests in Crimea and induces them to vote for independence with the subsequent accession to Russia.[499] Stoliarov does not picture public deliberations on the fate of Crimea, but shows an instant in which God-sent Zhanna ignites a mass movement, thereby creating a discursive bridge between two sublimities, which one can neither control, nor even comprehend: providential force, and people's wrath.

Pavel Krusanov, the leader of St Petersburg informal group of writers of "sacral SF," underscores supernatural and mystic

---

[497] Volodikhin, "Srednii tank v vashei spal'ne," *Literaturnaia Rossiia*, no. 48 (2003).
[498] Cf., for example, non-fiction discussion of possible scenarios of seizing Crimea and Ukraine in general in: Igor Berkut, Roman Vasilishin, *Brat* (Kiev, 2009).
[499] Andrei Stoliarov, *Zhavoronok*.

dimensions of an empire in his much acclaimed novel *Angel's Bite* (1999). Krusanov was one of the founders of the SF group of "St Petersburg fundamentalists," which was founded in 1998 on the platform of religious mysticism, Slavophile nationalism and rapture at an empire. Elsewhere Krusanov remarks that "an empire is full of will for expansion and destabilization of the world ... it is capable of super-natural effort which is practically useless, but which is directed towards making something forever."[500] On a related note, Roman Zlotnikov's *Long Live the Emperor!* pictures the coming to power in Russia of an immortal man of superior intellectual and moral qualities, who has witnessed and probably taken part in many of historical events on the planet during last two millennia. The reason for his enthronement in Russia is that humankind is ripe for an evolution into deep space, but that this can be done only if all peoples of Earth unite under a single authoritarian but benevolent power.

In Kantian theorization, the sense of sublimity is produced when the mind grasps the grandeur of a thing but consciousness fails to embrace its scale and complexity. By Edmund Burke's interpretation, you perceive sublimity when you, for example, observe a mortal danger from a position of safety. Both views direct us to link the sense of sublimity with detachment from the streamline of historical events, and with passivity in politics.

Abolishing people's agency in front of the "iron laws of geopolitics," SF all too often degenerates into a kind of conspiracy theory, featuring powerful but invisible forces behind all historical events.[501] In *The Last Tower of Troy* by Zakhar Oskotskii, the secret society of scientists nurtures ressentiment and bitter memory about the post-Soviet decades when impoverished academics and bandits took the upper hand. Having accumulated enormous financial, technological and intellectual resources, this society decides to isolate themselves completely from the rest of the population and if necessary to catapult themselves in a rocket to the other planet,

---

500 Krusanov, "Legionery nezrimoi imperii," in A. Sekatskii et al. (eds.) *Nezrimaia imperiia* (St Petersburg, 2005): 9.
501 Viktor Osipov and Gleb Kuznetsov, "Eto prosto fantastika!" *So-Obshchenie*, no. 12 (2003).

when the total war of all against all takes momentum on Earth. His latest SF book *Rosy Age of Morn* features analogous plot of "smart guys" (*razumniki*), the remnants of the Soviet intelligentsia, who initially planned a coup but soon became disillusioned about politics.[502]

In the same way, SF entertains the topics, connected with the power of special and intelligence services.[503] On the psychological plane of interpretation, special services create a zone in SF landscape, in which people's agency could be fictitiously reclaimed by means of abolishing the rule of law and institutional barriers.[504] In Oleg Divov's SF novel *Reject Control*, a special agency has a right to kill on spot, punish or send to labor camps anyone who is considered a criminal in circumvention of a normal procedure. The protagonist's family has once been sadistically killed by the bandits, so his work as a special agent, who violently suppresses any deviation on the streets of Moscow, is morally justified as the triumph of justice over formal legislation. This is also the triumph of a "simple person" over state bureaucracy, organized crime, corruption and big business — all those forces, which occupied so ominous place in the post-Soviet collective fantasies. The special services theme arises from the longing for control over one's own destiny, which is so dramatically absent in the lives and imaginations of post-Soviet producers and consumers of SF.

Biology and energy

Attenuation of agency and the advent of inoperosity in post-Soviet imagination makes discourses about "energy" a sore subject in SF. Writers find the most authoritative source on "energy" theorization in works by Lev Gumilev, the son of poets Nikolai Gumilev and

---

[502] Cf. Briz, *Krasnye*. Cf. the review on Volodikhin's novel *Polden' segodniashnei nochi* (Moscow, 2011): "This is a SF novel about conspiracy, which tells us that secret but powerful and terrifying forces act behind the surface of our everyday reality" (Roman Voznitsyn, "Retsenziia," *Nezavisimaia gazeta – Ex libris*, September 8, 2001: 6.

[503] Konstantin Frumkin, "Imperii i spetssluzhby v fantastike," *Svobodnaia mysl'* – *XXI vek*, no. 2 (2004): 76–83.

[504] Cf., for example, Oleg Izmerov, *Deti imperii*.

Anna Akhmatova, who in the 1970–80s came up with the concept of "passionarity," or "passion energy." This is a kind of vital force, which drives ethnics from the state of non-being to "passionary outburst" (defined by Gumilev as solar turbulence), expansion and climactic grandeur and preeminence as a world empire, to the stage of "passionary break off," to the period of "golden autumn" with fructifying culture, and back to the stage of homeostasis and nonexistence. The SF project "Ethnogenesis" creatively interpreted the theory of passionarity, enclosing the source of ethnic energy into animalistic-shaped "artifacts," magic objects left on Earth by some extraterrestrial civilization; possession of such an artifact imbues its owner with super-human abilities and faculties to actively interfere in the course of history. For example, Adolf Hitler had the figurine "Eagle"; as the plotline of the books in the series evolves, "simple people" regain the ability to influence history by means of possession of the figurines. Like belonging to the secret service, possession of the "artifacts" signify the ability to escape the horizon of inoperosity.

For example, energy discourses prevail in the novel *Russia the Damned* by Sergei Norka. In this book Russia's weakness of the 1990s is explained as a deliberate info-energetic attack of the Western enemy on the Russian population, which, as a result, demonstrated lack of enthusiasm, apathy, etc. In order to overcome this situation, a super-human magician with the help of a secret society of Russia's revival, generates "positive" energy, so that social activism grows and people start to strike and revolt.

The narrative of "vital energy" informs much of the post-Soviet SF concerned with either enhancing of people's bodily faculties, or violent infringement on humans' corporal integrity. Very often this strategy overlaps with the colonial theme. In Oskotskii's novel, for example, technologies stand behind both the immortality of the "First World" population, and physical extermination of the "Third World" people.[505] Similarly, in Gennady Prashkevich's *The*

---

505 On the theme of immortality in Russian culture: Irene Masin-Delic, *Abolishing Death: A Salvation Myth of Russian Twentieth-Century Literature* (Stanford: Stanford University Press, 1992).

Golden Billion novel, Essen-Goo—the residence of one billion of physically and genetically healthy, racially pure, and economically prosperous people, is pictured as a fortified island in the sea of the so called "freaks"—sickly victims of radiative and chemical pollution. Essen-Goo feeds billions of "freaks" up by some kind of genetically modified biological substance, which is reported to drastically affect their fertility. Furthermore, one of the subplots of *The Battle for Asgard* relates the story of Japanese scientist Tanaka, who wants to nurture a new race of super-humans, crossbreeding an African clairvoyant with a Slavic woman who has similarly exceptional faculties. Finally, Roman Zlotnikov's *Long Live the Emperor!* merges narratives about immortality, secret society and breeding a new race—all this in order to secure the restoration of monarchy in Russia. Ubiquity of narratives about raising a new species of humans testifies to the radical disillusionment in people's capabilities to master their life and environment, which runs through three stages of disempowerment: stripping of the political will, suppressing the procreative ability, and finally, negating the very right to existence.

If we drill down into the reasons for the thickening of discourse around the topic of biology, demography and procreation, we'll uncover a pack of interrelated metaphors, one of which deals with Russia as an organic body, dissected and dismembered in 1991, and another that pertains to the securitization of identity, which boils down to securitization of Russia's "body" due to the fact of ineliminable difficulty in defining Russia's cultural "core." The ultimate importance of the Russian demography, reproductivity, stability of families undergirds all recent public debates about the LGBT movement, adopting Russian orphans by foreigners, and implementation of the juvenile justice. The "Bastion" convention in January 2014 specifically discussed the need to preserve a traditional family, and launched a competition to encourage SF essays on this subject.[506]

---

506 Cf. diatribes against juvenile justice in: Viacheslav Rybakov, "Utopii i upravlentsy," *Neva*, no. 9 (2013): 133–134.

Ethno-national theme in post-Soviet SF undergoes the same biological reductionism, which provides writers with an effective literary hook; Russia's declining demography is contrasted by excessive fertility of "migrants" and Asian neighbors even in most liberal examples of SF (e.g. negative image of migrants in *Rosy Age of Morn* by Oskotskii).[507] Roman Zlotnikov's *Long Live the Emperor* is a case in point here; with migrantophobic remarks galore, this text features a scene in which a Russian heroine is raped and killed by Chechen men from the migrant quarter. In retribution, all its non-Russian population is locked in a barrack and burnt down alive.

Engaging with Strugatsky brothers

The majority of the writers of conservative SF belong to the generation, born in the 1960s, grown up in the late Soviet Union, and traumatized by its collapse and economic difficulties of the 1990s. For most of them, SF writers Arkady and Boris Strugatsky were literally teachers (e.g. for Viacheslav Rybakov and Eduard Gevorkian), or at least those who significantly shaped their personality, scope of interests, literary style, and ideological agenda. Strugatskies continue to be on the top of all rankings of fantastic literature.[508] Thus, profound engagement with brothers Strugatskies is an indelible earmark of post-Soviet SF. Strugatskies, however, could not be easily appropriated by the writers with conservative agenda because renowned brothers had a halo of liberalism and

---

[507] Cf. also explicitly migrantophobic pieces: Andrei Volos, *Maskavskaia Mekka* (Moscow, 2003 and 2005) and Elena Chudinova, *Mechet' Parizhskoi bogomateri*. The latter run through 5 editions and was translated into Serbian in 2006, having become one of the most popular SF books in Russia (Boris Lanin, "Voobrazhaemaia Rossiia v sovremennoi russkoi antiutopii," Mochizuki Tetsuo (ed.), *Beyond the Empire: Images of Russia in the Eurasian Cultural Context* (Sapporo: Slavic Research Center, 2008): 379–380.

[508] Their masterpieces continue to bring guaranteed profit for publishing houses (e.g. *Hard to Be a God* has been reprinted 57 times, *Monday Begins on Saturday* – 49). Ozon.ru, the largest online bookshop in Russia, returns 1200 hits on various items related to Strugatskies (cf with 1700 for Mikhail Bulgakov). Calculations are based on the webpages: www.ozon.ru and www.rsl.ru.

dissidence. So, for the conservative SF writers Strugatskies are not only a formative influence but also a challenge.

Even in terms of style, today's conservative SF is engaged in a protracted dispute with the Strugatsky brothers. Dmitry Volodikhin identifies his positive ideal as "Russian Victorianism," leaning heavily on the historical experience of the late imperial period. Specifically, he characterized this style as depiction of "patriarchal, benevolent despotism."[509] In his space operas Russia emerges as a powerful militaristic empire, an absolute monarchy, where the Orthodox Church plays a decisive role. This is the world, whose entourage resembles Japanese steam-punk, in which neatly dressed military officers, having received blessings from a capelin, throw their battle spaceships, bearing imperial insignia, into a deadly fight for ascendance in the Galaxy.[510] In a sense, this world is a complete repudiation of the Strugatsky's imperial theme. If the Soviet masters of SF consistently ridiculed boorish admiration of militarism and empire (e.g. in *Paren' iz preispodnei, A Kid from Hell*, 1974), conservative eu-topia eagerly aestheticezes the imperial sublimity.[511]

The most resonating theme in Strugatskies' books is the encounter between a more developed and a less developed civilization. Russian SF has always been sensitive to the problem of the contact with a superior (extraterrestrial) civilization, inheriting this concern from the Western experience of colonial encounter with the Oriental "Other." The reverted colonial situation, in which "we" are

---

509 "*Patriarkhal'nyi, blagodushnyi despotism.*" See: Volodikhin, "Viktorianskaia Rossiia," in P. Sviatenkov et al. *Politicheskoe pravoslavie: Strategicheskii zhurnal no. 2* (Moscow: APN, 2006): 252.
510 Cf. Konstantin Frumkin, "Imperii i spetssluzhby v fantastike," *Svobodnaia mysl' – XXI vek*, no. 2 (2004): 76–83.
511 Volodikhin implemented this ideal in his own SF novels, such as *Konkistador* (2004). Aleksandr Zorich developed the similar style in the book series *Zavtra voina* (2003–2008). "Aleksandr Zorich" is a pen-name of the duet of writers (Dmitry Gordievskii and Iana Botsman). The recent example of "Russian Victorianism" is Elena Chudinova's alternative history fantasy *The Viktors (Pobediteli)*, 2017. In this book Chudinova fleshes out the ideal of "benevolent despotism" in her imaginary imperial Russia of 1980s. She reproduces refined conversations of aristocrats, their ornate ways to eat delicate food, the atmosphere of sparsely populated Moscow of one-storeyed suburbs and gardens.

confronted by way more advanced "Others" who treat "us" exactly as "we" used to treat African and Asian aboriginals, haunted much of the Russian and Western SF from Kurt Lasswitz's *Auf Zwei Planeten* (1897) and H.G. Wells's *The War of the Worlds* (1897), to Aleksandr Bogdanov's *Red Star* (1908) and Strugatskies' *Ugly Swans* (1967). The Russian specificity consists in the fact that Russia had a *real* experience of contacting the superior "Other," the West, and thereby sensitized itself to a much greater extent to the Hegelian Master-Slave dialectics. Thus, Bogdanov's utopia recycled the old Slavophile creed that in spite of (or perhaps because of – see on this the next paragraph) the Western superiority Russia as a metonymy of the Earth contains a potential and a promise of much greater, radiant future than sophisticated but senile and declining Martian civilization.[512]

The Master and the Slave situation is problematized in Strugatskies' *Hard to Be a God* (1964), in which "we" represent a civilizational *Kulturträger*, but "our" moral right to interfere with a backward civilization is seriously questioned.[513] In a reverse situation, portrayed in Strugatskies' *Ugly Swans*, the Master and Slave dichotomy is posited in an original and intellectually powerful way. The book *Gadkie lebedi* (*Ugly Swans*, 1967) tells us about some unknown creatures "slimies" (*mokretsy*) characterized by superior intelligence and knowledge, who work as teachers in a boarding school and train kids to be like them. By doing so, they cause uproar from the people, who feel humiliated by the fact that their children willingly abandon them for strangers and their suspicious sciences. In the Strugatskies's story, humans are unpleasant, egoistic, petty bourgeois, but the reader nevertheless gets an ambivalent impression that in spite of all superiority of the slimies – also moral superiority, – the situation itself is morally crooked. This is because benevolent aliens inadvertently devalue the very existence of human

---

512 Mikhail Suslov, "Po tu storonu imperii: Prostranstvennye konfiguratsii identichnostei v rossiiskikh literaturnykh utopiiakh rubezha 19–20 vv.," *Ab Imperio*, no. 4 (2011): 325–356.
513 Howell, *Apocalyptic Realism*. See also Chapter 4 in this volume.

beings, nullify all achievements of the human race, and rob them even of their own children.[514]

Over time, the Strugatsky brothers developed deep moral and existential doubts about what they called "progressorism" — the idea that a superior, advanced society can (and should) interfere to improve (or "progress") a more backwards society.[515] However, it took the Strugatskys' followers in post-Soviet Russia to radicalize these doubts and transmogrify them into an unequivocal "no" to what they perceive as violent Westernization. In Volodikhin's and Gennady Prashkevich's account, "progressorism" in *Hard to Be a God* is unequivocally associated with the negation of traditionalism characteristic for the Russian liberal intelligentsia as a whole. Biographers point at the fact that eventually, "progressorism" leads to the "democracy for export" policies of the Western countries.[516]

Viacheslav Rybakov provided a sophisticated interpretation of "progressorism" by his analysis of the enigmatic book *The Snail on a Slope* (1966). The novel depicts a dystopian world of the Forest, where the "race" of moronic and brainless aboriginals dwell, being constantly harassed and exterminated by the superior "race" of Amazons who procreate by parthenogenesis, and these two in their turn are supervised by rational and bureaucratic "Administration."[517] Brother Strugatskies' moral indignation at this situation is expressed in the words of the protagonist: "What do I care if Hopalong [one of the locals] is a pebble in the millstones of their

---

514 Cf. "They [slimies] dismiss their lesser developed human brothers as one dismisses small children from a meaningful discussion ..." (Howell, *Apocalyptic Realism*, 111).
515 Mark Lipovetsky discussed the idea of "progressorism" from the perspective of the colonial studies at the conference "Radiant Futures: Russian Fantasy and Science" (Jordan Center for the Advanced Study of Russia at the New York University), 2016. Recordings are available at: https://www.youtube.com/watch?v=muXEwfjfjHE.
516 In the interpretation of these authors, in the 1960s, when the Strugatsky brothers were writing *Hard to Be a God*, and *The Snail on a Slope*, they voiced the same concerns, which bothers conservative intellectuals in post-Soviet Russia, and only later on, the Strugatsky adopted a more liberal and Westernized viewpoint.
517 One of the interpretation connects this plotline with the historical experience of genocides of the 20th century. See: Yvonne Howell, *Apocalyptic Realism: The Science Fiction of Arkady and Boris Strugatsky* (New York: P. Lang, 1994), 129–138.

progress? [...] I'll do everything I can to stop those millstones."[518] Yvonne Howell argues that the relation of Amazons to aboriginals stands for the Holocaust of the Jews and racial engineering in Nazi Germany, whereas Administration approximates Stalinism in its *mission civilisatrice* towards a semi-barbarian country under its jurisdiction.[519] In this context, Strygatskies' phrase about the pebble in the millstones reads as an indictment against an inhumane, totalitarian, and repressive regime.

Rybakov interpretation is manifestly different. He stresses that the keywords in the abovementioned phrase about Hopalong are "THEIR progress," meaning "horrendous sexless bitches."[520] He argues that the Amazons assumed the position of the progress, from which they view the Foresters as underdeveloped, whereas they themselves are even worse than just "underdeveloped," they are highly unnatural, lifeless hybrids[521], — an embodiment of the West in Rybakov's mental world. For him, the West cultivates sickly deviations while propagating them as signs of progress, so that new humans are growing up — wretched creatures who "cannot make love because they need stimulants and dildos, cannot give birth because they need in-vitro fertilization, cannot even die because they need euthanasia ... Is this progress?"[522] Comparing this kind of progress with cancer and calling to curtail it, Rybakov weaves together anti-Westernism, the civilizational approach, and a host of organic metaphors, characteristic of romantic nationalism

---

518 Translated from the Russian by Alan Meyers (Arkady and Boris Strugatsky, *The Snail on the Slope* (New York, 1980)). The same monologue of Kandid, the protagonist of the novel, stands in the interpretative center of the book *Brat'ia Strugatskie* by Volodikhin and Prashkevich. Volodikhin draws parallels between this indictment of inhumane progress with the position of late imperial Russian conservatives such as Konstantin Leont'ev, who claimed that "in order not to rot, Russia must be frozen" (Leont'ev, *Sobranie sochinenii* (Moscow: V.M. Sablin, 1912-1919), vol. 7, 124).

519 Howell, *Apocalyptic Realism*, 129-138.

520 Correspondence of October 5, 2015.

521 One can add that they are female; Strugatskies' repugnancy of women's rule (Diana Greene, "Male and Female in 'The Snail on the Slope' by the Strugatsky Brothers," *Modern Fiction Studies* 32, no. 1 (1986): 97-108) should be very much to the liking of Rybakov, for whom gynaecocracy stands for repulsive Western-style feminism.

522 From the correspondence of October 5, 2015.

(e.g. Slavophilism). Echoing speculations of intellectuals like Ivan Kireevskii from the mid-19th century, Rybakov maintains that each country has its own future;[523] when Russian tried (in the 1990s) to try on a "foreign future," it was immediately rejected by the very fabric of the Russian life and culture, just like an organism rejects an implanted organ.[524]

The moral dilemma of "progressors," identified by the Strugatsky Brothers in *The Ugly Swans* was pushed it one step farther by Konstantin Lopushanskii, known internationally for his Apocalyptic SF film *Letters from a Dead Man* (1986) and Viacheslav Rybakov. They scripted the cinematic version of this book in 2006. For Rybakov this was a tribute to his teachers, with whom he parted ways so decidedly after 1991, having charged them for "targeting a wrong target."[525] Unlike the original text, the film highlighted the unsolvability of the problem: in contradistinction to Strugatskies' plotline, the film shows that the humans finally physically destroy the *Slimies*.[526] So, the balance of watchers' sympathy is decisively tilted towards slimies, who are rendered as ugly and deformed in the book, but sport stylish black gowns in the cinematic version. In deviation to the book, slimies master esoteric spiritual skills, like levitation, and the thread of the film is their (failed) attempt to make themselves understandable for humans. Unlike in the book, the film ends with an air strike, carried out by the humans against the boarding school, which evidently kills aliens.[527] The protagonist

---

523 In his famous article "A Survey of Today's State of the [Russian] Literature" he elaborated a metaphor of the Western Enlightenment in Russia as a flower, torn from its roots and implanted on a foreign soil — the flower is going to wither and at the same time to block the growth of "native" plants (Ivan Kireevskii, "Obozrenie sovremennogo sostoianiia literatury," 1845, available at: https://azbyka.ru/otechnik/Ivan_Kireevskij/obozrenie-sovremennogo-sostojanija-literatury/).
524 Rybakov, *Rul' istorii*, 50. See also TV show "Noch' na piatom" (October 2, 2010), available at: http://vk.com/video85732658_169798829.
525 Rybakov, *Rul' istorii*, 231.
526 It should not be interpreted that Rybakov and Lopushanskii justified this action; the film is ambiguous about their own moral stance in the dilemma.
527 For example, closer to the end (1:26), one of the slimies regrets that they have had not enough time to make themselves understandable for humans. "I am sure, we could have been understood. Your kids have well understood us." This scene makes the audience feel for the slimies, doomed to perish because of

saves the kids, but they suffer from severe mental breakdown because their unlimited horizons of cognition and development, opened up by the slimies, became foreclosed as they returned to the world of humans and were treated with sedatives in a mental ward. The episode with an air strike reminds us of the NATO bombing of Serbia in 1999, and the entire story acquires a new resonance with the anti-Western agenda of the conservative SF. The parallel which emerges in front of our eyes is one between spiritually and morally superior but geopolitical weak "Russian civilization" and the violent ways of the global West, which instills conformity, cherishes reverence towards bare materialism and avarice, and nurtures myths of its civilizing mission on the planet.

Boris Mezhuev, one of the leading conservative intellectuals in the milieu of ISEPI came up with his original interpretation of *Obitaemyi ostrov* (*Inhabited Island*, 1971, translated into English as *Prisoners of War*, 1977). He departs from the "canon" of seeing Strugatskies as exemplary Soviet dissidents, and provides a scathing attack on them, blaming them for *not* being dissident enough. In brief, the novel's storyline describes a totalitarian order on a faraway planet, maintained by the massive propaganda and psychological manipulation of the planet's population. The instant reaction of the protagonist from the Earth is to destroy this horrendous regime at all cost. At some point, however, he encounters an agent of a superior galactic civilization, working on the planet under deep cover. The agent is likewise disgusted by the regime but he understands that its violent destruction would cause even greater pain to the people, and fights against the revolutionary plans of the Earthling.

Mezhuev argues that here the Strugatsky brothers expressed the ideal of "Enlightened authoritarianism" of the liberal intelligentsia, which in spite of all its iconoclasm and opposition, has always dreamt to build up a strategic partnership with the despotic state. In Mezhuev's view, this is precisely the idea of "progressorism" driven to its extreme. On the Russian soil, he argues,

---

human imperceptiveness and violent xenophobia. Volodikhin and Prashkevich also praised this cinematographic version of *Ugly Swans*, pointing at this very quotation as a summary of the film's message (Volodikhin, Gennady Prashkevich, *Brat'ia Strugatskie* (Moscow: Molodaia gvardiia, 2012)).

"progressorism" always winds up in the violence of the Westernized elite over the uncivilized grassroots. "The sin of the Strugatsky brothers, professed Mezhuev, was their idealization of the external foreign control" over the aboriginals.[528] He further mentions that reading the Strugatsky in the 1990s opened his eyes on the pernicious worldview of the liberal reformers of this period, who — until Putin consolidated his power — dreamt of a liberal dictatorship and worked on the transformation of Russia into a powerless deposit of natural resources for the global West.[529] Again, as in the example with Rybakov, an innocent space-opera plotline has gotten a new life as a commentary on geopolitics and Russia's national "true self" much in line with the Slavophile ideology.

The Strugatsky brothers almost certainly had no geopolitical metaphors in their minds, so it is all the more striking that their followers in our times straightforwardly identify a fantastic plot with ethical implications as a metaphor of geopolitical confrontation between Russia and the West.

Orthodox SF

Religious themes in SF do not necessarily dominate the plotline, but constitute an important part of the narrative's background of many a post-Soviet fantastic book. This religious entourage plays an important role in the fiction by Sergei Luk'ianenko, Viacheslav Rybakov, Andrei Stoliarov, Vadim Panov, Dalia Truskinovskaia, and dozens of others. In this section we will home in on a few selected SF stories which are directly and predominantly influenced by the Russian Orthodox Church, and which deal with two interrelated problems: 1) Russian Messianism and 2) friend/enemy distinction.

In her book *The Way of Cassandra* (2002) and its sequel *Lancelot's Pilgrimage* (2004) Voznesenskaia sets her adventure stories in

---

528 Boris Mezhuev, "Povest' o prosveshchennom avtoritarizme i gor'kikh plodakh reform" (August 30, 2016), politconservatism.ru. Available at: https://politcon servatism.ru/articles/povest-o-prosveshhennom-avtoritarizme-i-gorkih-plodah-reformy.

529 Cf. Leonid Fishman's interpretation of the Strugatsky's world as the deadlock of "total humanism" (Fishman, *Kartina budushchego u rossiiskikh fantastov* (Lipetsk, 2008): 24.)

the dystopian and Apocalyptic setting. Not dissimilar with the famous Vladimir Solov'ev's apocalyptic narrative in *Three Talks* (1899) the story portrays the last days of the world when Antichrist has come to power in the West and ousts religion and traditional morality from society. In accordance with the mythology politicized Orthodoxy, the Russian Empire remains impregnable for the evil deeds. Heroes of the both travelogues are fully embedded into society of Antichrist, and live thoughtless lives in the virtual space. However, when they are accidentally prodded into leaving their comfort zones, they wake up to endless evilness of the world where they have to live. Then, the memory about their Christian past or someone who keeps such memories serve as their lodestar in their perilous traveling through the world of natural catastrophes and demonic works. The protagonists redefine their place in society and their group of friends, and in spatial terms, the narrative boils down to the journey from the place where enemies dwell, to a peaceful harbor inhabited by friends — the last remaining Christians.[530]

Another example of anamnesis in religious SF comes from the space opera *The Ziggurat* by Iury Maksimov, the priest. It tells us about an interplanetary journey from the Earth to a technologically advanced civilization (which turns out to be the descendant of the ancient earthly people of Sumer), which traded its free will to demons in exchange for thorough knowledge about the universe. Demons literally possess almost everyone on that planet, and they also installed in the minds of the space travelers with one notable exception. The protagonist of the Russian origin appears to be conspicuously unavailable for the dark forces, and after laborious recollection of his past life he finds out that the only reason for his invulnerability is the fact that he had been baptized in his childhood. Armed with this knowledge, he baptizes his companions and embarks on a life of an ardent religious neophyte, ready to fight demons on the whole planet. Again, as in Voznesenskaia's narrative,

---

530 Voznesenskaia, *Put' Kassandry, ili Prikliucheniia s makaronami.* 3rd ed. (Moscow: Lepta-Press, 2005); Voznesenskaia, *Palomnichestvo Lanselota.* 2nd ed. (Moscow: Lepta-Press, 2004). On Voznesenskaia's "Orthodox fantasy" see: Tatiana Khoruzhenko, *Russkoe fentezi: Na puti k metazhanru.* Dissertation (Yekaterinburg: UrFU, 2015).

a formal and half-forgotten sign of belonging to the religious tradition (baptism) should be recollected and reinterpreted as the most important event in his life.[531]

The tragic moral dilemma, the earmark of the classic Russian literature, is alien to the post-Soviet conservative SF. There are racial interpretations of the "friends/enemies" divide in conservative SF, which is explored by Viktor Shnirel'man.[532] However, in most cases, actions in the narratives are powered by the territorial move between the camps of the "friends" and "enemies." This geopolitics of "us" versus "them" is preceded by the procedure of re-membering, who are the real friends and foes of the protagonist. It is characteristic that the very project of Orthodox SF becomes possible precisely when and as long as the universal enemy in the Christian worldview — demons — became territorialized.[533] The global empire of Antichrist in the books of Iuliia Voznesenskaia, or a planet, captured and possessed by demons in Iury Maksimov's novel, — are salient examples of how the universal enemy of universalist utopias acquires specific locality and enables us to draw a distinctive spatial line between "good friends" and "bad enemies." Geopolitization of the moral and religious problems was employed as early as in the 1990s by Iury Petukhov in his series of fantastic essays about *besoplanetiane* — demons-extraterrestrials. The narrative in this and analogous cases is built upon the plotline of penetration of borders, for example, on an assumption that *besoplanetiane* infiltrate into our world, or agents of the West are looking for newborn Antichrist on the territory of the Russian Empire. The problem of borderline separating "us" from "them" was specifically explored in the recent volume, edited by Dmitry Volodikhin and Sergei Chekmaev, *Russkii frontir* (*The Russian Frontier*, 2018). In an introductory essay, Volodikhin defines the main idea of the book as the dynamic and unstoppable expansion of the imaginary future Russian Empire in space, ideology and culture. He wraps up the paper by a catchy

---

531 Iury Maksimov, *Zikkurat* (Moscow: AST, 2008).
532 Viktor Shnirel'man, *Ariiskii mif v sovremennom mire* (Moscow: NLO, 2015), vol. 1: 208-271.
533 Utopia by its etymology — "u/eu+topos" — implies a specific territorial order.

phrase: "our borders in the future is the farewell to the borders."[534] Yet, with a more careful consideration it becomes clear that conservative SF requires borders, because spatialized "friend/enemy" distinctions are hardwired into the very logic of this ideological project. Irina Irtenina seems to understand it quite well.

Irtenina has been Volodikhin's comrade in arms, associated first, with RISI and now with the society Two-Headed Eage. She wrote a fairly bleak Orthodox SF novel *Belyi krest* (*The White Cross*), in which she is remarkably outspoken in her reflections and comments. In 2005 she penned a literary manifesto of Orthodox SF of sorts, arguing that its task would be to establish the "front line" not inside an individual (fighting with our own sins and passions), but inside the international world, contaminated by the "gangrene of anti-Christianity."[535] Continuing this thought, Irtenina mourns that Russia (back in 2005) "has no 'official', clearly designated and recognized enemies," and calls for having some in order to "keep Russia in shape." The ideology behind these words is the same trivial political Orthodoxy, well known by the panoply of Russian religious ideologues, who want to see Russia as a *Katechon*, a political powerful empire, providing the humanity with the "infrastructure of salvation" in face of the impending reign of Antichrist.[536]

In the book *Belyi krest*, however, Irtenina contemplates a more sophisticated interpretation of the "friend/enemy" dialectics. The narrative itself is a bunch of weird and unreadable fantasies about the future catastrophes with the bottom line of the Russian

---

534 Dmitry Volodikhin, "Geografiia budushchego," in Volodikhin and Chekmaev (eds.) *Russkii frontir* (Moscow: Izd-vo "E", 2018), 8.
535 "Liniia fronta prokhodit uzhe ne stol'ko vnutri lichnosti ... skol'ko vnutri mirovogo soobshchestva, porazhennogo gangrenoi antikhristianstva." See: Irina Irtenina, "Imperativ budushchego, ili Kak nam obustroit' pravoslavnyi literaturnyi masskul't (na primere fantastiki)", 2005, available at: http://fanread.ru/book/519182/?page=1.
536 Cf. "The powerful White Empire (here: reference to the White Guardism and Orthodoxy, but also probably to the racial whiteness) ... partakes in the clash of civilizations and withstands the pressure of the darkness, slowly but unstoppably moving on the world." See: Irtenina, "My vedem partizanskuiu voinu protiv antikhristovoi ideologii," available at: http://www.lepta-kniga.ru/ncd-5-11-45-1/cafe.html. On "political Orthodoxy" see, among others: Mitrofanova, *The Politicization of Russian Orthodoxy*. On geopolitical Messianism see Chapter 1 in this volume.

Orthodox Empire standing up to the degenerate West. In the end she says that the Orthodox Empire serves to the forces of good for as long as it maintains the border with the external evil (here: the West). However, when the Orthodox Empire prevails (and it should, by the very nature of things, because God helps it!) and embraces the entire world, there will be no inside and outside. This means that the Orthodox Empire will also absorb the evil, and "start to serve the darkness."[537] This ingenious and tantalizing remark, unfortunately, remains underdeveloped, but it allows us to understand that Irtenina is self-reflexive about the logic of Orthodox utopia, which by necessity produces geopolitical enemies.

Conclusions

Pre-revolutionary Russian SF was preoccupied with the "dark side of modernity"; it discussed possibilities of dehumanization and alienation in a rationally organized and bureaucratically administered, homogenous world; positing the question, how to maintain personal freedom, autonomy and justice in the age of "high imperialism," it often lapsed into pre-modern setting, not paying heed to the fact that this very question would have been senseless in this context. Post-Soviet SF shares the same premise as its precursors and inquires into the "dark side of post-modernity." However, today's SF writers contemplate the possibility of escaping from moral autonomy and cognitive uncertainty into a utopian land, where a strong external ethical system and comprehensive "rules of nature" reign. An imperial propensity, a geopolitical style of thinking, and discourses about "energy" demonstrate a retrospective lapsing of the contemporary Russian imagination back into a "steam punk" historical style. By so doing, SF undermines its own cultural foundation: driven by the acute sense of disempowerment, reduction to non-existence, and disintegration of post-Soviet subjectivity, Russian fandom fantasizes about such socio-political forms (empires in geopolitical struggle) which can only lead to further loss of agency. Quasi-post-colonial loss of agency is represented in SF as stealing

---

[537] "Imperia nachnet sluzhit' t'me." Irtenina, *Belyi krest* (Moscow: Eksmo, 2006).

of "our" enjoyment by the West cum Father. The problem with the post-Soviet SF consists in the imagery, that reclaiming this pleasure/agency from the West could be done only antagonistically — not through empowerment by the cultivation of people's political subjectivity, but through restoring the empire and taking "ours" by armed hand.

Part II

Imaginary Places

5 "Holy Russia"

Introduction

The idea has become established in the academic literature that in the current era of the "end of history" the geographical imagination is more important as a source of collective self-identification than historical conceptions.[538] This observation is especially accurate as applied to the spatial "sensitivity" of post-Soviet Russia, sharpened by the disintegration of the Soviet Union.[539] The Russian political elite is working on integration-oriented geopolitical projects that may overcome the "trauma" of the disintegration of empire (for example, as are the Eurasian Union and the "Russian World"). Trying to capture the geopolitical imagination of its contemporaries, the Russian Orthodox Church of the Moscow Patriarchate (henceforth, the ROC) actively participates in the discussion of these projects. At the same time, the ROC holds a trump card not possessed by the state: it has survived the disintegration of the Soviet Union without territorial losses, although its present-day leaders are inclined to agree with Vladimir Putin's words about a "geopolitical catastrophe."[540] Today the ROC actively presents itself as the sole integrative force in the space of the former Soviet Union, and this force has no intention of simply aligning itself with others' political schemes.[541]

The Church—in the person of its head, Patriarch Kirill—is developing its own geopolitical model—the "Holy Rus" project. First,

---

[538] R.J. Johnston, "One World, Millions of Places: The End of History and the Ascendancy of Geography," *Political Geography* 13, no. 2 (1994): 111–21.
[539] Clowes, *Russia on the Edge*; David Hooson, "Ex-Soviet Identities and the Return of Geography," in Hooson (ed.), *Geography and National Identity* (Cambridge, MA: Blackwell, 1994): 134–41.
[540] Metropolitan Hilarion (Alfeev), *Patriarkh Kirill: Zhizn' i mirosozertsanie* (Moscow: Eksmo, 2010): 90; Patriarch Kirill (Gundiaev), *Byt' vernym Bogu. Kniga besed so Sviateishim Patriarkhom Kirillom* (Moscow: Izd-vo Belorusskogo ekzarkhata, 2010): 279–80.
[541] Patriarch Kirill (Gundiaev), "Interv'iu zhurnalu 'Vnutri Vatikana'," *Ofitsial'nyi sait Moskovskogo patriarkhata*, April 19, 2006, available at: www.patriarchia.ru/db/text/106489.html; Kirill, *Byt' vernym Bogu*, 281.

investigation of "Holy Rus" as a concept and geopolitical metaphor within the ROC is important for understanding processes taking place in the contemporary ideological field: it is a point of conceptual growth, a place from which new elements enter into ideology. Second, in respect to the growing presence of the ROC in Russia's political life, it may be expected that the concept of "Holy Rus" will be made into a political instrument, just as the "Russian World" and Eurasianism have been made into political instruments. Finally, the true significance of "Holy Rus" lies in the ability of this project to influence the mass geopolitical imagination and, consequently, the processes by which collective identity is formed.

The works of Henri Lefebvre and his followers offer a theoretical basis for interpreting "Holy Rus" as a means by which the ROC seeks to transform and control space.[542] Such investigations emphasize that religion is not just situated in space but actively transforms it. In supporting the project of radically remaking society on Christian foundations, the ROC cannot help but assess the possibility of a radical reorganization of space. This kind of transformation is possible through the conceptualization of space in ideological constructions and through their mastery in everyday practices and in the imagination.

"Holy Russia" project

The metaphor of "Holy Russia," deeply engraved in Russian mythology and intellectual history, is on the increase in both lay and church discourses.[543] The central question of this chapter pertains to the exploration of the myth of "Holy Russia," restored and

---

542 Henri Lefebvre, *The Production of Space*, Kim Knott, "Spatial Theory and Method for the Study of Religion," *Temenos* 41, no. 2 (2005): 153–84.

543 For example, there is the publishing house in Moscow "New Holy Russia," the series of politically engaged encyclopedias "Holy Russia," edited by the Institute of Russian civilization in Moscow, a number of local newspapers of this title, some political pamphlets, associated with this term, such as: G. Ziuganov, *Sviataia Rus' i Koshcheevo tsarstvo* (Moscow: Rezerv, 2003), and even textbooks for religious secondary schools, e.g. L. Shevchenko, *Pravoslavnaia kul'tura. 6-i god obucheniia. Sviataia Rus'* (Moscow: Tsentr podderzhki kul'turno-istoricheskikh traditsii Otechestva, 2007).

promoted by the Russian Orthodox Church (ROC) and personally by Patriarch Kirill (Gundiaev), who was enthroned on February 1, 2009. The analytical framework would structure this examination of "Holy Russia" as a utopian "novum" of ambivalent status; it both liberates from cultural hegemony of the West, and claims to restore cultural hegemony of the "Orthodox civilization."[544] Thus, the "Holy Russian" mythology is not consistent in its decolonizing intention; it stops at the point where intellectual practices of decolonization should transform into post-colonial deconstruction of all hegemonic meta-narrations whatsoever.

Speaking about "Holy Russia" as utopia does not mean to denigrate the ideas of Patriarch Kirill and his collaborators;[545] by contrast, the interpretation of Kirill's thoughts as utopia means to highlight their ability to "estrange" reality and to break though the petrifying dominant mythology.[546] Kirill is himself reflexive about utopianism and its necessity,[547] arguing that it is important to have a dream, to be faithful to it and devote one's life to its implementation.[548] Kirill's recent moderate criticism of the government further aligns his ideas with utopianism much rather than with the docile pro-Putin crackdown on opposition.[549] This reasoning does not preclude the possibility that "Kirill's project" has been concocted in the

---

544 Darko Suvin, "Novum Is as Novum Does," in K. Sayer and J. Moore (eds.), *Science Fiction: Critical Frontiers* (Houndmills and London: Macmillan Press Ltd, 2000): 3–23.
545 Cf.: Aleksandr Verkhovskii speaks of Kirill's doctrine as a utopian (read: counter-productive) striving to restore pre-modern social configuration (Verkhovskii, "'Doctrina Kirilla' kak instrument izmeneniia identichnosti rossiiskogo obshchestva i Russkoi Pravoslavnoi Tserkvi," *Eurasian Review* 4 (November 2011): 19).
546 See on this interpretation of utopianism: Frederic Jameson, *Archaeologies of the Future: The Desire Called Utopia and Other Science Fiction* (New York: Verso, 2005); Moylan, *Demand the Impossible: Science Fiction and the Utopian Imagination*; Suvin, *Metamorphoses of Science Fiction*.
547 See, for example: Kirill, *Sviataia Rus' – vmeste ili vroz'? Patriarkh Kirill na Ukraine* (Moscow: Danilov muzhskoi monastyr', 2009): 217; P. Kuzenkov, "'Politika' i 'politiia' v vizantiiskoi traditsii," *Zhurnal Moskovskoi patriarkhii*, no. 7 (2011): 39.
548 Kirill, *Patriarkh i molodezh: Razgovor bez diplomatii* (Moscow: Danilov muzhskoi monastyr', 2009): 150; Kirill, "Kak sokhranit' svoiu mechtu?" *Zhurnal Moskovskoi Patriarkhii*, no. 7 (2009): 60–61.
549 Kirill, "Rozhdestvenskoe interv'iu," available at: http://www.patriarchia.ru/db/text/1932241.html.

Kremlin, but it definitely evokes intellectual forces and possibilities, potentially capable of destabilizing the regime.

The phrase "Holy Russia" (*Sviataia Rus'*) appeared in Kirill's programmatic enthronization speech and rapidly gained wide currency in his discourses throughout his three years in service of the Patriarch of the ROC, which highlights the importance of this metaphor in today's Russian Orthodoxy.[550] The very choice of the "Holy Russian" imagery is significant because of its historically entrenched anti-state overtones. First time the notion of "Holy Russia" is reported to appear in Prince Kurbsky's correspondence with Tsar Ivan the Terrible in 1570s, when it acquired distinctive dissident connotations as an "opposite to the myth of the ruler," and was further elaborated by the Slavophiles.[551] For the latter Holy Russia meant mostly the transcendental ideal to follow, and a metaphor, associated with relics, deposited in Russian monasteries and churches.[552] Kirill's predecessor Patriarch Aleksii II seems to embrace this interpretation.[553] Kirill, by contrast, understands "holiness" as an eternal quality of Russia, as its singular and immutable

---

550 Kirill, *Byt' vernym Bogu*, 10, 171, 325, 568–69; Hilarion, *Patriarkh Kirill: Zhizn' i mirosozertsanie* (Moscow: Eksmo, 2010): 116.
551 Michael Cherniavsky, "'Holy Russia': A Study in the History of an Idea," *American Historical Review* 63, no. 3 (1958): 621; Cherniavsky, *Tsar and People: Studies in Russian Myths* (New Haven: Yale University Press, 1961): 159–228; Peter Duncan, *Russian Messianism: Third Rome, Revolution, Communism and After* (London and New York: Routledge, 2000): 14–15.
552 See, for example: "If the Russian land was sometimes called 'Holy Russia', this is because of sacred relics, monasteries and churches, which were located there, and not because of the intertwining of state and church institutions" (Ivan Kireevskii, "O kharaktere prosveshcheniia Evropy i ego otnoshenie k prosveshcheniiu v Rossii," in Kireevskii, *Polnoe sobranie sochinenii* (Moscow: tip. P. Bakhmeteva, 1861): 263). Cf. celebrated verses by Aleksei Khomiakov: "Oh unworthy to be chosen, // Yet you were chosen. Cleanse yourself swiftly // In the waters of repentance, // Lest a twofold punishment // Should fall like a thunderbolt upon your head." (Khomiakov, "Rossii," in Khomiakov, *Stikhotvoreniia i dramy* (Leningrad: Sovetskii pisatel', 1969): 137. Translation from: Andrej Walicki, *The Slavophile Controversy: History of a Conservative Utopia in Nineteenth-Century Russian Thought* (Notre Dame: University of Notre Dame, 1975): 187. Our sources show that neo-Slavophiles of the late imperial period almost never used the term "Holy Russia."
553 Aleksii II, "Privetstvie uchastnikam II assamblei Russkogo mira," *Tserkovsnyi vestnik* 394, no. 21 (2008); *Zhurnal Moskovskoi Patriarkhii*, no. 2 (2008): 53; *Zhurnal Moskovskoi Patriarkhii*, no. 9 (2008): 36.

"spiritual and moral core,"[554] which manifested itself in the past, mostly in the Muscovite Tsardom, and which is to be "re-membered," "re-collected" and thereby restored in the future.[555] Thus, Kirill "geo-politicizes" and "de-historicizes" this metaphor, informing it with practical political meaning. He says that "Holy Russia is not a speculative concept, and not [merely] a part of our history. This is our present."[556] "Holy Russia" has its distinctive territory and borders; namely it includes Russia, Ukraine, Belarus, and on many occasions it is said to take in Moldova and less often—Kazakhstan.[557]

So, "Holy Russia" is located on the "canonical territory" of the ROC. This other spatial term frames geopolitical imagination in more or less tangible and rationalized juridical form. In an article published in 2005, archbishop Hilarion Alfeev (now Metropolitan) substantiated "canonical territory" as territory of exclusive jurisdiction of ROC. It does not mean that other confessions should be ousted from these lands, but Hilarion insists that missionary activity of other churches on "canonical territory" should be considered hostile proselytism if not overt imperialistic hegemony.[558] This territory includes Russia, Ukraine, Belarus, Moldova, Kazakhstan, Uzbekistan, Turkmenistan, Kirgizstan, Tajikistan, Estonia, Latvia, and Lithuania.[559] So this concept is basically reactive and defensive:

---

554 Kirill, *Propovedi, 2009–2010* (Sviato-Troitskaia Sergieva Lavra, 2010): 4, 6, 52. Cf.: Metropolitan Kliment, "Interv'iu *Rossiiskoi gazete*," January 12, 2012, available at: http://www.patriarchia.ru/db/text/1945937.html.
555 Kirill, *Byt' vernym*, 71, 78.
556 Kirill, "Doklad na Arkhiereiskom soveshchanii 2 fevralia 2010 g.," *Tserkov' i vremia*, no. 50 (2010) (http://www.mospat.ru/church-and-time/196); Hilarion, *Patriarkh Kirill*, 389. Cf. Kirill's remark that his visits to Ukraine were "the strongest spiritual experience and visible evidence of the unity of Holy Russia" (Kirill, *Propovedi*, January 7, 2010, 284).
557 E.g. Kirill, *Propovedi*, February 1, 2010, 308.
558 See on this, e.g.: John Anderson, "Putin and the Russian Orthodox Church: Asymmetric Symphonia?" *Journal of International Affairs* 61, no. 1 (2007): 193; Metropolitan Kirill, "Gospel and Culture," in J. Witte Jr. and M. Bourdeaux (eds.), *Proselytism and Orthodoxy in Russia: The New War for Souls* (Maryknoll, NY: Orbis Books, 1999): 72–76.
559 Hilarion, "Printsip 'kanonicheskoi territorii' v pravoslavnoi traditsii," 2005, available at: http://www.hilarion.ru/2010/02/25/1048. See also papers by then Metropolitan Kirill and then archbishop Hilarion, presented on December 1, 2007 in Moscow at the international conference "Local Church and Canonical

canonical territory, which generally coincides with the territory of the Soviet Union, symbolically stabilizes post-Soviet space.[560] The metaphor of "Holy Russia" shapes spatial imagination differently, in a way of practical political programming and active reforming.

"Holy Russia" emerges on the area, where territorially bounded notion of "canonical territory" and culturally bounded notion of the "Russian world" overlap. Due to its inescapably instrumentalized character as a political means to reinforce legitimacy of the Putin's regime in the eyes of foreigners, as well as its ethnically and religiously ambiguous status, the concept of the "Russian world" is much less popular in Kirill's discourses than "Holy Russia."[561] It appears sporadically mostly on special occasions, such as collaboration of the ROC with the foundation "Russian world,"[562] established in 2007 by the initiative of the Russian President in order to promote Russian language and culture abroad.

"Holy Russia," in his understanding, is held together by the common system or "matrix" of values and cultural foundations, implanted in "Kievan font" by St Prince Vladimir. These principles include ideas that the spiritual dominates over the material, and that there is good and evil, which everybody has the difficult task of having to to choose between.[563] Therefore, Kirill argues, in the center of these values lies an ideal of "holiness," which permeated

---

Territory: Canonical, Juridical and Inter-Confessional Aspects": Metropolitan Kirill, "Privetstvie mitropolita Kirilla," December 1, 2007], available at: http://www.mospat.ru/archive/38874.htm. For analysis of the concept of "canonical territory" see, e.g.: Daniel Payne, "Nationalism and the Local Church: The Sources of Ecclesiastical Conflict in the Orthodox Commonwealth," *Nationalities Papers* 35, no. 5 (2007): 831–852.

560 Kathy Rousselet, "L'Église orthodoxe russe et le territoire," *Revue d'études comparatives Est-Ouest* 35, no. 4 (2004): 153.
561 E.g.: Kirill, *Propovedi*, May 24, 2010, 447.
562 Kirill, "Vystupleniie na otkrytii III assamblei Russkogo Mira," *Zhurnal Moskovskoi Patriarkhii*, no. 12 (2009).
563 E.g.: Kirill, "Interv'iu dlia programmy 'Natsional'nyi interes'," November 25, 2009, available at: http://www.patriarchia.ru/db/text/949960.html. This idea was picked up by religious intellectuals of the conservative spectrum, who eagerly elaborate on the supremacy of the "Russian civilization" on the grounds that "the spirit always dominated over the material /concerns/" (Leonid Reshetnikov, "SShA visiat na voloske," *Argumenty i fakty*, February 2, 2016).

all aspects of Russian life in medieval and imperial periods, and also—although in considerably perverted form—in Soviet times.[564] It does not mean, he says, that all Russians were righteous people, but they measure their lives by the ideal of the righteousness.[565] In Kirill's thought, the "Holy Russian" community has also a transcendental dimension, that is the special relation of Russia as a geopolitical entity with the highest deity. God's divine grace, given due to the prayers of the Russian saints and just people, is what makes Russia "holy."[566] Another messianic metaphor employs the imagery of "Holy Russia" as the "earthly principality," which belongs to and resides under the protecting veil of the Mother of God.[567]

The fact that "Holy Russia" is politically split into several sovereign countries allows Patriarch Kirill to theorize a "new type of integration," which comes to replace the tradition of political centralization.[568] He argues that the "Russian world" could be organized on principally new foundations, which would blaze a new path of political reform, to be walked by the rest of the peoples on earth.[569] He is not very explicit, but we can assume that he means the principle of equal rights of all members of "Holy Russia."[570] The peacefulness of this process of integration is guaranteed by the fact that it is neither supposed to revise political borders of already sovereign countries, nor encroach on the existing national sovereignties.[571] The key element of such integration, however, does not

---

564 Kirill, *Propovedi*, 12, 52. Cf.: "Ideals of Holy Russia, though not connected with God, were actually present in culture of the Soviet people" (Kirill, *Propovedi*, September 11, 2009, 174).
565 Kirill, *Propovedi*, 520.
566 Kirill, "Sila Bozhestvennogo zakona," *Zhurnal Moskovskoi Patriarkhii*, no. 10 (2010): 27.
567 Kirill, *Propovedi*, October 14, 2009, 221.
568 Kirill, "Sem'ia narodov," 34; Kirill, *Propovedi*, 4.
569 Kirill, "Sem'ia narodov," *Zhurnal Moskovskoi patriarkhii*, no. 12 (2010): 35; Kirill, "Vystuplenie na otkrytii," 29–33.
570 *Zhurnal Moskovskoi Patriarkhii*, no. 12 (2009): 29–33. Cf.: "There should be no more 'seniors' and 'minors', leaders and followers [in our] brotherhood" (Hilarion, *Patriarkh Kirill*, 221).
571 Kirill, "Interv'iu Sviateishego Patriarkha Kirilla dlia ezhegodnika "Predstoiatel'," February 10, 2010, available at: http://www.patriarchia.ru/db/text/1065213.html; Kirill, "Interv'iu Sviateishego Patriarkha Kirilla programme

belong to the domain of politics; this is the specific spiritual atmosphere of Christian morality, a respectful attitude to foreigners and self-sacrificial service to "thy neighbor."[572]

This argumentation helps him to explain the collapse of the Russian and Soviet empires as the result of moral degradation of society and waning of religious enthusiasm and self-denial among Russians.[573] Kirill's attempt to bridge the gap between moral improvement and geopolitical perspectives of Russia deserves closer attention. He says that people like to live side by side with you when you are a good person. A good person is one who never oppresses you, or takes away your property, but instead gives you something. The same thing is true of an empire: when the imperial center gives more than it takes, the structure is stable. Thus, we have to learn how to give, to learn self-sacrificial service to our neighbors; which is the first precondition of integration.[574]

"Holy Russia" as a civilization

However, the most powerful instrument for maintaining the unity of "Holy Russia" is an attempt, though not thoroughly consistent, to de-ethnicize this metaphor. Kirill insists that "Holy Russia" is not based on ethnicity, because of inclusion of non-Slavic Moldovans and possibly Kazakhs. He further argues that whereas "Russians" are one nation, which includes *rossiiane* living in the Russian Federation (including the Great Russians and many other nationalities), Ukrainians and Belarusians, "Holy Russia" is geographically broader than "Russians" (the pan-Russian nation), because, for example, Moldovans belong to "Holy Russia" but not to the "Russians." According to a shrewd remark by David Harvey, the internal contradiction of spatial utopias consists in the fact that they "are

---

'Voskresnoe vremia'," January 31, 2010, available at: http://www.patriarchia.ru/db/text/1058792.html.
572 Kirill, *Propovedi*, November 4, 2009, 231. Cf. Kirill's television programme *Slovo pastyria*, aired on November 5, 2011 on *ORT (Public Russian Television) Channel*.
573 Kirill, *Byt' vernym*, 281.
574 Kirill, "Zadacha cheloveka: nesti mir Khristov v soznanie kazhdogo," *Zhurnal Moskovskoi patriarkhii*, no. 9 (2010): 33–34. See also: Hilarion, *Patriarkh Kirill*, 391–92.

typically meant to stabilize and control the processes that must be mobilized to build them"[575]. This observation precisely reflects the paradox of "Holy Russia": conceived as an intellectual instrument to arrest processes of nation-state making on the post-Soviet space, this project can be realized only if forces of nationalism are unleashed, as follows already from its name referring to Russia; to paraphrase the famous dictum of E. Gellner, "Holy Russia" could be only created by "holy Russian nationalism." Kirill, however, opposes nationalism as a non-Christian, pagan concept, detrimental to the dogma of unity.[576] From time to time Kirill voiced the necessity of patriotism as a geopolitical projection of Christian love to "thy neighbor," but he insists that patriotism must be "sanctified." His concept of "sanctified patriotism" (in Russian here, there is the play on words: *prosviashchennyi patriotism*, instead of *prosveshchennyi*, meaning enlightened) implied that the moral ideals of Scripture must always hover above any mundane, political attachments, thereby preventing patriotism from degenerating into nationalism.[577]

So, a closer look at Kirill's ideas cannot corroborate the vision of ROC as moving towards a more ethnically-bound religious identity.[578] Kirill re-launches the late imperial project of a pan-Russian nation; the meaningful difference is that tsarist government desired to consolidate it within a broader political entity, while Kirill is speaking about one nation, divided among several political entities. Although he consistently highlights the importance of observing

---

575 David Harvey, *Spaces of Hope* (Los Angeles: University of California Press, 2000): 173.
576 *Zhurnal Moskovskoi Patriarkhii*, no. 9 (2010): 34.
577 Kirill, *Byt' vernym*, 75; *Osnovy sotsial'noi kontseptsii Russkoi pravoslavnoi tserkvi* (2000), II.1, II.2, III.3; Kirill, "Interv'iu," July 23, 2009, available at: http://www.patriarchia.ru/db/text/702155.html; Kirill, "Aktual'nye voprosy tserkovnoi zhizni," *Zhurnal Moskovskoi patriarkhii*, no. 2 (2011): 29; "Zaiavlenie Sviateishego Sinoda," *Zhurnal Moskovskoi patriarkhii*, no. 7 (2011): 19. Cf. Kirill's television programme *Slovo pastyria*, aired on March 6, 2011 on *ORT (Public Russian Television) Channel*. See also: Verkhovskii, *Politicheskoe pravoslavie: Russkie natsionalisty i fundamentalisty, 1995–2001* (Moscow, 2003): 118–119.
578 Alexander Agadjanian, "Revising Pandora's Gifts: Religious and National Identity in the Post-Soviet Societal Fabric," *Europe-Asia Studies* 53, no. 3 (2001): 481–82.

current sovereignties, it cannot be denied that if his project of pan-nation-making succeeds, the existence of separate non-nation states—not supported by the nation and coinciding with the political boundaries—will become problematic.

All in all, "Holy Russian" imagery helps the ROC to dissociate its Messianic teaching from the state nationalism and imperialism and to distance from the "Moscow—the Third Rome" mythology as too much susceptible to the imperialist interpretation, to put it in Nikolai Berdiaev's words.[579] Kirill elaborated his position on "Moscow—the Third Rome" concept in 1995, when he argued that this mythology had been misinterpreted by the commentators; in fact it means not the claims for geopolitical hegemony but rather claims to be a Christian spiritual center, the place where religious values and morals reign.[580] The model of "Holy Russia" provides for a "third way" perspective between Westernism and Eurasianism, dominant in contemporary Russian public sphere.[581]

The utopia of "Holy Russia" is fecund with liberating and anti-colonial potential due to the possibility of interpreting it as a "covenant Messianism," to use Anthony Smith's seminal analysis.[582] If missionary peoples seek to transform the outer world according to what they perceive to be their divine revelation, covenant peoples look inwards and reflex on their ability to maintain the covenant and fulfill God's commandments as a precondition for being chosen.[583] So, covenant Messianism could provide the language of self-sufficiency, restoration of self-esteem and authenticity of one's own culture vis-à-vis the penetrating Western cultural hegemony. Already Slavophiles, who elaborated one of the first versions of anti-

---

579 Nikolai Berdiaev, *Russkaia ideia* (Paris: YMCA-Press, 1971): 12.
580 Kirill, *Byt' vernym*, 65.
581 Kirill capitalized on Eurasian terminology in 2001 (Verkhovskii, *Politicheskoe pravoslavie*, 42). Since then has rarely used it to designate territorial spread of Orthodoxy "on the immense vast of Eurasia" (Kirill, *Propovedi* July 22, 2010, 517; Alla Dobrosotskikh (ed.), *"Neizvestnyi" Patriarkh Kirill* (Moscow: Danilov muzhskoi monastyr', 2009): 103).
582 Anthony Smith, *Chosen Peoples* (Oxford: Oxford University Press, 2003): 49.
583 See also Chapter 1 in this volume.

colonial criticism,[584] tended towards covenant interpretation of Russian Messianism framed by the imagery of "Russian God."[585] Patriarch Kirill comprehensively elaborated this imagery when he devoted the whole sermon of 9 July 2009 to the concept of the covenant with God. He paralleled Russian history with the history of the Jews, implying that the Russians were the chosen people, dwelling in prosperous "Holy Russia," but in 1917 had betrayed Christ and apostatized from the true faith. This apostasy, he continued, was the catastrophe of universal importance which ended up by the genocidal Soviet regime, which took lives of tens of millions of Russians.[586] The idea of God's punishment for apostasy is a corollary of the covenant Messianism. So, Kirill picks on the discourses of sufferings during the Great Patriotic War in order to demonstrate that God chastised the whole of the people for its "deadly sin of apostasy, sacrilege, humiliation of the Church, sacred objects and faith."[587]

However, the revolution of 1917 is not the only one and perhaps even not the most dreadful act of apostasy, because it had been prepared by the previous two centuries of gradual secularization and Westernization, launched by the reforms of Peter the Great.[588] So, looking to history, when the initial fundamental condition of the covenant took their shape, Kirill discovers Russia's "golden age" not in the pre-revolutionary period but in the much more distant pre-Petrine past, when

> ... Our pious forefathers ... believed the material well-being to be not the end but the means for ... spiritual life ... There was no blind admiration for foreign experience [in Muscovite Russia] ... But there was no stagnation, isolation as well ... [Russia] always took care of its spiritual authenticity, spiritual individuality, and thereby critically assessed views from abroad.[589]

---

584 Etkind, *Internal Colonization. Russia's Imperial Experience* (Cambridge: Polity, 2011): 17, 140.
585 Cherniavsky, *The Tsar and People*, 177.
586 Kirill, *Propovedi*, 75–77. On Messianism in today's Orthodoxy in general (including laymen and religiously anxious intellectuals) see, e.g.: Mitrofanova, *The Politicization of Russian Orthodoxy*, 42–44.
587 Kirill, *Propovedi*, June 3, 2009; May 6, 2010, 57, 431.
588 Kirill, *Sviataia Rus'*, 218; Patriarch Kirill, *Byt' vernym*, 66.
589 Kirill, *Byt' vernym*, 64–65. Thus we have to qualify the analysis of Sabrina Ramet, according to which the "Orthodox geography of happiness" is located

Kirill's philosophy of history, based on covenant Messianism, means also that contemporary Russia is living through the second most important period in its history, which is associated with liberation from the Western hegemony in the forms of both secular imperialism and atheistic socialism.[590] *The Journal of Moscow Patriarchy* argues that the Church has to reconsider its missionary work; if in the previous centuries, the measure of success was the expansion of the so-called canonical territory, now this indicator is dated.[591] What was suggested instead is to "churchize" those people who already identify themselves with Orthodoxy, but do not attend services and actively participate in the life of a parish yet.[592]

"Holy Russian" Messianism helps to overcome not only "internal colonization,"[593] but also the Western cultural and political hegemony in time and in space, which is typical for religious Messianisms of the developing countries.[594] The "Holy Russian"

---

either before 1917 or before 1991. With Kirill's enthronization, situation has changed. See: Sabrina Ramet, "The Way We Were—and Should Be Again? European Orthodox Churches and the 'idyllic past'," in Byrnes, T. A. and Peter J. Katzenstein (eds.), *Religion in an Expanding Europe* (Cambridge, UK: Cambridge University Press, 2006): 151. Cf.: "By no means should we restore the pre-revolutionary situation [of the church-state relations]" (Hilarion, *Besedy*, 141).

590 Kirill, *Sviataia Rus'*, 38.
591 E. Murzin, "Svoboda i otvetstvennost'," *Zhurnal Moskovskoi patriarkhii*, no. 12 (2010): 22.
592 Kirill, "Missiia dolzhna byt' delom vsei tserkvi," *Zhurnal Moskovskoi Patriarkhii*, no. 12 (2010): 23–24; Kirill, "The Orthodox Church in the Face of World Integration: The Relation Between Tradition and Liberal Values," *The Ecumenical Review* 53 (2001): 4; Kirill, *Byt' vernym*, 167; Kirill, "Interv'iu Patriarkha Kirilla telekanalu 'Rossiia'," September 21, 2010, available at: http://www.patriarchia.ru/db/text/1280323.html; Kirill, "Interv'iu Sviateishego Patriarkha Kirilla telekanalu *Rossiia 24*," April 5, 2010, available at: http://www.patriarchia.ru/db/text/1131490.html.
593 The concept of internal colonization as regards Russian history has been fruitfully elaborated in: Etkind, *Internal Colonization*; Etkind, "Foucault i tezis vnutrennei kolonizatsii: Postkolonial'nyi vzgliad na sovetskoe proshloe," *Novoe Literaturnoe Obozrenie*, no. 49 (2001); Etkind, M. Mogil'ner, "Razgovor o neklassicheskom kolonializme," *Ab Imperio*, no. 1 (2011): 117–130; Etkind, "Bremia britogo cheloveka, ili vnutrenniaia kolonizatsiia Rossii," *Ab Imperio*, no. 1 (2002).
594 Vatro Murvar, "Messianism in Russia: Religious and Revolutionary," *Journal for the Scientific Study of Religion* 10, no. 4 (1971): 286–293; Vittorio Lanternari, *The Religion of the Oppressed: A Study of Modern Messianic Cults* (London: MacGibbon & Kee, 1963).

imagery strengthens feelings of self-esteem and dignity, injured by the collapse of the Soviet Union and the cultural hegemony of the secular West.

The utopia of "Holy Russia" underpins a "civilizational approach" to historiography, which helps the ROC's intellectuals to reject the universality of the Western notions of secular humanism, human rights and liberal democracy,[595] as well as to establish the principles of autonomy, importance and self-sustainability of "civilizations," the "Russian civilization" included, vis-à-vis their Western peer.[596] Postulating different yardsticks for different "civilizations," Kirill argues that countries which want to live up to their religious precepts must not be infringed or oppressed by those countries which maintain the human-rights-based, secular ideology. As stated in the "Foundations of Social Programme of ROC," and elaborated on by Kirill, the West is so fundamentally different a civilization to "ours" that applying the same norms would be unjust.[597]

However, postulating the difference of civilization is not enough, because it could not soothe the fear that "Russian civilization" is located on the periphery of the great civilizations of Europe and Asia, so it was necessary to find "contact points" of Russo-European interaction. The general assumption says that the Western civilization stemmed from Christianity, and the Orthodox religion, which was the faith of the European continent in the first thousand years AD, constitutes an important if not the bearing pillar of the

---

595 Marlene Laruelle, *In the Name of the Nation: Nationalism and Politics in Contemporary Russia* (New York: Palgrave Macmillan, 2009): 165; Verkhovskii, "Tserkovnyi proekt rossiiskoi identichnosti," in Laruelle (ed.) *Sovremennye interpretatsii russkogo natsionalizma* (Stuttgart: ibidem-Verlag, 2007): 171–188.

596 Kirill, *Byt' vernym*, 65, 95, 115; Agadjanian, "Breakthrough to Modernity, Apologia for Traditionalism: The Russian Orthodox View of Society and Culture in Comparative Perspective," *Religion, State and Society* 31, no. 4 (2003): 336–338; Rousselet, "L'Eglise orthodoxe russe," 157. On anti-Westernism in Orthodox discourses see: Vasilios Makrides, "Orthodox Anti-Westernism Today: A Hindrance to European Integration?," *International Journal for Study of the Christian Church* 9, no. 3 (2009): 209–224.

597 See on this: Verkhovskii, "'Bespokoinoe sosedstvo: Russkaia Pravoslavnaia Tserkov' i putinskoe gosudarstvo," in Verkhovskii, E. Mikhailovskaia, V. Pribylovskii, *Rossiia Putina: Pristrastnyi vzgliad* (Moscow: Panorama, 2003): 81–84; Makrides, "Orthodox Anti-Westernism Today," 211.

today's West. More than that, this twist of thought suggests that Orthodoxy is the most authentic European cultural tradition, which means that "Holy Russia" stands for its geopolitical center, its "Third Rome." Trying to substantiate Russia's cultural centrality in Europe, Kirill has to prejudice both the concept of covenant Messianism, and the concept of the autonomy of civilizations. First, to spite Huntington's (in)famous geopolitical analysis, Patriarch Kirill and the other ROC's leaders argue that the Orthodox countries are inseparable from the West,[598] and even responsible for what is going on in the West.[599] Thus, for example, the ROC's task is to arrest degradation of the Western civilization in spiritual, demographical and geopolitical aspects,[600] and to teach it the lesson of what can happen with the apostate people.[601] Second, parting with the principles of covenant Messianism, Kirill cedes to the spells of expansionist cultural imperialism and proclaims that Russia's history has transcendental meaning and universal importance: "Russia is the place, which is going to give a new life to the Universe," and to redeem humanity.[602]

The concept of "basic culture" explains in which sense the Russian-Western concordat is thinkable. In tune with the Western

---

598 Cf.: "Orthodoxy must be inscribed onto the spiritual and cultural space of the Western civilization" (Hilarion, *Besedy s mitropolitom Ilarionom* (Moscow: Eksmo, 2010): 97. And elsewhere: "We are not foreigners in the European Union ..." (Hilarion, *Besedy*, 294); Hilarion, *Tserkov' otkryta dlia kazhdogo: Vystupleniia i interv'iu mitropolita Ilariona (Alfeeva)* (Minsk: Belorusskaia Pravoslavnaia Tserkov', 2011): 36.
599 Igumen Filaret (Bulekov), "Russkaia Tserkov' v stolitse 'bol'shoi Evropy'," *Zhurnal Moskovskoi patriarkhii*, no. 10 (2010): 59–60; Metropolitan Hilarion, *Tserkov' otkryta*, 20, 26, 36; Hilarion (ed.), *Patriarkh Kirill*, 129, 481; Hilarion, *Besedy*, 300–303.
600 Kirill, "Vystuplenie na vstreche so studentami Kaliningradskikh vuzov," March 23, 2009, available at: http://www.patriarchia.ru/db/text/595733.html. See also: "Opredelenie Arkhiereiskogo Sobora," *Zhurnal Moskovskoi Patriarkhii*, no. 3 (2011): 72; Hilarion, *Besedy*, 111. Cf. Hilarion's reasoning that Western "anomic" Christianity cannot withstand the pressure of Islam, implying that only "firm and traditional" Christianity of the Russian ilk could do this (Hilarion, *Besedy*, 115).
601 Hilarion, *Patriarkh Kirill*, 482; *Zhurnal Moskovskoi patriarkhii*, no. 10 (2010): 59–60.
602 Kirill, *Byt' vernym*, 41; Dobrosotskikh (ed.) *"Neizvestnyi" Patriarkh*, 121–26; Hilarion, *Patriarkh Kirill*, 390.

neo-conservatives, it implies the importance of fundamental traditions, connected with Christian morality.⁶⁰³ Kirill professes that "basic culture" of different countries and even civilizations (which is, to be sure a contradiction in terms) is practically the same, so the more traditionally oriented a "civilization" is, the more grounds for intercultural dialogue and opportunities for peaceful co-existing it provides: "if these 'other' ways of life are based on their [peoples, nations] own traditions, then more often than not they are not perceived as dangerous for the Orthodox way of life."⁶⁰⁴ By the same token, breaking with "basic culture" makes people susceptible to hostility towards the alien cultures.⁶⁰⁵

Thus, traditional Russian anti-Catholic sentiments notwithstanding, the latter-day ROC has found many occasions to express its solidarity with Rome. Metropolitan Hilarion, the head of the External Relations Office, is especially explicit; he insists on the necessity of the "Orthodox-Catholic strategic alliance" against secularism.⁶⁰⁶ Another intellectual development is connected with the reframing of the image of the United States. Long viewed as a "Big Satan,"⁶⁰⁷ the United States as a fortress of traditional religiosity is often implicitly or explicitly juxtaposed to Northern Europe—a den of atheists.⁶⁰⁸ Probably we will witness the emergence of the US in religious minds as Holy Russia's strategic partner in the would-be "Inter-Traditional."

---

603 Kirill, *Patriarkh i molodezh'*, 98.
604 Kirill, "The Orthodox Church in the Face of World Integration: The Relation Between Tradition and Liberal Values," *The Ecumenical Review* 53, no. 4 (2001): 481. See also: Hilarion, *Patriarkh Kirill*, 217. See also: *Zhurnal Moskovskoi patriarkhii*, no. 2 (2009): 56.
605 Hilarion, "Vystuplenie Mitropolita Volokolamskogo Illariona na vstreche OBSE," September 12, 2011, available at: http://www.patriarchia.ru/db/text/1621587.html.
606 Hilarion, *Tserkov' otkryta*, 55, 82; Hilarion, *Patriarkh Kirill*, 422.
607 E.g.: Verkhovskii, *Politicheskoe pravoslavie*, 38.
608 *Zhurnal Moskovskoi patriarkhii*, no. 10 (2010): 62.

Mapping Kirill's pastoral visits

The concept of "Holy Russia" has been tested and honed by Kirill's semantically loaded visits to Ukraine in 2009-2011.[609] Nikolas Gvosdev quoted from the 19th-century historian A. N. Mouravieff, to describe the vast and often disunited territory of ancient Russia as held together as one whole "chiefly by their [metropolitans] travels and visitations"[610]; the same is true in regard to Kirill's thinking: his pastoral visits and pilgrimages weave the fabric of "Holy Russia." They produce "Holy Russia" by means of "re-membering" its sacrosanct geographical contours. Iu. Lotman uncovered the logic of a semiotic journey as a triple transfer from "here" to "there" in geographical terms; superimposed onto the shift between binary oppositions—between "home" and "foreign land" and "profane land" and "sacred place."[611]

According to this logic the very journey to Ukraine is represented as a feat of asceticism and self-denial; thus, Patriarch Aleksii II in Kirill's discourses was said to be traveling to Ukraine deadly ill; he had to terminate his visit because of this illness in the summer 2008 several months before his death. Kirill's own journey was obstructed by hostile forces, embodied by the President Iushchenko, nationalists and adepts of the dissident Ukrainian Orthodox Church of Kiev Patriarchate.[612]

Kirill's first pastoral visit to Ukraine took place on July 27–August 5, 2009, when he made his key geopolitical statements, timed to the anniversary of the baptism of St Vladimir. He started his visit

---

609 On symbolism of metropolitans' traveling in medieval Russia see: Boris Uspenskii, *Tsar' i patriarkh: Kharizma vlasti v Rossii (Vizantiiskaia model' i ee russkoe pereosmyslenie)* (Moscow: Iazyki russkoi kul'tury, 1998): 373-375. Pilgrimages are analyzed, for example, in: John Eade and M. Sallnow (eds.), *Contesting the Sacred: The Anthropology of Christian Pilgrimage* (London and New York: Routledge, 1991).
610 Nikolas Gvosdev, "Keeping the Faith: The Orthodox Church and Reintegration in Contemporary Eurasia," *Ab Imperio*, no. 2 (2000): 220.
611 Iury Lotman, *Semiosfera* (St Petersburg: Iskusstvo-SPB, 2000); conceptualization of "sacred places" is dominated by Eliade's analysis of sacred centers as intersections of divine and mundane forces (Mircea Eliade, "Sacred Places: Temple, Palace, 'Center of the World'," in *Patterns in Comparative Religion* (New York: World Publishing Co., 1963).
612 Kirill, *Sviataia Rus'*, 7-8.

in Kiev, which he called the Southern capital of Holy Russia, "our Jerusalem and Constantinople," the place where Russia was baptized.[613] Kiev represented three types of sacred place: the locus of supra-natural presence on earth through the first Russian monastery (Kiev Pechersk Lavra); a place of great historical importance (having seen the baptism of Russian people on the banks of Dnieper river); and the cradle of "Holy Russia," "from whence the Russian land came to be," in words of Nestor the Chronicler.[614]

On July 30 Kirill traveled to Sviatohirsk Lavra in the Donetsk region in the east of Ukraine. In his sermon Kirill compared the history of this monastery with the history of Russia in general; closed in 1787 by Catherine II and then again in 1918, Sviatohirst monastery was restored in 1992 as a "spiritual fortress" of "Holy Russia," thereby fitting to Kirill's historiosophic outline of Russian "illness" progressing through the 18th and 19th centuries, with its paroxysm in Soviet Russia and the subsequent convalescence[615]. On the next day in Gorlovka in the central Donbas area, the backbone of the Ukrainian heavy industry, Kirill referred to this region as "the holy land of Donbas."[616] On August 1, already in Simferopol, the patriarch spoke of Crimea as "the ancient land of Tavria," from whence St Cyril started to teach the Orthodox faith in Russian lands and where St Vladimir was baptized.[617] If the "holy Donbas area" is mostly the place where glorious and tumultuous events of Russian history took place, Crimea stands for another "hearth" of "Holy Russia," the place where religious enlightenment came on the Russian land.[618]

Kirill flew the next day to the Koretsky monastery in Volyn region in Western Ukraine, and then travelling to nearby Rovno. If

---

613 Kirill, *Sviataia Rus'*, 67; Kirill, *Propovedi*, July 28, 2009; October 4, 2009; February 25, 2010, 109, 207, 343.
614 "Nestor's Chronicle," in Leo Wiener (ed.), *Anthology of Russian Literature* (Honolulu: UP of the Pacific, 2001): 65.
615 Kirill, *Sviataia Rus'*, 137; Kirill, *Propovedi*, 112.
616 Kirill, *Propovedi*, July 31, 2009, 117; Kirill, *Sviataia Rus'*, 43.
617 Kirill, *Propovedi*, August 1, 2009, 121, 124; Kirill, *Sviataia Rus'*, 44–45; Kirill, "Interv'iu," July 31, 2009, available at: http://www.patriarchia.ru/db/text/709 499.html.
618 Kirill, *Sviataia Rus'*, 45, 140–141.

the Volyn region is the "foothold of Orthodoxy" in Western Ukraine, the Koretsky monastery is the "stronghold of Orthodoxy in Volyn."[619] Here among anti-Russian-oriented Western Ukrainians, his rhetoric acquired palpable military traits. Kirill completed his journey in Pochaev Lavra, further to the north from Rovno, which he assessed as a "holy Pochaev mountain," "one of the greatest spiritual centers of Russian Orthodoxy" and "the great shrine of Holy Russia," mystically sanctified by prayers of many generations of monks[620].

So, Ukrainian lands are sacred in three interconnected ways; they are the spring, the beginning of "Holy Russia," Russian Orthodoxy, statehood and religious enlightenment; they represent the spiritual center of "Holy Russia" — although located on its geographical periphery; and last but not least, Ukraine is the place, where asceticism and selfless devotion could be practiced. This last aspect establishes the parallels with the martyrdom of the first Christians. Like them, true believers in Ukraine, faithful to the Moscow Patriarchate, had to go to and perform services in catacombs; some of them pursued and threatened at knifepoint, as these original believers had been.[621]

The symbolic status of Ukraine displays the internal dynamism of spatial imagination; the focus of attention transfers from the fundamental binary opposition between "us" and "them" to the medieval geographical duality according to which territories are ranged on the scale of "sacred" to "sinful." Thus, Ukraine is represented as an essential part (even the "heart") of "Holy Russia," reigned over by aliens. Further disclosing the metaphor of "Holy Russia" in regard to Ukraine, it is necessary to stress that the postcolonial situation heightened the "center-periphery" sensibility, so that the spatial status of Ukraine is again destabilized: situated on the Russian border (the very name Ukraine is reminiscent of the Russian phrase *u kraia*, i.e. "on the edge"), it is nevertheless the center of "Holy Russia," its point of growth and the lieu of contestation

---

619 Kirill, *Propovedi*, August 3, 2009, 134–138.
620 Kirill, *Propovedi*, August 5, 2009, 147; Kirill, *Sviataia Rus'*, 167.
621 Kirill, *Sviataia Rus'*, 116, 197–198.

(us/them, holy/sinful), where the future of "Holy Russia" is being shaped.[622]

Kirill has traveled extensively in Russia too, but his highest esteem is reserved for Ukrainian sacred places. Only the "Moscow land" and the land of the Valaam monastery were honored by the epithet "holy."[623] Many other territories in Central Russia, the Urals and Siberia were designated by weaker epithets like "ancient" (Kolomna and Tver regions),[624] and "blessed" (Kursk region).[625] Only Kolyma evoked a stronger metaphor of "Russian Golgotha."[626] Novgorod stands for one of the "cultural centers of [medieval] Europe,"[627] and Karelia is said to bear "signs of God's presence."[628] This maps out the contours of "Holy Russia" as a space, where centers are located on the periphery: Kiev, Crimea, Sviatohirsk and Pochaev Lavras, Novgorod, Karelia, Kolyma and other "holy places" on the edge rim on the south, west, north-west and east the immense Russian hinterland with only "holy" Moscow and Valaam in the middle. The salient example of Kirill's thinking is his speech to the people of Kamchatka, in which he glibly avers that they live not on the periphery but "in the beginning of Russia."[629] This kind of spatial structuring marks a shift from the Soviet-type hierarchical imperial space to a "post-modern" space, organized as a decentralized network of sacred places, united by the same "matrix of values," transcending newly erected political differences.

The eccentric and network-like model of "Holy Russia" provides a more open structure with important outlets, "contact points" and points of conceptual growth on the periphery.[630] "Holy Russia" as an imaginary place where nation-states fail, opens up

---

622 Kirill, *Sviataia Rus'*, 214.
623 Kirill, *Propovedi*, September 1, 2009; July 9, 2010, 165, 495.
624 Kirill, *Propovedi*, September 13, 2009; July 1, 2010, 179, 482.
625 Kirill, *Propovedi*, September 24, 2009, 197.
626 Kirill, "My ne dolzhny zabyt' strashnyi urok proshlogo," September 1, 2011, available at: http://www.patriarchia.ru/db/text/1610887.html.
627 Kirill, *Propovedi*, September 20, 2009, 188.
628 Kirill, *Propovedi*, June 3, 2010, 454.
629 "Na Vostochnykh rubezhakh Rossii," *Zhurnal Moskovskoi patriarkhii*, no. 11 (2010): 25.
630 Cf. Kirill's sermon, saying that Pochaev mountain is a good place for "Holy Russia" to speak out its opinion to Europe (Kirill, *Propovedi*, August 5, 2009, 147.

horizons for new communities. This model, however, is self-contradictory in many aspects, and these contradictions put significant limitations on imagining the "novum." First, it helps to deconstruct Russian history as a history of Western colonialism, but it fails to deconstruct Russian geography likewise. Trying to preserve and restore "Holy Russia" as a geopolitical entity, Kirill and other ROC intellectuals neglect the fact that its territory was shaped by the colonial practices of the Russian empire, already "corrupt," "Westernized," and devoid of national authenticity. Second, the geographical anchoring of "Holy Russia" instrumentalizes it as a method of controlling certain portions of space, so this utopia is inseparable from the narrations of power and hegemony.[631] Third, historical and geographical aspects of this utopia could hardly be assembled together, because essentially postmodern, decentralized space of "Holy Russia" contradicts Kirill's modernist philosophy of history, based on Messianic meta-narrations of enslavement and subsequent liberation. Thus, in spite of Kirill's hopes, "Holy Russia" does not stop colonial practices, but perpetuates them in many aspects, such as the "internal re-colonization" of the Russian population by "re-churchizing" it, and claims to be cultural center of the Western civilization. "Holy Russia" is the utopia which fails to exit the vicious circle of de- and re-colonization towards the post-colonial imagination and spatial sensibility.

---

[631] On the religious way of controlling meanings and usages of space see, for example: Roger Stump, *Boundaries of Faith: Geographical Perspectives on Religious Fundamentalism* (Lanham: Rowman and Littlefield Publishers, 2000): 3; John O'Loughlin, G. Ó Tuathail (Gerard Toal), V. Kolossov, "Russian Geopolitical Culture and Public Opinion: The Masks of Proteus Revisited," *Transactions of the Institute of British Geographers, New Series* 30, no. 3 (2005): 322–325.

6 Continent Eurasia in Russian Geopolitical Imagination

Introduction

This chapter examines Eurasianism as an ideology of continentalism, which implies "right-sizing" the territorial basis of a political entity to a larger scale. Historically, different attempts of right-sizing and re-scaling[632] were associated with pan-nationalist and irredentist movements, expansionism, sphere-of-influence policies, integrationist projects, Messianisms and so on.[633] This chapter focalizes on continentalism as a specific type of enlarging the scale. Classics of geopolitical thought depicted enlarging the scale as a historically continuous and inevitable "tendency towards annexation and amalgamation."[634] Within this tendency, specificity of continentalism lies in the belief that there is or should be a close connection between a continent as a "natural" division of the planetary surface, and some kind of homogenous political entity.

Continentalism reflects on the deficiencies and limitations of the predominant form of imagining political subjects — a nation-state, which has been a by-default option for the largest part of the 20th century (since at least the Treaty of Versailles, 1919). Today this concept is being seriously challenged.[635] At present, more than half

---

[632] Alberto Alesina and E. Spolaore, *The Size of Nations* (Cambridge, Mass.: MIT Press, 2003); Brendan O'Leary, "The Elements of Right-Sizing and Right-Peopling the State," in B. O'Leary, Ian S. Lustick, and Thomas Callaghy (eds.), *Right-Sizing the State: The Politics of Moving Borders* (Oxford: Oxford University Press, 2001).

[633] Peter Duncan, *Russian Messianism: Third Rome, Holy Revolution, Communism and After* (London: Routledge, 2000); Karl Haushofer, *Geopolitik der Pan-Ideen* (Berlin: Zentral-Verlag, 1931); Hans Kohn, *Pan-Slavism: Its History and Ideology* (New York: Vintage Books, 1960); Louis Snyder, *Macro-Nationalisms: A History of the Pan-movements* (Santa Barbara: Praeger Pub Text, 1984).

[634] Friedrich Ratzel, "The Laws of Spatial Growth of States," in R. Kasperson and J. Minghi (eds.), *The Structure of Political Geography* (Chicago: Aldine Publishing Company, 1969 [1898]): 27.

[635] For the theoretical discussion on the matter from the post-Marxist position see: Michael Hardt and Antonio Negri, *Empire* (Cambridge, Mass.: Harvard University Press, 2001).

of the global trade is carried through regional trade agreements, whose numbers grew from 60 in 1992 to 303 in 2020.[636] These trade cooperation schemes are often fleshed out in a political form, which gives them greater security and international agency. The EU is understandably the most salient example, but we have to look at the "bigger picture" in order to understand the sheer scale of these processes and its dynamism: NAFTA (North-American Free Trade Agreement, 1994), SCO (Shanghai Cooperation Organization, 2001), AU (African Union, 2002), UNASUR (Union of South American Nations, 2008), EAU (Eurasian Economic Union, 2015), as well as a number of the regional cooperation programmes under the aegis of the United Nations, such as the Chernobyl Recovery and Development Programme. These organizations prioritize principles of neighborhood in inter-state relations over principles of cultural, linguistic, ethnic proximity, following the adage that a near neighbor is better than a distant relative. The neighborhood principle facilitates coalescence of the blocs of states of the continental dimensions. So, today, Africa, the Americas, Europe, Asia are becoming more than just geographical names, but political entities with a certain degree of internal cohesion.

Likewise, the growing importance of energy for the world economy gave a new impetus for the infrastructural integration of territorially contiguous states. The necessity to geographically connect producers of energy (most notably in Western Siberia and in the Persian Gulf) and its consumers by gas and oil pipelines gave rise to the "new continentalism" in Eurasia.[637] On a similar matter, expected growth of technologies of high-speed railways and concomitant infrastructure gives priority to the continental and transregional dimension of transportation. As of today, two networks of rapid railways in Western Europe and East Asia tend to connect into the mammoth pan-Eurasian system, traversing the vastness of

---

[636] "Facts and Figures," *World Trade Organization*, available at: http://rtais.wto.org/UI/PublicMaintainRTAHome.aspx.

[637] Kent Calder, *The New Continentalism: Energy and Twenty-First-Century Eurasian Geopolitics* (New Haven, Conn.: Yale University Press, 2012): xxix.

Russia, Mongolia and Kazakhstan under the aegis of the China-sponsored Silk Road Economic Belt initiative.[638]

The present chapter only tangentially speaks about "practical geopolitics" of continentalism, focusing mostly on the ideological and cultural aspects of imagining a continent.[639] More precisely, it approaches continentalism as political rhetoric, as a specific type of geopolitical metaphor, or more specifically, hyperbole.[640] As a figure of speech, hyperbole hypes up audiences by emotionally charged exaggerations. The purpose of hyperbole is to draw attention to a proposed vision, when a powerful alternative is also available.[641] In our case, continentalism fights the vision of Russia as a nation-state, by paralleling it to a whole continent. Geopolitical hyperbole, in this sense, aligns political bodies with powerful natural bodies and forces, such as tectonic platforms.[642]

Two central metaphors of human territoriality are the "springboard of opportunity" and the "shelter of security."[643] Leaning upon this theorization, the chapter discusses three interrelated hyperbolas of continentalism instead. First, continentalism offers a hyperbole of development (a "springboard of opportunity") by showing that the scale of enlargement has an effect on the qualitative leap in development of this territory. Second, continentalism is a hyperbole of autonomy (a "shelter of security").[644] This aspect points to

---

638 Mia M. Bennett, "The Silk Road Goes North: Russia's Role within China's Belt and Road Initiative," *Area Development and Policy* 1, no. 3 (2016): 341–351; Camille Brugier, "China's Way: The New Silk Road," *European Union Institute for Security Studies* 14 (2014): 1–4.
639 On the distinction between practical, formal and popular levels of geopolitical knowledge see: Gearóid Ó Tuathail, "Understanding Critical Geopolitics: Geopolitics and Risk Society".
640 Michael McCarthy and R. Carter, "'There's Millions of Them': Hyperbole in Everyday Conversation," *Journal of Pragmatics* 36, no. 2 (2004): 149–184.
641 Marc Swartz, "Hyperbole, Politics, and Potent Specification: The Political Uses of a Figure of Speech," in W. O'Barr and J. O'Barr (eds.), *Language and Politics* (The Hague: Mouton, 1976).
642 On the sublimity of imperial visions see: Harsha Ram, *The Imperial Sublime: A Russian Poetics of Empire* (Madison, Wis.: University of Wisconsin Press, 2006).
643 Colin Williams and A.D. Smith, "The National Construction of Social Space," 502–518.
644 On the relation of continentalism to the ideal of (geo)political autonomy see also: Andrés Rivarola Puntigliano, "'Geopolitics of Integration' and the Imagination of South America," *Geopolitics* 16, no. 4 (2011): 846–864.

the idea that the political subjectivity within the present territorial border of a given community is not well sustainable and that "we" need to extrapolate "our" agency into a greater scale in order to become a truly significant actor in world history. Finally, the chapter adds a third metaphor: continentalism could be seen as a hyperbole of authenticity, giving us a geographical frame within which we can imagine national regeneration, restoration of "our" authenticity and the fight with corruptive foreign influences.

The chapter is structured accordingly. It starts with a general examination of Eurasianism as a continentalism, then it discusses the idea of "naturalness" embedded into this ideology, and rounds up the discussion by zooming in on three continentalist hyperboles: the hyperbole of development, the hyperbole of autonomy and the hyperbole of authenticity.

Defining Eurasian continentalism

Modern-day geographers and scholars of critical geopolitics are apt to raise our awareness about the constructed nature of geographical phenomena, including continents. What we take as the primary geographical convention, grounded on the visual representation of the map from our childhood, may have not much to do with the actually important divisions of the landmasses.[645] Fluidity and the constructed nature of continents informed continentalism with inescapable ambiguities: there could be not one but several competing versions of the same continent.

Speaking about Eurasianist continentalism in Russia, we have to take into consideration that fact that Europe and Asia are culturally located on the diametrically opposite poles of the geo-cultural universe; they are more distant than the New and the Old Worlds, for that matter.[646] This makes imagination of the continent Eurasia, whose very name suggests an oxymoron of sorts, especially difficult and versatile. We can identify three rhetorical iterations of Eurasianist continentalisms: 1) "third continent"; 2) "Greater Eurasia"; 3) anti-Western Eurasia (see Table 2).

---

645 Lewis and Wigen, *The Myth of Continents*.
646 Larry Wolff, *Inventing Eastern Europe*.

Table 2. Contours of Eurasia

	Third continent	Greater Eurasia	Anti-Western Eurasia
Territory	Former Russian Empire	Europe, Asia, Russia	Russia and Asia
Ideology	Classic Eurasianism	"Liberal" neo-Eurasianism	Conservative neo-Eurasianism
Ideologues	Savitskii	Nazarbaev	Dugin
Institutional basis	Eurasian Economic Union	SCO+BRICS+EAU	SCO

First, Eurasia is imaginable as a separate, "third," continent, hitherto neglected by geographers, as neither Europe nor Asia. The "third continent" was envisaged by classic Eurasianists of the 1920s[647] as a space roughly coinciding with the territory of the former Russian Empire. Today, this vision instigates imagining of the Eurasian Economic Union (EAU), an impressive integrationist project embracing such former Soviet Union republics as Russia, Belarus, Kazakhstan, Armenia and Kyrgyzstan. However, the EAU is rarely framed as a "third continent"; more often, the political leadership of the post-Soviet countries is speaking about the EAU as an initiative, central for the integration of the whole of "Greater Eurasia." The most probable reason why Savitskii's scientific ruminations do not sound convincing for today's policy-makers is that the latter adopted bits and pieces of Eurasianism "second-hand," mediated by the Duginite circles and textbooks in geopolitics, in which Eurasia is differently constructed.

The second version of Eurasian continentalism leans upon the canon of geopolitical thinking, explicated by Hartford MacKinder, for whom the gist of the world history is reduced to the struggle between the continental and the maritime powers, or more precisely, between the geographical "pivot of history," the Eurasian heartland, and the Atlantic nations. The implications of this theory for Russia would be to think of this country as a "metonymy," the

---

647 Mark Bassin, "Russia between Europe and Asia: The Ideological Construction of Geographical Space," *Slavic Review* 50, no. 1 (1991): 1–17.

condensation of Eurasia, its linchpin and "pivot." This vision caters to the "great-power" ambitions of the post-Soviet Russian intellectuals who are pleased to imagine Russia as being on the forefront of the global processes, vested with a special mission and responsibility to protect the whole of Eurasia from the encroachments of "Atlanticists."[648] Evoking Karl Haushofer's idea of a continental bloc,[649] this interpretation of Eurasia produces the vision of the continent as a unity of Asiatic nations, as well as Russia with its post-Soviet vassals, but also Germany and probably other West European countries, willing to slip away from the hegemony of "Atlanticists."[650] In this case, the image of "Greater Eurasia" puts together otherwise hardly commensurable entities — Europe and Asia, — by means of establishing a new antagonistic border between "us" and "them" (maritime "Atlanticists").

Finally, in the vast majority of practical attempts to imaginatively construct Eurasia, there is a tendency to exclude Western Europe and to juxtapose Eurasia to the EU. The EU in the past decades likewise tends towards re-interpreting itself into a continental integration project, within which the terms "EU" and "Europe" would sound interchangeably. So, Eurasian continentalism is in this sense a counterpart of the EU,[651] ideologically capitalizing on abundant anti-Western and anti-European sentiments in Russia. This anti-Western Eurasianism highlights the importance of a strategic alliance between Russia and China.[652] However, the lofty visions of Russia as the "holder" of the geographical pivot in charge of the whole of Eurasia have a hard landing when it

---

648 Konstantin Aksenov and M. Bassin, "Mackinder and the Heartland Theory in Post-Soviet Geopolitical Discourse," *Geopolitics* 11, no. 1 (2006): 99–118.
649 Karl Haushofer, *Der Kontinentalblock: Mitteleuropa – Eurasien – Japan* (München: Frz. Eher Nachf, 1941); Rafael García Pérez, "El proyecto continental del Tercer Reich," *Revista de estudios políticos* 87 (1995): 259–284.
650 Aleksandr Dugin, *Osnovy geopolitiki. Geopoliticheskoe budushchee Rossii* (Moscow: Arktogeia, 1997); Dugin, *Voina kontinentov: Sovremennyi mir v geopoliticheskoi sisteme koordinat* (Moscow: Akademicheskii proekt, 2015).
651 Richard Sakwa, "Eurasian Integration: A Project for the 21st Century?" in V. S. David Lane (ed.), *The Eurasian Project and Europe: Regional Discontinuities and Geopolitics* (New York: Palgrave Macmillan, 2015).
652 Piotr Dutkiewicz and R. Sakwa, *Eurasian Integration: The View from Within* (Abingdon, Oxon: Routledge, 2015).

comes down to practical diplomacy because, for China, Russia is not merely an economically "younger sister," but also a partner of secondary importance compared to, for example, the United States.[653]

"Naturalness"

Unlike other types of state's right-sizing and scale-enlarging, continentalism is grounded on what is seen as "natural" divisions of the world, substantiated by geography, geology, botany, zoology, soil science and so on. In contrast to, for example, the logic of the spheres of influence, based on the state's political will[654], continentalists emphatically stress "naturalness" of their claim, and raise it to a position of a law of nature. The idea of "naturalness" of continentalism implies that continent is the highest-order "natural" division of the earth's surface, above which is only the planet as a whole. By extension, a continent-state is the largest "naturally" possible state, surpassed only by a utopian world state. In practice, more often than not, continentalism exists in its softer versions as an ideology supporting some kind of political or economic unity on the continental scale, such as the African Union or NAFTA. Yet, as an ideological project, continentalism always encapsulates a teleological perspective that someday in the future a state and a continent will overlap.

After the centralized Muscovite state had established its dominance over the other appanage principalities, it embarked upon a determined policy of territorial expansion to the South and East. Consolidation of the Russian Empire under Peter I and his successors temporally coincided with the intensive crystallization of the West European self-identification by contrasting it to the "East."[655] So it happened that the most significant geographical dichotomy for the Western debates became "Europe" and "Asia," whereas the

---

653 Bobo Lo, *Russia and the New World Disorder* (London: Brookings Institution Press, 2015).
654 Susanna Hast, *Spheres of Influence in International Relations: History, Theory and Politics* (New York: Routledge, 2016).
655 Iver B. Neumann, *Uses of the Other*; Wolff, *Inventing Eastern Europe*.

Russian Empire was constructed as a political entity, which internalized this dichotomy. During Peter I's reign the Urals emerged as the internal Russian border separating Europe and Asia. This geographical duality promoted the self-image of Russia as a European power, possessing its own vast Asiatic colony beyond the Urals.[656]

This "mental map" of Russia was seriously attacked by the classic Slavophiles, who challenged the role of the "West" as an undisputable trendsetter for Russia, and radically — prefiguring much of the 20th century anti-colonial criticism — supported non-Western nations under the rule of the Europeans. A decade later Russia suffered the shocking defeat in the Crimean war, and soon its territory began to contract. In 1867 Alaska was sold to the United States, and in 1905 Russia lost territories in the Far East to Japan. The political leadership and intelligentsia developed a sense of Russia's territorial precariousness, expressed by the vision of Russia as a colossus on feet of clay. Two factors, territorial vulnerability and inadequacy of the 18th-century self-image as a European master of the Asiatic slaves, prodded intellectuals of the second half of the 19th century to advance argumentation, which would demonstrate some kind of "natural tie" between the Russian state and its territories.

Quoting from Herodotus, historian Sergei Solov'ev started his monumental *History of Russia from the Ancient Times* (1851–1879) with a remark that pre-historical East Slavic tribes lived in accordance with the nature of their territory. Even today, he argued, the Russian Empire, was "natural" or "organic," because it had attained its great dimensions not by aggression and conquest as other great empires of history, but, as he insisted, by organic growth and spreading of the nation on a landscape without natural barriers.[657] Written in 1851, these words gave a keynote to the teaching of Eurasianists, whose main thrust, as this chapter purports to substantiate, was to establish a "natural" link between Russia's political sovereignty and territory. It has never been an easy task because, unlike Western kingdoms, Russia's Southern and Eastern borders

---

656 Bassin, "Russia between Europe and Asia."
657 Bassin, "Turner, Solov'ev, and the 'Frontier Hypothesis', 473–511; Sergei Solov'ev, *Istoriia Rossii s drevneishikh vremen* (Moscow: Mysl', 1959 [1851]), vol. 1.

were open and moving for the greatest part of its history, as well as the political centers of the country gravitated to different geographical locations.[658]

Nikolai Danilevsky's *Russia and Europe* (1871) was another attempt to do so; his vision resembles the American "Manifest Destiny," for he argues that the vast plains on both sides of the Urals had never been populated by a developed statehood and civilization—it is as if these lands had been waiting for Russia to come and apprehend them. He also powerfully criticizes the geographical convention to see the Urals as the natural divide between Europe and Asia; in fact, he professes, these low hilly mountains do not represent any geographically distinctive landscape. The Urals connects both sides of Russia rather than divides them, so it is safe to say that there is a single, relatively homogenous gigantic landmass, latitudinally spread from the Baltic to the Pacific under the protective wings of the Russian tsar.[659]

By the end of the 19th century, pan-Slavism became a powerful ally of the "geographical" interpretation of the Russian political subjectivity. In principle, pan-Slavism looked in a different direction, striving for an ethno-national substantiation of the Russian Empire, but some of its representatives, most notably Vladimir Lamanskii, adduced a geographical argument as well. Lamanskii is known for his theory of the "three worlds of Europe–Asia," in which he identified a continent-scale landmass between Europe proper and Asia proper, which remains mostly (but not exclusively) under the Russian jurisdiction.[660] Veniamin Tian-Shanskii, professional geographer, developed a similar vision in 1915.

Thus, when the circle of Eurasianists coalesced in Prague in 1921, all necessary intellectual ingredients were in the bowl.[661] The

---

[658] Bassin, "Turner, Solov'ev, and the 'Frontier Hypothesis'"; Nicholas Breyfogle, A. Schrader, W. Sunderland, *Peopling the Russian Periphery: Borderland Colonization in Eurasian History* (London: Routledge, 2007); Michael Khodarkovsky, *Russia's Steppe Frontier* (Bloomington: Indiana University Press, 2002).
[659] Nikolai Danilevsky, *Rossiia i Evropa* (St Petersburg: Glagol, 1995[1871]): 13–31, 47–49
[660] Vladimir Lamanskii, *Geopolitika panslavianstva* (Moscow: Institute of the Russian Civilization, 2010).
[661] Marlène Laruelle, *Russian Eurasianism*.

most remarkable alignment of the Russian statehood with a geographical entity of the continental scale was done by Petr Savitskii, who put forward and diligently developed during the next decade the theory of Russia as a continent of sorts. Other Eurasianists, such as Vladimir Vernadskii and Konstantin Chkheidze, similarly paralleled Russia to the United States, insisting on Russia's status as a "state-continent."[662]

In his response of 1921 to Nikolai Trubetskoi's study *Europe and Humankind*, Savitskii indulged in scientific studies, designed to prove the unity and homogeneity of the Russian "continent" in terms of climate, soil, geology, flora, etc. He pointed at the three greatplains—Russian, Siberian and Turkestan—which geographically constitute a single unified flat space, whose mean temperatures, average precipitations and other climatic parameters are sharply distinct from those of Europe and Asia. Savitskii extensively discusses conspicuous coincidences between the state borders of the Russian Empire as of 1914 and the low isothermal lines of January, as well as the huge oscillation amplitude of summer and winter temperatures. He further argues that the broad belt of black earth also connects cis- and trans-Ural lands. The same could be said about trans-Eurasian belts of taiga and tundra. All in all, "Russia, in terms of its spatial scale and geography, homogenous in all its parts and at the same time different from its neighbors, is a 'continent in itself'."[663] As follows from this passage, Savitskii inferred the political unity of Eurasia from its "natural," scientifically proven unity as a continent, separated from other continents not by spurious visual markers, but by solid facts, obtained from natural sciences.

In its extreme case, the "naturalness" of continentalism is observable in the theory of contemporary geopolitical theorist Vladimir Dergachev, who paralleled continents as cultural and political entities with tectonic plates, and aligned clashes of civilizations with the interactions of the tectonic plates: convergency,

---

662 Iury Gladkii, *Rossiia v labirintakh geograficheskoi sud'by* (St Petersburg: Izd-vo Aslanova, 2006): 505; Konstantin Chkheidze, "Liga natsii i gosudarstva-materiki," [1927], available at: http://www.politnauka.org/library/mpimo/chh.php.
663 Petr Saviskii, *Izbrannoe* (Moscow: ROSSPEN, 2010): 108.

divergency or transformism.[664] Aleksandr Prokhanov echoed these metaphors on the pages of the central Russian daily newspaper *Izvestiia*. He speculated about the reasons for the resilience of Eurasia, which in spite of wars and revolutions, repeatedly re-collected inself as a single state: "We can assume that this is the specificity of the tectonic plates, mountain ridges, rivers and winds ... in Eurasia."[665] Indeed, the reduction of the political to the "natural" is at the heart of continentalism. People cannot change the continent or a tectonic plate for that matter, people can only belong to it.

"Naturalness" of continentalisms competes with "historicality," lying behind other types of right-sizing. The most obvious rival to the idea of continent is the concept of a "civilization," which has enjoyed a resounding success in post-Soviet Russia.[666] Besides, in post-2014 Russian political discourses, Eurasianism as a continentalist doctrine is confronted with a powerful newcomer — the "Russian world" ideology, usually framed in "civilizational" terms. Speaking about interrelationship of these two ideologies, one can observe a recent tendency towards convergence. On the one hand, the "Russian world" is being reinterpreted in geographical rather than cultural terms so that it tends to designate the geopolitical sphere of presence and influence of Russia on the post-Soviet space.[667] On the other hand, Eurasianists have displayed a willingness to see Eurasia as by and large a civilizational community under the guidance of the Russians.[668] Thus, "naturalness" of the Eurasian imagery tends to merge together with "culturedness" of the "Russian world" project.

---

664 Dergachev, *Geopolitika*.
665 Aleksandr Prokhanov, "Zolotye bogini Evrazii," *Izvestiia*, 2 June 2014.
666 Fabian Linde, "The Civilizational Turn in Russian Political Discourse: From Pan-Europeanism to Civilizational Distinctiveness," *The Russian Review*, 75, no. 4 (2016): 604–625; Jutta Scherrer, *Kulturologie: Russland auf der Suche nach einer zivilisatorischen Identität* (Göttingen: Wallstein Verlag, 2003); Andrei Tsygankov, "Crafting the State-Civilization Vladimir Putin's Turn to Distinct Values," *Problems of Post-Communism* 63, no. 3 (2016): 146–158.
667 See chapters 7 and 8 in this volume.
668 Irina Kotkina, "Geopolitical Imagination and Popular Geopolitics, between the Eurasian Union and Russkii Mir," in M. Bassin and G. Pozo-Martin (eds.), *The Politics of Eurasianism: Identity, Popular Culture and Russia's Foreign Policy*.

This controversy between Eurasianism and the "Russian world" imagery shows that the idea of "naturalness" is seriously contested and thus requires additional rhetorical and ideological efforts to substantiate it. In the following paragraph we will discuss the hyperbole of development, one of the metaphors which necessarily supplement and accompany the "organic" argument of continentalism.

Hyperbole of development

Savitskii was arguably the first to explore the meaning of the continent as a springboard for development. In his oft-quoted essay of 1921 "Continent-Ocean," he advanced a pack of economic implications of seeing Eurasia as a third continent. Savitskii leaned upon statistics of the transaction costs for transportation by land and by sea, arguing that in foreseeable future, maritime trade routes would retain a crucial edge over land-based routes. This means that continental countries were doomed to lag behind sea powers in terms of economic competitiveness. Savitskii contemplates the possibility of eliminating this inherent disadvantage by isolating continental powers from the international, sea-based, economy.[669] Continuing this line of argumentation, Savitskii criticizes the decision of the tsarist government to acquire an outlet to the world ocean in the Far East. Those who ordered the construction of Dal'nii (now Dalian in China) had not understood, according to Savitskii, that the actual ocean was lying not in front of them on the seas, but behind their backs, in Russian lands, which was the ocean-continent of Eurasia.[670]

As a springboard of economic growth, continentalism is intimately connected with precariousness and weakness; indeed, somewhat counter intuitively we can call continentalism the weapon of the weak.[671] This aspect is already present in Savitskii's

---

669 Saviskii, *Izbrannoe*, 146.
670 Saviskii, *Izbrannoe*, 155.
671 Rivarola Puntigliano, "'Geopolitics of Integration'and the Imagination of South America"; Rivarola Puntigliano, "21st Century Geopolitics: Integration and

analysis of the continent-ocean as a naturally disadvantaged region, seeking to minimize its economic disadvantages by consolidating the intra-continental common market. As a "geopolitics of the weak," continentalism emerged powerfully and concomitantly among post-colonial integrationist movements in Africa and Latin America.[672]

As a "weapon of the weak" continentalism contains a tinge of the absurd; indeed, it sounds illogical that for boosting the development, a country would unite not with the strong and successful but with other weak and failed states. This absurdism of continentalist projects has been explored by a number of critics of Eurasianism, who pointed exactly at the inability to generate growth by applying the Eurasian continental scale to Russia's development. As a cinematic critical commentary of Eurasianism as a developmental project, let us consider the extravagant comedy film *Europe-Asia* (2008) by Ivan Dykhovichnyi. In this film the continental ambition of Russia is ridiculed for the utter inability to make sense of and to cope with this vast space, inherited from her imperial predecessors. The film depicts a meandering minor road in the woods of the Urals, traversing the symbolic border between Europe and Asia, where one loathsome temporary obelisk stands and another one is in the scaffoldings, being constructed by intoxicated workers. A group of fraudsters pretending to be celebrating a wedding near the obelisk, stop occasional travelers (a businessman in an expensive German car, a policeman, the Hungarian crew from the a crashed plane, Chinese petty traders on bicycles, a political agitator, a tourist bus with Americans, etc.), and extort money from them, but in the final scenes both the swindlers and their victims indulge in an orgy of hard drinking, hallucinations and dramatic

---

Development in the Age of 'Continental States'," *Territory, Politics, Governance* 5, no. 4 (2017): 1–17.
672 Fongot K.-Y. Kinni, *Pan-Africanism: Political Philosophy and Socio-Economic Anthropology for African Liberation and Governance: Caribbean and African American Contributions* (Bamenda: Langaa, 2015); Chris Landsberg, "Afro-Continentalism: Pan-Africanism in Post-Settlement South Africa's Foreign Policy," *Journal of Asian and African Studies* 47, no. 4 (2012): 436–448; Maano Ramutsindela, "Gaddafi, Continentalism and Sovereignty in Africa," *South African Geographical Journal* 91, no. 1 (2009): 1–3.

confessions. One of the inebriated protagonists intimates: "How can a man live, if his one leg is in Asia and another is in Europe? Where are his balls, then? (*everyone laughs*) Where is his brain and the rest of the body?"673

The film's symbolism reminds us of the tradition, especially salient in the late Soviet period, to erect monuments on the Europe-Asia border.674 Whereas imperial geography internalized the continental border for the purpose of arguing that Russia is a European power with Asiatic colonies, the "Europe-Asia" monuments of the Soviet Union symbolically projected its power and ideological influence on both continents. In the Soviet Union—the country whose very name avoids geographical allusions—maintenance of the geographical tradition of seeing the Urals as a divide between the continents emphasized universalism of the communist ideology and the lack of "natural" borders of the USSR. As the film *Europe-Asia* shows, present-day Russia's striving to span two continents smacks of absurdity and hallucination. It projects powerful irony against the hyperbole of development, perfectly amplified by Vladimir Iakunin's bombastic project.

Indeed, Iakunin's Eurasianist project is in a sense an extended response to the vision of Russia's Eurasian (failed) mission as Dykhovichnyi depicted it. Iakunin, an influential political figure during Putin's presidency and the long-term head of the Russian Railways (2005–2015), recently came up with a brand-new continentalism, called "Trans-Eurasian Project *Razvitie*"" (TEPR), which he propagated on many occasions such as the BRICS meetings and academic events.675 Iakunin has long been one of the major suppliers of the civilizational rhetoric on the Russian political horizon. Since 2002 he has been sponsoring the international forum for the Rhodes Island *The Dialogue of Civilizations*. In 2016, he founded a

---

673 Film *Evropa-Aziia* (2008), directed by Dmitry Dykhovichnyi.
674 A well-illustrated essay on "Europe-Asia" obelisks in the Urals is available here: http://ural-n.ru/p/obeliski-evropa-asia.html.
675 "V Ufe sostoialos' zasedanie delovogo soveta BRICS," July 8, 2015, available at: http://brics2015.ru/news/20150708/300825.html; "O zadachakh dlia nauki v proekte TEPR," March 13, 2014, available at: http://www.ras.ru/digest/show dnews.aspx?id=79ea6259-89b2-472d-964f-8c1fa34ba7eb.

research institution in Berlin with the same name and mission to facilitate "cooperation and partnership between civilizations."[676] TEPR is an attempt to align civilizationism and continentalism within the image of Great Eurasia. Iakunin pontificates that Russia should lead the integration process on the continent as a "state-civilization," capable of fostering unity and solidarity among neighboring civilizations of the continent.[677] Iakunin's project features the world map with four geo-economic zones: the Euro-Atlantic zone with the US and Western Europe as its major drivers, the Far Eastern zone (China, Japan, South Korea), Latin America and Africa. Iakunin draws the contours of the fifth, Eurasian zone, as an elongated oval, stretched approximately from the Adriatic Sea to the Okhotsk Sea, and embracing the most part of Russia, Central Asia, Eastern Europe, and probably also Mongolia, Northern China, Northern Iran and Turkey. This fifth zone is the Eurasian heartland, which, due to its latitudinal stretch between two oceans, comes in contact with all Eurasian "civilizations," be it China, Iran, India, Western Europe, Japan, or the Arab world.

The central idea for Iakunin is the difference between the concept of "growth" as quantitative increment and the concept of "development" as a qualitative change. Further on, he claims that the English word "development" does not reflect his understanding of the term, proposing to use the transliterated Russian word "*razvitie*," which in his vision, is more than just an economic category, because it implies also "spiritual and moral perfection of society." In somewhat esoteric language he insists that we "need to think in terms of *Razvitie* beyond economics" (*neobkhodimo nadekonomicheskoe myshlenie Razvitiem*), which would "restore Russia's [political] subjectivity as a state-civilization."[678] So TERP, in his words, is the way to incorporate the idea of super-economic, "moral and spiritual" development into the project of the Eurasian integration.[679]

---

676 https://doc-research.org/en/about-us/.
677 Vladimir Iakunin, "Integral'nyi proekt solidarnogo razvitiia na Evro-Asiatskom kontinente," March 11, 2014, available at: http://www.isprras.ru/pics/File/books%20-%2014/JAKUNIN-LAST.pdf.
678 Iakunin, "Integral'nyi proekt," 14–15.
679 Iakunin, "Integral'nyi proekt," 14–16.

Iakunin contextualizes TERP as one of Russia's "mega-projects." He establishes genealogy for his project by arguing that "development by mega-projects" is hardwired into the history of Russia with such iterations as the Medieval Orthodox Messianism (i.e. "Moscow as the Third Rome"), Peter I's sweeping Europeanization, and communist overhaul of the entire country.[680] Continuing this train of thought, Iakunin suggests that TERP be another "geo-economic, geopolitical and geo-cultural" mega-project, grounded in the Eurasianist worldview and principles of the "dialogue of civilizations." In the long run, he maintains, TERP would become a new center of global growth not only economically but also in terms of culture and morals. It is not entirely clear how Iakunin envisages the practical side of the project, but we have a few pointers in his report to assume that the key link is the infrastructural reconstruction, which would entail the creation of the belt some 300 kilometers in breadth crossing Eurasia on the latitude of the existing Trans-Siberian railway. In Iakunin's dream, this trans-continental "belt of development" incorporates other kinds of thruways, pipelines, concomitant industries and urban centers, as well as 25 million new working places and several dozens of trillions of Euro in investment.[681] Finally, TERP will become the global "future-zone," the point of growth on a planetary scale, which would usher into the world the new post- and re-industrial revolution. Elsewhere, Iakunin relates his ideas about the continent of development to the vision of "Greater Eurasia ... awakened from a hundred years of sleeping" thanks to the Chinese economic surge.[682]

In line with Iakunin's ruminations, the advocacy book by Evgeny Vinokurov and Alexander Libman maintains that "Eurasian continental integration could become a key developmental force" by means of unification of infrastructures and national

---

680 Iakunin, "Integral'nyi proekt," 16.
681 Iakunin, "Integral'nyi proekt," 25.
682 Nazira Kozhanova, "Astana Club discusses Eurasian region's role in future of global security," *The Astana Times*, November 12, 2019, available at: https://astanatimes.com/2019/11/astana-club-discusses-eurasian-regions-role-in-future-of-global-security/.

markets.[683] Iakunin's TERP is a rich coalescence of the most prominent ideological blocks characteristic of the country under Putin: it is Eurasianism, the language of "etnogenez," couched in Lev Gumilev's terms, classic realist geopolitics, Russian "cosmism," infatuation with mega-projects such as the Sochi Olympic Games of 2014, rhetoric of civilizations, and Slavophilism.[684] The logic of the continental integration by means of the belt of development parallels the examination of the role of the Eurasian steppe in Savitskii's writings. Iakunin's infrastructural belt and Savitskii's steppe roughly coincide visually, suggesting that by virtue of some kind of already given, "natural" quality of this region it is predestined to play the role of the integrator of Eurasia as a whole. In continuation with Iakunin's TEPR project, "Russian Railways" announced the construction of the high-speed railroad with the name "Eurasia" from Urumchi in China to Berlin, which is expected to be finished in 2026.[685]

Iakunin, who was the uncrowned king of the Russian railways for a decade, shrewdly revamped Savitskii by pointing at the "already given" infrastructural mega-project, the Trans-Siberian railroad as a "natural" precondition for the unity of the continent.[686]

---

683 Evgeny Vinokurov and A. Libman, *Eurasian Integration: Challenges of Transcontinental Regionalism* (Basingstoke: Palgrave Macmillan, 2012): 1–2. Vinokurov is the director of the Center for Integration Studies of the Eurasian Development Bank (EDB). Established in 2006 by the decision of Nursultan Nazarbaev, the President of Kazakhstan, EDB identifies its mission as a "support of integration in Eurasia" (https://eabr.org/en/about/).

684 Notably, Iakunin refers to Sergei Sharapov, who in the late 19th century came up with the proposal to build Trans-Siberian railway by means of the "paper ruble," that is freely minted currency, secured by the absolute power of the Russian tsar and by the expected future labor, which "paper rubles" would evoke (Mikhail Suslov, "The Lost Chance of Conservative Modernization: S.F. Sharapov in the Economic Debates of the Late Nineteenth to the Early Twentieth Century," *Acta Slavica Iaponica* 31 (2012): 31–54).

685 Sergei Kudiiarov, "Zamakh na trilliony," *Ekspert* 36, no. 1042 (2017). See also information about this project on the webpage of the Russian Railways: http://www.hsrail.ru/info/silkway/. Since 2017, there is no information about the progress of this project.

686 Cf. Trans-Siberian railroad will spur up the "inevitable process of economic collaboration and international integration of the states in Eurasia" (Sergei Tiurin, "Evraziiskii mnogougol'nik," *Torgovo-promyshlennye vedomosti*, September 8, 2014).

Unlike Savitskii, however, Iakunin's vision of Eurasia is a mixture of "liberal" and Duginite neo-Eurasianisms; he sees it as "Great Eurasia," a home to several civilizations, but in his criticism of the Western globalization, he tends to exclude Western Europe from his integrationist projects.

Hyperbole of autonomy

Continentalism as a hyperbole of development, discussed in the previous paragraph, is subject to powerful criticism and irony. Dykhovichnyi's film is one example; Vladislav Inozemtsev's article with the telling title "Eurasian Economic Union: Lost in Space"[687] is another. Today, continentalism capitalizes not so much on the tropes of development, but rather it becomes an ideological excrescence on the debates about security and sovereignty. Indeed, a union with a weak partner promises fewer possibilities to lose one's independence than a union with a strong ally. This issue did not attract much attention of the Eurasianists in the 1920s and became fully studied by their epigones in the post-Soviet decades. Today's Russian proponents of Eurasian continentalism draw heavily on the works of German theorists of geopolitics, especially Karl Haushofer, Carl Schmitt and Jordis von Lohausen, whose works were abundantly popularized, quoted and translated into Russian.[688]

Schmitt, who advanced the concept of *Großraum* ("large space"), is understandably the most interesting of them. Schmitt himself did not emphasize the continental dimension of a *Großraum* but he definitely had it in mind when he took the Monroe Doctrine as an early embodiment of his theory. Schmitt praised this doctrine for "decisionism" and non-universalism; namely, he pointed at the U.S. right to interpret the doctrine as it wished, and on the connection between a specific legal and political regime, established by the

---

[687] Vladislav Inozemtsev, "Evraziiskii Ekonomicheskii Soiuz: Poteriannye v prostranstve," *Polis*, no. 6 (2014): 71–82.
[688] Oleg Aronson, "Übersetzung und Politik. Carl Schmitt im heutigen Russland," in C. Engel and B. Menzel (eds.), *Kultur und/als Übersetzung. Russisch-deutsche Beziehungen im 20. Und 21. Jahrhundert* (Berlin: Frank&Timme, 2011): 57–76.

Monroe Doctrine, and the space of some specific quality—the American continent, the western hemisphere.[689] For Schmitt, *Großraum* signified the situation of exemption of some, relatively homogenous, territory from the universal legal norms.

Today, continentalist thinking is strategically allied with the conservative and religious communitarianism, which proposes Schmitt's vision of *Großräume* as an alternative to globalization.[690] These spaces should be large enough to sustain political subjectivity vis-à-vis the "Empire" (in Hardt and Negri's terms). The unity of "large spaces" is grounded on common cultural traditions and relations among kindred peoples.

Schmitt's thinking exerted crucial influence on the post-Soviet civilizationism and the official "sovereign democracy" doctrine, theorized by the Kremlin's chief ideologist between 2003 and 2011 Vladislav Surkov.[691] The ideological thread running through various visions of Eurasia as a "civilization" consists in the striving to exclude this territory from the internationally accepted model of the politics, and thereby to outlaw all possibilities of external interference into the Russian affairs. The vision of Eurasia as a community of common values was entertained already by the classic Eurasianists, who spoke about "brotherhood" and natural affinity among the Eurasian nations or even insisted on the existence of the

---

[689] William Hooker, *Carl Schmitt's International Thought: Order and Orientation* (Cambridge: Cambridge University Press, 2009); Claudio Minca and R. Rowan, "The Question of Space in Carl Schmitt," *Progress in Human Geography* 39, no. 3 (2015): 268–289; Rüdiger Voigt (ed.), *Großraum-Denken: Carl Schmitts Kategorie der Großraumordnung* (Stuttgart: Steiner, 2008).

[690] John Milbank and A. Pabst, *The Politics of Virtue: Post-Liberalism and the Human Future* (London; New York: Rowman and Littlefield, 2016); David Morrice, "The Liberal-Communitarian Debate in Contemporary Political Philosophy and Its Significance for International Relations," *Review of International Studies* 26, no. 2 (2000): 233–251; Michael Walzer, "The Moral Standing of States: A Response to Four Critics," *Philosophy and Public Affairs* 9, no. 3 (1980): 209–229.

[691] Ulrich Schmid, *Technologien der Seele: Vom Verfertigen der Wahrheit in der russischen Gegenwartskultur* (Frankfurt: Suhrkamp, 2015): 99–106; Gulnaz Sharafutdinova, "The Pussy Riot Affair and Putin's Démarche from Sovereign Democracy to Sovereign Morality," *Nationalities Papers* 42, no. 4 (2014): 615–621; Vladislav Surkov, *Suverenitet—eto politicheskii sinonim konkurentosposobnosti* (Moscow: Lenand, 2006).

single, multi-ethnic Eurasian nation.[692] Lev Gumilev's theory of *etnogenez* gave a new language with which to express this idea. His followers elaborate on the "complementarity" of the Eurasian ethnic communities.[693] Trying to figure out what exactly makes these peoples "complementary," Aleksandr Dugin referred to Schmitt's distinction between the continental and maritime nations.[694] For Schmitt, this distinction was a matter of morality, because the attachment to solid land, the necessity to establish a certain order in dividing lands for the purpose of their economic exploitation, requires some kind of moral fixity, whereas life on the seas fosters moral relativism and laxity. At the end of the day, and with the immense contribution from Dugin, the Eurasian community came to be seen as a community of moral traditionalism. This interpretation emerged at the right moment, when, during Putin's third term in power, the political leadership aligned itself with the ideology of conservatism and discourses of the traditional values.[695]

Conservative conceptualizations of the ongoing Eurasian integration processes generally follow the *Großraum*'s exceptionalism as well. For example, the conservative webpage "Russian idea," supported by the pro-Kremlin think tank *Institute for Socio-Economic and Political Studies* acclaimed the emergence of a new "macro-region" of the continental proportion "Central Eurasia," which includes Russia, China and Central Asian republics—basically all actors within the Shanghai Cooperation Organization (SCO). Oleg Barabanov, one of the coordinators of the Valdai discussion club, pointed to the common values shared by partners of SCO: "defense of sovereignty, defense of the development (sic!), and rights on our own civilizational choice."[696]

---

692 Nikolai Trubetskoi, *Izbrannoe* (Moscow: ROSSPEN, 2010), 457–459.
693 Bassin, *The Gumilev Mystique: Biopolitics, Eurasianism, and the Construction of Community in Modern Russia* (Ithaca: Cornell University Press, 2016).
694 Dugin, *Osnovy geopolitiki*.
695 Marcel van Herpen, *Putin's Propaganda Machine: Soft Power and Russian Foreign Policy* (Lanham: Rowman&Littlefield, 2016).
696 Oleg Barabanov, "Kornevoi strukturoi makroregiona Tsentral'noi Evrazii logichno iavlaietsia ShOS," 2015, available at: http://politconservatism.ru/interview/kornevoy-strukturoy-makroregiona-tsentralnoy-evrazii-logichno-y avlyaetsya-shos.

Traditionalism and the "complementarity" of the Eurasian nations were thoroughly examined in the alternative history book project by Khol'm van Zaichik (Viacheslav Rybakov and Igor Alimov), entitled *Eurasian Symphony*.[697] The similar interpretation of Eurasian continental unity is presented in the film *The Mongol* (2007) by Sergei Bodrov (Sr). The film, branded as a box-office hit, shows a period in the life of Genghis Khan before he conquered Eurasia. It features his romantic relationship, hardships in captivity, and struggle with other Mongol khans for ascendance. The film not only extols Genghis Khan for his political wisdoms but also shows unexpected aspects of his life as a loving and caring head of the family, faithful to his wife, protective to children, and always prioritizing the family over everything else in life. Striving for the political unity of his people, respectful to religion and always leaning on the traditions, on what the ancestors said and did, Genghis Khan emerges before our eyes as an ideal ruler of today's Russia. Different in representing the role of China in Eurasia (in *The Mongol* the Chinese, or to be more specific, the Tanguts, are portrayed as a decadent refined society), Bodrov and Khol'm van Zaichik concur in the vision of Eurasia as a locus of healthy traditionalism, benevolent authoritarianism and youthful militarism, — as a *Großraum*, exempted from the universal tendencies towards hedonism, mercantilism, and indulging human weaknesses.

Here the state of exemption is aligned with the conservative, or rather, palingenetic project of restoration, regeneration of the imaginary bygone past. So, continentalism as a hyperbole of autonomy is interlinked with the hyperbole of authenticity.

Hyperbole of authenticity

Various types of right-sizing the state serve the Romantic quest for lost ties with the nation's past. Reconnection with the authentic "soil" requires specific spatial imagery of this soil, which would embrace lost "cradles" of the political body (such as Serbia's relation to Kosovo, or Russia's to Kiev). Here I will argue that enlarging

---

697 See more on Eurasian Symphony in Chapter 7 in this volume.

the territorial scale can serve the same purpose, so that Eurasian continentalism emerges as a palingenetic ideology of sorts, calling for a nation to come back to its natural home, which is the whole continent. Here the hyperbole of authenticity rounds up the argument about continentalism as an organic tie between a state and a continent.

This palingenetic thrust is observable already in early Eurasianists, especially Nikolai Trubetskoy and George Vernadskii, who entertained an idea of Genghis Khan as a founding father of the Russian continental state. In sharp, even scandalous divergence from the historiographical orthodoxy, these intellectuals argued that the Empire of Mongols was historically first power of the continental scale in Eurasia, and Russia was lucky enough to bequeath this sense of continental dimension from the Golden Horde. The Russian state, which emerged from the crumbling blocks of the Empire of Mongols, "intuitively strove to restore this disrupted unity" of Eurasia.[698] Reimagining itself as a continent and restoring its unity means for Russia to come back to where it historically belongs: the great Eurasian steppe.

This continental comeback has a deep cultural meaning too, informed with the theory of Lev Gumilev, whose grip over public discourse and grassroots' opinion has been steadily growing in post-Soviet Russia. In a nutshell, Gumilev's theory of passionarity further develops the concept of place-development (*mestorazvitie*) by Savitskii. Gumilev firmly believed that there was an intimate relation between specific environmental factors and "etnogenez"; the development of an ethnos. He explicated his vision of a special vital energy in nations—*passionarnost'*, which emanates from the sun and randomly strikes an ethnos or a group of them, energizing them and causing an explosion-like expansionism and state-building. The most salient example for Gumilev was exactly the Mongols of the 13th century, whose *passionarnost'* was so blasting that it made this numerically insignificant and culturally backward nation the masters of Eurasia.

---

698 Trubetskoi, *The Legacy of Genghis Khan and Other Essays on Russia's Identity* (Ann Arbor: Michigan Slavic Publications, 1991).

Gumilevian *mestorazvitie* is at the center of the cinematic co-production between the crumbling Soviet Union and France *Urga: The Territory of Love* (aka *Close to Eden*, 1990). Directed by Nikita Mikhalkov, today one of the most vocal pro-Kremlin conservative ideologists, the film focalizes on the unnaturalness and non-organic character of the Western civilization in the Eurasian steppes. A cattle farmer is pressed to live an unauthentic life, in which he cannot make love to his wife because of the birth-control policies, in which he swaps horses for a bicycle, useless in the open fields, and watches television, displaying how feather grass waves in wind — as an absurdist substitution of the real life around him by a virtual projection on the screen. In a dream, the protagonist sees Genghis Khan with a retinue, suddenly emerging on the horizon, who orders to smash the TV set and asks: "Are you a Mongol? So where is your weapon? Where are your horses?"

In post-Soviet Russia, the rhetoric of continentalism, Eurasianism, authenticity and *passionarnost'* merge into a single tangle of images, according to which "going continental" implies also a move back to the roots and a kind of energizing and rejuvenation. This vision was elaborated in the film *The Target* (2011) by Aleksandr Zel'dovich (screenwriters Zel'dovich and popular writer Vladimir Sorokin). Sorokin is known for his creative engagement and ironic games with bits and pieces of the Russian conservative ideology, Eurasianism, *passionarnost'* and the like (cf. his recent book *Telluria*, 2013), and *The Target* is no exception. It portrays Russia of the nearest future, 2020, as a continental bridge, connecting Eurasia by the stunning engineering mega-project, the speedway Paris–Guangzhou. As one of the film's protagonists says: "This is not just a road, this is the blood system of the continent."[699] Russia in the film is thoroughly Sinicized, with its elite speaking fluent Chinese, donning traditional Chinese dresses, consuming Chinese food and doing business mostly with the Chinese.

The film revolves around "the target" — a cyclopean Soviet-era military construction somewhere in the Altai, designed to catch the energy of cosmos, the energy of vacuum. People who stay there,

---

699 Film *Mishen'* (2011), directed by Aleksandr Zel'dovich.

stop aging, they become mysteriously energized, adventurous, entrepreneurial, sexually insatiable, aggressive—basically "the target" serves as an illustration to Gumilev's vision of the cosmic energy of *passionarnost'*. Cinematic visualization of "the target" rings the bell too; the scenery features immense, sparsely populated, barren high-altitude plains under the clear sky, where, as we learn from the film, there is almost no precipitation, and where protagonists freeze at night and sweat during the day. This is fairly much an illustration to Savitskii's exposition of the "third continent," characterized by the flat woodless landscape, low precipitation, and a huge temperature interval.[700] So, the film masterfully forges together various continentalist images with the idea of "passionarity" and rejuvenation.

Conclusions

Russia's territorial dimensions as a contiguous empire, which at the apex of its expansion spanned 24 million square kilometers, its relative economic isolation and troubled relations with the West, made continentalism a logical way to image this country geopolitically. The "scientific" implications of continentalism rendered it especially applicable at times of the country's actual or imagined political weakening and precariousness. At these moments, be it the post-imperial or post-Soviet years, Eurasian continentalism offered "natural" legitimations for Russia's territorial possessions. The ideological meaning of various continentalist visions of Eurasia can have liberatory, anti-colonial and developmentalist aspects, which highlight the idea of the Eurasian solidarity vis-à-vis Western colonial masters. However, due to its connection with the Russian imperial legacy, Eurasian continentalism tends towards conservative, palingenetic moral exceptionalism in the spirit of Schmittean's *Großraum* and Mackinderian geopolitics.

---

700 Saviskii, *Izbrannoe*.

7 *Eurasian Symphony:* Geopolitical Imagination and Alternative History

Introduction

"Igor' Aleksandrovich! At the last census of population [in 2010] I indicated my nationality as 'Ordussian')))))) What is your attitude [to this] and how shall I live with this now)))))))))."[701] This was one of the questions, addressed to Sinologist and writer of Science Fiction (SF) Igor' Alimov at the internet-conference in October 2010. The fictitious nationality "Ordussian" refers to the literary franchise *Eurasian Symphony*, authored by Alimov and Viacheslav Rybakov under a collective pen-name "Khol'm van Zaichik." The series of seven books published between 2000 and 2005 describes a vast Eurasian power called Ordus', which in the alternative historical setting was formed in the 13th century from the Golden Horde (*Orda*, in Russian) and ancient Russia (*Rus'*, hence—"Ordus'"). The question from a person, who five years after this literary project was closed, still identifies herself with imaginary Ordus' to an extent that the made up nationality "Ordussian" would appear in the official papers of the national census, gives a keynote to the study on the intersection of the geopolitical fantasy and "real" politics.

Eurasian Symphony is seen here as both a diagnosis of today's Russian society and the instrument of its reproduction. As its authors mention elsewhere, the universe of Ordus' is the intellectual experiment of mastering forces of globalization, making sense of them; it is an attempt to contemplate a globalized world in which Russia—however this political entity is defined—continues to occupy an honorary—perhaps even primary—place, having successfully overcome problems characteristic of the present day reality.[702] In this sense, analyzing *Eurasian Symphony* is like doing a (dis)section of the Putin-era geopolitical culture, which exposes

---

701 http://www.piteropen.ru/conference/alimov.html. Original orthography.
702 Khol'm van Zaichik (Rybakov and I. Alimov), *Delo nezalezhnykh dervishei* (St Petersburg: Azbuka, 2001): 6; Zaichik, *Delo sud'i Di* (St Petersburg: Azbuka, 2003): 6.

contemporary dreams, fears, ideological nodal points, emotional tensions and hopes of the millions of the Russians. This dissection shows us some ideational tracks, on which the Russian society in the period of Putin's third presidency smoothly glided into the annexation of Crimea, the war in Donbas and confrontation with the West.

Viacheslav Rybakov maintains that *Eurasian Symphony* should not be seen as an ideal world, but rather as a method of attaching stereotypes and false assumptions on which our society is based.[703] This could be quite correct for the pivotal time on the turn of the 1990s into the 2000s when the franchise was conceived. Today, however, *Eurasian Symphony* reads as a political manifesto, or — to put it in terms suited to the authors — as a *pinying*, a reigning motto of the post-Yeltsin's decade and a half, which condenses preoccupation with geopolitics, antagonizing the West, securitization of the national identity, preoccupation with religion and faith, buttressing family values, castigating Ukraine, rapprochement with China and so forth. Indeed, many observers and Rybakov and Alimov themselves recognized that *Eurasian Symphony* had anticipated ("prophesied") many subsequent developments in Russian politics. Similarly to Vladimir Sorokin's anti-utopian prognostication in *Day of the Oprichnik* (2006), *The Sugar Kremlin* (2008) or in the recent futuristic video clip by punk-rock band *Leningrad* "Nikola" (2014), *Eurasian Symphony* astutely grasped the tendencies.[704] But, unlike the sarcastic gloom of liberal intellectuals, Rybakov and Alimov produced an optimistic fiction — a true utopia, which now has all grounds to reap its laurels.[705]

---

703 From the private correspondence, October 5, 2015.
704 https://www.youtube.com/watch?v=iV76RsmUag8.
705 Cf. their statement "we are fed up with anti-utopias." Viacheslav Rybakov, *Napriamuiu* (St Petersburg: Limbus Press, 2008): 46; Rybakov and Igor' Alimov, "Voprosy, chasto zadavaemye perevodchikam i ikh konsul'tantam," *FANtastika* 10 (2008): 97.

Emplotment and enjoyment in alternative history

Iskander Ismailov, PhD, professional historian from Kazan' reflects in this way on *Eurasian Symphony:*

> Reading these novels, you see that we lost an opportunity to create such a huge Eurasian empire, a state which would have been even bigger and more powerful than Russia ... There would have been neither xenophobia, nor [classifying] into "persons of Caucasian nationality" [*litso kavkazskoi natsional'nosti*]' ... There would have been no internal conflicts, no separatism, no religious intolerance ...[706]

This paper sees *Eurasian Symphony* as a dialogue between authors' geopolitical projects and the readers' visions and expectations. The genre of utopia has historically developed different strategies of engaging the audience and producing pleasure from its consumption,[707] beginning from a philosophical dialogue in its canonic masterpieces such as Thomas More's *Utopia* (1516) or Tommaso Campanella's *The City of the Sun* (1623), continuing in the form of a utopian romance such as Edward Bellamy's *Looking Backward, 2000–1887* (1888) and William Morris's *News from Nowhere* (1890), and later in the 20th century resulting in the "ambiguous utopias" by Ursula Le Guin and brothers Strugatskies.[708] An intellectual exercise of social critique in classic utopias was replaced by novelistic devices, which provided readers with a hero from our time and place with whom it was easy to identify in their exploration of a utopian terrain. The tension keeping the audience's attention was here between the present everyday life and the utopian alternative world. In contrast to this, "ambiguous utopias" of the 20th century attract readers' interest by staging the tension between a *utopian* protagonist and a *utopian* setting, which has been so successfully tested in a number of anti-utopian novels starting from Yevgeni Zamiatin's paradigmatic *We* (1920) to writings of brothers Strugatskies.

---

706 Aleksandr Gavrilenko, "Tatarskoe igo—bylo ili ne bylo?" *Elita Tatarstana: Kazan'*, June 3, 2011, available at: http://elitat.ru/society/tatarskoe-igo-bylo-ili-ne-bylo/.
707 Fitting, "Utopian Effect/Utopian Pleasure," *Utopian Studies* 4 (1991).
708 Suvin, "Locus, Horizon, and Orientation", 78.

In terms of the methods of emplotment *Eurasian Symphony* returns two steps back to a classic model of a utopias as a critical study of the imperfect present day society. Devoid of the romantic drama between a hero and its oppressive society, *Eurasian Symphony* is subtitled "There Are No Bad People." Thus, the main conflict of the narrative is coded in its juxtaposition to our present, in which, as we can assume, there is plenty of "bad people." The protagonists are vested with a single task—to preserve and maintain the status quo. Importantly, both central figures in *Eurasian Symphony* work for secret services and law enforcement institutions; they are not iconoclasts and (moral) revolutionaries but—by contrast—conservatives in thoughts and deeds. Revisiting the fundamentals of the Russian novelistic canon, Rybakov and Alimov produced a very static and "closed" utopia.[709]

The pleasure which readers extract from this kind of fiction is produced by the "inter-passive" consumption of enjoyment,[710] which the main protagonists, Bagatur and Bogdan experience in a perfectly organized society. *Eurasian Symphony*, thus, is perfectly escapist in its picturing the exact opposite to what is deemed to be characteristic of post-Soviet Russia: stability, wealth, security, social harmony and cohesion, brotherly communitarism, geopolitical might, self-esteem and preservation of cultural authenticity.[711] If we dig deeper into what constitutes pleasure of the ideal society,[712] we uncover not only amusing novelty (e.g. the combination of Russian, Turkic and Mongolic influences in the spirit of Eurasianism), but a soothing sensation of repetitiousness, because Ordus' is framed as a "considerably improved Soviet Union of our dreams."[713] As Viacheslav Rybakov pensively states, "[science] fiction is incapable

---

709 Fitting, "Positioning and Closure," 29.
710 Slavoj Zizek, "The interpassive subject," *Traverses*, 1998, awailable at: https://www.lacan.com/zizek-pompidou.htm.
711 Maria Iudanova, *Krizis kul'tury v sovremennoi russkoiazychnoi fantastike*. Dissertation (Moscow: RIK, 2012).
712 Suvin, "Locus, Horizon, and Orientation," 80.
713 Israel Shamir, "Nashe proshloe—delo nashego budushchego," *Novaia russkaia kniga*, no. 3-4 (2001). Available at: http://magazines.russ.ru/nrk/2001/3/shamir.html

of imagining anything which has not been previously invented in culture."⁷¹⁴

However, the main thrust of the franchise is diametrically opposed to this ostensible conservatism, since it is grounded on the assumption of the almost endless malleability of human nature with the help of rightful institutions, considerate legislation, as well as just and humane state power. Sharing the transformative pathos with classic utopias of the European Enlightenment, the ideological model of *Eurasian Symphony* functions in a completely different literary environment, shaped by the genre of alternative history. The concept of the therapeutic effect of the alternative history is a useful starting point,⁷¹⁵ which gives us a frame for understanding *Eurasian Symphony* as a specific mechanism of "re-membering" the defunct Soviet empire. As has been observed in scholarly studies, "all contemporary Russian fantasy novels have switched their attention from utopian futures to alternative concepts of history ... All writers are more or less preoccupied with the topic of the vanished empire."⁷¹⁶ For an alternative history this preoccupation becomes even more salient when authors revert to historical moments of Russia's imperial greatness, and contemplate possibilities to extend those moments into the present, as well as fictitiously eliminate factors, which in their opinion, prevented this greatness to last.⁷¹⁷

The narrative of *Eurasian Symphony* re-members the Soviet Union in the sense that it sutures together its cut members by means of finding a "bifurcation" point in the past when history "went wrong," resulting in the collapse of the USSR, and rectifies this "wrong." The trauma of 1991 is not represented here, but nevertheless experienced as a desire to undo what has been done.⁷¹⁸

---

714 Maria Cherniak, "Fantastika kak aktual'noe chtenie," *Bibliotechnoe delo* 16 (2013): 3.
715 Konstantin Sheiko and S. Brown, *History as Therapy: Alternative History and Nationalist Imaginings in Russia, 1991–2014* (Stuttgart: ibidem-Verlag, 2014): 31.
716 Menzel, "Russian Science Fiction and Fantasy Literature," in S. Lovell and Menzel (eds.), *Reading for Entertainment in Contemporary Russia: Post-Soviet Popular Literature in Historical Perspective* (München: Sagner, 2005): 149.
717 Sheiko and Brown, *History as Therapy*, 21.
718 Alexander Etkind, *Warped Mourning: Stories of the Undead in the Land of the Unburied* (Stanford: Stanford University Press, 2013): 14.

Importing a metaphor of the "chalk of destiny" from Timur Bekmambetov's SF film *Day Watch*, "Khol'm van Zaichik" writes with this chalk a new history in which what has been done has not been done: there was neither the violent Westernization of Peter I, nor the Bolsheviks' revolution, nor the bloody Great Patriotic War, nor the disintegration of Russia cum Soviet Union. In the universe of *Eurasian Symphony* the last war in Europe took place between France and Prussia in 1870/71.[719]

Like Fomenko's project of alternative history, *Eurasian Symphony* pictures the Russo-Turkish-Mongolian union as the real master of Eurasia.[720] The fictitious pivot of history in the world of *Eurasian Symphony* took place in the 1250s when Khan Sartak, the grandson of Genghis-Khan who adopted Christianity, concluded a treaty with Prince Aleksander of Neva, which stipulated the creation of a united state of Rus' and the Golden Horde on equal terms. Thus Ordus' was established. In historical reality Sartak died (perhaps was poisoned) around the year 1256, and this rapprochement never happened. In the end of the 14th century (in the fictitious universe) China joined Ordus' as its federative part and as one can assume, soon thereafter thanks to its advanced civilization, China became the cultural and political center of the state. In the fictitious present (e.g. the beginning of the 21st century) Ordus' includes almost the whole of the Eurasian continent "from the radiant tropics of Indo-China to chilly waters of Suomi Gulf [Gulf of Finland],"[721] and enjoys the international reputation of a prosperous and omnipotent empire although with a tinge of authoritarianism and negligence of the Western standard of liberal democracy and human rights. As follows from one fan-produced map of Ordus', only Western Europe, Japan and India remain beyond the orbit of the mammoth empire, with the capital in Khanbalyk (Beijing) and secondary centers in Alexandria on Neva (St Petersburg) and Karakorum (Kharkhorin, Mongolia).[722]

---

719 This war serves as a point of bifurcation for Rybakov's earlier tremendously popular experiment in alternative history *Gravity Flyer "Tsesarevich"* (1994).
720 Sheiko and Brown, *History as Therapy*, 213.
721 Zaichik, *Delo zhadnogo varvara* (St Petersburg: Azbuka, 2000), 7.
722 Fan-art "The Map of Ordus'," n.d., available at: https://vls-smolich.livejournal.com/146588.html.

Irony in *Eurasian Symphony*

Opposing their critics, Rybakov and Alimov used to say that *Eurasian Symphony* is not a political manifesto but an entertaining humorous reading. However, both laughter and un-laughter can be strategies of engaging with or resisting politics,[723] and to be sure, humor in "Khol'm van Zaichik," veering between good-natured kidding to vitriolic "stiob," is by and large political.[724] This is especially true given the importance of carnivalesque practice to Russian political culture.[725] The post-modern irony of Sorokin's *The One Day of Oprichnik* attacks the conservative turn in contemporary Russian politics, similarly to how late Soviet "stiob" operated in relation to the official discourse. Conservative SF also uses irony, perhaps even more actively than its liberal literary mainstream equivalent,[726] "smuggling" patriarchal values in undercover.[727]

Aleksei Yurchak's works out a useful understanding of irony as over-identification with the hegemonic discourse, which blurs the dividing line between wholehearted support and veiled mockery and effectively destabilizes the hegemonic power in a manner of brave solder Schwejk.[728] Thus, *Eurasian Symphony* assigns the role of the hegemonic master to the West, and provides over-identification with this imaginary Western discourses. Developing the mild

---

723 Dodds and P. Kirby, "It's Not a Laughing Matter: Critical Geopolitics, Humour and Unlaughter," *Geopolitics* 18, no. 1 (2012): 45–59; Moira Smith, "Humor, Unlaughter, and Boundary Maintenance," *Journal of American Folklore* 122, no. 2 (2009); 148–171.
724 "Stiob" is the Russian term for scathing mockery (Michael Klebanov, "Sergej Kurechin: The Performance of Laughter for the Post-Totalitarian Society of Spectacle. Russian Conceptualist Art in Rendezvous," *Russian Literature* 74, no. 1–2 (2013): 227–253; Mark Yoffe, "The Stiob of Ages: Carnivalesque Traditions in Soviet Rock and Related Counterculture," *Russian Literature* 74, no. 1–2 (2013)).
725 Fitting, "Utopian Effect/Utopian Pleasure," 92.
726 Yoffe, "The Stiob of Ages," 209.
727 Mark Lipovetsky, "Post-sots: Transformations of Socialist Realism in the Popular Culture of the Recent Period," *Slavic and East European Journal* 48, no. 3 (2004): 356–377; Boris Noordenbos, "Ironic Imperialism: How Russian Patriots Are Reclaiming Postmodernism," *Studies in East European Thought* 63, no. 2 (2011): 147–158.
728 Aleksei Yurchak, *Eto bylo navsegda, poka ne konchilos': Poslednee sovetskoe pokolenie* (Moscow: Novoe literaturnoe obozrenie, 2014): 489–490.

irony of *Eurasian Symphony*, Viacheslav Rybakov explained the rationale of his writings as follows: "to show that not everything which we usually and thoughtlessly consider progressive, is actually so."[729] There is nothing new; similarly to how Aleksandr Block wrote "yes, we are Scythians," "Khol'm van Zaichik" over-identifies with the imaginary Western perception of Russia as Orient, arguing, "yes, we are Ordus'." However, in the alternative world of Alimov and Rybakov, Ordus' accumulated such immeasurable cultural and material riches, that by comparison, Western Europeans seem pathetic barbarians. So the work cycle of irony is finished: starting from over-identification with the position, ascribed by the imaginary hegemon, and ending with complete destruction (or reversal) of this juxtaposition.

The idea of the moral and even technological superiority of Ordus' is framed ironically, as a complete reversal of the stereotype about Russian barbarity and Western civility, touched upon in Chapter 1. Here it is the other way round. To adduce one of the examples, the French second wife of the protagonist is condescendingly called "a beautiful barbarian," and the authors half-mockingly and with much enthusiasm and humor prove that even a Frenchwoman can be well cultured, tenderly loving, intelligent, and so on. The sexualised trope of a noble savage girl in the Western literature is thereby being reverted and addressed to the Westerners.[730] Another elegant vignette on the same topic concerns a lighter, mentioned in *Delo lis-oborotnei*. The Western detective gives a lighter to Bagatur, another key protagonist, as a sign of friendship and gratitude. Bagatur wants to thank him for the present by writing in the following way: "it is so pleasant to touch and reliable as if it had been produced in Ordus'." The authors emphasize this detail once again on the next page, saying that Bagatur was proud to write this ornate and agreeable phrase to his colleague, who "would certainly be flattered to know that the lighter is equal to Ordussian ones. Almost equal."[731] The authors stress the fact that

---

729 Correspondence of October 5, 2015.
730 Edward Said, *Orientalism* (London: Penguin, 2003).
731 Zaichik, *Delo lis-oborotnei* (St Petersburg: Azbuka, 2001): 184–186.

the superiority of Ordus' is so unquestionable and so much entrenched into Bagatur's mind, that he finds it to be the highest praise to say that a device produced abroad is almost as good as Ordussian.[732] The effect of irony is achieved by juxtaposing this firm belief with the reverse situation in "reality," when everything Western is taken as apriori better than Russian—hence the notorious Soviet-era campaign to fight with "idolatrous attitudes towards the West," which sounds as an echo in the ears of Soviet-born readers of the franchise.

Working similarly to the late Soviet stiob, this irony dislocates the source of hegemonic discourses from the home country—relocating it abroad, in the West. This could be compared to Go Koshino's argument that Ordus"s heterogeneity could only be sustainable by means of the "othering" of the West.[733] Aleksandr Dugin recently professed in a similar way, addressing the imaginary West: "You called us *gendarmes* of Europe. Yes, this is true. We are *gendarmes*. We maintain order, law, legality and security. We punish criminals and put rebels into irons. We are standing guard of the healthy family and justice. We defend culture and spirituality. [We defend] faith and morality. [We defend] identity and Tradition. We are holy *gendarmes*."[734] No doubt, the authors of *Eurasian Symphony* would endorse this statement completely.

Alimov and Rybakov develop a few methods of ironic overidentification in *Eurasian Symphony*. First, these are linguistic methods of creating the Ordus "newspeak" as a blend of ancient Russian and Chinese words, which effectively expels Western words. The car is *povozka*, the apartment is *terem*, a SUV, "jeep" in Russian, is Chinesified as *tsipuche*. All administrative titles are also Chinese, thus, a policeman is *lachzhun*. The gastronomic routine of Ordus is under the unquestionable influence of China, with only weak traces

---

732 Ordussian advanced technologies, the object of envy of the "Western barbarians", are also mentioned in *Delo zhadnogo varvara* (2000, 11).
733 Go Koshino, "Image of Empire and Asia in the Contemporary Science FIctions of Russia," *Acta Slavica Iaponica* 26 (2009): 188.
734 Dugin, *Ukraina: Moia voina. Geopoliticheskii dnevnik* (Moscow: Tsentrpoligraf, 2015): 40.

of European cuisine, so people drink *ergotou* instead of vodka or wine and eat oriental dumplings.

The second is blatant violation of shiboleths of the Western canon of civility, such as republicanism, or monogamy. Let's consider corporal punishment: the authors argue that it is unfair to penalize convicts by money because the imposition of the same fine on financially unequal people is not just, whereas all people equally suffer from physical pain. It is hard to decide, whether the authors really think that birch rods are better than fines, or whether they themselves would like to live in such a society, but by over-identifying with this marginal position in understanding of justice, they fight against universality of the human dignity thesis. So they could well be not serious about birch rods but they are very serious in their intention to question the Western canon of ethics.

The third is carefully staged Soviet nostalgia. Viacheslav Rybakov describes his ideal readers as working middle-aged intelligentsia with a Soviet background. This readership should be capable of grasping hints and jokes based on Soviet-era cultural products, but at the same time should be repelled by the kind of anti-Soviet and anti-Russian humor characteristic of refined intellectuals in dissident circles.[735] Authors constantly draw parallels between imaginary Ordus' and the Soviet past.[736] For example, there is a play on the Soviet detective canon, when all people are called comrades but criminals are called citizens, so you can see the change in person's status when a detective addresses him or her as

---

735 From correspondence, October 5, 2015. Rybakov's criticism of liberal intellectuals (called "sectarians") is staged in the book *Delo pobedivshei obez'iany* (Zaichik, 2002, p. 161), which reenacts the old Slavophile (cf. Konstantin Aksakov's essay "The Public and the People" from 1857) distinction between the imitative, Westernized, senseless "public", and the organic, authentic, wise "people" (Andrzej Walicki, *The Slavophile Controversy: History of a Conservative Utopia in Nineteenth-Century Russian Thought* (Oxford: Oxford University Press, 1975): 271–272).

736 Just a few of them, spotted in *Delo nepogashennoi luny*, are: a brand of the TV set is "Broad horizon" (cf. the most advanced type of the Soviet-era TV sets is "Horizon"); the producer of matches is named "Red Tenth Month" (cf. the Soviet match factory "Red Star" and the chocolate factory "Red October"); the advertising board in a Chinese restaurant offers large crayfish for 5 Choh (Chiao) and small for 3 Choh (cf. comedian Roman Kartsev's famous humoristic monologue from the 1970s: https://www.youtube.com/watch?v=PDM0GNgxPcM); cigarette's brand "Chernomor" (cf. Soviet cigarettes "Belomor"), and so on.

"citizen" not "comrade"; the same is in Ordus, a normative address is *edinochaiatel'*, which is—those who have similar goals, but when *edinochaiatel* commits a crime, they are called "subjects" of the emperor. For people born in the Soviet Union, these small allusions and parallels are dear and meaningful.

East and West in *Eurasian Symphony*

Without dramatism of Strugatskies' *Ugly Swans*[737] the book series of "Khol'm van Zaichik" tackles the same problem of communication with the Other, not lapsing into the Master and Slave conundrum. The solution which *Eurasian Symphony* offers lies in the intellectual range of ideas about "multiple modernities," and criticism of the idea of progress. In this sense, *Eurasian Symphony* is neither outlandish, nor original for a post-modern thought. In a dialogue between Bogdan, one of two key protagonist, and the Western detective, the latter voices the position profoundly alien to the authors: "There is only one culture, but some [nations] advanced on this track better than others ..." In counterpoint, Bogdan insists that there do not exist more or less cultured peoples; we can speak of different cultures.[738]

In spite of the proclaimed neutrality to different cultures, we can assuming from this that the world of Ordus' is grounded in a sense of moral superiority compared to the West. This idea is inscribed into the Dugin's speculations on the moral incompatibility of continental and maritime powers. The very lifestyle and economy of the former fosters respectful attitude to traditions, patriotism, loyalty to the state, and family values, whereas "sea powers" tend towards moral relativism, egoistic pursuit of success, neglecting traditions and so on. For example, on many instances in the universe of *Eurasian symphony*, the "Western barbarians" display sexual licentiousness.[739]

In the universe of "Khol'm van Zaichik," Khan Mamai and Prince Dmitry Ivanovich, in "historical reality" adversaries on the

---

737 See Chapter 4 in this volume.
738 Zaichik, *Delo sud'i Di*, 162.
739 Zaichik, *Delo lis-oborotnei*, 177.

Kulikovo field, fought together against the Polish-Lithuanian Commonwealth.[740] In *Eurasian Sympony's* somewhat playful interpretation, the decisive battle of this war took place near Prokhorovka village, where in 1943 the fierce tank battle with Wehrmacht took place, and the final defeat happened in Grunewald, where the Teutonic Order was crushed in 1410.[741] In this rendition, the theme of the eternal struggle of Russia against the Western aggressors is reenacted as the East-West antagonism, and as the manifestation of Russian solidarity with Asian peoples. With a reference to Halford Mackinder's celebrated essay "The Geographical Pivot of History" (1904), Rybakov and Alimov provide a geopolitical substantiation of this solidarity as a necessity to consolidate the continental landmass of Eurasia—primarily those occupied by Russia and China— in order to withstand the pressure of the maritime powers.[742] In his political journalism, Viacheslav Rybakov develops the idea of a never-ending contest between civilizations, comparing it to a car race: "how interesting indeed! [...] As if you were driving a powerful racing car, with excitement and mastery, you press for a faster speed, greater power and maneuverability from the unique ... mechanism [of your civilization]."[743] The authors proudly aver that *Eurasian Symphony* is the first "civilizational utopia," exploring the cultural variability of utopian ideals.[744]

Following the logic of a geopolitical style of thinking, the idea of the irreconcilable hostility of the West[745]—and specifically the US[746]—is embedded into the detective plotline of the *Eurasian Symphony*, in which crimes and criminals are invariably associated with the West or Western influences. Namely, the central motif of the

---

740 In his political journalism, Rybakov proposes to interpret the Kulikovo battle of 1380 as a fight in which the Russians and the Tartars, shoulder to shoulder, crushed the unlawful usurpers (the Western proxy) of the throne of the Golden Horde and reestablished "a constitutional order" both among the Mongols and the Russians (Rybakov, *Napriamuiu*, 137).
741 Zaichik, *Delo zhadnogo varvara* (St Petersburg: Azbuka, 2000): 74.
742 Zaichik, *Delo zhadnogo varvara*, 276.
743 Rybakov, *Rul' istorii*, 69.
744 Rybakov, *Napriamuiu*, 110.
745 Zaichik, *Delo pobedivshei obez'iany* (St Petersburg: Azbuka, 2002): 244.
746 Rybakov, *Rul' istorii*, 241.

West's plotting against Ordus' is explained by its craving for the immeasurable natural riches of the Empire.[747] For this purpose, Russia's enemies dream of splitting Eurasia and turning its wretched debris into obedient slaves.[748] Even the story debunking ethnic Russian nationalism revolves around an American, genetically-modified leech which transmits nationalist viruses when it bites.[749]

The most meaningful tension between East and West is inscribed into the very name of the franchise. The fact that *Eurasian Symphony* is written by "Khol'm van Zaichik," being inspired by the name of Dutch Orientalist Robert Hans van Gulik, establishes the West as a point of observation of the utopian landscapes to the East of Europe.[750] According to the tradition of the thinkers of the Enlightenment, the Orient served for intellectual experiments of estranging and critique of the present day reality. For example, Leibnitz marveled at the Chinese religious tolerance and practical morality, maintaining that that "we need missionaries from the Chinese" not the other way round.[751] The admiration of the Orient in "Khol'm van Zaichik" resembles the Sinophilia of the 18th century with its vision of China as a paragon of rationality, education and tolerance, represented as aesthetically exotic but attractive place. In Russia, however, the Sinophilia of Katherine the Great did not exclude emphatic self-identification as a part of the West, whereas the intellectual history of the 19th century brought about a more ambiguous vision of the East as both a place of backwardness and tyranny, and at the same time as a source for rejuvenation of Russia, and regaining Russia's cultural authenticity and distinctiveness from the West.[752]

---

747 Zaichik, *Delo zhadnogo varvara*, 212.
748 Rybakov, *Rul' istorii*, 114.
749 Zaichik, *Delo o polku Igoreve* (St Petersburg: Azbuka, 2001).
750 The name sounds a humorous note by contrasting its Western and Russian-styled parts. It could be roughly translated as "Holm van Bunny."
751 Jonathan Spence, *The Chan's Great Continent: China in Western Minds* (London: Penguin, 1999): 85.
752 David Schimmelpenninck van der Oye, "The East," in W. Leatherbarrow and D. Offord (eds.), *A History of Russian Thought*, 217–240.

The Russian school of Orientalist studies was established at the faculty of Oriental languages of St Petersburg University at the end of the 19th century, and struggled against the stereotypical image of the East as a realm of cruelty and barbarity. A purely Western academic enterprise in service to the Westernized Empire, this Orientalist school nevertheless asked meaningful questions about "othering" approaches to the East (questions which were later developed masterfully by Edward Said and Larry Wolff), and destabilized the "East and West" dichotomy as socio-political constructs. Headed by such scholars (of German origin) as V. Rosen, V. Bartold and S. Oldenburg, this school criticized Europocentrism and prefigured, and perhaps even influenced, many of the ideas of Eurasianists, especially those concerning Russia's cultural proximity to the world of Islam and the role of the Golden Horde in Russian history.[753]

Rybakov and Alimov, both professional Sinologists, graduated from the same Orientalist faculty (reorganized and renamed in 1944) in 1976 and 1986 respectively. Rybakov, affiliated at the Institute of Orientalism at the Russian Academy of Sciences, is a specialist in Medieval Chinese legislation, his recently defended (2009) Dr. habil. [*doktorskaia*] dissertation focuses on the Chinese bureaucracy of Tan period (618–907), whereas Alimov's Dr. habil. (2010) is devoted to the study of the written sources of the Song dynasty (960–1279). Thus, contrary to the intellectual thrust of classic Eurasianism to connect the history of Eurasia with the legacy of Genghis-Khan and Golden Horde, "Khol'm van Zaichik" relocates the attention to China, which completely changes the architecture and ideational underpinning of the Eurasian Union in their vision.

A conventional image of Eurasia implies the idea of unbounded virgin lands of unlimited possibilities, often represented visually as a barren steppe or wild desert, inhabited by nomads living in symbiosis with nature, as in Nikita Mikhalkov's film of 1991 *Close to Eden* (*Urga*). This vision is completely alien to *Eurasian Symphony*, which represents Eurasia as a densely populated land of

---

753 Vera Tolz, "*Sobstvennyi Vostok Rossii*": *Politika identichnostei i vostokovedenie v pozdneimperskii i rannesovetskii period* (Moscow: NLO, 2013).

ancient culture, sophisticated knowledge and minutely organized and well-ordered lifestyle. Written from the distinctively Western point of observation of the utopian landscape of Ordus', "Khol'm van Zaichik" recycles Chinese imagery for the construction of an alternative Russia and for staging an anti-Western critique. However, unlike the school of Russian academic Orientalism, the world of Ordus' is intended not to blur the distinction between the East and the West but to reinforce it, and to represent the East as way more developed and civilized than the West. The closest intellectual predecessor of this project could be found in late imperial *Vostochniki*, which envisaged an anti-Western coalition of colonial peoples, spearheaded by Russia. Or, even earlier, there is the example of classic Slavophiles with their sympathy for the colonized peoples of Africa and Asia. Anticipating later indictments of Alexander Blok, journalist Sergei Syromiatnikov (Sigma) professed in an imaginary dialogue with a German, "from now on, we will not stand up staunchly for Europe against Asia as we did when we defended [Europe] from the attack of the Tartars. We will come shoulder to shoulder with Asia because ... we have seen that you ... serve ... the devil."[754] The book series' central idea is that healthy traditionalism and religiosity make people happy and society — harmonious. The two pillars of Ordus — Confucianism and Orthodoxy — do not exclude Buddhism, Islam or Judaism from the public sphere.[755] This echoes the ruminations of early Eurasianists like Petr Savitskii, who argues that the common people of Russia have many things in common with the the grassroots of the East, which makes Russia "an Orthodox-Muslim, and an Orthodox-Buddhist" country.[756]

Here we approach a very consequential twist of logic in the construction of *Eurasian Symphony*. Unlike typical anti-colonial literature which changes the "polarity" of the colonial disposition to

---

754 Schimmelpenninck van der Oye, *Russian Orientalism: Asia in the Russian Mind from Peter the Great to the Emigration* (New Haven: Yale University Press, 2010); Sergei Syromiatnikov, *Opyty russkoi mysli* (St Petersburg: tip. A. S. Suvorina, 1901), vol. 1, 30.
755 *Delo napogashennoi luny* (2005), the last book in the series, was awarded the literary prize, established by the Russian Council of Muftis (2006).
756 Petr Savitskii, "Povorot k vostoku," in *Iskhod k vostoku. Filosofiia evraziistva* (Moscow: Dobrosvet, 2008 [1921]): 38.

diametrically opposite—although on the surface this is also the case, as we have seen in the previous paragraph: the West is barbarian and Ordus' is civilized—*Eurasian Symphony* conspicuously excludes Russia from the game. The fact that in Ordus' Russia proper plays a fairly insignificant role has been noted by a handful of critics. Indeed, what could be called "Russia" in the world of Ordus' is only its far North-Eastern part, the "ulus of Aleksandria," more than that, the capital is in Beijing (Khanbalyk), the imperial language is Mandarin, and Orthodoxy is only one among a number of confessions—perhaps even not the most publicly visible one, since even Orthodox believers deem it necessary to attend Confucian temple in order to resolve moral dilemmas. A utopian Russia cum Ordus' is, thus, bigger than Russia proper and at the same time much lesser than Russia in "reality." This exposes the dialectic pulsation of Eurasianist imagery between intimately interrelated self-belittling and self-aggrandizing.

In "Khol'm van Zaichik"'s narrative foundation of Ordus' (e.g. Aleksandr Nevskii's and Khan Sartak's brotherhood) is paralleled by the creation of the Soviet Union,[757] and evokes another instance of "kenotic" attitude in the Russian history—the "affirmative action empire."[758] The whole Ordus' project seems to be a re-enactment of the Soviet affirmative action model, revamped by an even more radical self-belittling of Russian geopolitical ambition and well developed practices of federalism. Unlike the Bolshevik project for dealing with the national question by means of "nationalization" (*korenizatsiia*), "Khol'm van Zaichik" highlights confessional heterogeneity instead of the national one. Ordus' is structured by religious communities, which may or may not coincide with national divisions.

---

[757] This parallelism is accentuated by the playful reference to a popular Ordussian song which sounds similar to the Soviet anthem, well engraved into the memory of Rybakov and Alimov's readers: "Unbreakable Union of freeborn Republics, \\ Great Russia has welded forever to stand" (Zaichik, *Delo zhadnogo varvara*, 2000, 104)).

[758] Terry Martin, *The Affirmative Action Empire: Nations and Nationalism in the Soviet Union, 1923–1939* (Ithaca: Cornell University Press, 2001).

The final result is, nevertheless, a Soviet-like "friendship of peoples." This principle is epitomized by the duet of protagonists, Bagatur, a Mongolian who confesses Buddhism, and Bogdan, a Russian Orthodox believer. Rybakov draws attention to an episode, which he penned in *Delo lis-oborotnei*. It relates the story of a friendship between an Orthodox and a Buddhist priest both living in Solovki island; their loving attitude towards each other is shown as a tacit mutual compassion, when an Orthodox regrets that his friend is likely to destroy his soul because of Buddhism, and a Buddhist similarly bemoans the fact that his friend is likely to never achieve nirvana because of his Christian convictions.[759] In Rybakov's vision, this compassion to the different, while being adamant in one's ancestral faith, represents the cornerstone of Ordus"s stability. It implies that all religions, whatever different they may seem, share a common ethical core, so the more faithful a believer is to his or her own religion, the more likely it is that he or she will find a common language with a representative of another religion.[760] In the interview, authors claimed that "van Zaichik is saving Russia" because it offers accommodation of difference, which is still pertinent to today's Russia, where "civilizational divides run inside [of Russia]."[761]

Fine-tuned to criticize Eurocentrism and the idea of progress, *Eurasian Symphony* does propose its own social ideal as well. The ideational glue that keeps Ordus' tight is Confucianism. In his Dr. habil. In his dissertation, Rybakov reconstructs the debates between Confucians and Legalists in ancient China, arguing that Legalists praised formal justice and the triumph of law and they failed, whereas Confucians proposed to lean on morals and patriarchal family, and they invented the magic formula of China's greatness. This is because moral people ("good people," cf. the subtitle of the franchise "There are no bad people") are more efficient as bureaucrats in an imperfect system than immoral people working within the formally perfect bureaucracy. He goes on to argue that family

---

759 Zaichik, *Delo lis-oborotnei*, 87.
760 Rybakov, *Rul' istorii*, 123.
761 Rybakov and Alimov, "Voprosy, chasto zadavaemye perevodchikam i ikh konsul'tantam," 97.

is the only institution which can produce moral, altruistic people, so the task of state builders should be to cherish families and to model the state as an extended patriarchal family, in which people don't steal public goods not because of the fear of punishment but because it would be disgracefully repugnant for them.[762] This family-centered ethics is the core of *Eurasian Symphony's* social ideal.

One of the corollaries from this is securitization of sacred objects. The plotline of the first novel in the series, *The Case of a Greedy Barbarian*, deals with the criminal investigation of the theft of one of the most sacred treasures of the empire, the Code of Chenghiz Khan. This case is represented as the utmost sacrilege, the gravest crime against the state that one can imagine. As the story progresses, the protagonists find out who has commissioned the offence — a certain Western businessman Shmoros — the literary counterpart of George Soros. Prefiguring much of the "sacrilege discourses" spurred by the Pussy Riot affair in 2012, this book centers on the inviolability of symbols of civilizational identity and on everlasting encroachments of the West on Russia's inner self, integrity and cultural authenticity. The sacrilegious attack on a venerated relic is considered to be the worst possible crime — since it constitutes an attempt to overthrow the existing order.[763] This resonates with the statements of Vsevolod Chaplin, former spokesman of the ROC, who in 2011 professed that sacred objects are more important than human rights, even than the right for life.[764]

Conclusions

In spite of its exotic entourage and shocking over-identification with a position of a "barbarous" East, *Eurasian Symphony* is paradoxically Western in its ideational structure. It follows the Western Orientalizing gaze on Asia as an outpost for the critical attack on

---

762 Rybakov, *Kitaiskaia biurokratiia perioda Tan (618–907 gg.) po materialam istoricheskikh i iuridicheskikh istochnikov*. Dissertation (St Petersburg, 2009): 37–51; Rybakov, *Rul' istorii*, 7, 79; Zaichik, *Delo sud'i Di*, 12.
763 Zaichik, *Delo zhadnogo varvara*, 82; Zaichik, *Delo pobedivshei obez'iany* (St Petersburg: Azbuka, 2002): 165.
764 Vsevolod Chaplin, "Tsennosti very, sviatyn', Otechestva — vyshe prav cheloveka," 2011, available at: http://pravovrns.ru/?p=4797

the present-day order and to stage the construction of the utopian alternative world. Fascinated with Chinese culture and Confucian ethics, authors of the book series instrumentalize this exoticism as typical Westerners, or even—Westernizers, because behind the façade of Ordus', one can discern two ideas originating in the European Enlightenment—the idea of endless social perfection and the idea of endless human development by means of applying external forces (e.g. institutions, legislations, etc.)

Following Rybakov's metaphor of progress as a cancer in the body of Western humankind,[765] one can assume that he reserved for himself the role of a surgeon, prepared to operate on the deceased with his scalpel of anti-Western irony. This means that—contrary to the pathos of "multiple modernities"—the position of *Eurasian Symphony* is a position of moral superiority verging on Western-style Messianism. This Western gazing of the East enables *Eurasian Symphony* to revisit the old concept of Russia as "true Europe."[766] Indeed, the intellectual thrust of the franchise pictures Ordus' as Russia's proxy, whose qualities make Russia an even better Europe than Europe proper: Ordus' is technologically advanced, multicultural, ethnically heterogeneous and religiously tolerant. At the same time, it is an absolutely law-abiding, well-functioning and well-ordered society, featuring developed local self-government and political participatory mechanisms. Hijacking Europeanness from the Europeans, Ordus' recycles Eurasianism for the purpose of re-membering (reconstructing) the Soviet Union as an alternative to the global West.

---

765 Cf. Chapter 4.
766 Iver Neumann, *Russia and the Idea of Europe*.

8 *"Novorossiia"* in Russian Geopolitical Culture

Introduction

The annexation of Crimea in March 2014 and the war in Donbas have made a strong impression on the popular imagination, and substantially changed the perception of Russia's place, role and mission in the world among the Russian population. Mass media and social networks have hyped up these events as Russia's return from historical obscurity and transformation from geopolitical periphery into international pivot. In today's Russia, people are preoccupied with space, territoriality, and cartography to an extend, which evokes Walter Benjamin's observations on Soviet Russia of the 1920s, when the map acquired iconic importance.[767] Disenchantment in communist teleology and attenuation of the liberal thrust to catch up with the West made spatial imagery of the country more pertinent and consequential than any futuristic projecting.[768] For the popular imaginary, territoriality gives both pain and hope, providing the corporeal metaphors of the dismembered body,[769] as well as geopolitical theories proving Russia's lasting international importance as long as it still possesses the Eurasian "heartland".[770] The unfinished work of mourning the victims of the past[771] has its compensatory flipside: the intensively going work of mourning of the lost limbs of Russia's geo-body.[772] As in the case of Crimea,

---

[767] Walter Benjamin, *Walter Benjamin: Selected Writings* (Harvard: Harvard University Press, 2005), vol. 2, 37.
[768] Edith W. Clowes, *Russia on the Edge*.
[769] Cf. Aleksandr Prokhanov's speech in support of the annexation of Crimea of March 18, 2014: "When we were half-dead, [the Westerners] dismembered us by chainsaws, [they] chopped off [our] hands, legs, ears ..." Available at: https://www.youtube.com/watch?v=VYV7TVuTTZ4.
[770] The term "heartland" comes from: Halford J. Mackinder, *Democratic Ideals and Reality* (Washington, DC: National Defense University Press, 1942 [1919]): 74–80.
[771] Etkind, *Warped Mourning*.
[772] Franck Billé, "Territorial Phantom Pains (and Other Cartographic Anxieties)," *Environment and Planning D: Society and Space* 32, no. 1 (2014): 163–178.

Eastern Ukraine has been the locus of undying territorial "phantom pains" for most of Russians. Hence, the armed pro-Russian rebellion in the region against the Ukrainian government has been widely discussed and almost unanimously supported in Russia.[773] The vision of "*Novorossiia*," which inspired the separatist movement, has shaped the geopolitical ideology of the "Russian world." It established the universal antagonistic border, constitutive for the whole of the imaginary community of the Russians. Together with "Crimea is ours!" concept, "*Novorossiia*" is the *territorial* concept, which defines the belonging to "us" or to the "fifth column."

"*Novorossiia*" in its present shape was a short-lived venture. It was mentioned in Putin's "direct line" phone-in of April 17, 2014,[774] then quickly fell out of favour with Russia's highest officials, yet has remained in the discourses of pro-Kremlin public intellectuals and in Donbas itself. After a visible spike in 2014, the term "*Novorossiia*" nearly had disappeared from Russian public debates by 2016.

On May 24, 2014 the self-proclaimed rebellious Donetsk People's Republic (DPR) and Luhansk People's Republic (LPR) established the confederative "Union of *Novorossiia*," labelled in the Russian media as a part of the broader Russian World. The results of the presidential elections in Ukraine (May 25, 2014) were a wake up call for supporters of "*Novorossiia*," because they revealed substantial support for President Poroshenko—and by extension for the idea of a united Ukraine—even in regions comprising they claimed as their historical lands. The Kremlin's reticence to openly support the pro-Russian separatists has led to a popular meme that "Putin

---

773 Julie Fedor, "Introduction: Russian Media and the War in Ukraine," *Journal of Soviet and Post-Soviet Politics and Society* 1, no. 1 (2015): 1–12; Stephen Hutchings, J. Szostek, "Dominant Narratives in Russian Political and Media Discourse during the Ukrainian Crisis," in A. Pikulicka-Wilczewska and R. Sakwa (eds.) *Ukraine and Russia: People, Politics, Propaganda and Perspectives* (Bristol: E-International Relations, 2015); Richard Sakwa, *Frontline Ukraine: Crisis in the Borderlands* (London: I.B. Tauris, 2014).
774 Vladimir Putin, "Priamaia liniia s Vladimirom Putinym," April 17, 2014, available at: http://kremlin.ru/events/president/news/20796.

is ditching *Novorossiia"* (*slivaet Novorossiyu*).[775] On May 18, 2015 Oleg Tsarev, speaker of the parliament of "*Novorossiia,*" proclaimed its break-up as a confederative state on grounds that its existence had not been stipulated in the Minsk agreements. "*Novorossiia*" is no longer central to ideological mobilization in the ongoing confrontation in Eastern Ukraine, but this concept belongs more or less to contemporary Russian and Ukrainian history. As such, an explanation is required as to why it was not a success story (if "success" is an appropriate word to describe an idea, which send hundreds and thousands of people to the carnage fields of Donbas).

The present chapter analyses, how the concept of "*Novorossiia*" is being used in popular discussions. It identifies concomitant ideas, visions and emotions, intimately related to spatial characteristics of this region (e.g. borders) as well as to the imbrication of historical and cultural legacies and memories associated with this place. The chapter focuses on how the digital environment and in particular social networks such as Facebook and Vkontakte mediate circulation of geopolitical knowledge and facilitate geopolitical identity making.

This study is based on analysis of the Russian-language sector of social networks, most notably facebook.com (36%), twitter.com (25%), vk.com (24%), and livejournal.com (12%),[776] with a particular focus on discussion threads about geopolitics. For data mining, Integrum Social Media service was used, which has monitored messages in social networks mentioning the keyword "*Novorossiia.*" The sample is drawn from the period between February 21 and March 8, 2015.[777] From more than 3000 messages collected by

---

[775] The expert community's opinion is that already in early summer 2014, Kremlin decided to reincorporate DPR and LPR into Ukraine in order to use them as its leverage on the otherwise recalcitrant country (Mikhail Zygar', *Vsia kremlevskaia rat': Kratkaia istoriia sovremennoi Rossii* (Moscow: Intellektual'naia literatura, 2016): 356).

[776] This distribution corresponds to the percentage of messages containing the keyword "*Novorossiia*" and does not reflect the popularity of each social network in Russia, where vk.com is the undisputed leader.

[777] The period is opportune for studying "*Novorossiia*" because after the second Minsk agreements (February 12, 2015) the frontline stabilized, and the life on the territory controlled by DPR and LPR got into a groove. Hence, the ideological construction around and about the concept of "*Novorossiia*" has become less

Integrum, some 300 were sampled for further work. The sample includes also manually collected statements (ca. 200) from the public discussion wall of the group *Tipichnyi Donetsk* on vk.com, monitored between July 2014 and August 2015. Those messages were chosen on the basis of their explicit intention to serve as arguments in geopolitical debates; technically this means that priority was given to polemical interjections rather than to the original posts. The sampling excluded quotations from the press and online agencies, as well as posts only tangentially dealing with geopolitical deliberation.

Methodological note: The brand *"Novorossiia"* and its ideological meaning

This research is informed by the approaches of critical geopolitical and conceptual history. For critical geopolitics, territory is not taken for granted; instead, it is understood as a social construct, resultant of many hegemonic projects, ideologies, policies and grassroots resistances.[778] The second methodological pillar is conceptual history. *"Novorossiia"* is considered here as a concept, which condenses and fixes different, often competing meanings, and informed with various non-representational experiences, metaphors, visuals, and feelings. In this capacity, a concept is used as an argument in political polemics with a certain illocutionary force. So, the essence of the logic of this research is to understand how, why and in which context people use the term *"Novorossiia,"* because by so doing, they work out its territory and borders.

This task requires heightened attention to conventional and minor ideological writing, rather than to the "great texts" or original speculations, which all too often emerge from the thrust to resist and overthrow the conventional wisdom. The paper insists that spatial concepts are also normative and illocutionary. *"Novorossiia"*

---

dependent on what is happening on the battlefields and more—on its ideological framing and popular imagination.

778 Henri Lefebvre, *State, Space, World: Selected Essays* (Minneapolis: University of Minnesota Press, 2009): 170; Tuathail, *Critical Geopolitics: The Politics of Writing Global Space*, 1.

"NOVOROSSIIA" 251

is a conceptual innovation intended to change some conventions and norms about thinking of the post-Soviet space for the purpose of legitimizing a specific course of political actions. Yet, it cannot change all conventions, it needs some conceptual "fulcrum" bequeathed from the historical legacies and memories. In this context we can speak of the "invention of the tradition":[779] usable pasts create usable spaces.

This approach brings together expert knowledge on "*Novorossiia*" and discussions about it in the online environment. Quantitatively digital social media have become the breeding ground for geopolitical concepts, outnumbering advocacy journalism and academia by orders.[780] The internet serves as the exclusive platform the political deliberation in Russia.[781] So, the largest work of the production of space is being done by the grassroots' internet users, acting in both capacities of consumers and producers of geopolitical knowledge (i.e. "prosumers"); the online commentators not merely passively reflect expert opinions, but actively produce new meanings.[782] This approach resonates with the studies of active audiences and their creative reception of cultural products. Scholars in this field argue that the flow of ideological signification is not unidirectional, i.e. from experts to grassroots; instead, political meanings are created in the process of communicative interaction with audiences.[783]

---

779 Eric Hobsbawm and T. Ranger, *The Invention of Tradition* (Cambridge: Cambridge University Press, 2012).
780 Suslov, "The 'Russian World' Concept in Online Debate during the Ukrainian Crisis," in Bassin and Suslov (eds.), *Eurasia 2.0: Post-Soviet Geopolitics in the Age of New Media* (Lanham: Lexington Press).
781 Evgeny Gorny, "Russian LiveJournal. The Impact of Cultural Identity on the Development of a Virtual Community," in H. Schmidt, K. Teubener and N. Konrafdova (eds.) *Control+ Shift. Public and Private Usages of the Russian Internet* (Norderstedt: Books on Demand, 2006).
782 This research acknowledges the massive participation of the paid pro-Kremlin commentators in the discussions, but for the study of the ideological conventional norms this is almost irrelevant: those "trolls" have to speak the common language, so to say, in order to meaningfully participate in the discussion and not just cry in the wilderness.
783 Jason Dittmer and K. Dodds, "Popular Geopolitics Past and Future: Fandom, Identities and Audiences," *Geopolitics* 13, no. 3 (2008); Dodds, "Popular Geopolitics and Audience Dispositions: James Bond and the Internet Movie

This chapter proposes to examine the geopolitical concept of "*Novorossiia*" as a cultural product, or a popular "brand," generated by the elite but capable of attracting attention and forming emotional bonds with its consumers. This "brand" has consolidated a relatively stable group of political activists, which—borrowing from fandom studies—could be called "fans" of "*Novorossiia*". Fans were recruited mostly from the already existing political fandom of President Putin.[784] This geopolitical fandom, based mainly online, functions as a mediation between the "*Novorossiia*" concept and relatively passive spectators of it on television. The fandom of "*Novorossiia*" has also generated the identity of "anti-fandom"—those whose very hatred of this cultural product means they unwillingly participate in promoting it.[785] Political activists in this interpretation could be seen as "fans of politics," whose consumption is culture-based, individual-oriented and highly emotional.[786]

This type of consumption requires that the consumable commodity is a brand, i.e. "a shortcut to consumer choice, enabling differentiation between broadly similar products."[787] Understanding "*Novorossiia*" as a territorial brand with regional, transnational and trans-border dimensions implies that inscribing ideological meaning onto a particular land creates the difference. The inscription highlights essential properties of the territory, which could be

---

Database (IMDb)," *Transactions of the Institute of British Geographers* 31, no. 2 (2006); Chih Y. Woon, "Popular Geopolitics, Audiences and Identities: Reading the 'War on Terror'in the Philippines," *Geopolitics* 19, no. 3 (2014).

784 Helena Goscilo (ed.), *Putin as Celebrity and Cultural Icon* (London: Routledge, 2013); Galina Nikiporets-Takigava and E. Pain, *Internet i ideologicheskie dvizheniia v Rossii* (Moscow: NLO, 2016).

785 Jonathan Gray, "New Audiences, New Textualities: Anti-Fans and Non-Fans," *International Journal of Cultural Studies* 6, no. 1 (2003): 64–81.

786 Catherine Burwell and M. Boler, "Calling on the Colbert Nation: Fandom, Politics and Parody in an Age of Media Convergence," *Electronic Journal of Communication* 18, no. 2 (2008): 3–25; Laurie Ouellette, "Branding the Right: The Affective Economy of Sarah Palin," *Cinema Journal* 51, no. 4 (2012): 185–191; Cornel Sandvoss, "Toward an Understanding of Political Enthusiasm as Media Fandom: Blogging, Fan Productivity and Affect in American Politics," *Participations* 10, no. 1 (2013): 252–296.

787 Margaret Scammell, "Political Brands and Consumer Citizens: The Rebranding of Tony Blair," *The Annals of the American Academy of Political and Social Science* 611, no. 1 (2007): 176–192.

easily consumed as a market commodity and at the same time recycled for the purpose of nation building.[788] The ideological "branding" of the territory follows the same logic as capitalist commodification of the qualitative aspects of space, discussed by Henri Lefebvre. "*Novorossiia*" in this sense possesses a space of specific market value—akin to the value of sun and sea or snow and mountains:[789] this is a huge adventure park, which used to supply in the 2014-2015 (today—to a lesser extent) spectators with their daily portion of adrenalin and provided a outlet for some, willing to escape the routine of the daily life.

However, commodification of "*Novorossiia*" is not untroubled, since—unlike many other territorial disputes in the post-Soviet space—there is no clear-cut ethnic, cultural and linguistic line between pro-Russian and pro-Ukrainian supporters in Donbas. Michael Gentile's findings have shown that the pre-war pro-Russian group in Luhansk tended to be somewhat less educated, less fluent in English, less tolerant to homosexualism, older and less satisfied with their lives than the pro-Ukrainian constituency,[790] but differences were actually very small. In fact there is a large group of well-educated people who know foreign languages and are relatively young, who nevertheless constituted fertile soil for the "*Novorossiia*" concept. As Elise Giuliano puts it, "ethnic and linguistic identities [in Ukraine] do not translate directly into political alienation from the central state,"[791] and neither do social identities in a broader sense. These recent studies are built upon previous examinations of identity-formation in Ukraine, which showed that even if there are two territorially bounded poles of identification (i.e. Crimea and Galicia), the largest part of the country represents an

---

788 Gert-Jan Hospers, "Borders, Bridges and Branding: The Transformation of the Øresund Region into an Imagined Space," *European Planning Studies* 14, no. 8 (2006): 1015–1033.
789 Lefebvre, *The Production of Space*; Harvey Molotch, "The Space of Lefebvre," *Theory and Society* 22, no. 6 (1993).
790 Michael Gentile, "West-Oriented in the East-Oriented Donbas: A Political Stratigraphy of Geopolitical Identity in Luhansk, Ukraine," *Post-Soviet Affairs* 31, no. 3 (2015): 201–223.
791 Elise Giuliano, "The Social Bases of Support for Self-determination in East Ukraine," *Ethnopolitics* 14, no. 5 (2015): 513–522.

unlimited spectrum of combined, mixed and complementary identities.[792]

All in all, the suggested approach intends to decisively connect cultural and intellectual history by seeing how a geopolitical concept of "*Novorossiia*" is being understood and contextualized by the audiences. From this we can infer whether this concept is capable of producing new political and geographical reality.

Where is *Novorossiia*? Territorial indeterminacy

Any social and conceptual framing of difference, such as the modern nation-state, requires a correspondent spatial delimitation[793] — for example an easily imagined border.[794] Cultural framing of a specific territory crucially depends on the availability of distinctive spatial landmarks (islands, mount ridges, valleys and so on), which can facilitate visualization of this territory and its differentiation from contiguous land.[795] The reverse should also be true: difficulties in successfully imagining and delineating an "alternative" territory impede on the construction of political difference. Unlike Crimea with its peninsular territoriality,[796] "*Novorossiia*" has no "natural" dividing

---

792 Lowell Barrington, "Russian-Speakers in Ukraine and Kazakhstan: 'Nationality', 'Population', or Neither?" *Post-Soviet Affairs* 17, no. 2 (2001): 129–158; Barrington and E.S. Herron, "One Ukraine or Many? Regionalism in Ukraine and Its Political Consequences," *Nationalities Papers* 32, no. 1 (2004): 53–86; Volodymyr Kulyk, "The Politics of Ethnicity in Post-Soviet Ukraine: Beyond Brubaker," *Journal of Ukrainian Studies* 26, 1–2 (2001): 197–221; Paul S. Pirie, "National Identity and Politics in Southern and Eastern Ukraine," *Europe-Asia Studies* 48, no. 7 (1996): 1079–1104; Stephen Shulman, "Competing versus Complementary Identities: Ukrainian-Russian Relations and the Loyalties of Russians in Ukraine," *Nationalities Papers* 26, no. 4 (1998): 615–632.

793 Mark Gottdiener, "A Marx for Our Time: Henri Lefebvre and the Production of Space," *Sociological Theory* 11, no. 1 (1993): 129–134; Reece Jones, "Whose Homeland? Territoriality and Religious Nationalism in Pre-partition Bengal," *South Asia Research* 26, no. 2 (2006): 115–131.

794 Andrew Abbott, "Things of Boundairies," *Social Research* 62, no. 4 (1995): 857–882.

795 Colin Williams and A. Smith, "The National Construction of Social Space," 502–518.

796 Crimea has been imagined as an island too, which is an ideal space for locating a utopia. Cf. Vasilii Aksenov's fantastic novel *Crimea the Island* (1979) and the journal of the same name, edited by Sergei Gradirovskii, one of the architects of the ideology of the "Russian world".

lines along geographical objects, ethnicity, language, religion or culture, being inscribed mostly on the historical maps.

In spite of attempts by ideologists to trace the genealogy of "*Novorossiia*" to Homer and represent it as the progenitor of the "Russian World,"[797] the historical master-narrative refers mostly to the Russian imperial past. The term "*Novorossiia*" emerged on March 22, 1764 when Catherine the Great issued a decree establishing a *guberniia* (region) called *Novorossiia* on the territories of Slavianoserbia (in today's Luhansk region), Kremenchug province and the "Ukrainian defence line." In the following few decades its territory was adjusted several times. The administrative reform of 1802 put an end to the official term "*Novorossiia*" on imperial maps, breaking the province into three gubernias (with centres in Nikolaev, Ekaterinoslav, and Crimea), the region of the Army of Don, and Bessarabia (**figure 7**). Yet, the word "*Novorossiia*" continued to circulate. For example, in 1865 the University of *Novorossiia* was established in Odessa. This town hosted the newspaper *Novorossiiskii Telegraf* (1869–1900). In 1838 the town of Novorossiysk was grounded in the Northern Caucasus (Krasnodar *krai* in today's Russia).

The imperial cartographic scholarship[798] also had conflicting accounts on *Novorossiia* and did not always consider it as a self-standing territorial entity. Konstantin Arsen'ev, for example, dissolved *Novorossiia* in the "steppe space" [*Stepnoe Prostranstvo*], embracing vast areas of Low Volga, the South Urals, and North Caspian guberniias.[799] The influential *Geographical and Statistical Dictionary of the Russian Empire* (1863–1885), edited by the famous traveller and scholar Petr Semenov Tian-Shanskii, has no entry on "*Novorossiia*" at all. Elsewhere, however, he mentioned *Novorossiia* consisting of Crimea, Kherson, Ekaterinoslav and Bessarabian

---

[797] Prokhanov, "Rossiia, sestra tvoia—*Novorossiia*," *Izborskii Klub: Russkie strategii* 17, no. 5 (2014).

[798] Marina Loskutova, "Regionalization, Imperial Legacy, and the Soviet Geographical Tradition," in Turoma and Waldstein (eds.), *Empire De/Centered: New Spatial Histories of Russia and the Soviet Union* (Farnham: Ashgate, 2013).

[799] Konstantin Arsen'ev, *Statisticheskie ocherki Rossii* (St Petersburg: Tip. Imp. Akad. Nauk, 1848).

guberniias.[800] From the 19th century *Novorossiia* was very loosely connected to the lands on the Northern shore of the Black Sea, speaking more to the idea of newness and renovation, rather than offering any precise spatial vision.

The difficulty of geographically locating "*Novorossiia*" becomes clear from the map in **figure 7**, which represents territories historically referred to as "*Novorossiia*" (in the 1800), onto which the map with the territory controlled by the insurgents (as of January 2015) is superimposed. It is easy to observe the expansionist potential, ingrained in the term "*Novorossiia*," and the fact that the territory of the pro-Russian rebellion is peripheral to historical *Novorossiia*, not including its core cities of Dnepropetrovsk, Kremenchug, Kirovograd, Odessa, Kherson and Nikolaev.

Figure 7. Map of *gubernia Novorossiia*, 1800, and the territory of the pro-Russian rebellion in Donbas.

Created by Maksim Domskii (reproduced with the permission).

Today, six years after the pro-Russian rebellion started in the spring of 2014, there are two dominant approaches to locating "*Novorossiia*" on the map. The first harks back to its (problematic)

---

800 See: *Entsiklopedicheskii slovar' Brokgauza i Efrona* (St Petersburg: Semenovskaia tipolit., 1899), vol. 27a.

imperial territorial outline, which sustains an interpretation of "*Novorossiia*" as part and parcel of the Russian World. For this version, the geographical outline of "*Novorossiia*" refers to the late 18th century cartography. The second capitalizes on Donbas territorial imagery and encapsulates a socialist reading of "*Novorossiia*" as a fortress in the fight against global, Ukrainian and—importantly!— Russian oligarchic capitalism. It has two geographical contours: the Donbas region and the whole of left-bank Ukraine. There is no impenetrable barrier between the imperial and the socialist versions, and ideologists used to juggle with both, according what their moment.

The imperial version has been promoted by right wing and nationalistic intellectuals, many of whom are members of the so-called Izborsk Club. Thus, Sergei Plekhanov and Mikhail Delyagin call "*Novorossiia*" the Piedmont of the Russian nation.[801] This vision resonates with Putin's Crimea speech of March 18, 2014, in which he described the Russian people as the biggest divided nation in the world. It also resonates with Putin's later "direct line" phone-in (April 17, 2014), during which he referred to historical *Novorossiia* as a precursor to the contemporary pro-Russian separatist movement. In the view of traditionalist commentator Egor Kholmogorov, *Novorossiia* is more than Donbas. For him, the latter is "simply a part of Russia" and nothing else.[802] Similarly, the iconic figure of the rebellion Igor' Strelkov (Girkin), whose views are dominated by anti-revolutionary traditionalism and Orthodoxy, preferred to speak of the "Russian Vande" on the South-East of Ukraine.[803] Meanwhile, ideologists with a socialist propensity, who extoll the

---

801 Mikhail Deliagin, "O nedaliekom budushchem Novorossii," in S. Plekhanov (ed.), *Novorossiia. Vosstavshaia iz pepla* (Moscow: Knizhnyi mir, 2014); Sergei Plekhanov, "Vosstavshaia iz pepla: Novorossiia mezhdu proshlym i budushchim," in Plekhanov (ed.), *Novorossiia. Vosstavshaia iz pepla*.
802 Egor Kholmogorov, "Putin napomnil Novorossii, gde ee dom," April 18, 2014, available at: http://zerkalokryma.ru/lenta/people/opinions/putin_napomn il_novorossii_gde_yeye_dom2/.
803 Mikhail Polikarpov, *Oborona Donbassa: Igor' Strelkov – uzhas banderovskoi khunty* (Moscow: Knizhnyi mir, 2014): 229.

region's Soviet-era heavy industry, centre their vision on Donbas as the pivot of "*Novorossiia*."[804]

Key public figures of the pro-Russian insurgency struggle with this ambiguity surrounding the territorial positioning of "*Novorossiia*," but—unlike Moscow-based "couch warriors"—they have something to lose: actual political control over some territory in the Luhansk and Donetsk regions. Pavel Gubarev, one of the most prominent activists in Donbas, has offered a much more precise geographical vision of what "*Novorossiia*" should be in the future. He distinguishes between "Larger *Novorossiia*" and "Larger *Novorossiia* Plus." The former coincides with the historical *gubernia Novorossiia*, i.e. the imperial version, whereas the latter includes the regions of Cherkassy, Poltava, Chernigov, Sumy and Kiev, that is the socialist version, embracing all of left-bank Ukraine. Importantly, for Gubarev this difference is pragmatic rather than ideological: it is good to have "Larger *Novorossiia* Plus," but if they are not so lucky, "Larger *Novorossiia*" would do equally well.[805] Gubarev's statement powerfully visualizes the covert cravings of the Russian ideologues to position "*Novorossiia*" as a project which excludes—territorially as well as ideologically—the existence of an independent Ukraine. The newspaper *Novorossiia*, the mouthpiece of DPR, has similarly voiced the idea of splitting Ukraine into large "*Novorossiia*" and pro-Russian Ukraine proper, which after a time would gradually be accepted into Russia.[806] In the official press of the insurgents, "*Novorossiia*" is used as a synonym for the DPR and LPR,[807] which makes "*Novorossiia*" a tool for displaying the threat of expansionism to the Kiev government.

---

[804] Sergei Glaz'ev, *Ukrainskaia katastrofa: Ot amerikanskoi agressii k mirovoi voine?* (Moscow: Knizhnyi mir, 2015).

[805] Pavel Gubarev, "Ideologiia dlia Novorossii: 'Kruglyi stol' v 'Izborskom klube'," *Zavtra*, September 18, 2014; Gubarev, "My vosstali i prognali oligarkhov k nastoiashchim rabam!," *Novaia zemlia: Zhurnal Izborskogo Kluba Novorossii*, October 1, 2014.

[806] A. Luganskii, "Debal'tsevskii 'kotel'—zloumyshlennaia 'peremoga'," *Novorossiia*, no. 24 (2015); Luganskii, "Samostiinyi Karfagen dolzhen byt' razrushen," *Novorossiia*, no. 28 (2015),

[807] D. Sedov, "*Novorossiia*: Novoe samosoznanie naroda," *Novorossiia*, no. 25 (2015).

In the spring of 2014 the leadership of the DPR held ambitious visions of their would-be country, proclaiming its belonging to the "Russian civilization" (sometimes referred to as the "Russian world" in the official documents of the republics), but also stipulating its independent geopolitical course towards the integration with the Eurasian Union, launched on January 1, 2015.[808] These statements sent a clear message to the Kremlin that republics did not see themselves as parts of the Russian Federation in its present shape, but rather as more autonomous players on the international arena. However, later on, when hopes for the mass pro-Russian movement in Eastern and Southern Ukraine faded away, the spokespeople of the DPR and LPR put a different emphasis by prioritizing the development of local, Donbas-based patriotism over "*Novorossiia*" patriotism. This became especially visible after the stabilization of the borderline between the two self-declared peoples' republics and Ukraine, following the Minsk agreements.[809] The newspaper *Novorossiia* repeatedly highlights the militiamen's professional connections to the Donbas coal region, describing them as "former tractor drives and miners," or "yesterday's steelmakers and pitmen."[810]

This kind of regional affinity required inventing a different—neither imperial nor Soviet—tradition. From the beginning of 2015 the elites of the DPR and LPR started to invest a lot of energy into popularizing the short-lived Donetsk-Krivoi Rog Republic (DKRR), which existed in February–March 1918 on the territories of Yekaterinoslav, Khar'kov, Luhansk, Donetsk, Zaporozh'e, and partially Sumy, Kherson, Nikolaev and Russian Rostov regions with its centre in Khar'kov (later Luhansk). On February 6, 2015 a memorandum was adopted by the DPR which acknowledges the historical ties between the DKRR and DPR, not even mentioning

---

[808] "Programma OPD 'Partiia Novorossii'", in A. Surnin (ed.), *Materialy dlia noveishei istorii Novorossii* (St Petersburg: Kvadrivium, 2014).
[809] On April 17, 2014 Gubarev issued an official statement, in which he consistently used the ambiguous term "people of Donbas and *Novorossiia*," without explaining whether these terms are synonymous, or nested, or overlapping (Surnin (ed.), *Materialy*, 123–125).
[810] Luganskii, "Samostiinyi Karfagen."

"*Novorossiia.*"[811] One of the leaders of the DPR, Andrei Purgin, proposed to make February 12, the day when this republic was proclaimed, a national holiday in the DPR.[812] In February 2015 Donetsk hosted a historical exhibition dedicated to this event. Following the same line, journalist Vsevolod Petrovskii,[813] of a socialist persuasion, reverentially referred to Lenin's support for the socialist DKRR. The DKRR fits the ideological agenda of the insurgency's leaders in three respects: as a 1) socialist, 2) independent state, 3) closely tied with Russia. However, from the viewpoint of geographical imagination, it only complicates already convoluted historical associations because the DKRR did not fully coincide territorially either with historical *Novorossiia*, or with today's "*Novorossiia.*"

The "where" of "*Novorossiia*" is arguably the most daunting question for pro-Russian intellectuals and grassroots online polemists alike. Their opponents quickly spotted the weak link in the chain of their argumentation and worked out a trolling strategy,[814] which consists of repeatedly asking an opponent to show "*Novorossiia*" on a map, as illustrated in the following example:

> What is *Novorossiia*?
> I am [looking for it] in Google maps ... Nothing (((
> Show me where it is on the map (((.[815]

The territorial perplexity associated with "*Novorossiia*" is expressed in countless posts by pro-Russian users. For them it is clear neither where "*Novorossiia*" should appear in the future, nor where it is located in the present. As one user succinctly put it, "the utmost idiocy is that people from the DPR and LNR do not know where the

---

811 "Memorandum DNR ob osnovakh gosudarstvennogo stroitel'stva, politicheskoi i istoricheskoi preemstvennosti," *Novorossiia*, no. 21 (2015).
812 "V Donetske pochtili pamiat' pervogo rukovoditelia Donetsko-Krivorozhskoi Sovetskoi Respubliki," *Novorossiia*, no. 22 (2015).
813 K. Nesterov, "Pamiati Vsevoloda Petrovskogo. Put' voina: ot Maidana do Donbassa," *Novorossiia*, no. 24 (2015).
814 Christopher Hopkinson, "Trolling in Online Discussions: From Provocation to Community-building," *Brno studies in English* 39, no. 1 (2013).
815 Sam Fisher's post on July 31, 2014, available at https://vk.com/donetsk. Cf. Zloy Banderovets's post on September 23, 2015, available at: https://vk.com/donetsk; Anastasia Alamaska's post on September 25, 2015, available at: https://vk.com/donetsk.

borders of *Novorossiia* start and where [they] end."⁸¹⁶ It is not uncommon for the whole of Ukraine to be referred to as "*Novorossiia*," perhaps with the exception of the "most inveterate regions."⁸¹⁷ One of the few controversial themes among pro-Russian users is whether "*Novorossiia*" should capture and incorporate Kiev, or whether it should be satisfied with expelling "fascists" from Donbas.⁸¹⁸ Another user is puzzled about whether Odessa should be incorporated into "*Novorossiia*" "or the Americans would not let it happen."⁸¹⁹ The geographical messiness of "*Novorossiia*" is further aggravated by its unclear relationship with Russia proper. Some users claim it to be ancient Russian lands;⁸²⁰ others support the idea of a state, independent from both Ukraine and Russia. Moreover, if the restoration of historical *Novorossiia* is at stake, Russia should also cede substantial parts of its territory, including Crimea, Rostov-on-Don region and Kuban. As an extravagant territorial projection of the idea of the "Russian Spring," some users suggest incorporating Russia into the territory of "*Novorossiia*."⁸²¹

The relation of Donbas to "*Novorossiia*" is as puzzling for online users as for public intellectuals. In spite of the attempts of the DPR to propagate Donbas patriotism, many users consciously neglect self-identification with Donbas in favour of "*Novorossiia*,"⁸²² because Donbas is framed as an old industrial, economically depressed region with low social prestige and associations with the unpopular workers' and communist movements (cf. "pathetic

---

816 Roman Tagiev's post on February 22, 2015, available at: http://vk.com/wall168439337_1387915.
817 Putingoodluck's post on March 8, 2015, available at: http://vk.com/wall-78275866_5164.
818 Sebastyan Pereyra's post on March 1, 2015, available at: http://vk.com/wall288332879_6054951; too_brutal's post on March 1, 2015, available at: http://vk.com/wall399557_13402.
819 frigeridga1975's post on March 8, 2015, available at: https://twitter.com/frigeridga1975/status/574516094951669760.
820 Yurii Zaitsev's post on March 8, 2015, available at: http://vk.com/wall238589801_6126698.
821 Aleksei Sharkov's post on March 2, 2015, available at: http://www.facebook.com/permalink.php?id=100003380105151&story_fbid=673157446140253.
822 Dimosha Milovanov's post on February 22, 2015, available at: http://vk.com/wall114654888_8234.

depressive Lugandon";[823] "half-destroyed Donbas, forgotten by God."[824] It is not infrequent to encounter ironic "Dambass" spelling of the term, which uneducated inhabitants who cannot correctly write the name of their region, or even—catering for the English-speaking audience—"Dumbass." In contrast, "*Novorossiia*" is reminiscent of a much more attractive imperial historical legacy and hints at the possibility of "rejuvenation" and "renaissance."

However, politically loaded terms *novoross* (i.e. a "New Russian") and "people of *Novorossiia*" are conspicuously rare. *Novoross* sounds especially weird to a Russian ear, whereas "people of *Novorossiia*" is somewhat more common. However, the most typical reference is to the "inhabitants of *Novorossiia*" (*zhiteli Novorossii*), which highlights their passive and geographical relation to "*Novorossiia*" as merely a spatial location. In this sense, the linguistic convention puts "*Novorossiia*" on a par with any Russian *oblast'*; the common phrase is, for example, "inhabitants of Perm krai," whereas there is no politically-coloured term to represent those "inhabitants" as a community. The political debate is centred on the name of the territory, not on the name of the people. As one user observes, "journalists do not know what to say. Sometimes they say 'inhabitants of *Novorossiia*', sometimes, obviously by the order from above, they flounder and say 'inhabitants of the South-East of Ukraine'. Hesitations, hesitations."[825]

Ideology of *Novorossiia*

Different political projects require different territories to sustain them.[826] From its very inception the concept of "*Novorossiia*" was informed with various competing ideologies both from the left and

---

823 Emiliozk's post on March 1, 2015, available at: http://emiliozk.livejournal.com/366964.html?thread=621684. The play on words parallels the name of the city Lugansk (Luhansk) with the obscene Russian gandon (condom).
824 Oleg Yakhnenko's post on March 8, 2015, available at: http://vk.com/wall276694117_1190041.
825 Andrei Solonnikov's post on February 22, 2015, available at: http://vk.com/wall244408971_101298.
826 Lefebvre, *State, Space, World*, 186.

right wings of the political spectrum,[827] which correspond to various outlines of its borders. Different versions of imperial and socialist territoriality roughly correspond to two main ideological argumentation threads in relation to "*Novorossiia*": traditionalism, which also embraces imperial monarchism, right-wing nationalism, and white-power racism on the one hand, and anti-globalism with concomitant ramifications of anti-oligarchic revolutionary stance, ideology of the grassroots' resistance, and Soviet nostalgia, on the other. However, more often than not, "*Novorossiia*" serves as a symbolic (and sometimes actual) meeting ground for the political extremes from the left and right. The common denominator for all these political speculations is the vision of "*Novorossiia*" as a locus of national regeneration ("palingenesis"). This interpretation points at the readiness to radically cast off all shackles and restore the perennial truths and "natural" order of things.[828]

Some regions, especially those associated with territorial "phantom pains" are being fetishized and become over-represented in the geopolitical imagination, acquiring contours of "a condensed symbol of the nation itself."[829] In Russia, where according to the aphorism of Vasilii Kliuchevskii, the center lies on the periphery, distant lands, sometimes outside of the state borders, quite often acquire exaggerated symbolic importance as places of regeneration.[830] The very name of "*Novorossiia*" ("*New* Russia") makes it a paradigmatic place of palingenetic hopes. For example, the leadership of DPR even insists that "*Novorossiia*" is not just a part of the Russian civilization but its most precious "pearl," the condensation

---

827 Laruelle, "The Three Colors of *Novorossiia*, or the Russian Nationalist Mythmaking of the Ukrainian Crisis," Post-Soviet Affairs 32, no. 1 (2015): 55–74.
828 Not digging into the discussion of the appropriateness of the term "fascism" in this context, it is obvious that "*Novorossiia*" imagery resonates within the large host of semi- and proto-fascist ideologies, such as neo-Eurasianism and Conservative Revolution, whose intellectual core is conditioned by the thrust towards national regeneration (Roger Griffin, The Nature of Fascism (London: Routledge, 1993); Andreas Umland, "Zhirinovskii as a Fascist: Palingenetic Ultra-Nationalism and the Emergence of the Liberal-Democratic Party of Russia in 1992–93," Forum für osteuropäische Ideen- und Zeitgeschichte 14, no. 2 (2010)).
829 Franck Billé, "Territorial Phantom Pains, 173.
830 Bassin, Imperial Visions: Nationalist Imagination and Geographical Expansion in the Russian Far East, 1840–1865 (Cambridge: Cambridge University Press, 1999).

of "Russianness," with its military glory, economic success and cultural heterogeneity. With a tinge of nostalgia for the socialist past, Pavel Gubarev calls "*Novorossiia*" the showcase of late Soviet prosperity. He identified his visions as a mixture of traditionalism and socialist-coloured futurism and called for an effort to "combine Orthodoxy with the roaring rocket's nozzles."[831]

In the same place Gubarev mentions that in order to understand his motivations, one has to read the Soviet-era SF novel *The Bull's Hour* (1968) by Ivan Efremov, depicting a Communist Earth expanding into the outer space. The utopian and futuristic connotations of the brand "*Novorossiia*" are obvious in the following examples. The leader of the pro-Russian militants, the "vice-Defense Minister" of the Donetsk People's Republic, Fedor Berezin, is a professional SF writer who has authored several dozens of books in the genres of "alternative history" and "military science fiction" (*voennaia fantastika*). Several other SF authors, such as Luhansk writers Gleb Bobrov, Andrei Kruz and Grigorii Savitskii, who had prophesied the military "clash of civilizations" in Ukraine, have joined or openly supported the pro-Russian insurgents. Capitalizing on the Soviet SF term "close aim fantasy," those authors publish in the book series called "Close combat fantasy" (*fantastika blizhnego pritsela – fantastika blizhnego boia*), implying an association of this kind of SF with the real-life military conflict. "*Novorossiia*" has become a post-Soviet "Free Republic of Fiume," a political *Gesamtkunstwerk* of sorts, combining utopian narrative, historical performance and bloody warfare.[832]

Gubarev's call to combine traditionalism and futurism has a resonance among all members of the Izborsk club. It also has parallels with the ideology of "atomic Orthodoxy,"[833] formulated by Orthodox activist Egor Kholmogorov, painter Aleksei Beliaev-

---

[831] Gubarev, *Fakel Novorossii* (St Petersburg: Piter, 2016): 7–9, 69.
[832] C. Young, "The Sci-Fi Writers' War", July 11, 2011, available at: http://www.slate.com/articles/news_and_politics/politics/2014/07/science_fiction_writers_predicted_ukraine_conflict_now_they_re_fighting.html. Cf. also (Il'ia Gerasimov, "Ukraine 2014: The First Postcolonial Revolution. Introduction to the Forum," *Ab Imperio*, no. 3 (2014)).
[833] Maria Engström, "Contemporary Russian Messianism and New Russian Foreign Policy," *Contemporary Security Policy* 35, no. 3 (2014).

Gintovt, and advocacy journalist Maksim Kalashnikov, whom Gubarev reverentially addressed to as his teacher. The religious implications of separatism in Eastern Ukraine have been picked up by the Orthodox publicist Kirill Frolov, for whom "*Novorossiia*" represents a springboard for the liberation of the whole Orthodox world from the fetters of secularism, as well as from a godless Ukraine dominated by "Uniates" (Greek-Catholics).[834] In this sense "*Novorossiia*" reconnects with Patriarch Kirill's vision of Holy Rus', i.e. the territorial projection of Russia's cultural fundamentals. This Holy Rus' imagery became a source of inspiration for the leadership of "*Novorossiia.*" It is enough to state that the Constitution of the Donetsk People's Republic, adopted on 3 June 2014, stipulates in the Preamble that the self-proclaimed republic is an "inseparable part of the Russian World as the Russian civilization," and that Orthodoxy is a pillar of the Russian World.

Likewise, Vitalii Aver'yanov depicts "*Novorossiia*" as the avant-garde of the culturally defined Russianness or the "Russian civilization," characterized by three main components: Russian identity, Orthodoxy and advanced industry.[835] Aver'yanov thus mixes up imperial and Soviet elements, placing industrial Donbas on an equal footing with Orthodox centres of historical *Novorossiia*. As Sergei Mironov concisely puts it in the same vein, "*Novorossiia*" nurtures two ideas: social justice and the importance of traditional values.[836] Following this line of argumentation, Egor Kholmogorov shrewdly draws parallels between "*Novorossiia*" and the American Western frontier. As a space of grassroots colonization, "*Novorossiia*" is Russia's America, a launchpad for any bold experiment[837] with a tinge of alternativeness and a futuristic thrust. In Maksim Kalashnikov's views, "*Novorossiia*" is the testing ground

---

[834] Kirill Frolov, *Sakral'nye smysly Novorossii: Tserkovnye i tsivilizatsionnye raskoly v Novorossii, na Podkarpatskoi Rusi i Ukraine* (St Petersburg: Aleteiia, 2015).

[835] Valery Aver'ianov, "Novorossiia—avangard natsii," in Plekhanov, S. (ed.), *Novorossiia. Vosstavshaia iz pepla* (Moscow: Knizhnyi mir, 2014).

[836] Sergei Mironov, "Novorossiia—Novaia Rossiia," July 31, 2014, available at: http://izvestia.ru/news/574606.

[837] Kholmogorov, "Putin napomnil Novorossii, gde ee dom," April 18, 2014, available at: http://zerkalokryma.ru/lenta/people/opinions/putin_napomn il_novorossii_gde_yeye_dom2/

for the most advanced industry, which can be developed in a socialist and protective environment: future-cities (*futuropolisy*), marine agriculture, *ekranoplany* (ground-effect ships), submerged hotels, seacoast farms and so on.[838] The revolutionary and socialist potential of "*Novorossiia*" has been highlighted by Sergei Glaz'ev, who parallels the resistance of Donbas to the Civil War in Spain: it is now on the frontline of a new world war against the global capitalist order.[839] For those intellectuals "*Novorossiia*" represents a territorialized ideology, or "a springboard of [political] opportunity."[840]

The similar narratives about Russian civilization and the Russian World lie behind Eurasianist visions of "*Novorossiia*." In the spirit of the "Conservative Revolution" and the European New Right movements, Aleksandr Dugin maintains that "*Novorossiia*" is a project whose far-reaching influence can transform the whole of Russia and Eurasia in general, because it signifies the revolutionary awakening of Russia's true self. Thus, "*Novorossiia*" is not a territory, it is "Russia's future."[841] But in order to sustain this spirit of radical return to civilizational roots and escape from the fetters of Modernity, "*Novorossiia*" should remain an independent state, not become part of Russia, whose oligarchs and Westernized intellectuals are likely to corrupt the newborn. Eurasianists, especially from the movement "Young Eurasia," cheerfully welcomed "*Novorossiia*" as a keystone in their Eurasian project, which should not necessarily become a part of Russia, but should rather co-exist alongside Russia within a broader integration project.[842] For Eurasianists, especially those under the influence of Lev Gumilev, "*Novorossiia*" represents the westernmost part of the Great Steppe, the cradle of the empire of Genghis Khan and the pivot of Eurasian identity. Historical connection of the lands to the north of the Black Sea with Golden Horde, Crimean khanate and Ottoman Empire

---

[838] Maksim Kalashnikov, "Novorossiia—zavtrashniaia real'nost'," in Plekhanov (ed.), *Novorossiia. Vosstavshaia iz pepla* (Moscow: Knizhnyi mir, 2014).
[839] Glaz'ev, *Ukrainskaia katastrofa*.
[840] Williams and Smith, "The National Construction of Social Space."
[841] Dugin, *Ukraina: Moia voina*.
[842] Iury Georgievskii, "Predannaia revoliutsiia Novorossii," June 26, 2014, posted at: http://eurasian-movement.ru/archives/11307 (no longer available).

additionally supplies the Eurasian imagination with the vision of "*Novorossiia*" as a place where the East meets the West.

An important ideological ingredient of thinking about "*Novorossiia*" is portraying it as a bastion against forces of globalization with a clear-cut geopolitical dimension. Most of those nationalistic intellectuals view *Novorossiia* as a trump card in the "big geopolitical game," in which the Russian civilization is withstanding the pressure of the global West. In July 2014 a group of patriotic organizations and geopolitical think-tanks under the guidance of Colonel-General Leonid Ivashov, the president of the Academy for Geopolitical Problems, prepared a "Military and Political Doctrine for the Struggle in *Novorossiia*," which depicts the rebellious region as the avant-garde of the Russian World in its war against "Atlantic civilization," and more specifically as part of the strategy to keep Ukraine in the Russian World.[843]

Similarly to "Crimea is ours" discourses, which have not been fully controlled by the government, "*Novorossiia*" is setting its own agenda, which may or may not cater to the demands of those in power. The state manifestly lacks powers to fix its meaning in one particular way, for example, along the lines of cultural conservatism which marks Vladimir Putin's third presidential term. However, unlike the "Crimea is ours!" campaign and such geopolitical brands as the "Russian world" or "Eurasian Union," which enjoy official support, "*Novorossiia*" has not managed to enlist the Russian elite into its "fandom." Besides, palingenetic connotations of its ideology over-represent this place as qualitatively most important territory of the imaginary "Russian world": as the point of growth, as a locus of regeneration, as a bastion of resistance to the universal evil forces, and so on. Understandably, over-representation of the region lying beyond the state borders of the Russian Federation challenges both official "strategic narratives"[844] on "sovereign democracy" and on the "vertical of power."

---

843 Leonid Ivashov, *Radikal'naia doktrina Novorossii* (Moscow: Algoritm, 2014).
844 Laura Roselle, A. Miskimmon and B. O'Loughlin, "Strategic Narrative: A New Means to Understand Soft Power," *Media, War & Conflict* 7, no. 1 (2014): 70–84.

Novorossiia in online debates

Online debates show that the most important method for making sense of "*Novorossiia*" ideologically consists in its "palingenetic" reading, which reduces the problem of blurred territoriality by depicting "*Novorossiia*" as a work-in-progress (*Novorossii byt'*).[845] The language of regeneration is salient in the following home-made verses, entitled *There Should Be Novorossiia!* (*Novorossii byt'!*), and circulating on the internet in March 2015:

> This is how the people have decided and ordered
> To restore to life a forgotten country.
> We remember [this country] and it lives in us,
> And [it] has been alive in all [previous] generations.
> So let it revive today again,
> And let it become our new house.
> And those who want to prevent us from this doing,
> We will convict according to new laws [of a crime].[846]

On the symbolic plane of interpretation, palingenetic project of "*Novorossiia*" is connected with the metaphors about constructing a new home, in contrast to the annexation of Crimea—which was framed as "returning home," i.e. to Russia. Both tropes of regeneration and building a new house somewhat exclude Russia from assuming the role of a representative of "*Novorossiia*," as happened in Crimea. Indeed, *There Should Be Novorossiia!* clearly stipulates that the initiative belongs to the people of "*Novorossiia*" and nobody else.

The trope of constructing a new home corresponds to a common metaphor of territory as "our property,"[847] which is one of the most developed in online debates. The metaphor of "property" creates emotional tension when "*Novorossiia*" is pictured as occupied or under threat of occupation by the enemy—hence the affective

---

[845] Yana Spas's post on March 8, 2015, available at: http://vk.com/wall6705 0309_288341.

[846] Fashizmynety's post on March 8, 2015, available at: http://vk.com/wall-40441936_20005.

[847] Tuomas Forsberg, "The Ground without Foundation: Territory as a Social Construct," 7–24.

promise: "We will never give you ['*Novorossiia*'] to anybody."[848] The "property" metaphor usefully distinguishes "us" from "them" by accusing the Ukrainian army and right-wing activists of "coming to our land"[849] or "invading our territory."[850] The task of the insurgent army is thus to "drive out fascists from our land,"[851] or "to kick the Ukrainian gangs [*ukrobandy*] beyond the borders of *Novorossiia*."[852] This metaphor resonates powerfully with historical reminiscences of the Great Patriotic War and the liberation of Ukraine from occupation by Nazi Germany. A common propagandistic device is to call the opponents "fascists," "banderites" and *karateli* (members of the SS' punitive expeditions against civil population).[853]

Fighting against *karateli* reconnects the property metaphor with the theme of renaissance in imagining "*Novorossiia*." In line with the ideological construction of "*Novorossiia*," the renaissance metaphor imparts a sense of a mission to the insurgency, so the common argument in online polemics is that "Crimea just left [Ukraine], but *Novorossiia* will scorch fascism from all occupied regions."[854] The sense of mission evokes a series of religious and pre-religious associations wherein "*Novorossiia*" is a sacral space, where super-natural forces are at play and where all normalcy is cancelled.[855] This interpretation evokes parallels with Giorgio

---

848 Fapacbk's post on March 1, 2015, available at: https://twitter.com/fapac bk/status/572138864208445441.
849 Juliya_shado's post on March 8, 2015, available at: http://vk.com/wall20 5799280_848.
850 Zhenechka Filimonova's post on March 8, 2015, available at: http://vk.com/ wall13918103_831412.
851 Vasily Petrov's post on February 12, 2015, available at: https://vk.com/wall-64487399?q=новороссия&w=wall-64487399_21412%2Fall.
852 Virita's post on March 8, 2015, available at: http://www.liveinternet.ru/ users/baroma/post355702992/#BlCom669759717.; cf. Elena Talashova's post on March 8, 2015, available at: http://vk.com/wall67448797_630525.
853 Elizaveta Gaufman, "Memory, Media, and Securitization: Russian Media Framing of the Ukrainian Crisis," *Journal of Soviet and Post-Soviet Politics and Society* 1, no. 1 (2015): 141–175; Alexandr Osipian, "Historical Myths, Enemy Images and Reginal Identity in the Donbass Insurgency (Spring 2014)," *Journal of Soviet and Post-Soviet Politics and Society* 1, no. 1 (2015): 109–140.
854 Allivdeaber's post on March 2, 2015, available at: https://twitter.com/allivde aber/status/572140080694870016.
855 René Girard, *La violence et le sacré* (Paris: Grasset, 1972).

Agamben's political philosophy, which maintains that political relations are based on the biopolitical practices of exclusion.[856] In this sense, a concentration camp serves as the most obvious explanatory model for the politics of DPR and LPR, being excluded both from the Ukrainian and Russian legal orders.

Following this framing, "*Novorossiia*" is a place marked by imagery of blood and sacrifice, with a special focus on the sacrificial death of children at the hands of Ukrainian solders and right-wing hitmen (cf. "children were torn into pieces …").[857] One user, drawing on the metaphor of "property," developed this idea as follows: "Get out from *Novorossiia, karateli*. God punishes you because you destroy Orthodox Churches there, and kill people of Donbas. You will go to hell …"[858] Likewise, a poem by a certain Anna Vasil'eva mentions blood and death many times, for example, here, addressing the Kiev administration:

> You have destroyed so many innocent [lives] there,
> How could you live with all this blood on your hands?![859]

Another poem mixes up themes of sacrificing children, "fascist *karateli*" occupying our land, and the geopolitical vision of Ukraine as a pawn in the big game of great powers (one of them is represented with a racist hint at Barack Obama):

> You are fascists on the service of the [U.S.] Department of State,
> You are led by the black master,
> You wear Nazi uniforms,
> You shoot in women and men.
> You bravely shoot in children too …[860]

---

856 Georgio Agamben, *Homo Sacer: Sovereign Power and Bare Life* (Stanford, Calif.: Stanford University Press, 1998).
857 Arship's post on February 21, 2015, available at: http://vk.com/wall16260 5065_90082.
858 Dana Zaborova's post on March 1, 2015, available at: http://vk.com/wall26879 6847_72.
859 Anastasiya Gromova's post on March 8, 2015, available at: http://vk.com/wall213819383_2391.
860 Bujhbkkj's post on February 21, 2015, available at: http://vk.com/wall1797 04429_1458.

Territorial imagination always utilizes a set of biopolitical metaphors, involving the image of a (predominantly female) body.[861] However, "*Novorossiia*" failed to develop "body" metaphors or a stable association with a female figure—partially because the spatial basis of the pro-Russian insurgency is Donbas, a word of the masculine gender in Russian, imaginatively connected with heavy industry and mining, i.e. with predominantly "men's business." A few instances of associating "*Novorossiia*" with feminine imagery are effectively counter-balanced by representing the typical insurgent as an epitome of masculinity. The already quoted poem *Novorossiia Should Be* frames it as follows:

> That guy who had simply cut coal,
> Has long joined the ranks of the militia.[862]

Whereas the symbol of the Crimean annexation/reunification is the girlish-looking public prosecutor Natalia Poklonskaia,[863] the Donbas rebellion has become represented by the iconic figure of "Babai the Cossack," an extravagant-looking bearded militiaman (see **figure 8**). Babai has evoked a wave of visual representations on social networks, which invariably highlight his masculine properties. One of them, for example, has the inscription "Europe has forgotten what a bearded victor looks like. Shall we remind them?," bringing to mind successful Russian military campaigns in Europe, most notably in 1813/14 and 1944/45. Babai's masculine imagery is connected with the idea of assertiveness, or "passionarity," couched in terms of Lev Gumilev's popular theory,[864] which has lent its idiosyncratic language to many spokesmen of "*Novorossiia*," including, among others, Pavel Gubarev. Instead of representing "*Novorossiia*" as a suffering fragile body in need of help, its present image as an aggressive warrior is easily incorporated into the narrative of the Donbas insurgency as Russia's military encroachment on the

---

861 Forsberg, "The Ground without Foundation"; Marina Warner, *Monuments and Maidens: The Allegory of the Female Form* (London: Vintage, 1996).
862 Fashizmynety's post on March 8, 2015, available at: http://vk.com/wall-40441936_20005.
863 Suslov, "Crimea Is Ours!"
864 Bassin, *The Gumilev Mystique*.

territorial integrity of Ukraine. Figures of armoured women do occasionally circulate on the internet, but none of them has risen to nationwide fame comparable to that of Natalia Poklonskaia. The conspicuous absence of female symbolism surrounding "*Novorossiia*" contributes to a failure to securitize the border of *Novorossiia*.[865] The irony of the situation is that unlike Natalia Poklonskaia, a resident of Crimea, both Strelkov and Babai are Russians from Moscow and Kuban' respectively. Their external provenance raises doubts about the subjectivity of "*Novorossiia.*"

Figures like Strelkov and Babai the Cossack (Aleksandr Mozhaev) became celebrities and icons of the insurgency, evoking all sorts of "fan-art," including cartoons. One cartoon, published in the group vk.com/superstrelkov, is entitled *Colonel Strelkov: A Hero Beyond Time*. It represents the separatist leader as a super-hero in the style of Captain America. The plotline features Strelkov as a colonel of the Russian Imperial Army during the First World War, who is severely wounded and teetering between life and death. A doctor offers him a mysterious remedy, which would heal him but make him a saint-like immortal person whose task would be to help Russia whenever enemies encroach on its territory. His first task in this new capacity is killing Hitler. In the first picture he is sent to Hitler's bunker; in the second he forces Hitler to take poison (the bubble reads: "Don't worry, history schoolbooks will say that you did it yourself"). In the third, Strelkov is rushing to his next feat, which is organizing protests in Simferopol in 2014, which would end up in breaking the Crimean peninsula away from Ukraine.[866] A similar appreciation group on vk.com is devoted to Babai the Cossack, depicted in a way that evokes associations with Fidel Castro and Cuban guerrillas (cf. **figure 8**).

---

865 Anne Norton, *Reflections on Political Identity* (Baltimore: Johns Hopkins University Press, 1988).
866 Cartoon about Strelkov. Source: https://vk.com/photo-72553817_334306875

Figure 8. Babai the Cossack.

Source: https://vk.com/kazak_babaj?w=wall-67949608_56184. Accessed 1 September 2015.

This kind of branding of "*Novorossiia*" has its flipside. The widespread vision of "*Novorossiia*" as a marketable project[867] contains latent self-delegitimizing potential because it imparts to the concept of "*Novorossiia*" a tinge of unreality, an association with something which is made-up and not natural or historically rooted. The idea of "*Novorossiia*" as a project generates a sense of disempowerment, because it suggests that people living in "*Novorossiia*" are not masters of their own lives. Instead they are merely soft clay in the hands

---

867 E.g. Dmitry Kozinkin's post on May 29, 2015, available at: https://vk.com/donetsk.

of mighty—and mostly externally located—Kremlin politicians. This attitude reveals a deeply seated distrust towards any political elite, represented as greedy scoundrels, for whom "*Novorossiia*" is just an occasion to fill pockets.[868] One user, who regularly posts on Donetsk's public chatroom on vk.com, wrote:

> I was with the militia and helped them when [it all] begun, [then] I guessed the Kremlin's riddle. They are using Donbas for their political purposes. Putin needed only Crimea. He uses us to make sacrifices for the purpose of trading with the West ...[869]

Online debaters have neither managed to elaborate a common territorial visualization of "*Novorossiia*," nor been successful in drawing a clear-cut historical genealogy. As a result, the territorial metaphors remain at a fairly basic level, mostly connected with the vision of "*Novorossiia*" as "our land" threatened by foreign occupants. Potentially powerful, this imagery has been undermined by an alternative Messianic and expansionist interpretation of "*Novorossiia*." Oscillation between two master-narratives of "*Novorossiia*" — "building our new home" and "returning home to Russia" — have effectively prevented the creation of political subjectivity on this territory.

Conclusions

Blurred, flexible "hyper-borders,"[870] capable of stretching, may be considered an advantage for governing Russia,[871] but they are detrimental to imagining "*Novorossiia*." Indeterminacy of its territorial parameters and the imbrication of ideological narratives prevented the production of a consistent popular image: "*Novorossiia*" is both a sacrifice and a political subject, a suffering female body and an

---

868 Alla Kutsenko's post on July 30, 2014, available at: https://vk.com/donetsk.
869 Vladimir Surkov's post on May 31, 2015, available at: https://vk.com/donetsk.
870 Paul Richardson, "Beyond the Nation and into the State: Identity, Belonging, and the 'Hyper-Border'," *Transactions of the Institute of British Geographers* 41, no. 2 (2016).
871 Gleb Pavlovskii, *Sistema RF v voine 2014 goda: De Principatu Debili* (Moscow: Evropa, 2014); Lara Ryazanova-Clarke, "The Discourse of a Spectacle at the End of the Presidential Term," in Goscilo (ed.), *Putin as Celebrity and Cultural Icon* (London: Routledge, 2013).

aggressively expansionist male force. From the viewpoint suggested in the beginning of the article, "*Novorossiia*" has failed to become a geopolitical brand, which could effectively create and explain the difference between the land and people of "*Novorossiia*" and the land and people of Ukraine (or for that matter—Russia). Without the ideological support for "*Novorossiia*" from official Russia, the leadership of DPR and LPR are now investing in an alternative territorial brand of "Donbas," which has had its setbacks but is in two aspects more felicitous (in terms of practical implementation) than "*Novorossiia*": its territory roughly coincides with the region, controlled by the self-proclaimed republics, and it refers to the much more historically and geographically stable borders of the Donbas mining area. Thus, "*Novorossiia*" continues to exist mainly in the discussions of the Russian right- and left-wing extremities, such as Izborsk club. These circles promote "palingenetic" imagery of "*Novorossiia*" as a place of national regeneration, which is salient and disturbing because it is fraught with violent and anti-liberal political courses of action.

Afterword: Amendments to the Constitution and Geopolitical Visions, 2020

On January 15, 2020, President Putin announced a constitutional reform in his annual address to the Russian parliament. In this speech, "absolute sovereignty" and national security were stressed. Putin specifically proposed to stipulate that national legislation would be higher than international laws, and dwelled on the ban for state functionaries to have a second citizenship or a residence permit. Summing up his address, Putin called to "create a solid, reliable, and invulnerable system that will be absolutely stable in terms of the external contour and will securely guarantee Russia's independence and sovereignty."[872] A few days thereafter, the law proposal on the amendments to the Constitution of 1993 was submitted to and accepted by the State Duma. In circumvention to the normal procedure, amendments to the Constitution were adopted by the referendum on July 1, 2020. Later on, the State Duma proposed to celebrate this date as the "Day of Russia's national interests."[873]

In continuation of Putin's proposals in the address, the revised Constitution included, among other things, a legal possibility for him personally to stay in power as Russia's President after the end of his present presidential term in 2024, as well as some changes to the power structure of the country. Most importantly, however, the amendments enshrined the new vision of the state ideology, in contradiction to the article 13 of the same Constitution, which solemnly declares: "Ideological diversity shall be recognized in the Russian Federation. No ideology shall be proclaimed as State ideology or as obligatory."[874]

---

[872] "Presidential Address to the Federal Assembly," *kremlin.ru*, January 15, 2020, available at: http://en.kremlin.ru/events/president/news/62582.
[873] N.a., "V Gosdume predlozhili 1 iulia ...", *IA Regnum*, July 2, 2020.
[874] In order to evade the obvious contradiction, the official language calls this not an ideology but the "set of values" (*nabor tsennostei*). See: Aleksandra Beluza, "Osnovnoi Zakon Rossii," *Rossiiskaia gazeta*, June 11, 2020.

This state ideology resulted from at least two decades of the political polylogue among the members of the elite and the non-liberal right- and left-wing opposition. Most of these debates were characterized by the salience of geopolitical topics. In contrast to the universalism of the Soviet-era ideology, these debates boil down to the treadmill of talks about Russian identity, Russia's place in the world, and relation to other nations, mostly in the West. Changes in the Constitution followed the conceptual change in Russian utopias and political science fiction. Whereas the Soviet-era fantasies tried to nail down major problems of humanity: preconditions for justice, equality, limits of cognition and perfection, future of human bodies and psyche, — post-Soviet science fiction elaborates on Russia's future greatness, restoration of the Soviet Union, revenge on Russia's geopolitical enemies, humiliation of the USA and so on. The revised Constitution is inspired not by dreams of a better society, but by geopolitical fears and security concerns. In this way, Russia's fundamental law became a projection of geopolitical imagination.

Indeed, the consensual understanding of the gist of amendments consists of the argument about reinforcing Russia's security and sovereignty. This was the primary concern of the working group on the amendments to the Constitution. One of its members, actor Vladimir Mashkov, voiced his concern about the Western political figures and analysts who, in his words, wait for the end of Putin's presidency in order to make territorial claims to Russia. In this connection, Mashkov proposed to enter a "ferroconcrete [*zhelezobetonnyi*, i.e. exceptionally strong] amendment" against the very possibility even to discuss territorial questions. Putin took up the word and admitted that he personally would have liked to have this "ferroconcrete amendment" in the Constitution.[875] This amendment became article 67.2¹ of the revised Constitution. It emphatically denies the possibility of secession and bans any calls for

---

875 Irina Korneeva, "Granitsa Mashkova," *Rossiiskaia gazeta*, March 31, 2020, available at: https://rg.ru/2020/03/31/vladimir-mashkov-territorialnaia-celostnost-dlia-menia-eto-ne-popravka-a-aksioma.html. The conversation is recorded in the following Youtube video of February 13, 2020: https://www.youtube.com/watch?v=mDtkyacqM_o.

separatism. On the grounds of this article, a criminal law on secession has been proposed as of July 2020,[876] as well as the revised version of the administrative prosecution for calls for separatism. The former penalizes any discourses about re-configuration of Russian borders, regardless of whether they are connected with calls for violent actions, or not.[877] In theory, this means that even an academic examination of this matter could be considered as liable to prosecution.

Mashkov's phrase, which by that time became a catchword, inspired the administration of Iuzhno-Sakhalinsk on the Kuril Islands to inaugurate the memorial plate, made of the reinforced concrete, with the etched text of this article. In this way, the "ferroconcrete amendment" became a monument, symbolically marking out one of Russia's contested territories.[878] However, the primary concern of this article was the unarticulated fear to lose Crimea. The perception of the territorial loss after the "greatest geopolitical catastrophe", the feeling of the lack of finality in Russia's present borders, and preposterous talks about Russia, which "does not end anywhere" — backfired by instilling a persistent sense of precarity of the present territorial arrangement.

The same article 67.2¹ declares that the Russian Federation "defends its sovereignty". By highlighting the need to maintain sovereignty, the revised Constitution encapsulates the long debates on "sovereign democracy" and inadvertently reveals doubts about Russia's independence vis-à-vis the "West". Dmitry Medvedev, for example, the long-term prime minister and now the deputy head of the Security Council of Russia, interpreted the constitutional reform in general as a provision for the "country's independence".[879]

---

[876] N.a., "Gosduma uzhestochit otvetstvennost'," *Vedomosti*, July 8, 2020, available at: https://www.vedomosti.ru/society/articles/2020/07/08/834220-gosduma a-uzhestochit.
[877] N.a., "Anonsirovano vvedenie administrativnoi preiuditsii," *Sova-center.ru*, July 8, 2020, available at: https://www.sova-center.ru/misuse/news/lawma king/2020/07/d42632/.
[878] N.a., "Putin otmetil 'zhelezobetonnuiu popravku' o neotchuzhdenii territorii," *Interfax*, July 3, 2020, available at: https://www.interfax.ru/russia/715823.
[879] Dmitry Medvedev, "Medvedev sviazal popravki v Konstitutsiiu ...," *Lenta.ru*, March 10, 2020, available at: https://lenta.ru/news/2020/03/10/suverenitet/.

Similarly, Sergei Markov, director of the pro-Kremlin think-tank "Institute of Political Research", saw amendments as a means to strengthen Russia's sovereignty. He believed that the constitutional reform was timely precisely because of the pandemic, which, in his opinion, revealed that "globalization was crumbling in front of our eyes" and national sovereignty is coming to the fore.[880] At the recorded meeting between President Putin and the working group on amendments, Konstantin Kosachev paralleled Russia in the 1990s to a "living organizm without skin, exposed to the hostile environment."[881]

One of the political studies professors from Chelyabinsk State University elaborated on the amendments in a way which highlighted the international pressure on Russia. He connected the fact that Russia possesses one third of the world deposits of natural resources with the sanctions imposed on the country after 2014. In his interpretation this happened because "the collective West" was at pains to prevent Russia from becoming an independent international subject and from entering into an alliance with China. He pointed at the decisions of the international courts that Russia had to pay large fees (for example, in connection with the YUKOS affair), arguing that the international jurisdiction has become an instrument of "hybrid warfare" against Russia. In this context, amendments aimed to counter the external threats by making international legislation subordinate to the domestic laws.[882] Another expert astutely observed (and praised) the tendency of the new Constitution to roll back processes of globalization and integration into the world community; "Russia is now being isolated [*zamykaetsia*] within its state borders".[883]

---

880 N.a., "Predlozheny vovremia," *AiF*, April 8, 2020. See also: Galina Gracheva, "Eksperty rasskazali, kakie popravki k Konstitutsii dlia Rossii vazhnee vsego," *Nezavisimaia gazeta*, June 8, 2020.
881 "Vstrecha Vladimira Putina s rabochei gruppoi," *Rossiia 24*, February 26, 2020, available at: https://www.youtube.com/watch?v=H2MAbcneFjg.
882 Vitalii Ivanov, S. Zyrianov et al., "Ekspertnyi klub Cheliabinska: Predlozheniia Presidenta po Izmeneniiu Konstitutsii ...," *Sotsium i vlast'* 82, no. 2 (2020): 115–116.
883 Remark by Aleksandr Fedotov, lecturer of history at the Cheliabinsk State University (Ivanov, Zyrianov et al., "Ekspertnyi klub," 122.

Concerns about independence were also implemented in article 67.1 (part 2¹) and article 71.т. The first introduces the new term "federal territory," which reflected on the perceived need to additionally securitize some parts of Russia, such as the Arctic or North Caucasus. The second stipulates that the state functionaries be prohibited from having a second citizenship or a residence permit in another country, or having accounts in foreign banks. Russia's independence is underpinned by the new Constitution in yet another way. The new article (79¹) defines Russia's international mission as "maintaining and reinforcing ... international peace and security, providing for the peaceful coexistence of states and nations, and barring [*nedopushchenie*] of the interference to the domestic affairs of a state."[884]

In contrast to the Constitution of 1993, the new amended version states that international legislation, which contradicts this Constitution, is null and void in the territory of the Russian Federation (79). This norm is not completely new. Previously (in 2013, 2016 and 2017) the Constitutional Court of the Russian Federation allowed Russia not to fulfil decisions of the European Court on Human Rights, when they do not comply with the Russian national legislation. In order to legitimize this substantial diversion from the Constitution (article 15), the judge of the Constitutional Court, Gadis Gadzhiev, introduced the concept "constitutional identity", which would take into account the national tradition, not falling into the extremities of "Westernized universalism" or radical isolationism. Gadzhiev proposed to identify the core of the identity-based legal traditions, and protect it from the international legislation in order to maintain national sovereignty.[885] The co-chair of the working group on the constitutional amendments, Andrei Klishas, saw this

---

[884] See the official version of the new Constitutution in: "Novyi tekst Konstitutsii s popravkami 2020," *Gosudarstvennaia Duma*, July 3, 2020, available at: http://duma.gov.ru/news/48953/.
[885] Gadis Gadzhiev, "Konstitutsionnaia identichnost' i prava cheloveka v Rossii," in *Pravo i gosudarstvo: Kul'turologicheskoe izmerenie* (St Petersburg: SPbGUP, 2017): 19–28, available at: http://www.ksrf.ru/ru/News/Documents/report_Гаджиев%20_2016.pdf.

change in the Constitution as the implementation of the concepts of "constitutional identity" and national sovereignty.[886]

Another amendment (67[1].3) prohibits "belittling of the importance of the feat of the people, defending the Fatherland," implying historical debates about the role of the Soviet Union in World War Two. The choice of words in meaningful. The word "belittling" (*umalenie*) has been stressed multiple times in the context of Russia being eternally in the hostile encirclement and suffering from the West's attacks and humiliations. Vladimir Putin, for example, supported this amendment, while pointing at the fact that "somebody wants to steal our Victory".[887] Another word, used in this kind of discourses, is "depreciation" (*prinizhenie*) of Russia's role in World War Two, which highlights the perception that the "West" is trying to subordinate and humiliate Russia.[888] This rhetoric inadvertently perpetuates the self-colonializing attitudes.

The head of the Security Council of the Russian Federation, Nikolai Patrishev put the question of constitutional reform in the context of the information war against Russia. In this interpretation, the "West" is trying to demoralize the Russian population by means of instilling Russophobe ideas and "demonization of the Russian history".[889] This point was further elaborated by another *silovik*, Sergei Naryshkin, the head of the External Intelligence Service. He dwelled on the argument that attempts to whitewash the Nazis and their allies (meaning: anti-Soviet resistance in Ukraine and the Baltic countries) "were coordinated from one center — beyond the ocean".[890] Similar statements, connecting Russia's national sovereignty with the Western "attack" on the historical memory, were made by Petr Tolstoi, deputy speaker of the State Duma, and Konstantin Kosachev, the head of the International

---

886 Andrei Klishas, "Suverenitet bez ogranichenii," *Rossiiskaia gazeta*, June 10, 2020.
887 Dmitry Laru, "Prostaia logika," *Izvestiia*, February 27, 2020.
888 N.a., "Prinizhaiushchikh rol' Rossii v pobede ...", *IA Regnum*, March 19, 2020, available at: https://regnum.ru/news/polit/2889343.html.
889 N.a., "V Kremle otsenili slova Patrusheva," *IA Regnum*, June 10, 2020, available at: https://regnum.ru/news/2977822.html
890 Elena Novoselova, "Istoriia bez oshibok," *Rossiiskaia gazeta*, June 25, 2020.

Affairs committee of the upper chamber of the Russian parliament.[891] In this way, the constitutional reform illustrates the conjoining of time and space in post-Soviet imagination. Concerns about history are being substantiated by references to the geopolitical competition and external threats.

The revised Constitution foregrounds the role of the Russian nation. On this issue, the working group on the amendments was tightrope walking, trying to avoid the pitfall of ethnically exclusive Russian nationalism, while at the same time trying to use nationalism's legitimization potential. On February 3, 2020, Konstantin Zatulin, the State Duma deputy, submitted a proposal to the working group on the amendments, to tailor the Constitution to the needs of the *russkii* nation. He argued that the Russian state had been grounded "by the initiative of the Russian [*russkii*] nation," and hence it should primarily take care of the well-being of the Russians. He emphasized that the point of the amendment was not to privilege the Russians, but to accept their political subjectivity and the importance of their national interests within the framework of the multinational country.[892] He suggested to change the Preamble of the Constitution accordingly, phrasing its beginning as: "we, the Russians [*russkie*], allied with other fraternal nations..."[893] This proposal was taken for a discussion at the political show "Vecher s Solov'evym" on February 12, and famous film director Karen Shakhnazarov, another member of the working group, vocally brushed away Zatulin's ideas on the grounds that they would foster separatism and preclude the possibility to add other, non-Russian countries to the territory of Russia.[894]

As the result of these debates, article 68.1 in its new edition does not mention the Russian [*russkii*] people explicitly, but instead it invents a euphemism "state-forming [*gosudarstvoobrazuiushchii*]

---

891 Petr Tolstoi, "Tsennosti budushchego," *Izvestiia*, June 26, 2020; Konstantin Kosachev, "Zhivoi organizm," *Izvestiia*, July 7, 2020.
892 Konstantin Zatulin, "Pustite russkikh v Konstitutsiiu," *Moskovskii komsomolets*, February 13, 2020.
893 Zatulin, "Pustite russkikh".
894 "Shakhnazarov o prirode natsional'nogo voprosa v Rossii," *Rossiia 24*, February 12, 2020, available at: https://www.youtube.com/watch?v=dogc1D41dbc.

nation." It literally says: "The official language of the Russian Federation on the whole of its territory is the Russian language as the language of the state-forming nation ..." This formula inaugurates the final demise of the construction of the inclusive civic "*rossiiskii* nation" and institutionalizes the trend to cautiously but persistently redefine the Russian identity in ethno-national terms. It also expectedly stirred up discontent of the non-Russian peoples, especially among the 5 million strong Tartar community.[895]

Amendments latched on to the geopolitical imagery of Russia as a unique civilization, yet they did not mention the term itself. The same article, which introduced the term "state-forming nation", also defined Russia as a "multinational union of peoples, equal in rights." Further, the new article 68.4 states that culture is the "unique legacy" of Russia's multinational people, and therefore protected by the state. Article 69.2 declared the state's obligation to protect "cultural originality [*samobytnost'*] of all peoples and ethnic communities of the Russian Federation." Discussions on these amendments were connected to the discourses about coherence of Russia's history, which unbreakably connects periods of Kiev Rus', Moscow Tsardom, Russian Empire, Soviet Union and present-day Russian Federation.[896] These ideas entered into article 67^1, parts 1 and 2 of the renewed Constitution. Taken as a whole, these changes advanced the vision of Russia as an organism, characterized by historical continuity, the fundamental role of the Russian culture, uniqueness and exceptional peacefulness and fraternity in relations among its nations. The role of the state is buttressed as that of a protecting shelter for this unique organism. This vision is by no means new to the Russian political elite. It has been tested throughout the post-Soviet period in such geopolitical constructions, as the "Russian world" project and the concept of Russia as a "state-civilization." The former found its way into the new Constitution

---

895 Kirill Antonov, I. Tiazhlov, "Gosudarstvoobrazumlivaiushchii narod," *Kommersant*, March 7, 2020.
896 On the discussion about this see speeches by the director of hermitage Mikhail Piotrovsky, head of the Education committee of the State Duma Viacheslav Nikonov, and film director Karen Shakhnazarov: "Vstrecha Vladimira Putina s rabochei gruppoi," *Rossiia 24*, February 26, 2020.

directly. By suggestion of Konstantin Zatulin, Viacheslav Nikonov and Konstantin Kosachev, the Constitution now declares the state's commitment to support compatriots abroad, stand for their rights and interests, and helps to preserve their "all-Russian cultural identity" (69.3).

In order to fight back against "propaganda of homosexualism," the new Constitution defined family as a "union of a man and a woman" (72.1.ж¹). This norm reflects the host of family-related metaphors with a distinctive geopolitical bearing. Paralleled to an extended family, Russia is imagined in this way, as an imperiled place of security, resisting the Western attempts to redefine the traditional family.[897] Additionally, members of the working group (for example, Aleksei Pushkov, member of the upper chamber of the Russian parliament) justified this amendment as a way in which Russia would officially assume the global "role of the leader in the fight for traditional values."[898]

Taken in their entirety, the amendments sum up many of the tendencies in the development of the geopolitical imagination in Russia over the past two decades. They crystallize geopolitical emotions of insecurity and precarity of Russia's present state and its borders. Amendments portray Russia as an ancient unique civilization, the central part of the "Russian world", surrounded by the hostile world. They enshrine Russia's position as the bastion of traditional family values, and identify Russia's "uniqueness" as a model of harmonious coexistence between nations and faiths inside the country. Amendments also lean on the old discussion about state sovereignty, while also making a decisive advance towards isolationism.

---

897 See, among others: Irina Souch, *Popular Tropes of Identity in Contemporary Russian Television and Film* (New York: Bloomsbury, 2017): 13–16.
898 "Putin na vstreche s rabochei gruppoi," *RT*, July 3, 2020, available at: https://www.youtube.com/watch?v=Z6VG-eAHWCc.

Index

Anti-globalism 112, 117, 143, 263
Anti-Westernism 74, 88, 116, 127, 160, 171, 195
Atlanticism 87
Barbarian 53, 62, 63, 64, 65, 66, 77, 149, 171, 234, 235, 237, 242, 244
'Bastion' (literary club) 146
Bastion 146, 166
Besieged fortress 44, 73
Biopolitics 97, 222
Byzantium, Byzantine Empire 46
Canonical territory 187, 188, 194
Civilization
    Civilization approach 89, 98, 156, 158, 159
    Civilizational choice 136, 137, 222
    Civilizational identity 60, 95, 133, 136, 137, 138, 244
    Clash of civilizations 112, 131, 143, 177, 264
    European civilization 63, 65
    Orthodox civilization 54, 111, 113, 114, 117, 131, 136, 185
    Slavic civilization 114
    State-civilization 24, 130
    Unique civilization 36, 68, 111, 126, 127, 128, 135, 284, 285
Colonization 42, 43, 93, 128, 149, 161, 194, 202, 265
Colored revolution 96, 97
'compatriots abroad' 58, 285
Conservatism 31, 35, 58, 73, 96, 125, 126, 127, 129, 135, 147, 222, 231, 267
Conspiracy theory 34, 35, 163

Continent 36, 55, 56, 60, 61, 195, 203, 205, 206, 207, 208, 209, 211, 212, 213, 214, 215, 217, 218, 219, 221, 224, 225, 226
Continentalism 37, 54, 55, 56, 203, 204, 205, 206, 207, 208, 209, 212, 213, 214, 215, 216, 217, 220, 223, 224, 225, 226
Diaspora 58, 102
Emigration 241
'End of history' 30, 104, 183
Eurasia
    'Greater Eurasia' 206, 207, 208, 218
    Eurasian continent 37, 41, 54, 60, 232
    Eurasian Economic Union (EAU) 23, 204, 207, 220
    Eurasian Heartland 207, 217
    Eurasian Symphony, book series 37, 38, 159, 223, 227, 228, 229, 230, 231, 232, 233, 234, 235, 237, 238, 239, 240, 241, 243, 244, 245
    Eurasianism 12, 23, 25, 37, 38, 56, 60, 87, 89, 90, 91, 95, 96, 99, 102, 127, 129, 158, 160, 184, 192, 203, 206, 207, 208, 211, 213, 214, 215, 219, 222, 225, 230, 240, 245
    Neo-Eurasianism 207, 263
Expansionism 28, 43, 68, 72, 91, 92, 93, 160, 203, 224, 258
Geographical determinism 27, 28, 56, 90
Geopolitical culture 22, 33, 36, 41, 47, 76, 111, 142, 227, 247
    Geopolitical concept 22, 25, 29, 37, 98, 251, 252, 254
    Geopolitical ideology 19, 248

Geopolitical imagination 11, 19, 22, 24, 25, 26, 27, 36, 37, 41, 43, 46, 47, 54, 77, 109, 183, 184, 187, 263, 278, 285
Geopolitical utopia 22
Geopolitical vision 19, 270
Geopolitics 9, 10, 11, 12, 17, 19, 20, 21, 23, 24, 25, 26, 27, 28, 29, 30, 31, 32, 33, 35, 36, 37, 38, 41, 47, 54, 55, 58, 59, 68, 79, 80, 81, 82, 83, 84, 85, 86, 87, 88, 89, 90, 91, 92, 93, 94, 95, 96, 97, 98, 99, 100, 101, 102, 103, 104, 105, 106, 107, 108, 109, 114, 115, 151, 156, 157, 163, 174, 176, 204, 205, 207, 208, 213, 214, 215, 219, 220, 226, 228, 233, 249, 250, 251
   Critical geopolitics 11, 12, 25, 26, 28, 29, 79, 80, 86, 87, 105, 206, 250
   Formal geopolitics 19
   Geopolitical risk 22
   Popular geopolitics 19
   Practical geopolitics 19, 205
   Realist (classic) geopolitics 27, 30, 35, 87, 91, 101
   Revisionist geopolitics 94, 107
Golden Horde 224, 227, 232, 238, 240, 266
Great power 9, 27, 53, 67, 103, 105, 107, 129, 156, 270
Great Power 60, 117
Großraum (large space) 37, 54, 55, 56, 58, 61, 220, 221, 222, 223, 226
Holy Russia (Sviataia Rus') 23, 25, 37, 44, 111, 183, 184, 185, 186, 187, 188, 189, 190, 191, 192, 193, 195, 196, 197, 198, 199, 200, 201, 202
Honor (in IR) 50, 67, 88, 151
Irredentism 116

Islam 70, 131, 140, 152, 196, 240, 241
Isolationism 24, 43, 53, 55, 59, 60, 103, 117, 134, 281, 285
Lebensraum (living space) 56
'Manifest Destiny' 211
Marxism-Leninism 10, 30
Mercator map 45
Messianism 43, 44, 67, 68, 69, 70, 72, 73, 74, 76, 116, 174, 177, 186, 192, 193, 194, 196, 203, 218, 245, 264
   'Third way' 120, 192
   Katechon 72, 73, 177
   Sonderweg (special road) 68
   Third Rome doctrine 68, 73, 186, 192, 196, 203, 218
Mestorazvitie (place of development) 100, 224, 225
Mimetic Westernization 47, 48
Monarchy 166, 168
Monroe Doctrine 220
Multiculturalism 24, 74, 89, 94, 112, 113
Nationalism 27, 49, 74, 115, 117, 120, 163, 191, 192, 239, 263, 283
Nation-state 56, 57, 125, 191, 201, 203, 205, 254
'Near abroad' 142
'New world order' 89
Nostalgia 160, 236, 263, 264
Novorossia 23, 37, 247, 248, 249, 250, 251, 252, 253, 254, 255, 256, 257, 258, 259, 260, 261, 262, 263, 264, 265, 266, 267, 268, 269, 270, 271, 273, 274
Orientalism 11, 63, 234, 240, 241
Ottoman Empire 68, 266
Pan-Slavism 160, 211

Patriotism 94, 108, 160, 191, 237, 259, 261
'passionarity' 99, 100, 101, 102, 165, 224, 226, 271
Periphery 20, 46, 54, 62, 66, 102, 154, 195, 200, 201, 247, 263
Progressory ('progressors', in science fiction) 157, 172
Recognition
    Struggle for recognition 67
Recognition (in IR) 24, 36, 41, 49, 50, 51, 53, 62, 67, 76, 77
    Struggle for recognition 47
    Struggle for recognition 49
    Struggle for recognition 53
Romantic nationalism 171
Russia as an Island, theory 59
Russian Orthodox Church 37, 119, 127, 130, 136, 174, 183, 185, 187
Russian World 12, 23, 54, 58, 84, 133, 183, 184, 248, 251, 255, 257, 265, 266, 267
Security
    Securitization 23, 37, 94, 127, 135, 139, 141, 150, 158, 166, 228, 244, 269

Spiritual security 94, 95, 136, 142
Slavophilism 49, 151, 172, 219
Soft power 51, 58
Soft Power 30, 52, 222, 267
Sovereign democracy 57, 58, 119, 120, 121, 122, 123, 124, 125, 137, 221, 267, 279
Sovereignty 24, 27, 33, 37, 55, 56, 57, 61, 95, 97, 108, 122, 124, 134, 135, 136, 210, 220, 222, 277, 278, 279, 280, 281, 282, 285
Soviet Union 10, 28, 29, 30, 35, 46, 81, 82, 91, 93, 97, 100, 104, 105, 108, 111, 113, 116, 122, 139, 152, 154, 158, 160, 167, 183, 188, 195, 207, 216, 225, 230, 231, 237, 242, 245, 255, 278, 282, 284
Sphere of influence 53, 124
Stigmatization (in IR) 49, 52, 67
'super-ethnos' 100
Trans-Siberian railway 218, 219
United Russia party 73, 120, 123
Westphalian system 49, 52

SOVIET AND POST-SOVIET POLITICS AND SOCIETY
Edited by Dr. Andreas Umland | ISSN 1614-3515

1   Андреас Умланд (ред.) | Воплощение Европейской конвенции по правам человека в России. Философские, юридические и эмпирические исследования | ISBN 3-89821-387-0

2   Christian Wipperfürth | Russland – ein vertrauenswürdiger Partner? Grundlagen, Hintergründe und Praxis gegenwärtiger russischer Außenpolitik | Mit einem Vorwort von Heinz Timmermann | ISBN 3-89821-401-X

3   Manja Hussner | Die Übernahme internationalen Rechts in die russische und deutsche Rechtsordnung. Eine vergleichende Analyse zur Völkerrechtsfreundlichkeit der Verfassungen der Russländischen Föderation und der Bundesrepublik Deutschland | Mit einem Vorwort von Rainer Arnold | ISBN 3-89821-438-9

4   Matthew Tejada | Bulgaria's Democratic Consolidation and the Kozloduy Nuclear Power Plant (KNPP). The Unattainability of Closure | With a foreword by Richard J. Crampton | ISBN 3-89821-439-7

5   Марк Григорьевич Меерович | Квадратные метры, определяющие сознание. Государственная жилищная политика в СССР. 1921 – 1941 гг | ISBN 3-89821-474-5

6   Andrei P. Tsygankov, Pavel A.Tsygankov (Eds.) | New Directions in Russian International Studies | ISBN 3-89821-422-2

7   Марк Григорьевич Меерович | Как власть народ к труду приучала. Жилище в СССР – средство управления людьми. 1917 – 1941 гг. | С предисловием Елены Осокиной | ISBN 3-89821-495-8

8   David J. Galbreath | Nation-Building and Minority Politics in Post-Socialist States. Interests, Influence and Identities in Estonia and Latvia | With a foreword by David J. Smith | ISBN 3-89821-467-2

9   Алексей Юрьевич Безугольный | Народы Кавказа в Вооруженных силах СССР в годы Великой Отечественной войны 1941-1945 гг. | С предисловием Николая Бугая | ISBN 3-89821-475-3

10 Вячеслав Лихачев и Владимир Прибыловский (ред.) | Русское Национальное Единство, 1990-2000. В 2-х томах | ISBN 3-89821-523-7

11 Николай Бугай (ред.) | Народы стран Балтии в условиях сталинизма (1940-е – 1950-е годы). Документированная история | ISBN 3-89821-525-3

12 Ingmar Bredies (Hrsg.) | Zur Anatomie der Orange Revolution in der Ukraine. Wechsel des Elitenregimes oder Triumph des Parlamentarismus? | ISBN 3-89821-524-5

13 Anastasia V. Mitrofanova | The Politicization of Russian Orthodoxy. Actors and Ideas | With a foreword by William C. Gay | ISBN 3-89821-481-8

14 Nathan D. Larson | Alexander Solzhenitsyn and the Russo-Jewish Question | ISBN 3-89821-483-4

15 Guido Houben | Kulturpolitik und Ethnizität. Staatliche Kunstförderung im Russland der neunziger Jahre | Mit einem Vorwort von Gert Weisskirchen | ISBN 3-89821-542-3

16 Leonid Luks | Der russische „Sonderweg"? Aufsätze zur neuesten Geschichte Russlands im europäischen Kontext | ISBN 3-89821-496-6

17 Евгений Мороз | История «Мёртвой воды» – от страшной сказки к большой политике. Политическое неоязычество в постсоветской России | ISBN 3-89821-551-2

18 Александр Верховский и Галина Кожевникова (ред.) | Этническая и религиозная интолерантность в российских СМИ. Результаты мониторинга 2001-2004 гг. | ISBN 3-89821-569-5

19 Christian Ganzer | Sowjetisches Erbe und ukrainische Nation. Das Museum der Geschichte des Zaporoger Kosakentums auf der Insel Chortycja | Mit einem Vorwort von Frank Golczewski | ISBN 3-89821-504-0

20 Эльза-Баир Гучинова | Помнить нельзя забыть. Антропология депортационной травмы калмыков | С предисловием Кэролайн Хамфри | ISBN 3-89821-506-7

21 Юлия Лидерман | Мотивы «проверки» и «испытания» в постсоветской культуре. Советское прошлое в российском кинематографе 1990-х годов | С предисловием Евгения Марголита | ISBN 3-89821-511-3

22 Tanya Lokshina, Ray Thomas, Mary Mayer (Eds.) | The Imposition of a Fake Political Settlement in the Northern Caucasus. The 2003 Chechen Presidential Election | ISBN 3-89821-436-2

23 Timothy McCajor Hall, Rosie Read (Eds.) | Changes in the Heart of Europe. Recent Ethnographies of Czechs, Slovaks, Roma, and Sorbs | With an afterword by Zdeněk Salzmann | ISBN 3-89821-606-3

24 *Christian Autengruber* | Die politischen Parteien in Bulgarien und Rumänien. Eine vergleichende Analyse seit Beginn der 90er Jahre | Mit einem Vorwort von Dorothée de Nève | ISBN 3-89821-476-1

25 *Annette Freyberg-Inan with Radu Cristescu* | The Ghosts in Our Classrooms, or: John Dewey Meets Ceauşescu. The Promise and the Failures of Civic Education in Romania | ISBN 3-89821-416-8

26 *John B. Dunlop* | The 2002 Dubrovka and 2004 Beslan Hostage Crises. A Critique of Russian Counter-Terrorism | With a foreword by Donald N. Jensen | ISBN 3-89821-608-X

27 *Peter Koller* | Das touristische Potenzial von Kam"janec'–Podil's'kyj. Eine fremdenverkehrsgeographische Untersuchung der Zukunftsperspektiven und Maßnahmenplanung zur Destinationsentwicklung des „ukrainischen Rothenburg" | Mit einem Vorwort von Kristiane Klemm | ISBN 3-89821-640-3

28 *Françoise Daucé, Elisabeth Sieca-Kozlowski (Eds.)* | Dedovshchina in the Post-Soviet Military. Hazing of Russian Army Conscripts in a Comparative Perspective | With a foreword by Dale Herspring | ISBN 3-89821-616-0

29 *Florian Strasser* | Zivilgesellschaftliche Einflüsse auf die Orange Revolution. Die gewaltlose Massenbewegung und die ukrainische Wahlkrise 2004 | Mit einem Vorwort von Egbert Jahn | ISBN 3-89821-648-9

30 *Rebecca S. Katz* | The Georgian Regime Crisis of 2003-2004. A Case Study in Post-Soviet Media Representation of Politics, Crime and Corruption | ISBN 3-89821-413-3

31 *Vladimir Kantor* | Willkür oder Freiheit. Beiträge zur russischen Geschichtsphilosophie | Ediert von Dagmar Herrmann sowie mit einem Vorwort versehen von Leonid Luks | ISBN 3-89821-589-X

32 *Laura A. Victoir* | The Russian Land Estate Today. A Case Study of Cultural Politics in Post-Soviet Russia | With a foreword by Priscilla Roosevelt | ISBN 3-89821-426-5

33 *Ivan Katchanovski* | Cleft Countries. Regional Political Divisions and Cultures in Post-Soviet Ukraine and Moldova| With a foreword by Francis Fukuyama | ISBN 3-89821-558-X

34 *Florian Mühlfried* | Postsowjetische Feiern. Das Georgische Bankett im Wandel | Mit einem Vorwort von Kevin Tuite | ISBN 3-89821-601-2

35 *Roger Griffin, Werner Loh, Andreas Umland (Eds.)* | Fascism Past and Present, West and East. An International Debate on Concepts and Cases in the Comparative Study of the Extreme Right | With an afterword by Walter Laqueur | ISBN 3-89821-674-8

36 *Sebastian Schlegel* | Der „Weiße Archipel". Sowjetische Atomstädte 1945-1991 | Mit einem Geleitwort von Thomas Bohn | ISBN 3-89821-679-9

37 *Vyacheslav Likhachev* | Political Anti-Semitism in Post-Soviet Russia. Actors and Ideas in 1991-2003 | Edited and translated from Russian by Eugene Veklerov | ISBN 3-89821-529-6

38 *Josette Baer (Ed.)* | Preparing Liberty in Central Europe. Political Texts from the Spring of Nations 1848 to the Spring of Prague 1968 | With a foreword by Zdeněk V. David | ISBN 3-89821-546-6

39 *Михаил Лукьянов* | Российский консерватизм и реформа, 1907-1914 | С предисловием Марка Д. Стейнберга | ISBN 3-89821-503-2

40 *Nicola Melloni* | Market Without Economy. The 1998 Russian Financial Crisis | With a foreword by Eiji Furukawa | ISBN 3-89821-407-9

41 *Dmitrij Chmelnizki* | Die Architektur Stalins | Bd. 1: Studien zu Ideologie und Stil | Bd. 2: Bilddokumentation | Mit einem Vorwort von Bruno Flierl | ISBN 3-89821-515-6

42 *Katja Yafimava* | Post-Soviet Russian-Belarussian Relationships. The Role of Gas Transit Pipelines | With a foreword by Jonathan P. Stern | ISBN 3-89821-655-1

43 *Boris Chavkin* | Verflechtungen der deutschen und russischen Zeitgeschichte. Aufsätze und Archivfunde zu den Beziehungen Deutschlands und der Sowjetunion von 1917 bis 1991 | Ediert von Markus Edlinger sowie mit einem Vorwort versehen von Leonid Luks | ISBN 3-89821-756-6

44 *Anastasija Grynenko in Zusammenarbeit mit Claudia Dathe* | Die Terminologie des Gerichtswesens der Ukraine und Deutschlands im Vergleich. Eine übersetzungswissenschaftliche Analyse juristischer Fachbegriffe im Deutschen, Ukrainischen und Russischen | Mit einem Vorwort von Ulrich Hartmann | ISBN 3-89821-691-8

45 *Anton Burkov* | The Impact of the European Convention on Human Rights on Russian Law. Legislation and Application in 1996-2006 | With a foreword by Françoise Hampson | ISBN 978-3-89821-639-5

46 *Stina Torjesen, Indra Overland (Eds.)* | International Election Observers in Post-Soviet Azerbaijan. Geopolitical Pawns or Agents of Change? | ISBN 978-3-89821-743-9

47 *Taras Kuzio* | Ukraine – Crimea – Russia. Triangle of Conflict | ISBN 978-3-89821-761-3

48 *Claudia Šabić* | „Ich erinnere mich nicht, aber L'viv!" Zur Funktion kultureller Faktoren für die Institutionalisierung und Entwicklung einer ukrainischen Region | Mit einem Vorwort von Melanie Tatur | ISBN 978-3-89821-752-1

49 *Marlies Bilz* | Tatarstan in der Transformation. Nationaler Diskurs und Politische Praxis 1988-1994 | Mit einem Vorwort von Frank Golczewski | ISBN 978-3-89821-722-4

50 *Марлен Ларюэль (ред.)* | Современные интерпретации русского национализма | ISBN 978-3-89821-795-8

51 *Sonja Schüler* | Die ethnische Dimension der Armut. Roma im postsozialistischen Rumänien | Mit einem Vorwort von Anton Sterbling | ISBN 978-3-89821-776-7

52 *Галина Кожевникова* | Радикальный национализм в России и противодействие ему. Сборник докладов Центра «Сова» за 2004-2007 гг. | С предисловием Александра Верховского | ISBN 978-3-89821-721-7

53 *Галина Кожевникова и Владимир Прибыловский* | Российская власть в биографиях I. Высшие должностные лица РФ в 2004 г. | ISBN 978-3-89821-796-5

54 *Галина Кожевникова и Владимир Прибыловский* | Российская власть в биографиях II. Члены Правительства РФ в 2004 г. | ISBN 978-3-89821-797-2

55 *Галина Кожевникова и Владимир Прибыловский* | Российская власть в биографиях III. Руководители федеральных служб и агентств РФ в 2004 г.| ISBN 978-3-89821-798-9

56 *Ileana Petroniu* | Privatisierung in Transformationsökonomien. Determinanten der Restrukturierungs-Bereitschaft am Beispiel Polens, Rumäniens und der Ukraine | Mit einem Vorwort von Rainer W. Schäfer | ISBN 978-3-89821-790-3

57 *Christian Wipperfürth* | Russland und seine GUS-Nachbarn. Hintergründe, aktuelle Entwicklungen und Konflikte in einer ressourcenreichen Region| ISBN 978-3-89821-801-6

58 *Togzhan Kassenova* | From Antagonism to Partnership. The Uneasy Path of the U.S.-Russian Cooperative Threat Reduction | With a foreword by Christoph Bluth | ISBN 978-3-89821-707-1

59 *Alexander Höllwerth* | Das sakrale eurasische Imperium des Aleksandr Dugin. Eine Diskursanalyse zum postsowjetischen russischen Rechtsextremismus | Mit einem Vorwort von Dirk Uffelmann | ISBN 978-3-89821-813-9

60 *Олег Рябов* | «Россия-Матушка». Национализм, гендер и война в России XX века | С предисловием Елены Гощило | ISBN 978-3-89821-487-2

61 *Ivan Maistrenko* | Borot'bism. A Chapter in the History of the Ukrainian Revolution | With a new Introduction by Chris Ford | Translated by George S. N. Luckyj with the assistance of Ivan L. Rudnytsky | Second, Revised and Expanded Edition ISBN 978-3-8382-1107-7

62 *Maryna Romanets* | Anamorphosic Texts and Reconfigured Visions. Improvised Traditions in Contemporary Ukrainian and Irish Literature | ISBN 978-3-89821-576-3

63 *Paul D'Anieri and Taras Kuzio (Eds.)* | Aspects of the Orange Revolution I. Democratization and Elections in Post-Communist Ukraine | ISBN 978-3-89821-698-2

64 *Bohdan Harasymiw in collaboration with Oleh S. Ilnytzkyj (Eds.)* | Aspects of the Orange Revolution II. Information and Manipulation Strategies in the 2004 Ukrainian Presidential Elections | ISBN 978-3-89821-699-9

65 *Ingmar Bredies, Andreas Umland and Valentin Yakushik (Eds.)* | Aspects of the Orange Revolution III. The Context and Dynamics of the 2004 Ukrainian Presidential Elections | ISBN 978-3-89821-803-0

66 *Ingmar Bredies, Andreas Umland and Valentin Yakushik (Eds.)* | Aspects of the Orange Revolution IV. Foreign Assistance and Civic Action in the 2004 Ukrainian Presidential Elections | ISBN 978-3-89821-808-5

67 *Ingmar Bredies, Andreas Umland and Valentin Yakushik (Eds.)* | Aspects of the Orange Revolution V. Institutional Observation Reports on the 2004 Ukrainian Presidential Elections | ISBN 978-3-89821-809-2

68 *Taras Kuzio (Ed.)* | Aspects of the Orange Revolution VI. Post-Communist Democratic Revolutions in Comparative Perspective | ISBN 978-3-89821-820-7

69 *Tim Bohse* | Autoritarismus statt Selbstverwaltung. Die Transformation der kommunalen Politik in der Stadt Kaliningrad 1990-2005 | Mit einem Geleitwort von Stefan Troebst | ISBN 978-3-89821-782-8

70 *David Rupp* | Die Rußländische Föderation und die russischsprachige Minderheit in Lettland. Eine Fallstudie zur Anwaltspolitik Moskaus gegenüber den russophonen Minderheiten im „Nahen Ausland" von 1991 bis 2002 | Mit einem Vorwort von Helmut Wagner | ISBN 978-3-89821-778-1

71 *Taras Kuzio* | Theoretical and Comparative Perspectives on Nationalism. New Directions in Cross-Cultural and Post-Communist Studies | With a foreword by Paul Robert Magocsi | ISBN 978-3-89821-815-3

72 *Christine Teichmann* | Die Hochschultransformation im heutigen Osteuropa. Kontinuität und Wandel bei der Entwicklung des postkommunistischen Universitätswesens | Mit einem Vorwort von Oskar Anweiler | ISBN 978-3-89821-842-9

73 *Julia Kusznir* | Der politische Einfluss von Wirtschaftseliten in russischen Regionen. Eine Analyse am Beispiel der Erdöl- und Erdgasindustrie, 1992-2005 | Mit einem Vorwort von Wolfgang Eichwede | ISBN 978-3-89821-821-4

74 Alena Vysotskaya | Russland, Belarus und die EU-Osterweiterung. Zur Minderheitenfrage und zum Problem der Freizügigkeit des Personenverkehrs | Mit einem Vorwort von Katlijn Malfliet | ISBN 978-3-89821-822-1

75 Heiko Pleines (Hrsg.) | Corporate Governance in post-sozialistischen Volkswirtschaften | ISBN 978-3-89821-766-8

76 Stefan Ihrig | Wer sind die Moldawier? Rumänismus versus Moldowanismus in Historiographie und Schulbüchern der Republik Moldau, 1991-2006 | Mit einem Vorwort von Holm Sundhaussen | ISBN 978-3-89821-466-7

77 Galina Kozhevnikova in collaboration with Alexander Verkhovsky and Eugene Veklerov | Ultra-Nationalism and Hate Crimes in Contemporary Russia. The 2004-2006 Annual Reports of Moscow's SOVA Center | With a foreword by Stephen D. Shenfield | ISBN 978-3-89821-868-9

78 Florian Küchler | The Role of the European Union in Moldova's Transnistria Conflict | With a foreword by Christopher Hill | ISBN 978-3-89821-850-4

79 Bernd Rechel | The Long Way Back to Europe. Minority Protection in Bulgaria | With a foreword by Richard Crampton | ISBN 978-3-89821-863-4

80 Peter W. Rodgers | Nation, Region and History in Post-Communist Transitions. Identity Politics in Ukraine, 1991-2006 | With a foreword by Vera Tolz | ISBN 978-3-89821-903-7

81 Stephanie Solywoda | The Life and Work of Semen L. Frank. A Study of Russian Religious Philosophy | With a foreword by Philip Walters | ISBN 978-3-89821-457-5

82 Vera Sokolova | Cultural Politics of Ethnicity. Discourses on Roma in Communist Czechoslovakia | ISBN 978-3-89821-864-1

83 Natalya Shevchik Ketenci | Kazakhstani Enterprises in Transition. The Role of Historical Regional Development in Kazakhstan's Post-Soviet Economic Transformation | ISBN 978-3-89821-831-3

84 Martin Malek, Anna Schor-Tschudnowskaja (Hgg.) | Europa im Tschetschenienkrieg. Zwischen politischer Ohnmacht und Gleichgültigkeit | Mit einem Vorwort von Lipchan Basajewa | ISBN 978-3-89821-676-0

85 Stefan Meister | Das postsowjetische Universitätswesen zwischen nationalem und internationalem Wandel. Die Entwicklung der regionalen Hochschule in Russland als Gradmesser der Systemtransformation | Mit einem Vorwort von Joan DeBardeleben | ISBN 978-3-89821-891-7

86 Konstantin Sheiko in collaboration with Stephen Brown | Nationalist Imaginings of the Russian Past. Anatolii Fomenko and the Rise of Alternative History in Post-Communist Russia | With a foreword by Donald Ostrowski | ISBN 978-3-89821-915-0

87 Sabine Jenni | Wie stark ist das „Einige Russland"? Zur Parteibindung der Eliten und zum Wahlerfolg der Machtpartei im Dezember 2007 | Mit einem Vorwort von Klaus Armingeon | ISBN 978-3-89821-961-7

88 Thomas Borén | Meeting-Places of Transformation. Urban Identity, Spatial Representations and Local Politics in Post-Soviet St Petersburg | ISBN 978-3-89821-739-2

89 Aygul Ashirova | Stalinismus und Stalin-Kult in Zentralasien. Turkmenistan 1924-1953 | Mit einem Vorwort von Leonid Luks | ISBN 978-3-89821-987-7

90 Leonid Luks | Freiheit oder imperiale Größe? Essays zu einem russischen Dilemma | ISBN 978-3-8382-0011-8

91 Christopher Gilley | The 'Change of Signposts' in the Ukrainian Emigration. A Contribution to the History of Sovietophilism in the 1920s | With a foreword by Frank Golczewski | ISBN 978-3-89821-965-5

92 Philipp Casula, Jeronim Perovic (Eds.) | Identities and Politics During the Putin Presidency. The Discursive Foundations of Russia's Stability | With a foreword by Heiko Haumann | ISBN 978-3-8382-0015-6

93 Marcel Viëtor | Europa und die Frage nach seinen Grenzen im Osten. Zur Konstruktion ‚europäischer Identität' in Geschichte und Gegenwart | Mit einem Vorwort von Albrecht Lehmann | ISBN 978-3-8382-0045-3

94 Ben Hellman, Andrei Rogachevskii | Filming the Unfilmable. Casper Wrede's 'One Day in the Life of Ivan Denisovich' | Second, Revised and Expanded Edition | ISBN 978-3-8382-0044-6

95 Eva Fuchslocher | Vaterland, Sprache, Glaube. Orthodoxie und Nationenbildung am Beispiel Georgiens | Mit einem Vorwort von Christina von Braun | ISBN 978-3-89821-884-9

96 Vladimir Kantor | Das Westlertum und der Weg Russlands. Zur Entwicklung der russischen Literatur und Philosophie | Ediert von Dagmar Herrmann | Mit einem Beitrag von Nikolaus Lobkowicz | ISBN 978-3-8382-0102-3

97 Kamran Musayev | Die postsowjetische Transformation im Baltikum und Südkaukasus. Eine vergleichende Untersuchung der politischen Entwicklung Lettlands und Aserbaidschans 1985-2009 | Mit einem Vorwort von Leonid Luks | Ediert von Sandro Henschel | ISBN 978-3-8382-0103-0

98 Tatiana Zhurzhenko | Borderlands into Bordered Lands. Geopolitics of Identity in Post-Soviet Ukraine | With a foreword by Dieter Segert | ISBN 978-3-8382-0042-2

99   *Кирилл Галушко, Лидия Смола (ред.)* | Пределы падения – варианты украинского будущего. Аналитико-прогностические исследования | ISBN 978-3-8382-0148-1

100 *Michael Minkenberg (Ed.)* | Historical Legacies and the Radical Right in Post-Cold War Central and Eastern Europe | With an afterword by Sabrina P. Ramet | ISBN 978-3-8382-0124-5

101 *David-Emil Wickström* | Rocking St. Petersburg. Transcultural Flows and Identity Politics in the St. Petersburg Popular Music Scene | With a foreword by Yngvar B. Steinholt | Second, Revised and Expanded Edition | ISBN 978-3-8382-0100-9

102 *Eva Zabka* | Eine neue „Zeit der Wirren"? Der spät- und postsowjetische Systemwandel 1985-2000 im Spiegel russischer gesellschaftspolitischer Diskurse | Mit einem Vorwort von Margareta Mommsen | ISBN 978-3-8382-0161-0

103 *Ulrike Ziemer* | Ethnic Belonging, Gender and Cultural Practices. Youth Identitites in Contemporary Russia | With a foreword by Anoop Nayak | ISBN 978-3-8382-0152-8

104 *Ksenia Chepikova* | ‚Einiges Russland' - eine zweite KPdSU? Aspekte der Identitätskonstruktion einer postsowjetischen „Partei der Macht" | Mit einem Vorwort von Torsten Oppelland | ISBN 978-3-8382-0311-9

105 *Леонид Люкс* | Западничество или евразийство? Демократия или идеократия? Сборник статей об исторических дилеммах России | С предисловием Владимира Кантора | ISBN 978-3-8382-0211-2

106 *Anna Dost* | Das russische Verfassungsrecht auf dem Weg zum Föderalismus und zurück. Zum Konflikt von Rechtsnormen und -wirklichkeit in der Russländischen Föderation von 1991 bis 2009 | Mit einem Vorwort von Alexander Blankenagel | ISBN 978-3-8382-0292-1

107 *Philipp Herzog* | Sozialistische Völkerfreundschaft, nationaler Widerstand oder harmloser Zeitvertreib? Zur politischen Funktion der Volkskunst im sowjetischen Estland | Mit einem Vorwort von Andreas Kappeler | ISBN 978-3-8382-0216-7

108 *Marlène Laruelle (Ed.)* | Russian Nationalism, Foreign Policy, and Identity Debates in Putin's Russia. New Ideological Patterns after the Orange Revolution | ISBN 978-3-8382-0325-6

109 *Michail Logvinov* | Russlands Kampf gegen den internationalen Terrorismus. Eine kritische Bestandsaufnahme des Bekämpfungsansatzes | Mit einem Geleitwort von Hans-Henning Schröder und einem Vorwort von Eckhard Jesse | ISBN 978-3-8382-0329-4

110 *John B. Dunlop* | The Moscow Bombings of September 1999. Examinations of Russian Terrorist Attacks at the Onset of Vladimir Putin's Rule | Second, Revised and Expanded Edition | ISBN 978-3-8382-0388-1

111 *Андрей А. Ковалёв* | Свидетельство из-за кулис российской политики I. Можно ли делать добро из зла? (Воспоминания и размышления о последних советских и первых послесоветских годах) | With a foreword by Peter Reddaway | ISBN 978-3-8382-0302-7

112 *Андрей А. Ковалёв* | Свидетельство из-за кулис российской политики II. Угроза для себя и окружающих (Наблюдения и предостережения относительно происходящего после 2000 г.) | ISBN 978-3-8382-0303-4

113 *Bernd Kappenberg* | Zeichen setzen für Europa. Der Gebrauch europäischer lateinischer Sonderzeichen in der deutschen Öffentlichkeit | Mit einem Vorwort von Peter Schlobinski | ISBN 978-3-89821-749-1

114 *Ivo Mijnssen* | The Quest for an Ideal Youth in Putin's Russia I. Back to Our Future! History, Modernity, and Patriotism according to Nashi, 2005-2013 | With a foreword by Jeronim Perović | Second, Revised and Expanded Edition | ISBN 978-3-8382-0368-3

115 *Jussi Lassila* | The Quest for an Ideal Youth in Putin's Russia II. The Search for Distinctive Conformism in the Political Communication of Nashi, 2005-2009 | With a foreword by Kirill Postoutenko | Second, Revised and Expanded Edition | ISBN 978-3-8382-0415-4

116 *Valerio Trabandt* | Neue Nachbarn, gute Nachbarschaft? Die EU als internationaler Akteur am Beispiel ihrer Demokratieförderung in Belarus und der Ukraine 2004-2009 | Mit einem Vorwort von Jutta Joachim | ISBN 978-3-8382-0437-6

117 *Fabian Pfeiffer* | Estlands Außen- und Sicherheitspolitik I. Der estnische Atlantizismus nach der wiedererlangten Unabhängigkeit 1991-2004 | Mit einem Vorwort von Helmut Hubel | ISBN 978-3-8382-0127-6

118 *Jana Podßuweit* | Estlands Außen- und Sicherheitspolitik II. Handlungsoptionen eines Kleinstaates im Rahmen seiner EU-Mitgliedschaft (2004-2008) | Mit einem Vorwort von Helmut Hubel | ISBN 978-3-8382-0440-6

119 *Karin Pointner* | Estlands Außen- und Sicherheitspolitik III. Eine gedächtnispolitische Analyse estnischer Entwicklungskooperation 2006-2010 | Mit einem Vorwort von Karin Liebhart | ISBN 978-3-8382-0435-2

120 *Ruslana Vovk* | Die Offenheit der ukrainischen Verfassung für das Völkerrecht und die europäische Integration | Mit einem Vorwort von Alexander Blankenagel | ISBN 978-3-8382-0481-9

121 *Mykhaylo Banakh* | Die Relevanz der Zivilgesellschaft bei den postkommunistischen Transformationsprozessen in mittel- und osteuropäischen Ländern. Das Beispiel der spät- und postsowjetischen Ukraine 1986-2009 | Mit einem Vorwort von Gerhard Simon | ISBN 978-3-8382-0499-4

122 *Michael Moser* | Language Policy and the Discourse on Languages in Ukraine under President Viktor Yanukovych (25 February 2010–28 October 2012) | ISBN 978-3-8382-0497-0 (Paperback edition) | ISBN 978-3-8382-0507-6 (Hardcover edition)

123 *Nicole Krome* | Russischer Netzwerkkapitalismus Restrukturierungsprozesse in der Russischen Föderation am Beispiel des Luftfahrtunternehmens „Aviastar" | Mit einem Vorwort von Petra Stykow | ISBN 978-3-8382-0534-2

124 *David R. Marples* | 'Our Glorious Past'. Lukashenka's Belarus and the Great Patriotic War | ISBN 978-3-8382-0574-8 (Paperback edition) | ISBN 978-3-8382-0675-2 (Hardcover edition)

125 *Ulf Walther* | Russlands „neuer Adel". Die Macht des Geheimdienstes von Gorbatschow bis Putin | Mit einem Vorwort von Hans-Georg Wieck | ISBN 978-3-8382-0584-7

126 *Simon Geissbühler (Hrsg.)* | Kiew – Revolution 3.0. Der Euromaidan 2013/14 und die Zukunftsperspektiven der Ukraine | ISBN 978-3-8382-0581-6 (Paperback edition) | ISBN 978-3-8382-0681-3 (Hardcover edition)

127 *Andrey Makarychev* | Russia and the EU in a Multipolar World. Discourses, Identities, Norms | With a foreword by Klaus Segbers | ISBN 978-3-8382-0629-5

128 *Roland Scharff* | Kasachstan als postsowjetischer Wohlfahrtsstaat. Die Transformation des sozialen Schutzsystems | Mit einem Vorwort von Joachim Ahrens | ISBN 978-3-8382-0622-6

129 *Katja Grupp* | Bild Lücke Deutschland. Kaliningrader Studierende sprechen über Deutschland | Mit einem Vorwort von Martin Schulz | ISBN 978-3-8382-0552-6

130 *Konstantin Sheiko, Stephen Brown* | History as Therapy. Alternative History and Nationalist Imaginings in Russia, 1991-2014 | ISBN 978-3-8382-0665-3

131 *Elisa Kriza* | Alexander Solzhenitsyn: Cold War Icon, Gulag Author, Russian Nationalist? A Study of the Western Reception of his Literary Writings, Historical Interpretations, and Political Ideas | With a foreword by Andrei Rogatchevski | ISBN 978-3-8382-0589-2 (Paperback edition) | ISBN 978-3-8382-0690-5 (Hardcover edition)

132 *Serghei Golunov* | The Elephant in the Room. Corruption and Cheating in Russian Universities | ISBN 978-3-8382-0570-0

133 *Manja Hussner, Rainer Arnold (Hgg.)* | Verfassungsgerichtsbarkeit in Zentralasien I. Sammlung von Verfassungstexten | ISBN 978-3-8382-0595-3

134 *Nikolay Mitrokhin* | Die „Russische Partei". Die Bewegung der russischen Nationalisten in der UdSSR 1953-1985 | Aus dem Russischen übertragen von einem Übersetzerteam unter der Leitung von Larisa Schippel | ISBN 978-3-8382-0024-8

135 *Manja Hussner, Rainer Arnold (Hgg.)* | Verfassungsgerichtsbarkeit in Zentralasien II. Sammlung von Verfassungstexten | ISBN 978-3-8382-0597-7

136 *Manfred Zeller* | Das sowjetische Fieber. Fußballfans im poststalinistischen Vielvölkerreich | Mit einem Vorwort von Nikolaus Katzer | ISBN 978-3-8382-0757-5

137 *Kristin Schreiter* | Stellung und Entwicklungspotential zivilgesellschaftlicher Gruppen in Russland. Menschenrechtsorganisationen im Vergleich | ISBN 978-3-8382-0673-8

138 *David R. Marples, Frederick V. Mills (Eds.)* | Ukraine's Euromaidan. Analyses of a Civil Revolution | ISBN 978-3-8382-0660-8

139 *Bernd Kappenberg* | Setting Signs for Europe. Why Diacritics Matter for European Integration | With a foreword by Peter Schlobinski | ISBN 978-3-8382-0663-9

140 *René Lenz* | Internationalisierung, Kooperation und Transfer. Externe bildungspolitische Akteure in der Russischen Föderation | Mit einem Vorwort von Frank Ettrich | ISBN 978-3-8382-0751-3

141 *Juri Plusnin, Yana Zausaeva, Natalia Zhidkevich, Artemy Pozanenko* | Wandering Workers. Mores, Behavior, Way of Life, and Political Status of Domestic Russian Labor Migrants | Translated by Julia Kazantseva | ISBN 978-3-8382-0653-0

142 *David J. Smith (Eds.)* | Latvia – A Work in Progress? 100 Years of State- and Nation-Building | ISBN 978-3-8382-0648-6

143 *Инна Чувычкина (ред.)* | Экспортные нефте- и газопроводы на постсоветском пространстве. Анализ трубопроводной политики в свете теории международных отношений | ISBN 978-3-8382-0822-0

144 *Johann Zajaczkowski* | Russland – eine pragmatische Großmacht? Eine rollentheoretische Untersuchung russischer Außenpolitik am Beispiel der Zusammenarbeit mit den USA nach 9/11 und des Georgienkrieges von 2008 | Mit einem Vorwort von Siegfried Schieder | ISBN 978-3-8382-0837-4

145 *Boris Popivanov* | Changing Images of the Left in Bulgaria. The Challenge of Post-Communism in the Early 21st Century | ISBN 978-3-8382-0667-7

146 *Lenka Krátká* | A History of the Czechoslovak Ocean Shipping Company 1948-1989. How a Small, Landlocked Country Ran Maritime Business During the Cold War | ISBN 978-3-8382-0666-0

147 *Alexander Sergunin* | Explaining Russian Foreign Policy Behavior. Theory and Practice | ISBN 978-3-8382-0752-0

148 *Darya Malyutina* | Migrant Friendships in a Super-Diverse City. Russian-Speakers and their Social Relationships in London in the 21st Century | With a foreword by Claire Dwyer | ISBN 978-3-8382-0652-3

149 *Alexander Sergunin, Valery Konyshev* | Russia in the Arctic. Hard or Soft Power? | ISBN 978-3-8382-0753-7

150 *John J. Maresca* | Helsinki Revisited. A Key U.S. Negotiator's Memoirs on the Development of the CSCE into the OSCE | With a foreword by Hafiz Pashayev | ISBN 978-3-8382-0852-7

151 *Jardar Østbø* | The New Third Rome. Readings of a Russian Nationalist Myth | With a foreword by Pål Kolstø | ISBN 978-3-8382-0870-1

152 *Simon Kordonsky* | Socio-Economic Foundations of the Russian Post-Soviet Regime. The Resource-Based Economy and Estate-Based Social Structure of Contemporary Russia | With a foreword by Svetlana Barsukova | ISBN 978-3-8382-0775-9

153 *Duncan Leitch* | Assisting Reform in Post-Communist Ukraine 2000–2012. The Illusions of Donors and the Disillusion of Beneficiaries | With a foreword by Kataryna Wolczuk | ISBN 978-3-8382-0844-2

154 *Abel Polese* | Limits of a Post-Soviet State. How Informality Replaces, Renegotiates, and Reshapes Governance in Contemporary Ukraine | With a foreword by Colin Williams | ISBN 978-3-8382-0845-9

155 *Mikhail Suslov (Ed.)* | Digital Orthodoxy in the Post-Soviet World. The Russian Orthodox Church and Web 2.0 | With a foreword by Father Cyril Hovorun | ISBN 978-3-8382-0871-8

156 *Leonid Luks* | Zwei „Sonderwege"? Russisch-deutsche Parallelen und Kontraste (1917-2014). Vergleichende Essays | ISBN 978-3-8382-0823-7

157 *Vladimir V. Karacharovskiy, Ovsey I. Shkaratan, Gordey A. Yastrebov* | Towards a New Russian Work Culture. Can Western Companies and Expatriates Change Russian Society? | With a foreword by Elena N. Danilova | Translated by Julia Kazantseva | ISBN 978-3-8382-0902-9

158 *Edmund Griffiths* | Aleksandr Prokhanov and Post-Soviet Esotericism | ISBN 978-3-8382-0903-6

159 *Timm Beichelt, Susann Worschech (Eds.)* | Transnational Ukraine? Networks and Ties that Influence(d) Contemporary Ukraine | ISBN 978-3-8382-0944-9

160 *Mieste Hotopp-Riecke* | Die Tataren der Krim zwischen Assimilation und Selbstbehauptung. Der Aufbau des krimtatarischen Bildungswesens nach Deportation und Heimkehr (1990-2005) | Mit einem Vorwort von Swetlana Czerwonnaja | ISBN 978-3-89821-940-2

161 *Olga Bertelsen (Ed.)* | Revolution and War in Contemporary Ukraine. The Challenge of Change | ISBN 978-3-8382-1016-2

162 *Natalya Ryabinska* | Ukraine's Post-Communist Mass Media. Between Capture and Commercialization | With a foreword by Marta Dyczok | ISBN 978-3-8382-1011-7

163 *Alexandra Cotofana, James M. Nyce (Eds.)* | Religion and Magic in Socialist and Post-Socialist Contexts. Historic and Ethnographic Case Studies of Orthodoxy, Heterodoxy, and Alternative Spirituality | With a foreword by Patrick L. Michelson | ISBN 978-3-8382-0989-0

164 *Nozima Akhrarkhodjaeva* | The Instrumentalisation of Mass Media in Electoral Authoritarian Regimes. Evidence from Russia's Presidential Election Campaigns of 2000 and 2008 | ISBN 978-3-8382-1013-1

165 *Yulia Krasheninnikova* | Informal Healthcare in Contemporary Russia. Sociographic Essays on the Post-Soviet Infrastructure for Alternative Healing Practices | ISBN 978-3-8382-0970-8

166 *Peter Kaiser* | Das Schachbrett der Macht. Die Handlungsspielräume eines sowjetischen Funktionärs unter Stalin am Beispiel des Generalsekretärs des Komsomol Aleksandr Kosarev (1929-1938) | Mit einem Vorwort von Dietmar Neutatz | ISBN 978-3-8382-1052-0

167 *Oksana Kim* | The Effects and Implications of Kazakhstan's Adoption of International Financial Reporting Standards. A Resource Dependence Perspective | With a foreword by Svetlana Vlady | ISBN 978-3-8382-0987-6

168 *Anna Sanina* | Patriotic Education in Contemporary Russia. Sociological Studies in the Making of the Post-Soviet Citizen | With a foreword by Anna Oldfield | ISBN 978-3-8382-0993-7

169 *Rudolf Wolters* | Spezialist in Sibirien Faksimile der 1933 erschienenen ersten Ausgabe | Mit einem Vorwort von Dmitrij Chmelnizki | ISBN 978-3-8382-0515-1

170 *Michal Vít, Magdalena M. Baran (Eds.)* | Transregional versus National Perspectives on Contemporary Central European History. Studies on the Building of Nation-States and Their Cooperation in the 20th and 21st Century | With a foreword by Petr Vágner | ISBN 978-3-8382-1015-5

171 *Philip Gamaghelyan* | Conflict Resolution Beyond the International Relations Paradigm. Evolving Designs as a Transformative Practice in Nagorno-Karabakh and Syria | With a foreword by Susan Allen | ISBN 978-3-8382-1057-5

172 *Maria Shagina* | Joining a Prestigious Club. Cooperation with Europarties and Its Impact on Party Development in Georgia, Moldova, and Ukraine 2004–2015 | With a foreword by Kataryna Wolczuk | ISBN 978-3-8382-1084-1

173 *Alexandra Cotofana, James M. Nyce (Eds.)* | Religion and Magic in Socialist and Post-Socialist Contexts II. Baltic, Eastern European, and Post-USSR Case Studies | With a foreword by Anita Stasulane | ISBN 978-3-8382-0990-6

174 *Barbara Kunz* | Kind Words, Cruise Missiles, and Everything in Between. The Use of Power Resources in U.S. Policies towards Poland, Ukraine, and Belarus 1989–2008 | With a foreword by William Hill | ISBN 978-3-8382-1065-0

175 *Eduard Klein* | Bildungskorruption in Russland und der Ukraine. Eine komparative Analyse der Performanz staatlicher Antikorruptionsmaßnahmen im Hochschulsektor am Beispiel universitärer Aufnahmeprüfungen | Mit einem Vorwort von Heiko Pleines | ISBN 978-3-8382-0995-1

176 *Markus Soldner* | Politischer Kapitalismus im postsowjetischen Russland. Die politische, wirtschaftliche und mediale Transformation in den 1990er Jahren | Mit einem Vorwort von Wolfgang Ismayr | ISBN 978-3-8382-1222-7

177 *Anton Oleinik* | Building Ukraine from Within. A Sociological, Institutional, and Economic Analysis of a Nation-State in the Making | ISBN 978-3-8382-1150-3

178 *Peter Rollberg, Marlene Laruelle (Eds.)* | Mass Media in the Post-Soviet World. Market Forces, State Actors, and Political Manipulation in the Informational Environment after Communism | ISBN 978-3-8382-1116-9

179 *Mikhail Minakov* | Development and Dystopia. Studies in Post-Soviet Ukraine and Eastern Europe | With a foreword by Alexander Etkind | ISBN 978-3-8382-1112-1

180 *Aijan Sharshenova* | The European Union's Democracy Promotion in Central Asia. A Study of Political Interests, Influence, and Development in Kazakhstan and Kyrgyzstan in 2007–2013 | With a foreword by Gordon Crawford | ISBN 978-3-8382-1151-0

181 *Andrey Makarychev, Alexandra Yatsyk (Eds.)* | Boris Nemtsov and Russian Politics. Power and Resistance | With a foreword by Zhanna Nemtsova | ISBN 978-3-8382-1122-0

182 *Sophie Falsini* | The Euromaidan's Effect on Civil Society. Why and How Ukrainian Social Capital Increased after the Revolution of Dignity | With a foreword by Susann Worschech | ISBN 978-3-8382-1131-2

183 *Valentyna Romanova, Andreas Umland (Eds.)* | Ukraine's Decentralization. Challenges and Implications of the Local Governance Reform after the Euromaidan Revolution | ISBN 978-3-8382-1162-6

184 *Leonid Luks* | A Fateful Triangle. Essays on Contemporary Russian, German and Polish History | ISBN 978-3-8382-1143-5

185 *John B. Dunlop* | The February 2015 Assassination of Boris Nemtsov and the Flawed Trial of his Alleged Killers. An Exploration of Russia's "Crime of the 21st Century" | ISBN 978-3-8382-1188-6

186 *Vasile Rotaru* | Russia, the EU, and the Eastern Partnership. Building Bridges or Digging Trenches? | ISBN 978-3-8382-1134-3

187 *Marina Lebedeva* | Russian Studies of International Relations. From the Soviet Past to the Post-Cold-War Present | With a foreword by Andrei P. Tsygankov | ISBN 978-3-8382-0851-0

188 *Tomasz Stępniewski, George Soroka (Eds.)* | Ukraine after Maidan. Revisiting Domestic and Regional Security | ISBN 978-3-8382-1075-9

189 *Petar Cholakov* | Ethnic Entrepreneurs Unmasked. Political Institutions and Ethnic Conflicts in Contemporary Bulgaria | ISBN 978-3-8382-1189-3

190 *A. Salem, G. Hazeldine, D. Morgan (Eds.)* | Higher Education in Post-Communist States. Comparative and Sociological Perspectives | ISBN 978-3-8382-1183-1

191 *Igor Torbakov* | After Empire. Nationalist Imagination and Symbolic Politics in Russia and Eurasia in the Twentieth and Twenty-First Century | With a foreword by Serhii Plokhy | ISBN 978-3-8382-1217-3

192 *Aleksandr Burakovskiy* | Jewish-Ukrainian Relations in Late and Post-Soviet Ukraine. Articles, Lectures and Essays from 1986 to 2016 | ISBN 978-3-8382-1210-4

193 *Natalia Shapovalova, Olga Burlyuk (Eds.)* | Civil Society in Post-Euromaidan Ukraine. From Revolution to Consolidation | With a foreword by Richard Youngs | ISBN 978-3-8382-1216-6

194 *Franz Preissler* | Positionsverteidigung, Imperialismus oder Irredentismus? Russland und die „Russischsprachigen", 1991–2015 | ISBN 978-3-8382-1262-3

195 *Marian Madeła* | Der Reformprozess in der Ukraine 2014-2017. Eine Fallstudie zur Reform der öffentlichen Verwaltung | Mit einem Vorwort von Martin Malek | ISBN 978-3-8382-1266-1

196 *Anke Giesen* | „Wie kann denn der Sieger ein Verbrecher sein?" Eine diskursanalytische Untersuchung der russlandweiten Debatte über Konzept und Verstaatlichungsprozess der Lagergedenkstätte „Perm'-36" im Ural | ISBN 978-3-8382-1284-5

197 *Alla Leukavets* | The Integration Policies of Belarus and Ukraine vis-à-vis the EU and Russia. A Comparative Case Study Through the Prism of a Two-Level Game Approach | ISBN 978-3-8382-1247-0

198 *Oksana Kim* | The Development and Challenges of Russian Corporate Governance I. The Roles and Functions of Boards of Directors | With a foreword by Sheila M. Puffer | ISBN 978-3-8382-1287-6

199 *Thomas D. Grant* | International Law and the Post-Soviet Space I. Essays on Chechnya and the Baltic States | With a foreword by Stephen M. Schwebel | ISBN 978-3-8382-1279-1

200 *Thomas D. Grant* | International Law and the Post-Soviet Space II. Essays on Ukraine, Intervention, and Non-Proliferation | ISBN 978-3-8382-1280-7

201 *Slavomír Michálek, Michal Štefansky* | The Age of Fear. The Cold War and Its Influence on Czechoslovakia 1945–1968 | ISBN 978-3-8382-1285-2

202 *Iulia-Sabina Joja* | Romania's Strategic Culture 1990–2014. Continuity and Change in a Post-Communist Country's Evolution of National Interests and Security Policies | With a foreword by Heiko Biehl | ISBN 978-3-8382-1286-9

203 *Andrei Rogatchevski, Yngvar B. Steinholt, Arve Hansen, David-Emil Wickström* | War of Songs. Popular Music and Recent Russia-Ukraine Relations | With a foreword by Artemy Troitsky | ISBN 978-3-8382-1173-2

204 *Maria Lipman (Ed.)* | Russian Voices on Post-Crimea Russia. An Almanac of Counterpoint Essays from 2015–2018 | ISBN 978-3-8382-1251-7

205 *Ksenia Maksimovtsova* | Language Conflicts in Contemporary Estonia, Latvia, and Ukraine. A Comparative Exploration of Discourses in Post-Soviet Russian-Language Digital Media | With a foreword by Ammon Cheskin | ISBN 978-3-8382-1282-1

206 *Michal Vít* | The EU's Impact on Identity Formation in East-Central Europe between 2004 and 2013. Perceptions of the Nation and Europe in Political Parties of the Czech Republic, Poland, and Slovakia | With a foreword by Andrea Pető | ISBN 978-3-8382-1275-3

207 *Per A. Rudling* | Tarnished Heroes. The Organization of Ukrainian Nationalists in the Memory Politics of Post-Soviet Ukraine | ISBN 978-3-8382-0999-9

208 *Kaja Gadowska, Peter Solomon (Eds.)* | Legal Change in Post-Communist States. Progress, Reversions, Explanations | ISBN 978-3-8382-1312-5

209 *Paweł Kowal, Georges Mink, Iwona Reichardt (Eds.)* | Three Revolutions: Mobilization and Change in Contemporary Ukraine I. Theoretical Aspects and Analyses on Religion, Memory, and Identity | ISBN 978-3-8382-1321-7

210 *Paweł Kowal, Georges Mink, Adam Reichardt, Iwona Reichardt (Eds.)* | Three Revolutions: Mobilization and Change in Contemporary Ukraine II. An Oral History of the Revolution on Granite, Orange Revolution, and Revolution of Dignity | ISBN 978-3-8382-1323-1

211 *Li Bennich-Björkman, Sergiy Kurbatov (Eds.)* | When the Future Came. The Collapse of the USSR and the Emergence of National Memory in Post-Soviet History Textbooks | ISBN 978-3-8382-1335-4

212 *Olga R. Gulina* | Migration as a (Geo-)Political Challenge in the Post-Soviet Space. Border Regimes, Policy Choices, Visa Agendas | With a foreword by Nils Muižnieks | ISBN 978-3-8382-1338-5

213 *Sanna Turoma, Kaarina Aitamurto, Slobodanka Vladiv-Glover (Eds.)* | Religion, Expression, and Patriotism in Russia. Essays on Post-Soviet Society and the State. ISBN 978-3-8382-1346-0

214 *Vasif Huseynov* | Geopolitical Rivalries in the "Common Neighborhood". Russia's Conflict with the West, Soft Power, and Neoclassical Realism | With a foreword by Nicholas Ross Smith | ISBN 978-3-8382-1277-7

215 *Mikhail Suslov* | Geopolitical Imagination. Ideology and Utopia in Post-Soviet Russia | With a foreword by Mark Bassin | ISBN 978-3-8382-1361-3

ibidem.eu